MW00558965

Cambridge Latin Course

Unit 4

FIFTH EDITION

CAMBRIDGE
UNIVERSITY PRESS

CAMBRIDGE
UNIVERSITY PRESS

University Printing House, Cambridge CB2 8BS, United Kingdom

One Liberty Plaza, 20th Floor, New York, NY 10006, USA

477 Williamstown Road, Port Melbourne, VIC 3207, Australia

314–321, 3rd Floor, Plot 3, Splendor Forum, Jasola District Centre, New Delhi – 110025, India

79 Anson Road, #06–04/06, Singapore 079906

Torre de los Parques, Colonia Tlacoquemécatl del Valle, Mexico City CP 03200, Mexico

Cambridge University Press is part of the University of Cambridge.

It furthers the University's mission by disseminating knowledge in the pursuit of education, learning and research at the highest international levels of excellence.

www.cambridge.org
Information on this title: www.cambridge.org/9781107070981

The Cambridge Latin Course is an outcome of work jointly commissioned by the Cambridge School Classics Project and the Schools Council © Schools Council 1970, 1982 (succeeded by the School Curriculum Development Committee © SCDC Publications 1988).

© University of Cambridge School Classics Project 2001, 2015

This publication is in copyright. Subject to statutory exception and to the provisions of relevant collective licensing agreements, no reproduction of any part may take place without the written permission of Cambridge University Press.

First published 1970
Second edition 1982
Third edition 1988
Fourth edition 2001
Fifth edition 2015
20 19 18 17 16 15 14 13 12 11 10 9 8 7 6 5

Printed in Mexico by Editorial Impresora Apolo, S.A. de C.V.

ISBN 978-1-107-07098-1 Hardback
ISBN 978-1-316-64623-6 Hardback +8 Year Website Access
ISBN 978-1-107-09829-9 Hardback +6 Year Website Access
ISBN 978-1-107-09830-5 Hardback +1 Year Website Access
ISBN 978-1-107-69327-2 Paperback
ISBN 978-1-107-09825-1 Paperback +1 Year Website Access

Cover photograph: coin Head of Domitian © British Museum; background Nezabudkina / Shutterstock
Maps and plans by Robert Calow / Eikon
Illustrations by Joy Mellor, Leslie Jones, Peter Kesteven, Neil Sutton, and Lisa Jiang.

Additional resources for this publication at www.cambridge.org/9781107070981

Cambridge University Press has no responsibility for the persistence or accuracy of URLs for external or third-party internet websites referred to in this publication, and does not guarantee that any content on such websites is, or will remain, accurate or appropriate. Information regarding prices, travel timetables, and other factual information given in this work is correct at the time of first printing but Cambridge University Press does not guarantee the accuracy of such information thereafter.

Contents

Acknowledgments

The authors and publishers acknowledge the following sources of copyright material and are grateful for the permissions granted. While every effort has been made, it has not always been possible to identify the sources of all the material used, or to trace all copyright holders. If any omissions are brought to our notice, we will be happy to include the appropriate acknowledgments on reprinting.

p. 1, © Art Images / Getty Images; p. 5 *b*, © Jackie and Bob Dunn, www.pompeiiinpictures.com. Su concessione del Ministero dei Beni e delle Attività Culturali e del Turismo - Soprintendenza Speciale per i Beni Archeologici di Pompei, Ercolano e Stabia.; pp. 5 *t*, 62 *b*, © Photo Scala, Florence/Fotografica Foglia - courtesy of the Ministero Beni e Att. Culturali; pp. 9 *t*, 18, © Lautaro / Alamy; p. 9 *b*, © Getty Images / AFP PHOTO / LAURENT KALFALA; p. 11, © De Agostini Picture Library / G. Dagli Orti / Bridgeman Images; p. 12, © Museo Archeologico Nazionale, Naples, Italy / Mondadori Portfolio/Electa/Luigi Spina / Bridgeman Images; pp. 13 *t*, 15, 21, 78, 94, 149, © Photo Scala, Florence; pp. 25 *t*, 44 *b*, 47, 60 *t*, 61, 64, 71 *t*, 95, 99, 109, 113 *t*, 121 *t*, *b*, 122, 148, 161, 215, 218, 232, 235, 236, 244, © The Trustees of The British Museum; pp. 25 *b*, 123, © Musée National du Bardo, Le Bardo, Tunisia / Bridgeman Images; p. 26, © Getty images / Print Collector; p. 28, © Werner Forman Archive / Bridgeman Images; pp. 29, 184, 195, 231, © DEA / G. DAGLI ORTI / Getty Images; pp. 36, / 37 *t*, 83, © akg-images / Peter Connolly; pp. 37 *b*, 81 *tl*, *br*, *bl*, 82 156, With the permission of Ministry of Cultural Heritage and Activities - Superintendence for the Colosseum, the Roman National Museum and the Archaeological area of Rome; p. 42, © PRISMA ARCHIVO / Alamy Stock Photo; p. 46, © iStock / Getty images / ssuni; p. 60 *b*, © Biblioteca Apostolica Vaticana, Vatican City / Bridgeman Images; pp. 62 *t*, 65, 79 *b*, 243, © Louvre, Paris, France / Bridgeman Images; p. 71 *b*, © Glyn Genin / Alamy Stock Photo; p. 79 *t*, Courtesy of Carol Rumford; p. 81 *tr*, © Yale University Press; p. 96, © Museo Archeologico Nazionale, Firenze / Bridgeman Images; pp. 104, 118, 241, © akg-images; p. 107 *l*, © Edifice / Bridgeman Images; p. 107 *r*, © Timgad, Algeria / © Gerard Degeorge / Bridgeman Images; p. 108, © Forum, Rome, Italy / Bridgeman Images; p. 119, © Bertl123 / Shutterstock; p. 125, Courtesy of the Thomas Fisher Rare Book Library, University of Toronto; p. 133, © Museum of Fine Arts, Boston; p. 137, Courtesy of the Holkham Estate, Holkham; p. 138, © Ancient Art & Architecture Collection Ltd / Alamy; p. 139, © Somerset County Museum; p. 150, © The Granger Collection / TopFoto; p. 163, © Musée des Beaux-Arts, Caen, France / Bridgeman Images; p. 164, © Pompei - Segreteria Scientifica akg-images / Erich Lessing; pp. 165, 169, 180, Courtesy of Justine Hopkins; p. 170, © Hellenic Ministry of Culture and Sports /Archaeological Receipts Fund; p. 175, © Fitzwilliam Museum, University of Cambridge, UK / Bridgeman Images; p. 183, © Musées Royaux des Beaux-Arts de Belgique, Brussels, Belgium / Bridgeman Images; p. 185, © Photo © RMN-Grand Palais (musée du Louvre) / Gérard Blot; p. 187, © akg-images / Nimatallah; p. 189, © DEA / G. NIMATALLAH / Getty Images; p. 192, © Museo Archeologico Nazionale, Naples, Italy / Mondadori Portfolio/Electa/Sergio Anelli / Bridgeman Images; p. 200, © DEA / A. DAGLI ORTI / Getty Images; p. 201, © Christie's Images / Photo © Christie's Images / Bridgeman Images; p. 202, © Private Collection / Photo © Christie's Images / Bridgeman Images; p. 203, © Ny Carlsberg Glyptotek; p. 204, © Photo Scala, Florence - courtesy of the Ministero Beni e Att. Culturali; p. 205, © University College of Wales, Aberystwyth, Wales / Bridgeman Images; p. 211, © iStock / edella; p. 216, © Romisch-Germ. Museum, Cologne; p. 217, © Photo Scala, Florence/bpk, Bildagentur fuer Kunst, Kultur und Geschichte, Berlin; p. 223, © akg-images / John minimum; p. 232 *r*, © DEA PICTURE LIBRARY / Getty Images; p. 234, © Musei Capitolini, Rome, Italy / Bridgeman Images; p. 239, © iStock / Angelafoto; p. 250 *t*, © Shutterstock / LianeM; p. 250 *b*, © De Agostini Picture Library / A. Dagli Orti / Bridgeman Images; p. 253, © akg-images / Erich Lessing; p. 254, © PjrTravel / Alamy.

All other photography by R.L. Dalladay.

'Musée des Beaux Arts' reproduced by permission of Faber and Faber Ltd from *Collected Poems* by W.H. Auden. Copyright 1940 and renewed 1968 by W.H. Auden; reprinted from *W.H. Auden: Collected Poems* by W.H. Auden, edited by Edward Mendelson, by permission of Random House, Inc. Richmond Lattimore's translation of Homer's *Iliad* is reproduced by permission of the University of Chicago Press, copyright 1951 © 1962 by the University of Chicago, all rights reserved.

The current edition of the *Cambridge Latin Course* is the result of over forty years of research, classroom testing, feedback, revision, and development. In that period millions of students, tens of thousands of teachers, hundreds of experts in the fields of Classics, history, and education, and dozens of authors have contributed to make the Course the leading approach to reading Latin that it is today.

To list everyone who has played a part in the development of the *Cambridge Latin Course* would be impossible, but we would particularly like to thank individuals and representatives from the following organizations, past and present:

British Museum
British School at Rome
Butser Iron Age Farm, England
Castell Henllys, Wales
Council for British Archaeology
Department of Education and Science, London
Fishbourne Palace, England
Herculaneum Conservation Project
Her Majesty's Inspectorate of Schools
North American Cambridge Classics Project
Nuffield Foundation
Qualifications and Curriculum Authority, London
Queen Mary University of London, Department of Classics
Schools Council, London
Southern Universities Joint Board for School Examinations, England
St Matthias College of Education, Bristol
Swedish Pompeii Project
University of Bradford, Department of Classics
University of Cambridge, Faculty of Classics
University of Cambridge, Faculty of Education
University of Cambridge School Classics Project Advisory Panel
University College Cardiff, Classics Department
University College London, Centre for the History of Medicine
University College London, Department of Greek and Latin
University of Leeds, Department of Classics
University of Leeds, School of Education
University of London, Institute of Education
University of Manchester, Department of Art History and Visual Studies
University of Massachusetts at Amherst, Department of Classics
University of Nottingham, Department of Classics
University of Nottingham, School of Education
University of Oxford, Department of Education
University of Oxford, Faculty of Classics
University of Oxford, School of Archaeology
University of Wales, School of Archaeology, History and Anthropology
University of Warwick, Classics Department
Welsh Joint Education Committee

RUS

ex urbe

When you have read this story, answer the questions on the next page.

Mānius Acīlius Glabriō salūtem dīcit Lupō amīcō.
quid agis, mī Lupe, in vīllā tuā rūsticā? quid agit Helvidius,
fīlius tuus?

    quotiēns dē tē tuāque vīllā cōgitō, tibi valdē invideō; nam in
urbe nusquam est ōtium, nusquam quiēs. ego quidem multīs   5
negōtiīs cotīdiē occupātus sum. prīmā hōrā ā clientibus meīs
salūtor; inde ad basilicam ōrātiōnēs habitum vel ad cūriam
ōrātiōnēs audītum contendō; aliquandō amīcōs vīsitō, vel ab eīs
vīsitor; per tōtum diem officia prīvāta vel pūblica agō. at tū
intereā in rīpā flūminis vel in umbrā arboris ōtiōsus fortasse   10
iacēs, et dum ego strepitū urbis vexor, tū carmine avium
dēlectāris. sed satis querēlārum!

    Imperātor Domitiānus triumphum heri dē Germānīs ēgit.
pompa, per tōtam urbem prōgressa, ā multīs laudābātur, ā
nōnnūllīs dērīdēbātur. aliī, mīrābile dictū, "spectāculum   15
splendidissimum" clāmābant. "Imperātor noster, pater vērus
patriae, gentēs barbarās iam superāvit; Germānī per viās urbis
iam in triumphō dūcuntur!" aliī tamen "spectāculum rīdiculum"
susurrābant. "illī quī per viās dūcuntur haudquāquam Germānī
sunt, sed servī, ex prōvinciā Hispāniā arcessītī et vestīmenta   20
Germāna gerentēs!"

    litterae cotīdiē ā Britanniā exspectantur, ubi Agricola bellum
contrā Calēdoniōs gerit. Calēdoniī crēduntur ferōcissimī
omnium Britannōrum esse, terribilēs vīsū audītūque. dē
Calēdoniā ipsā omnīnō incertus sum, mī Lupe. utrum pars est   25
Britanniae an īnsula sēiūncta?

    ad cōnsilium Imperātōris adesse saepe iubeor. invītus pāreō;
quotiēns enim sententiam meam ā Domitiānō rogor, difficile est
mihi respondēre; turpe vidētur mentīrī, perīculōsum vēra loquī.
nam iussū istīus tyrannī multī bonī damnātī sunt.   30

    audīvistīne umquam poētam Valerium Martiālem
recitantem? ego quidem recitātiōnibus eius saepe adsum; tū sī
eum audīveris, certē dēlectāberis. versūs eius semper ēlegantēs,
nōnnumquam scurrīlēs sunt. eum tamen ideō reprehendō, quod
Imperātōrem nimium adulātur.   35

    quandō rūre discēdēs, mī Lupe? quandō iterum tē in urbe
vidēbimus? cum prīmum ad urbem redieris, mē vīsitā, quaesō;
sī tē mox vīderō, valdē dēlectābor. valē.

salūtem dīcit	*sends good wishes*
quid agis?	*how are you? how are you doing?*
invideō: invidēre	*envy*
ōtium	*leisure*
ōrātiōnēs habitum	*(in order) to give speeches*
ōrātiōnēs audītum	*(in order) to hear speeches*
officia: officium	*duty*
prīvāta: prīvātus	*private*
querēlārum: querēla	*complaint*
triumphum … ēgit: **triumphum agere**	*celebrate a triumph*
dē Germānīs	*over the Germans*
mīrābile dictū	*strange to say*
patriae: patria	*country, homeland*
litterae	*letters, correspondence*
Calēdoniōs: Calēdoniī	*Scots*
utrum … est … an?	*is it … or?*
sēiūncta: sēiūnctus	*separate*
cōnsilium	*council*
turpe: turpis	*shameful*
mentīrī	*lie, tell a lie*
tyrannī: tyrannus	*tyrant*
recitātiōnibus: recitātiō	*recital, public reading*
nōnnumquam	*sometimes*
ideō … quod	*for the reason that, because*
reprehendō: reprehendere	*blame, criticize*
adulātur: adulārī	*flatter*
rūre: rūs	*country, countryside*
cum prīmum	*as soon as*
quaesō	*I beg, i.e. please*

Questions

1 Who is writing this letter? To whom is it written?

2 Where is Lupus?

3 **nam … quiēs** (lines 4–5). What is Glabrio complaining about here?

4 In lines 6–9 (**prīmā hōrā … pūblica agō**), Glabrio explains why he is so busy every day. Write down two of the reasons he gives.

5 **at tū … dēlectāris** (lines 9–12). How does Glabrio imagine that his friend is spending his time?

6 What public event has just taken place in Rome?

7 What two different reactions did it get from the people (lines 14–15)?

8 "**illī … haudquāquam Germānī sunt**" (lines 19–20). If they were not Germans, who did some people think they were?

9 What is going on in Britain (lines 22–23)?

10 What has Glabrio heard about the Scots?

11 What problem does Glabrio have about the geography of Scotland (lines 25–26)?

12 What order does Glabrio often receive (line 27)?

13 Why does he find it difficult to give the emperor his opinion (line 29)?

14 **versūs eius … adulātur** (lines 33–35). What is Glabrio's opinion of the work of the poet Martial?

15 What evidence is there in this letter to show that Glabrio and Lupus are close friends? Make two points.

dum ego strepitū urbis vexor, tū carmine avium dēlectāris.

vīta rūstica

C. Helvidius Lupus salūtem dīcit Acīliō Glabriōnī amīcō.
cum epistulam tuam legerem, mī Glabriō, gaudium et dolōrem
simul sēnsī. gaudiō enim afficiēbar, quod tam diū epistulam ā tē
exspectābam; dolēbam autem, quod tū tot labōribus
opprimēbāris.

dolēbam: dolēre *grieve, be sad*

    in epistulā tuā dīcis tē valdē occupātum esse. ego quoque,
cum Rōmae essem, saepe negōtiīs vexābar; nunc tamen vītā
rūsticā dēlector. nam rūrī iūcundissimum est forās īre aliquandō
per agrōs equitātum, aliquandō fundum īnspectum. crās in silvīs
proximīs vēnābor; vīcīnī enim crēdunt aprum ingentem ibi latēre.
nōn tamen omnīnō ōtiōsus sum; nam sīcut tū ā clientibus tuīs
salūtāris atque vexāris, ita ego ā colōnīs meīs assiduē vexor.

rūrī *in the country*
iūcundissimum: iūcundus
                pleasant
forās *outside, outdoors*
vēnābor: vēnārī *hunt*
vīcīnī: vīcīnus *neighbor*
sīcut ... ita *just as ... so*
colōnīs: colōnus *tenant farmer*
rēctē *rightly*
affirmat: affirmāre *declare*

    rēctē dīcis Calēdoniōs omnium Britannōrum ferōcissimōs
esse. amīcus meus Silānus, quī cum Agricolā in Britanniā nūper
mīlitābat, dīcit Calēdoniōs in ultimīs partibus Britanniae
habitāre, inter saxa et undās. quamquam Calēdoniī ferōcissimē
pugnāre solent, Silānus affirmat exercitum nostrum eōs vincere
posse. crēdit enim Rōmānōs nōn modo multō fortiōrēs esse
quam Calēdoniōs, sed etiam ducem meliōrem habēre.

    dē poētā Martiāle tēcum cōnsentiō: inest in eō multum
ingenium, multa ars. ego vērō ōlim versibus Ovidiī poētae
maximē dēlectābar; nunc tamen mihi epigrammata Martiālis
magis placent.

vērō *indeed*
epigrammata: epigramma
                epigram

    in epistulā tuā Helvidium, fīlium meum, commemorās. quem
tamen rārissimē videō! nam in hāc vīllā trēs diēs mēcum
morātus, ad urbem rediit; suspicor eum puellam aliquam in

aliquam: aliquī *some*

*sīcut tū ā clientibus tuīs
salūtāris atque vexāris, ita ego
ā colōnīs meīs assiduē vexor.*

urbe vīsitāre. quīndecim iam annōs nātus est; nihil cūrat nisi puellās et quadrīgās. difficile autem est mihi eum culpāre; nam ego quoque, cum iuvenis essem – sed satis nūgārum!

nunc tū mihi graviter admonendus es, mī Glabriō. in epistulā 30 tuā dē quōdam virō potentī male scrībis, quem nōmināre nōlō. tibi cavendum est, mī amīce! perīculōsum est dē potentibus male scrībere. virī potentēs celeriter īrāscuntur, lentē molliuntur. nisi cāveris, mī Glabriō, damnāberis atque occīdēris. sollicitus haec scrībō; salūs enim tua mihi magnae cūrae est. valē. 35

quadrīgās: quadrīga *chariot*
nūgārum: nūgae *nonsense, foolish talk*
admonendus es: admonēre *warn, advise*
male *badly, unfavorably*
nōmināre *name, mention by name*
īrāscuntur: īrāscī *become angry*

A country farm

This small farm (**vīlla rūstica**) at Boscoreale, near Pompeii, was buried by Vesuvius in AD 79. It was possible for the archaeologists to trace the holes where the vines were planted and vines have now been planted there again. The wine was fermented in buried jars (below), which were then covered with lids to store it.

Farmers were recommended to have enough jars to store their wine for up to five years, so as to sell at the time when prices were highest.

The owner of this sort of farm would probably have let it out to a tenant (**colōnus**) to run.

About the language: indirect statement

1 In Unit 1, you met sentences like these:

"mercātor multam pecūniam habet."
The merchant has a lot of money.

"ancillae cibum parant."
The slave girls are preparing the food.

In each example, a statement is being *made*. These examples are known as **direct statements**. Notice the nouns **mercātor** and **ancillae** and the verbs **habet** and **parant**.

2 In Stage 35, you have met sentences like these:

scīmus **mercātōrem** multam pecūniam **habēre**.
We know the merchant to have a lot of money.
Or, in more natural English:
We know that the merchant has a lot of money.

crēdō **ancillās** cibum **parāre**.
I believe the slave girls to be preparing the food.
Or, in more natural English:
I believe that the slave girls are preparing the food.

In each of these examples, the statement is not being made, but is being *reported* or *mentioned*. These examples are known as **indirect statements**. Notice that the nouns **mercātōrem** and **ancillās** are now in the *accusative* case, and the verbs **habēre** and **parāre** are now in the *infinitive* form.

3 Compare the following examples:

direct statements	*indirect statements*
"captīvī dormiunt."	centuriō dīcit **captīvōs dormīre**.
The prisoners are asleep.	*The centurion says that the prisoners are asleep.*
"Lupus in vīllā rūsticā habitat."	audiō **Lupum** in vīllā rūsticā **habitāre**.
Lupus is living in his country villa.	*I hear that Lupus is living in his country villa.*

4 Further examples of direct and indirect statements:

a "hostēs appropinquant."
b nūntius dīcit hostēs appropinquāre.
c "Agricola bellum in Calēdoniā gerit."
d audiō Agricolam bellum in Calēdoniā gerere.
e rhētor affirmat fīlium meum dīligenter labōrāre.
f domina crēdit fugitīvōs in silvā latēre.
g scīmus mīlitēs nostrōs semper fortiter pugnāre.
h dīcisne patrōnum tuum esse virum līberālem?

Word patterns: nouns and adjectives

1 Study the form and meaning of the following nouns and adjectives:

ōtium	*idleness, leisure*	ōtiōsus	*idle, at leisure*
spatium	*space*	spatiōsus	*spacious, large*
fōrma	*beauty*	fōrmōsus	*beautiful*

2 Using paragraph 1 as a guide, complete the table below.

līmus	*mud*	līmōsus	. . . .
herba	. . . .	herbōsus	*grassy*
bellum	. . . .	bellicōsus	*aggressive, warlike*
furor	*madness*	furiōsus	. . . .
damnum	. . . .	damnōsus	*harmful, damaging*
pretium	. . . .	pretiōsus	. . . .
perīculum	. . . .	perīculōsus	. . . .
odium	. . . .	odiōsus	. . . .
iniūria	. . . .	iniūriōsus	. . . .

3 Match each of the following Latin adjectives with the correct English translation:

Latin: fūmōsus, iocōsus, ventōsus, perfidiōsus, annōsus
English: treacherous, smoky, fond of jokes, old, blown by the winds

4 Many Latin **-ōsus** adjectives come into English as words ending in "-ose" or "-ous." Give an English adjective and its meaning for each of the following Latin adjectives. Use the meaning of the Latin word in your definitions.

   verbōsus, studiōsus, dēliciōsus, cōpiōsus, victōriōsus

Tenants bringing gifts to the villa owner.

Practicing the language

1 Complete each sentence with the most suitable verb from the box below, using the correct form of the future tense. Then translate the sentence. Do not use any verb more than once.

terrēbit	reficiet	dabit	pugnābit	dūcet
terrēbunt	reficient	dabunt	pugnābunt	dūcent

 a hī fabrī sunt perītissimī; nāvem tuam celeriter . . . .
 b crās dominus lībertātem duōbus servīs . . . .
 c leōnēs, quī ferōciōrēs sunt quam cēterae bēstiae, spectātōrēs fortasse . . . .
 d sī templum vīsitāre vīs, hic servus tē illūc . . . .
 e frāter meus, gladiātor nōtissimus, crās in amphitheātrō . . . .

2 Turn each of the following pairs into one sentence by replacing the word in **boldface** with the correct form of the relative pronoun **quī, quae, quod**. Use paragraph 8 on page 268 to help you. Then translate the sentence.

 For example: prō templō erant duo virī. **virōs** statim agnōvī.
 This becomes: prō templō erant duo virī, **quōs** statim agnōvī.
                  *In front of the temple were two men, **whom** I recognized at once.*

 a in fundō nostrō sunt vīgintī servī. **servī** in agrīs cotīdiē labōrant.
 b in hāc vīllā habitat lībertus. **lībertum** vīsitāre volō.
 c prope iānuam stābat fēmina. **fēminae** epistulam trādidī.
 d audī illam puellam! **puella** suāviter cantat.
 e in viā erant multī puerī. **puerōrum** clāmōrēs senem vexābant.
 f vīdistīne templum? **templum** nūper aedificātum est.

3 Select the participle which agrees with the noun in **boldface**. Then translate the sentence.

 a **hospitēs**, dōna pretiōsissima . . . . , ad vīllam prīncipis contendēbant. (ferentēs, ferentia)
 b versūs **poētae**, in forō . . . . , ab omnibus audītī erant. (recitantis, recitantium)
 c **pecūniā** . . . . , fūr in silvam cucurrit. (raptā, raptō, raptīs)
 d **sacerdōtibus**, ē templō . . . . , victimās ostendimus. (ēgressōs, ēgressīs)
 e **nāvēs**, in lītore . . . . , īnspicere volēbam. (īnstrūcta, īnstrūctae, īnstrūctās)
 f **puer**, canem . . . . , arborem quam celerrimē cōnscendit. (cōnspicātus, cōnspicāta, cōnspicātum)
 g fēminae **mīlitēs** vīdērunt captīvum . . . . (pulsantem, pulsātōs, pulsātūrōs)
 h puella nesciēbat cūr **pater** ancillam . . . . , esset. (pūnītūrus, pūnītūra, pūnītūram)

Country villas

Many wealthy Romans, like Lupus on pages 2–5, owned both a town house in Rome and at least one villa in the country. There they could escape from the noise and heat of the city, especially during the unhealthy months of late summer, and relax from the pressures of private business and public duties.

Some of these country houses were fairly close to Rome; their owners could get a day's work done in the city and then travel out to their villa before nightfall. The villas were generally either on the coast, like Pliny's villa at Laurentum, or on the hills around Rome, for example at Tibur, where the Emperor Hadrian owned the most spectacular mansion of all, surrounded by specially constructed imitations of buildings that had impressed him on his travels.

An emperor's villa

Hadrian's villa near Tibur, 19 miles (30 kilometers) from Rome: a vast, sprawling complex covering 300 acres (120 hectares). The photograph of the model shows only part of it.

There were two theaters and three bath buildings; huge state rooms contrasted with more homely quarters for the emperor's private use. He loved to enjoy the landscape. A terrace (top, foreground) has views over a valley he called the Vale of Tempe after a famous Greek beauty spot. An outdoor dining room (below) looks over a canal which may have recalled the Canopus at Alexandria.

Other country villas were further afield. A popular area was Campania; the coastline of the Bay of Naples was dotted with the villas of wealthy men, while vacation resorts such as Baiae had a reputation for fast living and immorality.

Country villas naturally varied in design, but they usually contained some or all of the following features: a series of dining and reception rooms for entertaining guests, often with extensive views of the surrounding countryside; a set of baths, heated by hypocausts, containing the full range of apodyterium, tepidarium, caldarium, and frigidarium; long colonnades where the owner and his friends might walk, or even ride, sheltered from the rain or from the direct heat of the sun; and extensive parkland, farmland, or gardens, preferably with plenty of shade and running water. In a corner of the estate there might be a small shrine, dedicated to the protecting gods.

Pliny's letters include descriptions of two of his villas. Although detailed, the descriptions are not always clear, and many scholars have tried to reconstruct the plans of the villas, without reaching agreement. An attempt at the plan of Pliny's Laurentine villa is shown below, together with a model based on the plan. Among

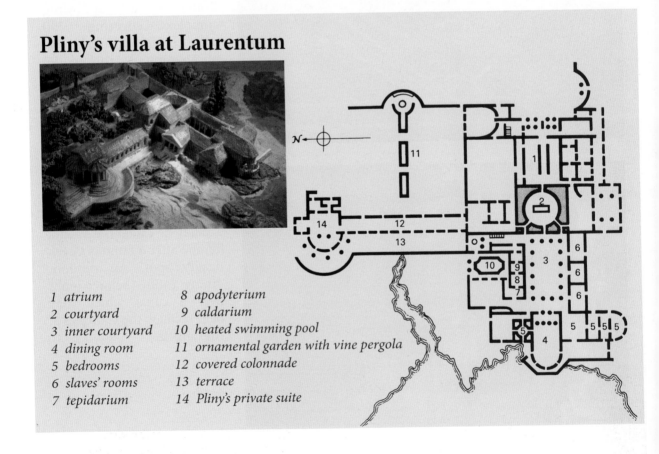

Pliny's villa at Laurentum

1 atrium
2 courtyard
3 inner courtyard
4 dining room
5 bedrooms
6 slaves' rooms
7 tepidarium
8 apodyterium
9 caldarium
10 heated swimming pool
11 ornamental garden with vine pergola
12 covered colonnade
13 terrace
14 Pliny's private suite

the villa's special features were the heated swimming pool (10), the big semicircular recess at the end of the chief dining room (4), designed to provide the dinner guests with an impressive panorama of the sea, and the covered colonnade (12) leading to Pliny's private suite (14). This suite was Pliny's own addition to the building, and it provided him with quiet and privacy; at the noisy mid-winter festival of the Saturnalia, for example, Pliny could retire to his suite while his slaves enjoyed themselves in the main villa, so that he did not get in the way of their celebrations and they did not disturb his peace.

Country pursuits

One of the most popular recreations for a wealthy Roman on his country estate was hunting. Hares, deer, or wild boar were tracked down and chased into nets where they could be speared to death. Long ropes, to which brightly colored feathers were attached, were slung from trees to cut off the animal's retreat and frighten it back towards the nets. The actual chasing was often left to slaves and dogs, while the hunter contented himself with waiting at the nets and spearing the boar or deer when it had become thoroughly entangled. Pliny, for example, in reporting a successful expedition on which he caught three boars, says that he took his stilus and writing tablets with him to the hunt and jotted down ideas under

The hunter (bottom left) *has been gored by the cornered boar.*

People with fishing rods (left and center) in a Pompeian painting of a seaside villa.

the inspiration of the woodland scene while he waited for the boars to appear. But although Pliny's description of hunting is a very peaceful one, the sport still had its dangers: a cornered boar might turn on its pursuers, and a hunter who was slow with his spear might be gashed severely, even fatally.

Fishing also seems to have been popular, and could easily be combined with rowing or sailing, either on the sea (in the Bay of Naples, for example) or on such lakes as the Lucrine lake, famous for its fish and its oysters. A lazier method of fishing is described by Martial, who refers to a villa with a bedroom directly overlooking the sea, so that the occupant could drop a fishing line from the window and catch a fish without even getting out of bed.

Some of Pliny's letters describe his daily routine at his country villas. He spent most of his time in gentle exercise (walking, riding, or occasionally hunting), working on a speech or other piece of writing, dealing with his tenant farmers (**colōnī**), entertaining friends, dining, or listening to a reading or to music. He often spent part of the afternoon reading a Greek or Latin speech aloud "for the sake of both voice and digestion." (Pliny often spoke in the law courts and the senate, and he was naturally anxious to keep his voice in good trim.)

The economy of the villa

A country villa of this kind, however, was not just for vacation relaxation: it was an important investment. Often there was a farm attached to the house, and the property would usually include an extensive area of land which the owner might farm himself or lease to tenant farmers. In the ancient world, by far the commonest way of investing money was to buy land. It is not surprising that many of Pliny's letters deal with the day-to-day problems of land management. He agonizes over whether to buy a neighboring piece of land, fertile and conveniently situated but long neglected; he asks the emperor to excuse him from Rome so that he can be on one of his estates at a time

Tenants paying their rent.

when the tenancy is changing hands; and when his tenants get into difficulties and are heavily in debt, he arranges for them to pay their rent with part of their crops rather than in cash. He likes to present himself as an ignorant amateur with no interest in the running of his villas, but some of his comments give the impression that he was in fact enthusiastic, practical, and shrewd. One of his villas brought him an income of 400,000 sesterces a year. If you compare this with the annual pay of a centurion – about 6,000 sesterces a year – and remember that Pliny owned other villas and property, you can see that he was a very successful landowner.

What country activities can you find in this picture?

Vocabulary checklist 35

ager, agrī, m.	field
an	or
utrum ... an	whether ... or
carmen, carminis, n.	song
caveō, cavēre, cāvī	beware
culpō, culpāre, culpāvī	blame
inde	then
magis	more
male	badly, unfavorably
moror, morārī, morātus sum	delay
multō	much
nusquam	nowhere
quandō?	when?
quidem	indeed
quotiēns	whenever
rūs, rūris, n.	country, countryside
simul	at the same time

A grand country villa, with symmetrical wings and a formal garden in front. A painting in Pompeii.

RECITATIO

Stage 36

Marcus Valerius Mārtiālis

I

in audītōriō exspectant multī cīvēs. adsunt ut Valerium Mārtiālem,
poētam nōtissimum, recitantem audiant. omnēs inter sē colloquuntur.
subitō signum datur ut taceant; audītōrium intrat poēta ipse.
audītōribus plaudentibus, Mārtiālis scaenam ascendit ut versūs suōs
recitet.   5

Mārtiālis: salvēte, amīcī. (*librum ēvolvit.*) prīmum
                        recitāre volō versūs quōsdam nūper dē
                        Sabidiō compositōs.

complūrēs audītōrēs sē convertunt ut Sabidium, quī in ultimō sellārum
ōrdine sedet, spectent.   10

Mārtiālis: nōn amo tē, Sabidī, nec possum dīcere quārē.
                         hoc tantum possum dīcere – nōn amo tē.

audītor: (*cum amīcīs susurrāns*) illōs versūs nōn
                        intellegō. cūr poēta dīcere nōn potest quārē
                        Sabidium nōn amet?   15
prīmus amīcus: (*susurrāns*) scīlicet poēta ipse causam nescit.
secundus amīcus: (*susurrāns*) minimē, poēta optimē scit quārē
                        Sabidium nōn amet: sed tam foeda est causa
                        ut poēta eam patefacere nōlit.

aliī audītōrēs: st! st!   20

audītōriō: audītōrium
    auditorium, hall (used for
    public readings)
colloquuntur: colloquī
                talk, chat
audītōribus: audītor
    listener, (pl.) audience
ēvolvit: ēvolvere *unroll, open*
compositōs: compōnere
    compose, make up
complūrēs *several*

st! *hush!*

prīmus amīcus:	hem! audītōrēs nōbīs imperant ut taceāmus.
Mārtiālis:	nunc dē Laecāniā et Thāide, fēminīs
	"nōtissimīs": (*audītōrēs sibi rīdent.*)

Thāis habet **nigrōs**, niveōs Laecānia **dentēs.***
    quae ratiō est? . . .   25

| audītor: | (*interpellāns*) . . . ēmptōs haec habet, illa suōs! |

Mārtiālis, valdē īrātus, dē scaenā dēscendit ut audītōrem vituperet.

Thāide *ablative of* Thāis

quae?: quī? *what?*
ratiō *reason*
haec . . . illa *this one (Laecania)*
                 . . . that one (Thais)

Mārtiālis:	ego poēta sum, tū tantum audītor. ego hūc
	invītātus sum ut recitem, tū ut audiās.
	(*subitō audītōrem agnōscit.*) hem! scio quis sīs. 30
	tū Pontiliānus es, quī semper mē rogās ut
	libellōs meōs tibi mittam. at nunc, mī
	Pontiliāne, tibi dīcere possum quārē semper
	mittere recūsem. (*ad scaenam reversus,*
	recitātiōnem renovat.) 35

cūr nōn mitto **meōs** tibi, Pontiliāne, **libellōs**?
    nē mihi tū mittās, Pontiliāne, tuōs!

renovat: renovāre
         continue, resume

*omnēs praeter Pontiliānum rīdent. Pontiliānus autem tam īrātus est ut
ē sellā surgat. ad scaenam sē praecipitāre cōnātur ut Mārtiālem pulset,
sed amīcī eum retinent.*   40

*Some noun-and-adjective phrases, in which an adjective is separated by one
word or more from the noun which it describes, are shown in **boldface**.

II

Mārtiālis, quī iam ūnam hōram recitat, ad fīnem librī appropinquat.

Mārtiālis:	postrēmō pauca dē prīncipe nostrō, Domitiānō Augustō, dīcere velim. aliquōs versūs nūper dē illā aulā ingentī composuī quae in monte Palātīnō stat:

> aethera contingit **nova** nostrī prīncipis **aula**;
> clārius in **tōtō** sōl videt **orbe** nihil.
> **haec**, Auguste, tamen, quae vertice sīdera pulsat,
> pār **domus** est caelō sed minor est dominō.

plūrimī audītōrēs vehementissimē plaudunt; animadvertunt enim Epaphrodītum, Domitiānī lībertum, in audītōriō adesse. ūnus audītor tamen, M'. Acīlius Glabriō, tālī adulātiōne offēnsus, nōn modo plausū abstinet sed ē sellā surgit et ex audītōriō exit. quā audāciā attonitus, Mārtiālis paulīsper immōtus stat; deinde ad extrēmam scaenam prōcēdit ut plausum excipiat. ūnus tamen audītor exclāmat:

audītor:	sed quid dē mē, Mārtiālis? epigramma dē mē compōnere nunc potes?
Mārtiālis:	dē tē, homuncule? quis es et quālis?
audītor:	nōmine Diaulus sum. artem medicīnae nūper exercēbam . . .
alius audītor:	. . . at nunc vespillō es!

omnēs rīdent; rīdet praesertim Mārtiālis.

Mārtiālis:	bene! nunc epigramma accipe, mī Diaule:

> nūper erat medicus, nunc est vespillo Diaulus.
> quod vespillo facit, fēcerat et medicus.

cachinnant multī; ērubēscit Diaulus. Mārtiālis, recitātiōne ita perfectā, ex audītōriō ēgreditur, omnibus praeter Diaulum plaudentibus. servī ingressī audītōribus vīnum cibumque offerunt.

---

prīncipe: prīnceps *emperor*

monte Palātīnō: mōns
    Palātīnus *the Palatine hill*

aethera *accusative of* **aethēr**
    sky, heaven
contingit: contingere *touch*
clārius . . . nihil
    nothing more splendid
orbe: orbis *globe, world*
vertice: vertex *top, peak*
sīdera: sīdus *star*
pār *equal*
minor . . . dominō
    smaller than its master
animadvertunt: animadvertere
    notice

M'. = Mānius
adulātiōne: adulātiō *flattery*
abstinet: abstinēre *abstain*
ad extrēmam scaenam
    to the edge of the stage
vespillō *undertaker*

quod = id quod *what*
et = etiam *also*

The Emperor Domitian's palace overlooking the Circus Maximus.

About the language 1: present subjunctive

1 In Unit 3, you met the imperfect and pluperfect tenses of the subjunctive:

   imperfect
   haruspex aderat ut victimam **īnspiceret**.
   The soothsayer was there in order that he might examine the victim.
     Or, in more natural English:
   The soothsayer was there to examine the victim.

   pluperfect
   rēx prīncipēs rogāvit num hostēs **vīdissent**.
   The king asked the chieftains whether they had seen the enemy.

2 In Stage 36, you have met sentences like these:

   cīvēs conveniunt ut poētam **audiant**.
   The citizens are gathering in order that they may hear the poet.
     Or, in more natural English:
   The citizens are gathering to hear the poet.

   Mārtiālis dīcere nōn potest quārē Sabidium nōn **amet**.
   Martial is unable to say why he does not like Sabidius.

   The form of the verb in **boldface** is the **present subjunctive**.

3 Further examples:

   a cognōscere volō quid illī fabrī aedificent.
   b tam saevus est dominus ut ancillās semper pūniat.
   c in agrīs cotīdiē labōrō ut cibum līberīs meīs praebeam.
   d nōn intellegimus quārē tālī hominī crēdās.

4 Compare the present subjunctive with the present indicative:

	present indicative (3rd person singular and plural)		*present subjunctive* (3rd person singular and plural)	
first conjugation	portat	portant	portet	portent
second conjugation	docet	docent	doceat	doceant
third conjugation	trahit	trahunt	trahat	trahant
fourth conjugation	audit	audiunt	audiat	audiant

   The present subjunctive of all four conjugations is set out in full on page 272 of the Language information section.

5 For the present subjunctive of irregular verbs, see page 282.

epigrammata Mārtiālia

The following epigrams, and also the ones which appeared on pages 16–18, were written by Marcus Valerius Martialis (Martial) and published between AD 86 and 101.

I *dē Tuccā, quī saepe postulat ut Mārtiālis libellōs sibi dōnet*
    exigis ut **nostrōs** dōnem tibi, Tucca, **libellōs**.
        nōn faciam: nam vīs vēndere, nōn legere.

dōnet: **dōnāre** *give*
exigis: **exigere** *demand*
nostrōs: **noster = meus** *my*

Why does Martial refuse Tucca's demand?

II *dē Sextō, iuvene glōriōsō*
    dīcis amōre tuī **bellās** ardēre **puellās**,
        quī faciem sub aquā, Sexte, natantis habēs.

glōriōsō: **glōriōsus** *boastful*
bellās: **bellus** *pretty*
faciem: **faciēs** *face*

Judging from Martial's description, what impression do you have of Sextus' appearance?

III *dē Symmachō medicō discipulīsque eius centum*
    languēbam: sed tū comitātus prōtinus ad mē
        vēnistī **centum**, Symmache, **discipulīs**.
    centum mē tetigēre **manūs** Aquilōne **gelātae**;
        nōn habuī febrem, Symmache: nunc habeō.

discipulīs: **discipulus** *pupil, student*
languēbam: **languēre** *feel weak, feel ill*
prōtinus *immediately*
tetigēre = tetigērunt: **tangere** *touch*
Aquilōne: **Aquilō** *North wind*
gelātae: **gelāre** *freeze*
febrem: **febris** *fever*

Why do you think Martial repeats the word **centum** (lines 2–3) and uses the phrase **Aquilōne gelātae** (line 3)?

*centum mē tetigēre manūs
Aquilōne gelātae.*

IV *dē Catullō, quī saepe dīcit Mārtiālem hērēdem sibi esse*
  hērēdem tibi mē, Catulle, dīcis.
  nōn crēdam nisi lēgerō, Catulle.

When will Martial believe Catullus' promise? Why do you think he will believe it then, but not believe it earlier?

V *dē Quīntō, quī Thāida lūscam amat*
  "Thāida Quīntus amat." "quam Thāida?" "Thāida lūscam."
  ūnum oculum Thāis nōn habet, ille duōs.

Thāida *accusative of* **Thāis**
lūscam: lūscus *one-eyed*
quam?: quī? *which?*

What do the last two words suggest about
a Quintus **b** Thais?

VI *dē Vacerrā, quī veterēs poētās sōlōs mīrātur*
  mīrāris **veterēs**, Vacerra, sōlōs
  nec laudās nisi mortuōs **poētās**.
  ignōscās petimus, Vacerra: tantī
  nōn est, ut placeam tibī, perīre.

mīrātur: mīrārī *admire*
ignōscās petimus = petimus ut
  nōbīs ignōscās
tantī nōn est . . . perīre *it is not*
  worth dying

Do people like Vacerra still exist nowadays?

Christ shown as a Roman reading from a book.

About the language 2: word order

1 From Stage 3 on, you have met phrases in which an adjective is placed next to the noun it describes:

ad **silvam obscūram**	*to the dark wood*
contrā **multōs barbarōs**	*against many barbarians*
in **flūmine altō**	*in the deep river*

2 In Unit 3, you met phrases in which an adjective is separated by a preposition from the noun which it describes:

tōtam per **urbem**	*through the whole city*
omnibus cum **mīlitibus**	*with all the soldiers*
hōc ex **oppidō**	*from this town*

3 In Stage 36, you have met sentences like these:

cūr nōn mitto **meōs** tibi, Pontiliāne, **libellōs**?
Why do I not send you my writings, Pontilianus?

aethera contingit **nova** nostrī prīncipis **aula**.
The new palace of our emperor touches the sky.

This kind of word order, in which an adjective is separated by one or more words from the noun which it describes, is particularly common in verse.

Further examples:

a dēnique centuriō **magnam** pervēnit ad **urbem**.

b nox erat, et **caelō** fulgēbat lūna **serēnō**. (*From a poem by Horace*)

c flūminis in rīpā nunc **noster** dormit **amīcus**.

4 In each of the following examples, pick out the Latin adjective and say which noun it is describing:

a atque iterum ad Trōiam magnus mittētur Achillēs. (*Virgil*)
And great Achilles will be sent again to Troy.

b ergō sollicitae tū causa, pecūnia, vītae! (*Propertius*)
Therefore you, money, are the cause of an anxious life!

c rōbustus quoque iam taurīs iuga solvet arātor. (*Virgil*)
Now, too, the strong plowman will unfasten the yoke from the bulls.

5 Translate the following examples:

a *On a journey*
cōnspicimus montēs atque altae moenia Rōmae.

b *Cries of pain*
clāmōrēs simul horrendōs ad sīdera tollit. (*Virgil*)

c *A foreigner*
hic posuit nostrā nūper in urbe pedem. (*Propertius*)

d *Preparations for battle*
tum iuvenis validā sustulit arma manū.

e *The foolishness of sea travel*
cūr cupiunt nautae saevās properāre per undās?

moenia *city walls*
horrendōs: horrendus *horrifying*
properāre *hurry*

Pick out the adjective in each example and say which noun it is describing.

Word patterns: combinations

1 Notice how Latin sometimes combines two or more words into one:

animadvertere *to notice* (a combination of **animus** *mind*, **ad** *to*, and **vertere** *turn*).
To notice is to turn the mind towards.

ēgregius *excellent* (a combination of **ē** *out of* and **grex, gregis** *flock*).
An excellent person stands out from the flock.

amphitheātrum *amphitheater* (a combination of **ambō** *both* and **theātrum** *theater*).
An amphitheater is a double theater (with an arena in the middle).

2 Using paragraph 1 as an example, explain how the following Latin words were formed and how they came to have the meaning they have acquired:

agricola, aquaeductus, aquilifer, duodecim, intervallum, mandāre, merīdiēs, omnipotēns, ūnivira, valedīcere, versipellis.

Practicing the language

1 Complete each sentence with the correct word. Then translate the sentence.

   a Mārtiālis versum dē Imperātōre compōnere . . . . (cōnābātur, ēgrediēbātur)

   b mīlitēs ducem ad ultimās regiōnēs Britanniae . . . . (sequēbantur, suspicābantur)

   c omnēs senātōrēs dē victōriā Agricolae . . . . (adipīscēbantur, loquēbantur)

   d cūr fēminam . . . . ut ad urbem revenīret? (cōnspicābāris, hortābāris)

   e clientēs, quī patrōnum ad forum . . . . , viam complēbant. (comitābantur, proficīscēbantur)

   f nēmō mē, quī multōs cāsūs . . . . , adiuvāre volēbat. (patiēbar, precābar)

2 Translate each sentence. Then change the words in **boldface** from singular to plural. Use the tables on pages 258–267 and 280 to help you.

   a tribūnus **centuriōnem callidum** laudāvit.

   b frāter meus, postquam **hoc templum** vīdit, admīrātiōne affectus est.

   c senex **amīcō dēspērantī** auxilium tulit.

   d ubi **est puella**? **eam** salūtāre volō.

   e iuvenis, **hastā ingentī** armātus, aprum saevum petīvit.

   f **puer**, **quem** heri pūnīvī, hodiē labōrāre nōn **potest**.

   g mē iubēs **rem difficilem** facere.

   h mīlitēs **flūmen altum** trānsiērunt.

3 Complete each sentence with the most suitable verb from the box below, using the correct form. Then translate the sentence. Do not use any verb more than once.

occīdit	accēpit	iussit	recitāvit	dūxit
occīdērunt	accēpērunt	iussērunt	recitāvērunt	dūxērunt
occīsus est	acceptus est	iussus est	recitātus est	ductus est
occīsī sunt	acceptī sunt	iussī sunt	recitātī sunt	ductī sunt

   a senātor ā servō . . . .

   b poēta multōs versūs dē Imperātōre . . . .

   c captīvī per viās urbis in triumphō . . . .

   d clientēs pecūniam laetissimē . . . .

   e lībertus ad aulam contendere . . . .

recitātiōnēs

Although most Latin literature was designed initially for reading, many authors presented their work to a listening audience first. For example, a poet might choose a convenient spot, such as a street corner, a barber's shop, or a colonnade in the forum, and recite his poems to anyone who cared to stop and listen. Like any kind of street performance or sales talk, this could be very entertaining or very annoying for the passersby. In an exaggerated but colorful complaint, Martial claims that a poet called Ligurinus used to recite continually at him, whether he was eating dinner, hurrying along the street, swimming in the baths, or using the public lavatories, and that even when he went to sleep, Ligurinus woke him up and began reciting again.

An author reading from a scroll.

Often, however, a writer's work received its first reading in a more comfortable place than the street corner, with a carefully chosen group of listeners rather than a casual collection of passersby. A natural audience for a writer was his patron, if he had one, and his patron's family and friends. For example, Virgil read sections of his poem the *Aeneid* to the Emperor Augustus and to Augustus' sister Octavia, who is said to have fainted when Virgil reached a part of the poem which referred to her dead son Marcellus. A writer might also invite friends to his house and read his work to them there. This kind of reading sometimes took place at a dinner party. If the host was an accomplished and entertaining writer, this would add to the guests' enjoyment of the meal; but some hosts made great nuisances of themselves by reading boring or feeble work to their dinner guests.

Mosaic showing the poet Virgil, with the Aeneid *on his lap. The two female figures are goddesses, the Muses of epic poetry and tragedy.*

The public reading of a writer's work often took place at a special occasion known as a **recitātiō**, like the one on pages 16–18, in which an invited audience had a chance to hear the author's work and could decide whether or not to buy a copy or have a copy made. The recitatio might be given at the writer's house, at the house of his patron, or in a hall (**audītōrium**) especially rented for the purpose. Invitations were sent out. A raised platform for the **recitātor** was erected at one end of the hall. In the front rows cushioned chairs were set out for the more distinguished guests. Behind them were placed benches, and, if the recitatio was a very grand occasion, even tiered seats on temporary scaffolding. Slaves gave out programs to the audience as they arrived. All these expenses were met by the author or his patron. If the writer was unscrupulous or over-anxious, he might even plant friends or hired clappers in the audience with instructions to applaud at appropriate passages.

When all was ready, the reading started. Generally the author himself read his work, though there were exceptions. Pliny the Younger, for example, knew that he was bad at reading poetry; so although he read his speeches himself, he had his poems read by a freedman. The writer, specially dressed for the occasion in a freshly laundered toga, stepped forward and delivered a short introduction (**praefātiō**) to his work, then sat to read the work itself. The recital might be continued on a second and third day, sometimes at the request of the audience.

Things did not always go smoothly at recitationes. The Emperor Claudius, when young, embarked on a series of readings from his own historical work, but disaster struck when an enormously fat man joined the audience and sat down on a flimsy bench, which collapsed beneath him; in the general laughter it became impossible for the reading to continue. Pliny records a more serious incident during the reign of Trajan. A historian, who had announced that he would continue his reading in a few days' time, was approached by a group of people who begged him not to read the next passage because they knew it would be dealing with some fairly recent events in which they had been involved. It is possible that the author concerned was the historian Tacitus, describing the misdeeds of the Emperor Domitian and his associates. The historian granted the request and canceled the next installment of the reading. However, as Pliny pointed out, canceling the recitatio did not mean that the men's misdeeds would stay unknown: people would be all the more curious to read the history, in order to find out why the recitatio had been canceled.

Statuette of a man reading from a scroll. With his prominent ears, he could have been intended as a caricature of Claudius.

Pliny, who gave recitationes of his own work and also regularly attended those of other people, was very shocked at the frivolous way in which some members of the audience behaved: "Some of them loiter and linger outside the hall, and send their slaves in to find out how far the recitatio has gotten; then, when the slaves report that the author has nearly finished his reading, they come in at last – and even then they don't always stay, but slip out before the end, some of them sheepishly and furtively, others boldly and brazenly." Pliny was more impressed by the response of his wife to his recitals: "Whenever I recite, she sits nearby but behind a curtain, and listens with greedy ears to the audience singing my praises."

The attitude of Romans toward recitationes varied. While Pliny the Younger attached great importance to public readings, Martial, once he was an established poet, laughed at them. By then public recognition of Martial's literary qualities was so assured that he could afford to disregard the success of the recitatio. Seneca wrote that when the author asked the audience, "Shall I read some more?" they usually replied, "Yes, please do," but privately they were praying for the man to be struck dumb. Juvenal sarcastically includes recitationes among the dangers and disadvantages of life in Rome, together with fires and falling buildings. In fact, the work read out must have varied enormously in quality: occasional masterpieces, a sprinkling of good-to-middling work, and plenty of trash.

However, in first-century Rome, when every copy of a book had to be produced individually by hand, recitationes filled a real need. They enabled the author to bring his work to the notice of many people without the expense and labor of creating large numbers of copies. From the response of the listeners, the author could learn if his work was worth publishing. From a discerning audience, the author could obtain comments and criticism that would help in the final revision of his work. There was a danger, however, that the exaggerated applause of a clique might encourage the conceit of an indifferent author. An even more serious criticism of recitationes is that they encouraged writers to think too much about impressing their patron or their audience. One author admitted that much of what he wrote was done not because it pleased him but because it would please his audience.

From the audience's point of view, recitationes were useful. It was far harder in Roman than in modern times to go into a library or a bookstore, run one's eye over the titles and covers, sample the contents of a few likely-looking books, and make a selection. The physical nature of a Roman book (see illustration on page 21) meant that there was no such thing as a cover; the title was printed not on a convenient part of the book but on a label attached to it, which was often lost; and the act of unrolling and reading a book, then rerolling it ready for the next reader, was so laborious that sampling and browsing were virtually impossible. The recitatio allowed the author to present his work to an audience conveniently, economically, and (if he was a good reader) attractively.

A reconstruction of a Roman gentleman's library, with cupboards for the scrolls and a statue of Minerva, goddess of wisdom.

Vocabulary checklist 36

animadvertō, animadvertere,
  animadvertī, animadversus — *notice, take notice of*
arma, armōrum, n. pl. — *arms, weapons*
causa, causae, f. — *reason, cause*
discipulus, discipulī, m. — *pupil, student*
dōnō, dōnāre, dōnāvī, dōnātus — *give*
extrēmus, extrēma, extrēmum — *farthest*
fīnis, fīnis, m. — *end*
ignis, ignis, m. — *fire*
mīror, mīrārī, mīrātus sum — *admire, wonder at*
nē — *that … not, in order that … not*
niger, nigra, nigrum — *black*
praesertim — *especially*
praeter (+ACC) — *except*
recitō, recitāre, recitāvī, recitātus — *recite, read out*
tangō, tangere, tetigī, tāctus — *touch*
vetus, *gen.* veteris — *old*

Inkwell, pen, and scroll, showing its label.

CONSILIUM

Stage 37

Agricola, Calēdoniīs victīs, epistulam nūntiō dictat. in hāc epistulā Agricola victōriam Rōmānōrum Imperātōrī nūntiat.

1 "exercitus Rōmānus Calēdoniōs superāvit!"

Agricola dīcit exercitum Rōmānum Calēdoniōs superāvisse.

2 "multī hostēs periērunt, paucī effūgērunt."

Agricola dīcit multōs hostēs periisse, paucōs effūgisse.

3 "aliae gentēs nūntiōs iam mīsērunt quī pācem petant."

Agricola dīcit aliās gentēs nūntiōs mīsisse quī pācem petant.

epistula

Cn. Iūlius Agricola Domitiānō Imperātōrī salūtem dīcit.
septimus annus est, domine, ex quō pater tuus, dīvus
Vespasiānus, ad prōvinciam Britanniam mē mīsit, ut barbarōs
superārem. tū ipse, audītīs precibus meīs, iussistī Calēdoniōs
quoque in populī Rōmānī potestātem redigī. nunc tibi nūntiō
exercitum Rōmānum magnam victōriam rettulisse. bellum est
cōnfectum; Calēdoniī sunt victī.

 initiō huius aestātis, exercitus noster ad ultimās partēs
Britanniae pervēnit. hostēs, adventū nostrō cognitō, prope
montem Graupium sē ad proelium īnstrūxērunt. ibi mīlitēs
nostrī, spē glōriae adductī, victōriam nōmine tuō dignam
rettulērunt. incertum est quot hostēs perierint; sciō tamen
paucissimōs effūgisse. explōrātōrēs meī affirmant nōnnūllōs
superstitēs, salūte dēspērātā, etiam casās suās incendisse atque
uxōrēs līberōsque manū suā occīdisse.

 dē bellō satis dīxī. nunc pāx firmanda est. ego ipse Britannōs
hortātus sum ut templa, fora, domōs exstruant; filiīs prīncipum
persuāsī ut linguam Latīnam discant. mōrēs Rōmānī ā Britannīs
iam adsūmuntur; ubīque geruntur togae.

 ūna cūra tamen mē sollicitat. timeō nē inquiēta sit Britannia,
dum Hibernia īnsula in lībertāte manet. quod sī Hibernōs
superāverimus, nōn modo pācem in Britanniā habēbimus, sed
etiam magnās dīvitiās comparābimus; audiō enim ex
mercātōribus metalla Hiberniae aurum multum continēre.
equidem crēdō hanc īnsulam legiōne ūnā obtinērī posse. mīlitēs
sunt parātī; signum Imperātōris alacriter exspectātur. valē.

5 **Cn.** = **Gnaeus**

 **in ... potestātem redigī: in
  potestātem redigere**
   bring under the control
**victōriam rettulisse: victōriam
  referre** *win a victory*
10 **initiō: initium** *beginning*
aestātis: aestās *summer*
proelium *battle*

15

 firmanda est: firmāre
   strengthen, establish

 adsūmuntur: adsūmere *adopt*
20 **sollicitat: sollicitāre** *worry*
timeō nē *I am afraid that*
inquiēta: inquiētus *unsettled*
Hibernia *Ireland*
quod sī *but if*
aurum *gold*
25 **equidem** *indeed*
 obtinērī: obtinēre *hold*
 alacriter *eagerly*

*Drawing of a coin (a brass sestertius) issued shortly after the battle of
Mons Graupius.*

amīcī prīncipis

When you have read this story, answer the questions on the next page.

diē illūcēscente, complūrēs senātōrēs in aulam Domitiānī
conveniēbant. nam Domitiānus cōnsilium suum ad aulam
arcessī iusserat. L. Catullus Messālīnus, vir maximae
auctōritātis, et Q. Vibius Crispus, senātor septuāgintā annōs   **Q. = Quīntus**
nātus, dum Imperātōrem exspectant, anxiī inter sē   5
colloquēbantur.

Messālīnus: cūr adeō perturbāris, mī Crispe? nōn intellegō
             quārē anxius sīs.
Crispus: nōn sine causā perturbor. ego enim prīmus ā
             Domitiānō sententiam rogābor, quia cōnsulāris   10   **cōnsulāris** *ex-consul*
             sum nātū maximus. at nisi sciam quārē
             Domitiānus nōs arcessīverit, sententiam bene
             meditātam prōpōnere nōn poterō.   **meditātam: meditārī** *consider*
Messālīnus: difficile est mihi tē adiuvāre, mī amīce. nescio
             enim quārē Domitiānus nōs cōnsulere velit. aliī   15   **putant: putāre** *think*
             dīcunt nūntium ē Britanniā advēnisse; aliī putant
             Germānōs rebellāvisse; aliī crēdunt ministrōs   **ministrōs: minister** *servant,*
             Epaphrodītī coniūrātiōnem dēprehendisse. nōn   *agent*
             tamen tibi timendum est; tū enim es senātor   **dēprehendisse: dēprehendere**
             summae auctōritātis.   20   *discover*
Crispus: id quod dīcis fortasse vērum est. nihilōminus mihi
             semper difficile est intellegere quāle respōnsum
             Domitiānus cupiat. sēnsūs enim vērōs dissimulāre   **sēnsūs: sēnsus** *feeling*
             solet. sī tamen tū mē adiūveris, sēcūrus erō. vīsne,
             quicquid dīxerō, sententiam similem prōpōnere?   25   **quicquid** *whatever*
Messālīnus: minimē! perīculum mihi ipsī facere   **similem: similis** *similar*
             haudquāquam volō. nihil dīcam priusquam
             Epaphrodītī sententiam audīverō.
Crispus: sed –
Messālīnus: tacē, mī amīce! adest Imperātor.   30

Questions

1 At what time of day did this conversation take place?
2 Why were the senators gathering in the palace?
3 Which Latin word shows how Messalinus and Crispus were feeling (lines 3–6)?
4 **ego enim … maximus** (lines 9–11). Who will be asked for an opinion first? Why?
5 What does he need to know before he can give a well-considered opinion (lines 11–13)?
6 Messalinus mentions three rumors he has heard (lines 15–18). What are they?
7 **nōn tamen … auctōritātis** (lines 18–20). How does Messalinus try to reassure Crispus?
8 What favor does Crispus ask from Messalinus (lines 24–25)?
9 Why does Messalinus refuse (lines 26–27)?
10 What impression do you get in this passage of
   a Domitian
   b Epaphroditus?
   Make one point about each character and support your answer by referring to the text.

About the language 1: indirect statement (perfect active infinitive)

1 Compare the following direct and indirect statements:

direct statements
"servus fūgit."
"The slave has fled."

indirect statements
dominus crēdit servum **fūgisse**.
The master believes the slave to have fled.
Or, in more natural English:
The master believes that the slave has fled.

"Rōmānī multa oppida dēlēvērunt."
"The Romans have destroyed
many towns."

audiō Rōmānōs multa oppida **dēlēvisse**.
*I hear that the Romans have destroyed
many towns.*

The form of the verb in **boldface** is known as the **perfect active infinitive**.

2 Further examples:

a "hostēs castra in rīpā flūminis posuērunt."
b centuriō dīcit hostēs castra in rīpā flūminis posuisse.
c "Rōmānī magnam victōriam rettulērunt."
d in hāc epistulā Agricola nūntiat Rōmānōs magnam victōriam rettulisse.
e clientēs putant patrōnum ex urbe discessisse.
f scio senātōrem vīllam splendidam in Campāniā aedificāvisse.

3 Compare the perfect active infinitive with the perfect active indicative:

perfect active indicative (1st person singular)		*perfect active infinitive*	
portāvī	*I have carried*	portāvisse	*to have carried*
docuī	*I have taught*	docuisse	*to have taught*
trāxī	*I have dragged*	trāxisse	*to have dragged*
audīvī	*I have heard*	audīvisse	*to have heard*

cōnsilium Domitiānī

I

dum senātōrēs anxiī inter sē colloquuntur, ingressus est
Domitiānus vultū ita compositō ut nēmō intellegere posset
utrum īrātus an laetus esset. eum sequēbātur Epaphrodītus,
epistulam manū tenēns.

Domitiānus, ā senātōribus salūtātus, "nūntius," inquit, "nōbīs 5
epistulam modo attulit, ā Cn. Iūliō Agricolā missam. in hāc
epistulā Agricola nūntiat exercitum
Rōmānum ad ultimās partēs
Britanniae pervēnisse et magnam
victōriam rettulisse. affirmat bellum 10
cōnfectum esse. Epaphrodīte,
epistulam recitā."

epistulā recitātā, Domitiānus, ad
Crispum statim conversus,
"quid," inquit, "dē hāc Agricolae 15
epistulā putās? quid mihi suādēs?"

Crispus diū tacēbat; superciliīs
contractīs quasi rem cōgitāret, oculōs
humī dēfīxit. dēnique:
"moderātiōnem," inquit, "suādeō." 20
Domitiānus "breviter," inquit, "et prūdenter locūtus es; tua
tamen sententia amplius est explicanda."
priusquam Crispus respondēret, A. Fabricius Vēientō, cēterīs
paulō audācior, interpellāvit. veritus tamen nē Domitiānum
offenderet, verbīs cōnsīderātīs ūsus 25
est:

"cognōvimus, domine, Calēdoniōs
tandem victōs esse. Agricola tamen
hāc victōriā nimis ēlātus est. nam
crēdit īnsulam Hiberniam facile 30
occupārī posse; ego autem putō
Agricolam longē errāre; Hibernī enim
et ferōcēs et validī sunt. sī cōpiae
nostrae trāns mare in Hiberniam
ductae erunt, magnō perīculō 35
obicientur. revocandus est Agricola."
quibus verbīs offēnsus, M'. Acīlius
Glabriō, "equidem valdē gaudeō," inquit, "Calēdoniōs superātōs
esse. sī Hibernia quoque ab Agricolā victa erit, tōtam Britanniam
in potestāte nostrā habēbimus. absurdum est Agricolam 40
revocāre priusquam Britannōs omnīnō superet! quis nostrōrum
ducum est melior quam Agricola? quis dignior est triumphō?"

modo *just now*
suādēs: suādēre *advise, suggest*
**superciliīs contractīs: supercilia
    contrahere** *draw eyebrows
        together, frown*
moderātiōnem: moderātiō
        moderation, caution
breviter *briefly*
prūdenter *prudently, sensibly*
amplius *more fully*
A. = Aulus
veritus: verērī *be afraid, fear*
cōnsīderātīs: cōnsīderātus
        careful, well-considered
ūsus est: ūtī *use*
ēlātus *excited, carried away*
cōpiae *forces*
obicientur: obicere
        put in the way of, expose to

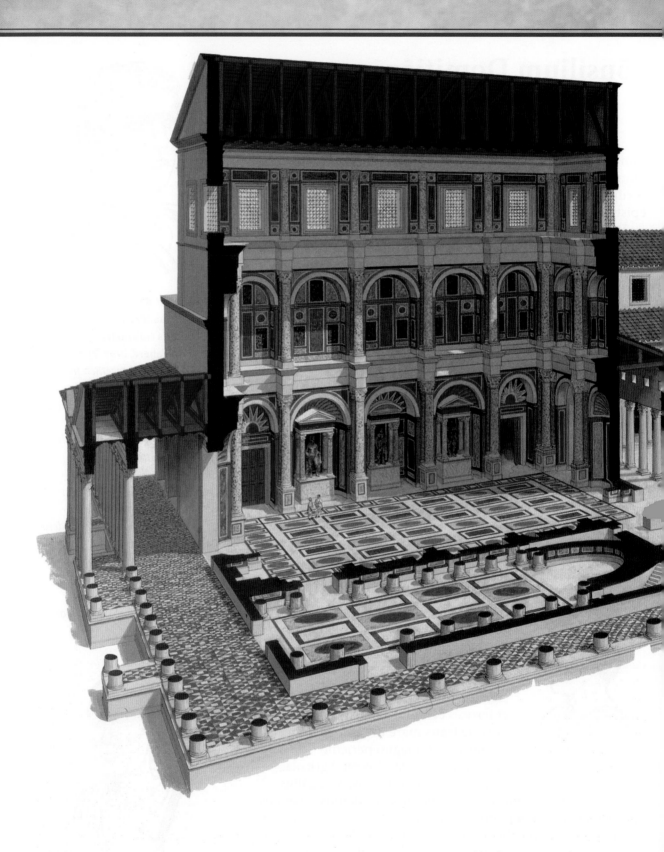

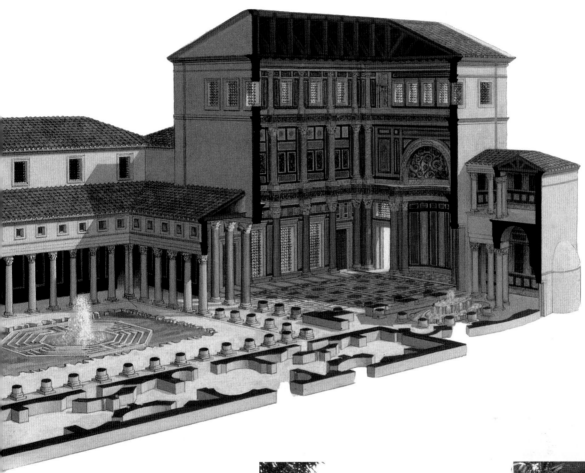

Above: *A reconstruction of part of Domitian's enormous palace on the Palatine hill. At the left there is a large hall* (aula) *where the emperor's consilium might have met. It was flanked by two other large rooms. In the center is a peristylium with a fountain, and on the right, a vast dining room.*

Right: *The remains of the porch in front of the large hall (at the left in the reconstruction). Built of brick-faced concrete, the palace was covered in colored marbles.*

II

cētērī, audāciā Glabriōnis obstupefactī, oculōs in
Imperātōrem dēfīxōs tenēbant nec quicquam dīcere audēbant.
ille tamen nec verbō nec vultū sēnsūs ostendit. deinde
Epaphrodītus, ad Glabriōnem
conversus,   5

"num comparās," inquit, "hanc
inānem Agricolae victōriam cum
rēbus splendidīs ab Imperātōre
nostrō gestīs? nōnne audīvistī, mī
Glabriō, Imperātōrem ipsum   10
proximō annō multa mīlia
Germānōrum superāvisse? num
oblītus es prīncipēs Germānōs,
catēnīs vīnctōs, per viās urbis in
triumphō dēductōs esse?"   15
tum Messālīnus, simulatque
haec Epaphrodītī verba audīvit,
occāsiōne ūsus,
"scīmus," inquit, "nūllōs hostēs ferōciōrēs Germānīs esse,
nūllum ducem Domitiānō Augustō esse meliōrem. scīmus etiam 20
Agricolam in prōvinciā septem
annōs mānsisse. ipse affirmat tam
fidēlēs sibi legiōnēs esse ut ad
Hiberniam sine timōre prōgredī
possit. cavendum est nōbīs! timeō nē 25
Agricola, spē imperiī adductus, in
Ītaliam cum legiōnibus reveniat
bellumque contrā patriam gerat.
num Glabriō cupit Agricolam fierī
Imperātōrem? Agricola, meā   30
sententiā, revocandus, laudandus,
tollendus est."

Glabriō nihil respondit. nōn enim
dubitābat quīn Imperātōrem
graviter offendisset. Messālīnī sententiam cētērī senātōrēs   35
alacriter secūtī sunt.
Domitiānus autem nūllum signum dedit neque odiī neque
gaudiī neque invidiae. cōnsiliō tandem dīmissō, in ātriō sōlus
mānsit; multa in animō dē Glabriōne atque Agricolā volvēbat.

---

comparās: comparāre *compare*

gestīs: gerere *achieve*

proximō: proximus *last*

oblītus es: oblīvīscī *forget*

imperiī: imperium *power*

fierī *to become, to be made*

tollendus: tollere
    remove, do away with
nōn … dubitābat quīn
    did not doubt that

invidiae: invidia *jealousy, envy*

About the language 2: indirect statement (perfect passive infinitive)

1 Compare the following direct and indirect statements:

direct statements	*indirect statements*
"captīvī līberātī sunt."	scio captīvōs **līberātōs esse**.
"The prisoners have been freed."	I know the prisoners to have been freed.
	Or, in more natural English:
	I know that the prisoners have been freed.
"nūntius ab Agricolā missus est."	lībertus dīcit nūntium ab Agricolā **missum esse**.
"A messenger has been sent by Agricola."	The freedman says that a messenger has been sent by Agricola.

The form of the verb in **boldface** is known as the **perfect passive infinitive**.

2 Further examples:

a "multī Calēdoniī occīsī sunt."

b in hāc epistulā Agricola nūntiat multōs Calēdoniōs occīsōs esse.

c "templum novum in forō exstrūctum est."

d mercātōrēs dīcunt templum novum in forō exstrūctum esse.

e audiō lībertātem omnibus servīs datam esse.

f nauta crēdit quattuor nāvēs tempestāte dēlētās esse.

3 Compare the perfect passive indicative and the perfect passive infinitive:

perfect passive indicative *(1st person singular)*		*perfect passive infinitive*	
portātus sum	I have been carried	portātus esse	to have been carried
doctus sum	I have been taught	doctus esse	to have been taught
tractus sum	I have been dragged	tractus esse	to have been dragged
audītus sum	I have been heard	audītus esse	to have been heard

Notice that the perfect passive infinitive contains the perfect passive participle (**portātus**, etc.), which changes its ending in the usual way to agree with the noun it describes:

videō cibum **parātum** esse.	videō nāvēs **parātās** esse.
I see that the food has been prepared.	I see that the ships have been prepared.

Word patterns: frequentatives

1 Study the form and meaning of the following verbs:

agere	*to drive*	agitāre	*to chase*
volāre	*to fly*	volitāre	*to flit, to fly about*
habēre	*to have*	habitāre	*to have possession of, to inhabit*

The verbs in the second column are called **frequentatives**. They indicate repeated or more intense action than the basic verb from which they are formed.

2 Using paragraph 1 as a guide, complete the following table:

dīcere	. . . .	dictāre	*to dictate*
salīre	*to jump*	saltāre	. . . .
haerēre	. . . .	haesitāre	. . . .
. . . .	. . . .	clāmitāre	*to cry out violently*
. . . .	*to sleep*	. . . .	*to fall asleep*

3 Give the meaning for the following frequentative verbs:

cantāre, captāre, cōgitāre, iactāre, pulsāre, ventitāre, vīsitāre.

4 The verb **dubitāre** is a combination of **duo** and **habitāre**. Explain how it comes to have the meanings given in the vocabulary checklist for this Stage.

Practicing the language

1 Complete each sentence with the most suitable word from the box below, and then translate.

audītō   aedificābātur   poterant   prōcēdere   Imperātōrī   esset

a in summō monte novum templum . . . .

b nūntius, simulatque advēnit, ... epistulam trādidit.

c strepitū . . . . , cōnsul ē lectō surrēxit.

d facile cognōvī quis auctor pugnae . . . .

e putō pompam per forum iam . . . .

f post proelium paucī Calēdoniī effugere . . . .

2 Translate the first sentence of each pair. Then, with the help of page 270, complete the second sentence with a passive form of the verb to express the same idea. Finally, translate the second sentence.

For example: senātōrēs Domitiānum timent.
 Domitiānus ā senātōribus timē… .

Translated and completed, this becomes:
 senātōrēs Domitiānum timent.
 The senators fear Domitian.
 Domitiānus ā senātōribus timētur.
 Domitian is feared by the senators.

a dux equitēs iam incitat.
 equitēs ā duce iam incita… .

b exercitus noster oppidum mox dēlēbit.
 oppidum ab exercitū nostrō mox dēlē… .

In sentences **c–f**, nouns as well as verbs have to be completed. Refer if necessary to the table of nouns on pages 258–259.

c multī cīvēs lūdōs spectābunt.
 lūdī ā multīs cīv… spectā… .

d puellae ātrium ōrnant.
 ātrium ā puell… ōrnā… .

e puer victimās ad āram dūcēbat.
 victimae ad āram ā puer… dūcē… .

f mercātor ancillam accūsābat.
 ancill… ā mercātor… accūsā… .

3 Translate each sentence into Latin by selecting correctly from the list of Latin words.

a *The barbarians have been surrounded by our army.*

| barbarī | ad exercitum | nostrō | circumventus est |
| barbarīs | ab exercitū | noster | circumventī sunt |

b *A certain senator is trying to deceive you.*

| senātōrī | quīdam | tē | dēcipit | cōnātur |
| senātor | quidem | tuī | dēcipere | cōnantur |

c *She was lying hidden, in order to hear the old men's conversation.*

| latēbat | ut | sermōnem | senem | audīvisset |
| latuerat | nē | sermō | senum | audīret |

d *The same clients will be here tomorrow.*

| eōsdem | cliēns | crās | aderunt |
| eīdem | clientēs | cotīdiē | aberunt |

e *The instigator of the crime did not want to be seen in the forum.*

| auctor | scelerī | in forum | vidēre | volēbat |
| auctōrem | sceleris | in forō | vidērī | nōlēbat |

The emperor's council

Among the people who took part in the government of the empire were the members of the emperor's **cōnsilium** (council), often referred to as **amīcī** (friends) of the emperor.

The consilium did not have a fixed membership; it was simply made up of those people whom the emperor invited to advise him on any particular occasion. Some men were regularly asked to meetings of the consilium; others were asked occasionally. Many would be experienced and distinguished men of senatorial rank, who had reached the top of the career ladder described on pages 43–45. Some men of equestrian rank might also be invited, such as the commander of the praetorian guard. When there was a change of emperor, the new emperor usually invited some new members to meetings of the consilium, but also found it convenient to continue using some of the previous emperor's advisers. In many cases the new emperor had himself attended the previous emperor's consilium.

The matters on which the emperor asked his consilium for advice were naturally varied. The consilium might, for example, be summoned in moments of crisis, such as the discovery of a conspiracy against the emperor's life; or it might be consulted on the delicate question: "Who should be the emperor's heir?" Sometimes the emperor would want advice about military decisions or foreign affairs. The story on pages 35 and 38, in which Domitian asks his advisers about Agricola's letter from Britain, is fictitious, but it would not have been odd or unusual for the consilium to have discussed such a question.

Relief showing an emperor dealing with affairs of state, seated on a platform in front of the Basilica Iulia in the Forum.

However, the commonest task of the amici was to advise the emperor while he was administering the law. For example, they might join him when he was hearing an appeal by a condemned prisoner, or settling a property dispute between two or more parties. After the people concerned had stated their case, the emperor would ask for the **sententia** (opinion) of each member of the consilium in turn; he might then retire for further thought, and would finally announce his decision. He was not bound to follow the majority opinion of the consilium, and could even ignore their advice altogether. In theory, the amici were free to give their opinions firmly and frankly; but under some emperors it could be dangerous to speak one's mind too openly. During Domitian's reign a number of amici used their position as members of the consilium to increase their own power and to spread rumors and accusations about their enemies; it was said of one man that he could "slit a throat with a whisper."

Some of the cases which were heard by the Emperor Trajan are described by Pliny, who was sometimes invited to Trajan's consilium. They include a charge of adultery against a military tribune's wife and a centurion, and a dispute in a small town in Gaul where the local mayor had abolished the town's annual games. It is clear from Pliny's account that even quite trivial cases were sometimes referred to the emperor for decision; most Roman emperors were kept very busy, and needed the help of their amici in order to cope with the workload.

The senatorial career

Most of the amici taking part in the discussion on pages 35 and 38 would have successfully followed a career known as the senatorial **cursus honōrum** (series of honors or ladder of promotion), in which members of the senatorial class competed with each other for official posts in the Roman government. These official positions were arranged in a fixed order. As a man worked his way through them, his responsibilities and status steadily increased. Some posts were compulsory, so that a man who had not held a particular post was not allowed to proceed to a higher one, except by special favor of the emperor. Some positions also had age restrictions. To gain a position **suō annō** (in one's year) meant at the earliest possible age. The most successful men got to the top of the ladder of positions while the rest dropped out at various points along the way.

Some officials, such as the consuls, were chosen by the emperor; others were elected by the senate. Even in those posts where the choice was made by the senate, the emperor still had great influence, since he could "recommend" to the senate particular candidates for election.

By the time of Domitian, the most important stages in the cursus honorum were as follows:

Holders of the senior posts – aediles, praetors, and consuls – had the honor of sitting in an ivory-inlaid "curule chair."

The senatorial cursus honorum

1 **vīgintīvir**. Every year twenty young men were chosen as vigintiviri, who served for a year in Rome as junior officials, assisting with such tasks as the management of the law courts and prisons, and the minting of the Roman coinage.

2 **tribūnus mīlitum**. In the following year, each of the young men went abroad on military service as an officer in a legion.

3 **quaestor**. On returning to Rome, a man who wanted to progress further in the cursus honorum would aim at the quaestorship. This position involved the management of sums of public money and was usually (but not always) held in Rome. It lasted for one year and was important because it qualified a man for entry into the senate, which met regularly to discuss and decide government business.

4 **tribūnus plēbis** or **aedīlis**. After a compulsory interval of a year, an ex-quaestor who wanted further promotion had a choice. He might aim to become one of the ten tribunes of the people, whose original responsibility had been to act as helpers and advisers of the common people (**plebs**), but whose tasks had been greatly reduced by the time of Domitian. Alternatively, he could try to be appointed as one of the six aediles, who were responsible for the upkeep of public buildings, baths, sewers, and roads.

5 **praetor**. The chief task of the praetors was to supervise the Roman law courts. A man who had held the praetorship also became eligible for certain important posts abroad; for example, he might command a legion, or govern one of the twenty-eight provinces (but not the ten most important ones). Governorships of provinces were normally held for a period of three years.

6 **cōnsul**. The highest post in the cursus honorum was the consulship. There were only two consuls at any one time, but they changed at intervals during the year. They presided at meetings of the senate, and had a general responsibility for supervising government business. The ablest ex-consuls became governors of the ten most important provinces; some men, through exceptional ability or by favor of the emperor, achieved further distinctions, including second or even third consulships.

C PLINIO L F
OVF CAECILIO
SECVNDO COS
AVGVR CVR ALV TIB
ET RIP ET CLOAC VRB
PRAEF AER SAT
PRAEF
AER MIL Q IMP
SEVIR EQ R TR MIL
LEG III GALL XVIRO
STL IVD FL DIVI T AVG
VERCELLENSES

Above: *An inscription, with transcript, setting out the career of Pliny, found in a town where he had a villa. It was set up in his honor by the people of Vercellae. His final posting, to Bithynia, must have come later (coin of Nicaea in Bithynia, below).*

This system enabled the emperor to see who the best men were. It also showed him whether a man had any special skills which made him suitable for a particular job or province. For example, Agricola was a good soldier, while Pliny was an expert in financial matters; each man was given work that offered him opportunities to use his particular gifts. The careers of both men are given below. They differ from each other in the early stages, because Agricola did not become a vigintivir and had an unusually long period as a military tribune. Pliny's career looks somewhat fuller than Agricola's; this is partly because Agricola's governorship of Britain was exceptionally lengthy, and partly because Agricola held no post at all between his recall from Britain and his death.

Career of Agricola

AD	
40	birth
58–61	tribunus militum in Britain
64	quaestor in Asia
66	tribunus plebis
68	praetor
70–73	legatus Legionis XX in Britain
74–76	legatus (governor) of Aquitania
77	consul
78–84	legatus (governor) of Britain
93	death

Career of Pliny

AD	
61 or 62	birth
?82	vigintivir (with responsibility for one of the law courts)
?83	tribunus militum in Syria
90	quaestor in Rome
92	tribunus plebis
93	praetor
94–96	praefectus aerarii militaris (in charge of the military treasury)
98–100	praefectus aerarii Saturni (in charge of the treasury of the god Saturn)
100	consul
103	augur (honorary priesthood, held simultaneously with other positions)
104–106	curator Tiberis (responsible for flood precautions, drainage, etc., in connection with Tiber river)
109–111	legatus Augusti in Bithynia (a special governorship by personal appointment of the emperor)
111	death

Several of the above dates, especially in the early part of Pliny's career, are approximate and uncertain.

Vocabulary checklist 37

complūrēs, complūra	*several*
dignus, digna, dignum	*worthy, appropriate*
discō, discere, didicī	*learn*
dīvus, dīvī, m.	*god*
dubitō, dubitāre, dubitāvī	*hesitate, doubt*
exercitus, exercitūs, m.	*army*
fīō, fierī, factus sum	*become, be made*
oblīvīscor, oblīvīscī, oblītus sum	*forget*
odium, odiī, n.	*hatred*
patria, patriae, f.	*country, homeland*
paulō	*a little*
perturbō, perturbāre, perturbāvī, perturbātus	*alarm, disturb*
proelium, proeliī, n.	*battle*
puto, putāre, putāvī	*think*
revocō, revocāre, revocāvī, revocātus	*recall, call back*
sēcūrus, sēcūra, sēcūrum	*without a care*
tempestās, tempestātis, f.	*storm*
trāns (+ACC)	*across*
validus, valida, validum	*strong*

Pliny's experience as Prefect of the Treasury of Saturn (housed in this temple overlooking the Forum Romanum) prepared him for sorting out the considerable financial problems of Bithynia.

NUPTIAE

Stage 38

Imperātōris sententia

When you have read this story, answer the questions on the next page.

in aulā Domitiānī, T. Flāvius Clēmēns, adfīnis Imperātōris, cum Domitiānō anxius colloquitur. Clēmēns semper cum Imperātōre cōnsentīre solet; verētur enim nē idem sibi accidat ac frātrī, quī iussū Imperātōris occīsus est.

		adfīnis *relative, relation by marriage*

Domitiānus: decōrum est mihi, mī Clēmēns, tē līberōsque tuōs 5
honōrāre. ego ipse, ut scīs, līberōs nūllōs habeō
quī imperium post mortem meam exerceant.
cōnstituī igitur fīliōs tuōs in familiam meam
ascīscere. cognōmina "Domitiānum" et
"Vespasiānum" eīs dabō; praetereā rhētorem 10
nōtissimum eīs praeficiam, M. Fabium
Quīntiliānum. prō certō habeō Quīntiliānum eōs
optimē doctūrum esse.

Clēmēns: grātiās maximās tibi agō, domine, quod mē
fīliōsque meōs tantō honōre afficis. ego semper – 15

Domitiānus: satis! pauca nunc dē Pōllā, fīliā tuā, loquī velim.
crēdō Pōllam quattuordecim annōs iam nātam
esse. nōnne necesse est nōbīs eam in
mātrimōnium collocāre?

Clēmēns: domine – 20

Domitiānus: virum quendam cognōvī quī omnī modō fīliā tuā
dignus est. commendō tibi Sparsum, senātōrem
summae virtūtis quī magnās dīvitiās possidet.

Clēmēns: at, domine, iam quīnquāgintā annōs nātus est
Sparsus. 25

Domitiānus: ita vērō! aetāte flōret.

Clēmēns: at bis mātrimōniō iūnctus, utramque uxōrem
repudiāvit.

Domitiānus: prō certō habeō eum numquam cognātam
Imperātōris repudiātūrum esse. quid multa? 30
prōmittō Sparsum tibi generum grātissimum
futūrum esse. haec est sententia mea, quam sī
dissēnseris mūtābō. sed prius tibi explicandum
erit quārē dissentiās.

adfīnis *relative, relation by marriage*
idem ... ac *the same ... as*

ascīscere *adopt*
cognōmina: cognōmen *surname, additional name*

afficis: afficere *treat*

quattuordecim *fourteen*

virtūtis: virtūs *virtue*

aetāte flōret: aetāte flōrēre *be in the prime of life*
bis *twice*
iūnctus: iungere *join*
utramque: uterque *each, both*
repudiāvit: repudiāre *divorce*
cognātam: cognāta *relative (by birth)*
quid multa? *what more is there to say?, in short*
generum: gener *son-in-law*
grātissimum: grātus *acceptable, pleasing*
mūtābō: mūtāre *change*

prō certō habeō
Quīntiliānum eōs
optimē doctūrum esse.

Questions

1 What is taking place in the palace?

2 What attitude does Clemens always take toward Domitian? Why?

3 What is Domitian proposing to do (lines 5–6)?

4 What problem does he have (lines 6–7)?

5 How has he decided to solve it (lines 8–9)?

6 What arrangements will he make about the boys' education? What guarantee does he make to Clemens (lines 10–13)?

7 What proposal does Domitian make about Polla? Why does he think it is the right time to make it?

8 **commendō … possidet** (lines 22–23). Why does Domitian recommend Sparsus?

9 What is the first objection Clemens makes to Sparsus (lines 24–25)? What do you think of Domitian's reply?

10 What is Clemens' second objection (lines 27–28)? Do you think Domitian's answer is convincing (lines 29–30)? Give a reason.

11 **haec est … dissentiās** (lines 32–34). What does Domitian say he will do if Clemens disagrees? What condition does he attach? Do you think Clemens will disagree? Give a reason.

12 What does this story tell us about Domitian's attitude to his family? Make two points.

Pōlla

Pōlla, fīlia Clēmentis, fortūnam suam queritur; māter Flāvia eam cōnsōlārī cōnātur.

Pōlla:	quam crūdēlis est pater meus, quī mē Sparsō nūbere iussit! quid faciam, māter? num putās mē istī senī umquam nūptūram esse? scīs mē alium quendam amāre.
Flāvia:	ō dēliciae, nōlī lacrimāre! dūra est vīta; necesse est pārēre eīs quī nōs regunt. crēdō tamen Sparsum satis grātum et benignum tibi futūrum esse.
Pōlla:	cūr mē ita dēcipis? scīs eum esse senem odiōsum. scīs etiam eum duās uxōrēs iam repudiāvisse. at tū, māter, sententiā Imperātōris nimis movēris; nihil dē mē cūrās, nihil dē Helvidiō quem amō.
Flāvia:	num tū tam audāx es ut istī amōrī indulgeās? iste enim Helvidius gentī nostrae est odiō. num oblīta es avum eius, cum Vespasiānum Imperātōrem graviter offendisset, in exiliō occīsum esse? mihi crēde, mea Pōlla! melius est cēdere quam frūstrā resistere.

Lines numbered: 5, 10, 15

queritur: querī *lament, complain about*
cōnsōlārī *console*
nūbere *marry*
quid faciam? *what am I to do?*

regunt: regere *rule*

odiōsum: odiōsus *hateful*

movēris: movēre *move, influence*
indulgeās: indulgēre *give way to*
avum: avus *grandfather*
exiliō: exilium *exile*

Sculptures of Roman married couples often show that the man was older than the woman.

About the language 1: indirect statement (future active infinitive)

1 Compare the following direct and indirect statements:

direct statements	indirect statements
"hostēs mox pugnābunt."	crēdimus hostēs mox **pugnātūrōs esse**.
"The enemy will fight soon."	*We believe the enemy to be going to fight soon.*
	Or, in more natural English:
	We believe that the enemy will fight soon.
"senex perībit."	medicus dīcit senem **peritūrum esse**.
"The old man will die."	*The doctor says that the old man will die.*

The form of the verb in **boldface** is known as the **future active infinitive**.

2 Further examples:

a "multī āthlētae crās certābunt."
b praecō dīcit multōs āthlētās crās certātūrōs esse.
c "fīliae mox advenient."
d māter crēdit fīliās mox adventūrās esse.
e suspicor ancillam tē dēceptūram esse.
f mercātor spērat sē magnās dīvitiās comparātūrum esse.

3 Study the way in which the future active infinitive is formed:

portātūrus esse	*to be about to carry*
doctūrus esse	*to be about to teach*
tractūrus esse	*to be about to drag*
audītūrus esse	*to be about to hear*

Notice that the future active infinitive contains a participle (**portātūrus**, etc.) which changes its ending in the usual way to agree with the noun it describes:

puer dīcit patrem crās **reventūrum** esse.
The boy says that his father will return tomorrow.

puer dīcit fēminās crās **reventūrās** esse.
The boy says that the women will return tomorrow.

prīdiē nūptiārum

nox est. crās nūptiae Pōllae et Sparsī celebrābuntur. Pōlla per hortum patris errat. crēdit sē sōlam esse; ignōrat Helvidium advēnisse. quī, hortum clam ingressus, Pōllam querentem audit; inter arborēs immōtus stat.

Pōlla:	quid faciam? Helvidius trēs diēs iam abest, neque scio quō ille ierit. intereā tōtam domum nostram videō ad nūptiās meās odiōsās parārī. ō Helvidī, ēripe mē ex hīs malīs!
Helvidius:	*(subitō prōgressus)* id libenter faciam. nēmō mē prohibēbit.
Pōlla:	*(gaudiō et pavōre commōta)* Helvidī! quō modō hūc vēnistī? sī hīc captus eris, interficiēris. fuge, priusquam pater meus tē cōnspiciat!
Helvidius:	fugiam vērō, sed nōn sine tē. fuge mēcum, mea Pōlla! tē ex hīs malīs ēripiam, sīcut tū modo precābāris.
Pōlla:	quō modō fugere possumus? tū ipse scīs mē semper custōdīrī. nūptiās odiōsās nūllō modō vītāre possum. parentēs, Imperātor, lēgēs mē iubent cōguntque Sparsō nūbere.
Helvidius:	minimē, mea Pōlla! tibi polliceor mē moritūrum esse priusquam ille senex tē uxōrem dūcat. nōbīs procul ex hāc urbe fugiendum est, ubi parentēs tuī nōs invenīre numquam poterunt.
Pōlla:	distrahor et excrucior. hūc amor, illūc pietās mē trahit.
Helvidius:	nōlī timēre, mea Pōlla! tē numquam dēseram, semper servābō.
Flāvia:	*(intrā domum)* Pōlla! Pōlla, ubi es?
Pōlla:	ēheu! ā mātre vocor. audī, mī Helvidī! haec ultima verba tibi dīcō; nōn enim putō mē umquam tē iterum vīsūram esse. crās ego Sparsō nūbam. est mihi nūlla spēs fugae. sed quamquam Sparsus mē uxōrem ductūrus est, mī Helvidī, iūrō mē tē sōlum amāre, iūrō mē ... *(lacrimās retinēre frūstrā cōnātur)* tē semper amātūram ... *(vōx dēficit.)*
Helvidius:	*(dextram Pōllae arripiēns)* Pōlla, deōs testor Sparsum tē uxōrem numquam ductūrum esse. cōnfīde mihi, mea Pōlla! *(Pōllam ardenter amplexus, Helvidius abit.)*
Pōlla:	*(incerta utrum spēret an timeat)* dea Fortūna, servā eum!

Line numbers: 5, 10, 15, 20, 25, 30, 35, 40

prīdiē *the day before*

errat: errāre *wander*

ēripe: ēripere *rescue, snatch away*

uxōrem dūcat: uxōrem dūcere *take as a wife, marry*

distrahor: distrahere *tear apart, tear in two*

hūc ... illūc *this way ... that way, one way ... another way*

pietās *duty*

intrā *inside*

iūrō: iūrāre *swear*

dēficit: dēficere *fail, die away*

dextram: dextra *right hand*

arripiēns: arripere *seize*

testor: testārī *call to witness*

ardenter *passionately*

About the language 2: perfect subjunctive

1   In Stage 36, you met the present subjunctive:

> incertus sum ubi Mārtiālis hodiē **recitet**.
> *I am not sure where Martial **is reciting** today.*

2   In Stages 37 and 38, you have met sentences like these:

> cognōscere volō quārē Domitiānus nōs **vocāverit**.
> *I want to find out why Domitian **has called** us.*

> senātor nescit quō modō Imperātōrem **offenderit**.
> *The senator does not know how he **has offended** the emperor.*

The form of the verb in **boldface** is the **perfect subjunctive**.

3   Further examples:

  a crās cognōscēmus quantam pecūniam parentēs nōbīs relīquerint.
  b centuriō scīre vult num senex equum cōnspexerit.
  c Pōlla nescit quō Helvidius ierit.
  d uxor mē cotīdiē rogat quārē hanc vīllam ēmerim.
  e incertī sumus utrum barbarī castra oppugnāverint an fūgerint.

4   Compare the perfect subjunctive with the perfect indicative:

perfect indicative	*perfect subjunctive*
portāvī	portāverim
portāvistī	portāverīs
portāvit	portāverit
portāvimus	portāverīmus
portāvistis	portāverītis
portāvērunt	portāverint

Perfect subjunctive forms of **doceō**, **trahō,** and **audiō** are given on page 272 of the Language information section.

5   For the perfect subjunctive of irregular verbs, see page 282.

cōnfarreātiō

cōnfarreātiō *wedding ceremony*

I

diēs nūptiārum adest. Pōlla, veste nūptiālī ōrnāta, in cubiculō suō stat.
māter eam īnspicit.

veste: vestis *clothing, clothes*
nūptiālī: nūptiālis *wedding*

Flāvia:	nunc tē verte ad mē, Pōlla! flammeum firmē capitī superpositum est? (*Pōllam lacrimāre videt.*) ō mea fīlia, tibi haud lacrimandum est; diē nūptiārum nōn decōrum est lacrimāre.

flammeum *veil*
superpositum est: superpōnere
place on

servus Clēmentis: (*ingressus*) domina, iussus sum vōs ad sacrificium arcessere. dominus meus dīcit victimam iam ēlēctam esse, haruspicēs parātōs adstāre. nūntius quoque iam adest, quī dīcit Imperātōrem, comitante Sparsō, mox adventūrum esse.

Flāvia: bene! nūntiā dominō tuō nōs statim ad ātrium prōcessūrās esse.

Flāvia et Pōlla ad ātrium prōcēdunt, ubi multī amīcī, familiārēs, clientēs iam adsunt. intrat Sparsus, multīs comitantibus servīs; deinde ingreditur ipse Domitiānus. Pōlla, valdē commōta, ad Sparsum dūcitur; dextrās sollemniter iungunt. inde Domitiānus, ut Pontifex Maximus, ad medium ātrium prōcēdit ut sacrificium Iovī faciat. victima ā Domitiānō sacrificātur; precēs Iovī et Iūnōnī offeruntur. Pōlla tamen adeō perturbātur ut precēs audīre vix possit.

Pontifex Maximus *Chief Priest*

Iūnōnī: Iūnō *Juno (goddess of marriage)*

Sparsus: (*Pōllam perturbārī animadvertit.*) nōlī timēre, mea Pōlla! age! cōnsīde in hāc sellā. nunc cōnfarreātiōnem celebrābimus.

Domitiānus: (*lībum farreum Sparsō et Pōllae offerēns*) hoc lībum sacrum cōnsūmite!

lībum farreum *cake made from grain*

Sparsus et Pōlla lībum sacrum cōnsūmunt.

Domitiānus: tacēte vōs omnēs, quī adestis! vōbīs prōnūntiō hanc virginem nunc in manum huius virī convenīre.

spectātōrēs: fēlīciter! fēlīciter!
Domitiānus: nunc cēdite testibus! tabulae nūptiālēs signandae sunt.

in manum … convenīre
pass into the hands of
fēlīciter! *good luck!*
tabulae nūptiālēs *marriage contract, marriage tablets*

tabulīs signātīs, omnēs ad triclīnium prōcēdunt, ubi cēna sūmptuōsa parāta est.

5

10

15

20

25

30

35

Sparsus Pōllam perturbārī animadvertit.

II

sōle occidente, servī Pōllam domum Sparsī dēdūcere parant, ubi
Sparsus, prior profectus, iam eam exspectat. chorus mūsicōrum
carmen nūptiāle cantāre incipit.

chorus: ō Hymēn Hymenaee, iō!
           ō Hymēn Hymenaee!   5
Flāvia: mea fīlia, sīc tē amplexa valedīcō. valē, mea Pōlla, valē!

servī, ut mōs est, puellam ā mātre abripiunt. puerī, quī facēs ardentēs
ferunt, Pōllam forās dēdūcunt. magnā comitante turbā pompa per viās
prōgreditur.

chorus: tollite, ō puerī, facēs!   10
           flammeum videō venīre.
           ō Hymēn Hymenaee, iō!
           ō Hymēn Hymenaee!

prior *earlier*
chorus *chorus, choir*
mūsicōrum: mūsicus *musician*
Hymēn *and* **Hymenaee:**
    Hymenaeus *Hymen*
    (*Roman god of weddings*)
valedīcō: valedīcere *say*
               good-bye
abripiunt: abripere *tear away*
               from
forās *out of the house*

III

tandem pompa domum Sparsī, flōribus ōrnātam, advenit. quī, domō
ēgressus, Pōllam ita appellat:

Sparsus:	siste! quis es tū? quō nōmine hūc venīs?	**siste: sistere** *stop, halt*
Pōlla:	ubi tū Gāius, ego Gāia.	

quibus verbīs sollemnibus dictīs, subitō magnus clāmor audītur; ē   5   **sollemnibus: sollemnis**
mediā turbā ērumpit iuvenis, pugiōne armātus, quī praeceps in   *solemn, traditional*
Sparsum ruit.

iuvenis:	nunc morere, Sparse! (*Sparsum ferōciter pugiōne petit.*)	**morere!** *die!*
Sparsus:	subvenīte! subvenīte!	

ingēns strepitus orītur; servī accurrunt; aliī spectātōrēs Sparsō   10   **orītur: orīrī** *rise, arise*
servīsque subveniunt, aliī immōtī et obstupefactī stant. Pōlla tamen,
iuvene Helvidiō agnitō, pallēscit. servī Helvidium, tandem
comprehēnsum, firmē retinent.

Sparsus: (*exclāmāns*) illum agnōscō! Helvidius est, homō īnfestissimus gentī Imperātōris. eum ad Imperātōrem *15* dūcite! prō certō habeō Domitiānum eī poenam aptissimam excōgitātūrum esse. (*Pōlla horrēscit.*) nōlī timēre, mea Pōlla! ille iuvenis īnsānus numquam iterum nōs vexābit. nunc tibi tempus est domum tuam novam intrāre. *20*

excōgitātūrum esse: excōgitāre
invent, think up
horrēscit: horrēscere *shudder*

Sparsus Pōllam bracchiīs tollit ut eam trāns līmen portet. Helvidius ad Domitiānum abdūcitur.

About the language 3: indirect statement (present passive infinitive)

1 In Stage 34, you met the present passive infinitive, used in sentences like these:

laudārī volō.
I want to be praised.

sonitus **audīrī** nōn poterat.
The sound was unable to be heard.

2 In Stage 38, you have met the present passive infinitive in indirect statements. Study the following examples:

direct statements
"vexāris."
"*You are annoyed.*"

indirect statements
scio tē **vexārī**.
I know you to be annoyed.
Or, in more natural English:
I know that you are annoyed.

"multī mīlitēs exercentur."
"*Many soldiers are being trained.*"

audīmus multōs mīlitēs **exercērī**.
We hear that many soldiers are being trained.

3 Further examples:

a "cēna splendida in vīllā iam parātur."
b prō certō habeō cēnam splendidam in vīllā iam parārī.
c "cōnsul morbō gravī afflīgitur."
d senātōrēs dīcunt cōnsulem morbō gravī afflīgī.
e audiō fīliōs Clēmentis ā Quīntiliānō cotīdiē docērī.
f amīcus meus affirmat tē numquam ab Imperātōre laudārī, saepe culpārī.

4 The forms of the present passive infinitives are set out on page 275.

amor et mātrimōnium

I *dē amīcō mūtābilī*

> difficilis facilis, iūcundus acerbus es īdem:
>> nec tēcum possum vīvere nec sine tē.
>>> *Martial*

How does Martial emphasize the contradictions in his friend's character and the effect they have on himself?

mūtābilī: mūtābilis
changeable, contradictory
facilis *here = easy-going*
iūcundus *pleasant*
acerbus *harsh, disagreeable*
īdem *here = you, the same person*

II *dē Chloē, quae septem marītīs nūpsit*

> īnscrīpsit tumulīs septem scelerāta virōrum
>> "sē fēcisse" Chloē. quid pote simplicius?
>>> *Martial*

What does Chloe mean by **sē fēcisse**? What meaning does Martial suggest?

The following lines are taken from a longer poem, possibly written by Petronius, Nero's **arbiter ēlegantiae** (adviser on good taste).

tumulīs: tumulus *tomb*
scelerāta: scelerātus *wicked*
virōrum: vir *here = husband*
quid pote? *what could be?*
simplicius: simplex *simple*

III *dē Cupīdine, deō potentī*

> ecce tacent vōcēs hominum strepitusque viārum
>> et volucrum cantūs turbaque fīda canum:
>>> sōlus ego ex cūnctīs paveō somnumque torumque
>>>> et sequor imperium, magne Cupīdo, tuum.

What contrasts do you find between the first two and the last two lines? What impression are you given of the god Cupid?

volucrum: volucris *bird*
cantūs: cantus *song*
fīda: fīdus *faithful*
cūnctīs: cūnctus *all*
paveō: pavēre *dread, fear*
somnum: somnus *sleep*
-que … -que *both … and*
torum: torus *bed*
imperium *here = command*

The Romans often decorated their walls, floors, and (as here) their crockery with pictures of lovers.

Word patterns: Compounds of *facere*

1 Study the following verb forms:

facere	*to make*	perficere	*to complete (to do thoroughly)*
afficere	*to affect (to do to)*	reficere	*to repair (to make again)*
efficere	*to accomplish (to carry out)*		

What happens to the form of **facere** following the prefix in each of the other verbs?
What other verbal compounds of **facere** have we met?

2 Other compounds of **facere** follow different patterns. Explain the meaning for each of the following:

aedificium, beneficium, carnifex, grātificārī, patefacere, pontifex, praefectus, sacrificium

Practicing the language

1 Complete each sentence with the correct word. Then translate the sentence.

a cognōscere volō ubi fīlius vester . . . . (habitet, habitent)
b tot gemmās ēmistī ut nūllam pecūniam iam . . . . (habeās, habeātis)
c strēnuē labōrāmus ut opus ante lūcem . . . . (perficiam, perficiāmus)
d tam fessus est amīcus meus ut longius prōgredī nōn . . . . (possit, possint)
e māter nescit quārē puellae in viā . . . . (clāmēs, clāmet, clāment)
f iterum vōs rogō num hunc virum . . . . (agnōscam, agnōscās, agnōscātis)

2 Translate the first sentence. Then change it from a direct statement to an indirect statement by completing the second sentence. Finally, translate the second sentence.

For example:
puer labōrat.   dominus putat puerum labōr... .
Translated and completed, this becomes:
puer labōrat.   dominus putat puerum labōrāre.
The boy is working.   The master thinks that the boy is working.

a multae vīllae ardent!   c medicus tēcum cōnsentit.
senex dīcit multās vīllās ard... .   crēdō medicum tēcum consent... .
b centuriō appropinquat.
mīlitēs putant centuriōnem appropinqu... .

In sentences **d–f**, nouns as well as verbs have to be completed. Refer if necessary to the table of nouns on pages 258–259.

d rēx in illā aulā habitat.   f puella dentēs nigrōs habet.
scio rēg... in illā aulā habit... .   Martiālis dīcit puell... dentēs nigrōs hab... .
e servī iam dormiunt.
fūr crēdit serv... iam dorm... .

Marriage

A Roman girl was normally married by the age of twenty, with the daughters of elite families often married as young as twelve; men probably married aged twenty-five to thirty. If the husband had been married previously, like Sparsus in the story on page 48, there might be a wide difference in age between the man and his wife.

The husband was normally chosen for the girl by her father or guardian. According to the law, the consent of both the bride and the groom had to be given. However, it is unlikely that a daughter would have found it easy to defy the wishes of her **paterfamiliās**. If all the requirements of age and consent were met, then the girl's father would negotiate with the family of her future husband about the **dōs** (dowry); this was a payment (in money or property or both) made by the bride's family to the husband.

At the ceremony of betrothal or engagement (**spōnsālia**), the father of the bride made a promise of marriage, on his daughter's behalf, to the father of the groom, or, if the husband-to-be were independent, to the man himself. Gifts were exchanged, and a ring was placed on the third finger of the girl's left hand. The Roman belief that a nerve ran directly from this finger to the heart initiated this custom, which is still practiced in many countries. Family and friends were present as witnesses, and the ceremony was followed by a party.

Under Roman law, there were two different sorts of marriage. In the first, which was known as marriage **cum manū**, the bride ceased to be a member of her father's family and passed completely into the

Above: *Gold betrothal ring.*

Below: *Traditionally, girls were supposed to be unwilling to leave the safety of their parents' home for marriage. This painting shows a veiled bride, seated on the marriage bed, being coaxed by the goddess Persuasion, while another goddess and human wedding attendants make preparations.*

manus (control) of her husband; any property she possessed became her husband's, and although he could divorce her, she could not divorce him. A couple could enter into marriage cum manu in various ways; one was by an ancient ceremony known as **cōnfarreātiō**, in which the bride and bridegroom together ate a sacred cake made of **far** (grain). This ceremony was used only by a few aristocratic families and had almost died out by the end of the first century AD. However, on page 54, Polla is married by confarreatio because she is related to the Emperor Domitian.

By the first century, marriage cum manu had become far less common than the other type of marriage, which was known as marriage **sine manū**. In this type of marriage, the bride did not pass into the manus of her husband; legally, she was still regarded as a member of her father's family (even though she was now no longer living with them); she could possess property of her own and she could divorce her husband. It was very easy for a couple to enter into marriage sine manu; all they needed to do was to live together after declaring their intention of being man and wife.

On the evening before her wedding day, the bride took off her **lūnula**, a moon-shaped locket or amulet worn on a chain around the neck. She had worn this since shortly after birth as a protection against evil but now she removed it, perhaps as a sign that she was leaving her childhood behind. The groom would already have dedicated his **bulla** to his family's lares when he became a citizen at about the age of seventeen.

Whether a couple became married cum manu or sine manu, they usually celebrated their wedding with some of the many customs and ceremonies that were traditional among the Romans. Some of these are mentioned in the story of Polla's wedding to Sparsus on pages 54–57: the flame-colored bridal veil (**flammeum**); the sacrifice and the taking of the omens by a haruspex; the signing of the marriage contract, witnessed by the wedding guests; the symbolic joining of hands (**iūnctiō dextrārum**); the wedding feast (**cēna nūptiālis**) at the bride's house; the ancient custom of pretending to pull the bride away from her mother by force; the torch-lit procession to the bridegroom's house; the wedding song; the calling out of noisy greetings and coarse jokes to the bridegroom; the traditional words of the bride to her husband, **ubi tū Gāius, ego Gāia** (*Where you are Gaius, I am Gaia*); the anointing of the doorposts with oil; and the custom of carrying the bride across the threshold of her new home. Other traditions and ceremonies included the careful arrangement of the bride's hair, parted with the point of a spear and then divided into six plaits; the presentation of fire and water by the bridegroom to the bride; and the undressing of the bride by **mātrōnae ūnivirae** (women who had had only one husband).

The chief purpose of Roman marriage, as stated in marriage contracts and in various laws, was the obvious one of producing

Pictures of weddings very often show the joining of hands (iūnctiō dextrārum).

A woman suckling her baby while her husband looks on.

and bringing up children. The Roman government often made efforts to encourage marriage and large families; in particular, the Emperor Augustus introduced a law which imposed penalties on those who remained unmarried (for example, by forbidding them to receive legacies) and offered special privileges to married couples who produced three or more children. Nevertheless, the birthrate in Rome dropped steadily from the second century BC onwards, especially among the senatorial class.

A Roman wife had fewer legal rights than her husband. In the eyes of the law, unless she had three children (four if she was a freedwoman), she was under the authority of either her husband or her father (or guardian), depending on whether she had been married *cum manu* or *sine manu*. She could not vote in elections, take an active part in public or political life, sit on a jury, or plead in court. But in some ways a first-century Roman wife had more freedom than women in other countries, and enjoyed a higher status than they did. She was not restricted to the home but could visit friends, go to the theater and the baths, and accompany her husband to dinner parties (unlike the women of classical Athens, for example). Her traditional day-to-day task, the running of the household, was regarded by most Romans as important and valuable, and a woman could gain great prestige and respect for the way in which this task was carried out; in many aristocratic and wealthy families, running the house was a highly complicated and demanding job, involving the management and supervision of a large number of domestic slaves.

Our knowledge of Roman married life is very incomplete. We know far less about the poor than about the wealthy upper classes,

A wife could go to a party with her husband (painting in Pompeii).

and have hardly any information on married life from the wife's point of view, because most of what is written in Latin was written by men. Nevertheless, the writings of Roman authors include many references to married life. The following letter, for example, was written by Pliny to his wife Calpurnia:

The strength of my longing for you is hard to believe. Love is the reason above all others. Another reason is that we are not used to being separated. I spend most of the night awake, picturing you. During the day, at the times when I usually come to see you, my feet guide me to your room; then I turn sadly back, sick at heart.

Calpurnia was Pliny's third wife. At the time of their marriage, she was about fifteen and he was in his early forties. In another letter, he writes about Calpurnia:

From sheer affection for me, she keeps copies of my speeches, reads them over and over again and even learns them by heart. She is tortured with worry when I appear in court, and is overcome with relief when the case is over. Whenever I give a recitatio, she listens from behind a curtain waiting eagerly for comments of approval. As for my poems, she sets them to music and sings them, taught not by some musician but by love, the best of teachers.

A letter by Cicero describes an incident from the stormy relationship between his brother Quintus and Quintus' wife Pomponia:

We lunched at Arcanum. When we got there, Quintus said, perfectly politely, "Pomponia, you invite the women, and I'll get the slave-boys together." There was nothing to be cross about, as far as I could see, in either what he said or the way he said it. But, within everyone's hearing, Pomponia replied, "What, me? I'm only a stranger here!" – just because Quintus had made arrangements for the lunch without telling her, I suppose. "There you are," said Quintus. "That's what I have to put up with every day." I hid my feelings. We sat down to eat; she refused to join us. Quintus sent her some food from the table; she sent it back. The following day, Quintus told me that she had refused to sleep with him and had continued to behave as she had done at lunchtime.

Roman married life is also referred to in numerous epitaphs, written in memory of husbands and wives. There are extracts from three of them below.

HERE LIES
AMYMONE,
WIFE OF MARCUS,
MOST GOOD AND
MOST BEAUTIFUL,
WOOL-SPINNER,
DUTIFUL, MODEST,
CAREFUL, CHASTE,
HOME-LOVING.

I HAVE
WRITTEN THESE
WORDS SO THAT
THOSE WHO READ
THEM MAY REALISE
HOW MUCH WE
LOVED EACH
OTHER.

TO MY DEAREST WIFE
WITH WHOM I LIVED
TWO YEARS, SIX
MONTHS, THREE DAYS,
TEN HOURS.

Vocabulary checklist 38

certus, certa, certum	certain, infallible
prō certō habēre	know for certain
clam	secretly, in private
cōpiae, cōpiārum, f. pl.	forces
dextra, dextrae, f.	right hand
ēripiō, ēripere, ēripuī, ēreptus	rescue, snatch away
familia, familiae, f.	household
grātus, grāta, grātum	acceptable, pleasing
ignōrō, ignōrāre, ignōrāvī	not know about
iungō, iungere, iūnxī, iūnctus	join
lēx, lēgis, f.	law
līmen, līminis, n.	threshold, doorway
nūbō, nūbere, nūpsī (+ DAT)	marry
orior, orīrī, ortus sum	rise, arise
polliceor, pollicērī, pollicitus sum	promise
prohibeō, prohibēre, prohibuī, prohibitus	prevent
queror, querī, questus sum	lament, complain about
regō, regere, rēxī, rēctus	rule
vereor, verērī, veritus sum	be afraid, fear
vērō	indeed
virgō, virginis, f.	virgin

A beautiful marble container provided by one of the emperor's freedmen for the ashes of his wife, Vernasia Cyclas.

STUDIA

Stage 39

hērēdēs prīncipis

I

in aulā Imperātōris, duo puerī in studiīs litterārum sunt occupātī. alter
puer, Titus nōmine, fābulam nārrāre cōnātur; alter, nōmine Pūblius,
intentē audit. adest quoque puerōrum rhētor, M. Fabius Quīntiliānus.
Titus Pūbliusque, fīliī Clēmentis ac frātrēs Pōllae, nūper hērēdēs
Imperātōris factī sunt.   5

studiīs: studium *study*
litterārum: litterae *literature*

Titus: (*fābulam nārrāns*) deinde Iuppiter, rēx deōrum,
                sceleribus hominum valdē offēnsus, genus
                mortāle magnō dīluviō dēlēre cōnstituit. prīmō
                eī placuit dē caelō fulmina spargere, quae tōtam
                terram cremārent. timēbat tamen nē deī ipsī, sī   10
                flammae ad caelum ā terrā ascendissent, eōdem
                ignī cremārentur. dīversam ergō poenam impōnere
                māluit.

genus mortāle
            the human race
dīluviō: dīluvium *flood*
fulmina: fulmen *thunderbolt*
cremārent: cremāre
            burn, destroy by fire
dīversam: dīversus *different*

Titō nārrante, iānua subitō aperītur. ingreditur Epaphrodītus. puerī
anxiī inter sē aspiciunt; Quīntiliānus, cui Epaphrodītus odiō est,   15
nihilōminus eum cōmiter salūtat.

Quīntiliānus: libenter tē vidēmus, Epaphro–
Epaphrodītus: (*interpellāns*) salvēte, puerī. salvē tū, M. Fabī.
                hūc missus sum ut mandāta prīncipis nūntiem.
                prīnceps vōbīs imperat ut ad sē quam celerrimē   20
                contendātis.
Quīntiliānus: verba tua, mī Epaphrodīte, nōn intellegō. cūr
                nōs ad Imperātōrem arcessimur?

Epaphrodītus, nūllō respōnsō datō, puerōs Quīntiliānumque per aulam
ad Imperātōris tablīnum dūcit. puerī, timōre commōtī, extrā tablīnum   25
haesitant.

Quīntiliānus:	(*timōrem suum dissimulāns*) cūr perturbāminī, puerī?
Pūblius:	bonā causā perturbāmur. Imperātor enim nōs sine dubiō castīgābit vel pūniet.
Quīntiliānus:	nimis timidus es, Pūblī. sī prūdenter vōs gesseritis, neque castīgābiminī neque pūniēminī.

(line 30 at right)

castīgābit: castīgāre *scold, reprimand*
vōs gesseritis: sē gerere *behave, conduct oneself*

II

Quīntiliānus et puerī, tablīnum ingressī, Domitiānum ad mēnsam sedentem muscāsque stilō trānsfīgentem inveniunt. Domitiānus neque respicit neque quicquam dīcit. puerī pallēscunt.

muscās: musca *fly*
respicit: respicere *look up*

Domitiānus:	(*tandem respiciēns*) nōlīte timēre, puerī. vōs nōn pūnītūrus sum – nisi mihi displicueritis. (*muscam aliam trānsfīgit; dēnique, stilō dēpositō, puerōs subitō interrogat:*) quam diū discipulī M. Fabiī iam estis?
Titus:	(*haesitāns*) d-duōs mēnsēs, domine.
Domitiānus:	nōbīs ergō tempus est cognōscere quid didiceritis. (*ad Pūblium repente conversus*) Pūblī, quid herī docēbāminī?
Pūblius:	versūs quōsdam legēbāmus, domine, quōs Ovidius poēta dē illō dīluviō fābulōsō composuit.
Domitiānus:	itaque, versibus Ovidiānīs herī lēctīs, quid hodiē facitis?
Pūblius:	hodiē cōnāmur eandem fābulam verbīs nostrīs nārrāre.
Quīntiliānus:	ubi tū nōs arcessīvistī, domine, Titus dē īrā Iovis nārrātūrus erat.
Domitiānus:	fābula scīlicet aptissima! eam audīre velim. Tite, nārrātiōnem tuam renovā!
Titus:	(*fābulam timidē renovāns*) Iu-Iuppiter nimbōs ingentēs dē ca-caelō dēmittere cōnstituit. statim Aquilōnem in ca-cavernīs Aeoliīs inclūsit, et Notum līberāvit. quī madidīs ālīs ēvolāvit; ba-barba nimbīs gravābātur, undae dē capillīs fluēbant. simulatque Notus ēvolāvit, nimbī dēnsī ex aethere cum ingentī fragōre effūsī sunt. sed tanta erat Iovis īra ut imbribus caelī contentus nōn esset; auxilium ergō ā frātre Neptūnō petīvit. quī cum terram tridente percussisset, illa valdē tremuit viamque patefēcit ubi undae fluerent. statim flūmina ingentia per campōs apertōs ruēbant.
Domitiānus:	satis nārrāvistī, Tite. nunc tū, Pūblī, nārrātiōnem excipe.

(line numbers at right: 5, 10, 15, 20, 25, 30, 35)

displicueritis: displicēre *displease*

didiceritis: discere *learn*
repente *suddenly*

fābulōsō: fābulōsus *legendary, famous*
Ovidiānīs: Ovidiānus *of Ovid*

nārrātiōnem: nārrātiō *narration*
nimbōs: nimbus *rain cloud*
cavernīs: caverna *cave, cavern*
Aeoliīs: Aeolius *Aeolian*
inclūsit: inclūdere *shut up*
Notum: Notus *South wind*
ālīs: āla *wing*
gravābātur: gravāre *load, weigh down*
imbribus: imber *rain*
Neptūnō: Neptūnus *Neptune (Roman god of the sea)*
tridente: tridēns *trident*
campōs: campus *plain*
excipe: excipere *take over*

Pūblius:	iamque inter mare et tellūrem nūllum discrīmen erat; mare ubīque erat, neque ūlla lītora habēbat. hominēs exitium effugere cōnābantur. aliī montēs ascendērunt; aliī, in nāvibus sedentēs, per agrōs illōs rēmigāvērunt quōs nūper arābant; hic suprā segetēs aut tēcta vīllārum mersārum nāvigāvit; ille in summīs arboribus piscēs invēnit. lupī inter ovēs natābant; leōnēs fulvī undīs vehēbantur. avēs, postquam terram diū quaerēbant ubi cōnsistere possent, tandem in mare fessīs ālīs dēcidērunt. capellae gracilēs –

40

45

Pūbliō hoc nārrantī Domitiānus manū significat ut dēsistat. diū tacet, puerīs anxiīs exspectantibus. Quīntiliānus verētur nē puerī Imperātōrī nōn placuerint. tandem ille loquitur.

50

Domitiānus:	fortūnātī estis, Pūblī ac Tite; nam, ut decōrum est prīncipis hērēdibus, ab optimō rhētore docēminī, quī optima exempla vōbīs prōposuit. sī vōs, puerī, causās vestrās tam fācundē dīxeritis quam Ovidius versūs composuit, saepe victōrēs ē basilicā discēdētis; ab omnibus laudābiminī.
Titus:	(*timōre iam dēpositō*) nōnne ūna rēs tē fallit, domine? nōs sumus hērēdēs tuī; nōnne igitur nōs, cum causās nostrās dīxerimus, nōn saepe sed semper victōrēs discēdēmus et ab omnibus laudābimur?

55

60

Quīntiliānus ērubēscit. Domitiānus, audāciā Titī obstupefactus, nihil dīcit. tandem, rīdēns vel rīsum simulāns, puerōs rhētoremque dīmittit; deinde, stilō resūmptō, muscās iterum trānsfīgere incipit.

tellūrem: tellūs *land, earth*
discrīmen *boundary, dividing line*

rēmigāvērunt: rēmigāre *row*
arābant: arāre *plow*
hic … ille *this man … that man, one man … another man*
suprā *over, on top of*
aut *or*
mersārum: mergere *submerge*
piscēs: piscis *fish*
ovēs: ovis *sheep*
fulvī: fulvus *tawny*
capellae: capella *she-goat*
gracilēs: gracilis *graceful*
causās … dīxeritis: causam dīcere *plead a case*
fācundē *fluently, eloquently*

fallit: fallere *escape notice of, slip by*

simulāns: simulāre *pretend*
resūmptō: resūmere *pick up again*

ab omnibus laudābiminī.

About the language 1: fearing clauses

1 Study the following examples:

> timeō **nē inquiēta sit Britannia**, dum Hibernia īnsula in lībertāte manet.
> *I am afraid that (lest, in case) Britain may be unsettled, as long as the island of Ireland remains free.*

> timēbat Iuppiter **nē deī ipsī eōdem ignī cremārentur**.
> *Jupiter feared that the gods themselves might be consumed by the same fire.*

> Quīntiliānus verētur **nē puerī Domitiānō nōn placuerint**.
> *Quintilian is afraid that the boys have not pleased Domitian.*

> Glabriō timēbat **nē Imperātōrem graviter offendisset**.
> *Glabrio was afraid that he had seriously offended the emperor.*

The groups of words in **boldface** are known as **fearing clauses**. The verb in a fearing clause in Latin is always subjunctive. Because a fear can be for the past, the present, or the future, you must pay particular attention to the tense of the subjunctive verb.

2 In fearing clauses, the conjunction **nē** means *that* (*lest/in case*) and the negative is **nē … nōn**. Occasionally the negative can be **ut**, e.g.

> Quīntiliānus verētur **ut** puerī Domitiānō **placuerint**.
> *Quintilian is afraid that the boys have not pleased Domitian.*

3 Further examples:

 a timeō nē genus mortāle deōs fallere cōnātum sit.
 b Domitia, fragōre audītō, verita est nē Paris dē arbore cecidisset.
 c timēbāmus nē diūtius dubitāvissēmus.
 d anxiane erās ut tē hīs malīs ēriperem?

This coin shows the infant son of Domitian among the stars with the description **dīvus Caesar**, *divine Caesar. This suggests that the coin was issued after the child's death as emperors and members of their families were often posthumously proclaimed as gods. Domitian and Domitia only had one son and therefore Domitian later took on Titus and Publius as his heirs.*

sed tanta erat Iovis īra ut imbribus caelī contentus nōn esset; auxilium ergō ā frātre Neptūnō petīvit.
This Greek bronze sculpture from the fifth century BC stands over 6.5 feet (2 meters) tall and was found in a shipwreck. It is disputed whether it portrays Jupiter or Neptune. The figure would have hurled a thunderbolt or trident from his right hand.

versūs Ovidiānī

The story of the flood, told by Publius and Titus on pages 66–68, is based on the following lines written by the poet Ovid. When you have read them, answer the questions on the next page. At the start of the extract, the god Jupiter is about to punish the human race for its wickedness by submerging the earth in a great flood.

prōtinus **Aeoliīs** Aquilōnem claudit in **antrīs.***
ēmittitque Notum; **madidīs** Notus ēvolat **ālīs**;
barba gravis nimbīs, **cānīs** fluit unda **capillīs**.
fit fragor; hinc **dēnsī** funduntur ab aethere **nimbī**.
   nec **caelō** contenta **suō** est Iovis īra, sed illum
caeruleus frāter iuvat auxiliāribus undīs.
ipse tridente suō terram percussit, at illa
intremuit mōtūque viās patefēcit aquārum.
exspatiāta ruunt per apertōs **flūmina** campōs.
   iamque mare et tellūs nūllum discrīmen habēbant:
omnia pontus erant, dēerant quoque lītora pontō.
occupat hic collem, **cumbā** sedet alter **aduncā**
et dūcit rēmōs illīc, ubi nūper arābat;
ille suprā segetēs aut **mersae** culmina **vīllae**
nāvigat, hic **summā** piscem dēprendit in **ulmō**.
nat lupus inter ovēs, **fulvōs** vehit unda **leōnēs**,
quaesītīsque diū terrīs, ubi sistere possit,
in mare **lassātīs** volucris vaga dēcidit **ālīs**.
et, modo quā **gracilēs** grāmen carpsēre **capellae**,
nunc ibi **dēfōrmēs** pōnunt sua corpora **phōcae**.

antrīs: antrum *cave*

cānīs: cānus *white*
fit: fierī *be made, occur*
5   hinc *then, next*
caeruleus *from the deep blue sea*
iuvat: iuvāre *help, assist*
auxiliāribus: auxiliāris *additional*
intremuit: intremere *shake*
10   exspatiāta: exspatiārī *extend, spread out*
pontus *sea*
dēerant: dēesse *be lacking, be missing*
collem: collis *hill*
cumbā: cumba *boat*
15   aduncā: aduncus *curved*
rēmōs: rēmus *oar*
illīc *there, in that place*
culmina: culmen *roof*
dēprendit = dēprehendit: dēprehendere *discover*
ulmō: ulmus *elm tree*
nat: nāre *swim*
lassātīs: lassāre *tire, weary*
vaga: vagus *wandering*
quā *where*
grāmen *grass*
carpsēre = carpsērunt: carpere *chew, nibble, crop*
dēfōrmēs: dēfōrmis *ugly, inelegant*
phōcae: phōca *seal*

* Some noun-and-adjective phrases, in which an adjective is separated by one word or more from the noun which it describes, are shown in **boldface**.

Questions

1 **prōtinus … Notum** (lines 1–2). What two things did Jupiter do?
2 **madidīs … capillīs** (lines 2–3). In this description of the South wind, how does Ovid emphasize that he brings rain? Make three points.
3 **fit … nimbī** (line 4). What happened when the South wind appeared?
4 Who came to Jupiter's assistance (lines 5–6)? What was his name?
5 What did he do?
6 What results did this have (lines 7–9)?
7 How does Ovid emphasize the vastness of the flood (line 11)?
8 **dūcit rēmōs** (line 13). Where is this man rowing?
9 **ille … nāvigat** (lines 14–15). Where is this one sailing?
10 **hic … piscem dēprendit** (line 15). What is remarkable about this?
11 **nat lupus inter ovēs** (line 16). What is strange about the relationship of these animals?
12 **quaesītīs … ālīs** (lines 17–18). What happened to the birds? Why?
13 What is the connection between the goats and seals (lines 19–20)?
14 Which Latin word in line 20 is used to contrast with **gracilēs** in line 19?
15 How does Ovid vary his subject-matter? Give three examples taken from the text.

Questions for discussion

1 Which detail or incident in this passage can you picture most vividly?
2 Which seems to you to be the better description of Ovid's account: "serious" or "light-hearted"?

About the language 2: word order (continued)

1 In Stage 36, you met verse sentences like this:

> exigis ut **nostrōs** dōnem tibi, Tucca, **libellōs**.
> *You demand that I should give you my books, Tucca.*

The adjective **nostrōs** is separated from the noun which it describes (**libellōs**).

2 In Stage 39, you have met sentences in which one noun-and-adjective phrase is followed by another:

> ***caeruleus frāter*** iuvat **auxiliāribus undīs**.
> *His brother from the deep blue sea helps him with additional waves.*

Further examples:

a *arbore* sub *magnā* **parva** latēbat **avis**.
b *vertice* dē *summō* **liquidōs** mōns ēvomit **ignēs**.

liquidōs: liquidus	*liquid*
ēvomit: ēvomere	*spit out, spew out*

Study the pattern formed by the pairs of noun-and-adjective phrases in each of the above sentences. Similar patterns are often formed in English verse by rhymes at the ends of lines. For example:

> A man he was to all the country ***dear***,
> And passing rich with forty pounds a ***year***;
> Remote from towns he ran his godly **race**,
> Nor e'er had changed, nor wished to change his **place**.

3 You have also met sentences in which one noun-and-adjective phrase is placed inside another one:

> nunc ibi **dēfōrmēs** pōnunt *sua corpora* **phōcae**.
> *Now the ugly seals rest their bodies there.*

Further examples:

a **in mediōs** vēnit *iuvenis fortissimus* **hostēs**.
b cōnstitit ante **oculōs** *pulchra puella* **meōs**.

Compare the arrangement of the noun-and-adjective phrases in the previous sentences with the arrangement of the rhyming lines in such verse as the following:

> Ring out, wild bells, to the wild **sky**,
>   The flying cloud, the frosty **light**;
>   The year is dying in the **night**:
> Ring out, wild bells, and let him **die**.

4 In each of the following examples, pick out the Latin adjectives and say which nouns they are describing:

   a aure meā ventī murmura rauca sonant.
      The hoarse murmurs of the wind sound in my ear.

   b iam nova prōgeniēs caelō dēmittitur altō. (*Virgil*)
      Now a new generation is being sent down from high heaven.

   c nōn fuit ingeniō Fāma maligna meō. (*Ovid*)
      Fame has not been unkind to my talent.

   d agna lupōs audit circum stabula alta frementēs. (*Ovid*)
      The lamb hears the wolves howling around the tall sheepfolds.

   e atque opere in mediō laetus cantābat arātor.
      And the happy plowman was singing in the middle of his work.

   f vincuntur mollī pectora dūra prece. (*Tibullus*)
      Hard hearts are won over by soft prayer.

5 Translate the following examples:

   a *A cry for help*
      at puer īnfēlīx mediīs clāmābat in undīs.

   b *An echo*
      reddēbant nōmen concava saxa meum.

   c *Travel plans*
      nunc mare per longum mea cōgitat īre puella. (*Propertius*)

   d *Evening*
      maiōrēsque cadunt altīs dē montibus umbrae. (*Virgil*)

concava: concavus *hollow*

Pick out the adjectives in each example and say which nouns they are describing.

Word patterns: verbs and nouns

1 Study the form and meaning of each of the following verbs and nouns:

nōmināre	*nominate, name*	nōmen	*name*
volvere	*turn, roll*	volūmen	*roll of papyrus, scroll*
unguere	*anoint, smear*	unguentum	*ointment*

2 Following the example of paragraph 1, complete the following table:

certāre	*compete*	certāmen	. . . .
crīmināre	*accuse*	crīmen	. . . .
arguere	. . . .	argūmentum	*proof, argument*
impedīre	. . . .	impedīmentum	*hindrance, nuisance*
vestīre	*clothe, dress*	vestīmenta	. . . .
ōrnāre	. . . .	ōrnāmentum	. . . .
torquēre	. . . .	tormentum	. . . .

Practicing the language

1 In each sentence, replace the noun in **boldface** with the correct form of the noun in parentheses. Then translate the sentence.

Use the table of nouns on pages 258–259 to help you, if necessary; you may also need to consult the Vocabulary to find out the genitive singular of 3rd declension nouns, as a guide to forming the other cases.

   a subitō Pōlla **Flāviam** vīdit. (māter)
   b nūntius **uxōrī** epistulam trādidit. (fēmina)
   c senātōrēs ad aulam **Domitiānī** contendēbant. (Imperātor)
   d iuvenis **Agricolae** tōtam rem nārrāvit. (dux)
   e ingēns multitūdō **Rōmānōrum** in amphitheātrō conveniēbat. (cīvis)
   f poēta **audītōribus** paucōs versūs recitāvit. (amīcus)

2 Complete each sentence with the correct verb. Then translate the sentence.

   a fessus sum! cotīdiē ā centuriōne labōrāre . . . . (iubeor, teneor)
   b tū semper bene recitās; semper ā rhētore . . . . (parāris, laudāris)
   c nōlī dēspērāre, mī amīce! mox . . . . (spectāberis, līberāberis)
   d maximē gaudeō; crās enim ab Imperātōre . . . . (honōrābor, vituperābor)
   e cum in urbe habitārem, strepitū continuō . . . . (audiēbar, mittēbar, vexābar)
   f medicus tē sānāvit, ubi morbō gravī . . . . (afficiēbāris, dēcipiēbāris, dūcēbāris).

3 Translate the first sentence. Then change it from a direct statement to an indirect statement by completing the second sentence. Finally, translate the second sentence.

For example: hostēs advēnērunt.
                nūntius dīcit hostēs advēn... .
Translated and completed, this becomes:
                hostēs advēnērunt.
                The enemy have arrived.
                nūntius dīcit hostēs advēnisse.
                The messenger says that the enemy have arrived.

In sentences **a–c**, a perfect *active* infinitive is required. For examples of the way in which this infinitive is formed, see page 34, paragraph 3.

a Imperātor sententiam mūtāvit.
    cīvēs crēdunt Imperātōrem sententiam mūtāv... .

b nautae nāvem ingentem comparāvērunt.
    mercātor dīcit nautās nāvem ingentem comparāv... .

c fabrī mūrum optimē refēcērunt.
    putō fabr... mūrum optimē refēc... .

In sentences **d–f**, a perfect *passive* infinitive is required. For examples of the way in which it is formed, see page 37, paragraph 3. Note that the first part of this infinitive (e.g. **parātus** in **parātus esse**) changes its ending to agree with the noun it describes.

For example: epistulae missae sunt.
                crēdō epistulās miss... ....
Translated and completed, this becomes:
                epistulae missae sunt.
                The letters have been sent.
                crēdō epistulās missās esse.
                I believe that the letters have been sent.

d victima ā pontifice ēlēcta est.
    spectātōrēs putant victimam ā pontifice ēlēct... ....

e multī amīcī ad cēnam vocātī sunt.
    sciō multōs amīcōs ad cēnam vocāt... ....

f captīvus occīsus est.
    mīlitēs dīcunt captīv... occīs... ....

Authors, readers, and listeners

After a Roman writer had recited his work to his patron or friends, or to a wider audience at a recitatio, as described in Stage 36, he had to decide whether or not to make it available to the general public. If he decided to go ahead, his next step was to have several copies made. If he or his patron owned some sufficiently educated slaves, they might be asked to make copies for the author to distribute among his friends. Cicero sent volumes of his work to his banker friend, Atticus, who had many such **librāriī**. Alternatively, the author might offer his work to the **bibliopōlae**, the booksellers, whose slaves would make a number of copies for sale to the public.

Most Roman booksellers had their shops in the Argiletum, a street which ran between the Forum Romanum and the Subura. Books were fairly inexpensive. A small book of poems might cost 5 sesterces if it were an ordinary copy, 20 sesterces if it were a deluxe edition made of high-quality materials. Martial tells us that his first book of epigrams, about 700 lines, sold for 20 sesterces. After the work had been copied, all money from sales of the book belonged to the booksellers, not to the author. We do not know if the booksellers ever paid anything to an author for letting them copy his work.

The Argiletum, where the book shops were, is the long street emerging from the Forum at top left, passing through the narrow Forum Transitorium which Domitian began, and running down to the bottom right in the crowded Subura district.

One result of these arrangements for copying and selling books was that there was no such thing in Rome as a professional writer; no author could hope to make a living from his work. Some of the people who wrote books were wealthy amateurs like Pliny, who made most of his money as a landowner and wrote as a hobby; others, like Martial, depended on patrons for support. Writers fit into the general client–patron system we learned about in Unit 3. An author, unlike ordinary **clientēs**, however, could offer his **patrōnus** a wider reputation, a chance for perpetual **dignitās**.

Sometimes the emperor became an author's patron. For example, the poets Virgil and Horace were helped and encouraged first by the Emperor Augustus' friend, Maecenas, and then by Augustus himself. Other authors, however, got into trouble with the emperor. Ovid, for instance, was sent into exile by Augustus because he had been involved in a mysterious scandal in the emperor's own family and because he had written a poem entitled *Ars Amatoria* (*The Art of Love*), a witty and light-hearted guide for young men on the conduct of love affairs. The *Ars Amatoria* greatly displeased Augustus, who had introduced a number of laws for the encouragement of respectable marriage, and Ovid was exiled to a distant part of the empire for the rest of his life. Under later emperors, such as Domitian, it was safest for an author to publish nothing at all, or else to make flattering remarks about the emperor in his work, as Martial did in his poem on page 18 (lines 6–9).

Some works of Latin literature reached a wide public. For example, thousands of people saw the comic plays of Plautus when

Choosing a book.

they were performed in the theater. But most Roman authors wrote for a small, highly educated group of readers who were familiar not only with Latin literature, but also with the literature of the Greeks.

Schoolboys, like Publius and Titus in the story on pages 66–68, and perhaps a few girls as well, were introduced by their teachers to the study of both Greek and Roman authors. The famous educator and orator, Quintilian (*c.* AD 35 – *c.* 100), was the first teacher to obtain a salary from the state when he was appointed instructor of rhetoric by Vespasian. Besides Domitian's adopted sons, Quintilian taught Pliny the Younger. The most influential of Quintilian's books, *The Education of an Orator*, covered education from infancy to the level of the experienced speaker. The book also included a long list of recommended Greek and Latin authors, with comments on each one. For example, he wrote: "Ovid is light-hearted even on serious subjects and too fond of his own cleverness, but parts of his work are excellent."

Latin literature played an important part in Roman education. Roman education, in turn, played an important part in the writing of Latin literature. Most Roman authors had received a thorough training from a **rhētor**, who taught them how to express themselves persuasively and artistically, how to choose words and rhetorical devices that would have maximum effect on an audience, and how to organize a speech. This training had a great influence on the way Latin literature was written.

Above: *The poet Horace was given this farm in the Sabine Hills by his patron, Maecenas.* Below: *A boy practicing public speaking. Round his neck he wears a* bulla, *a child's locket containing an amulet.*

An important difference between Latin and modern literature is that most modern literature is written for silent reading, whereas Latin literature was often written to be read aloud. The three reasons for this have already been mentioned: first, the easiest way for an author to tell the public about his work was to read it aloud to them; second, most authors had received extensive training in public speaking and this affected the way they wrote; third, many Romans when reading a book, would read it aloud or have it read to them.

The fact that Latin literature was written for speaking aloud, and not for silent reading, made a great difference to the way Roman authors wrote. They expressed themselves in ways that would sound effective when heard, not just look effective when read. For example, suppose a Roman author wished to say, in the course of a story:

The unfortunate boy did not see the danger.

He might express this quite straightforwardly:

puer īnfēlīx perīculum nōn vīdit.

But he might, especially in poetry, choose a more artistic word order. For instance, he might place the emotional word **īnfēlīx** in the prominent first position in the line, juxtapose the alliterative **perīculum** and **puer**, and separate the adjective from its noun.

īnfēlīx perīculum puer nōn vīdit.

Again, the author might prefer a more dramatic way of expressing himself. He might address the character in the story as if he were physically present, and put a question to him:

heu, puer īnfēlīx! nōnne perīculum vidēs?
Alas, unfortunate boy! Do you not see the danger?

On the printed page, especially in English translation, such artistic variations as these may sometimes appear rather strange to a modern reader. When they are read aloud in Latin, however, the effect can be very different. To read Latin literature silently is like looking at a page of written music; it needs to be performed aloud for full effect.

Domitian's palace

The Emperor Domitian was a great builder. He finished Vespasian's Colosseum and gave Rome a stadium and a new forum (the Forum Transitorium) as well as many smaller buildings. He restored much of Rome after a serious fire. But his greatest building was his own palace, on the Palatine hill.

Fragment of a floor made by cutting white and colored marbles and red and green porphyry to an elaborate pattern.

The side of the palace overlooking the Circus Maximus.

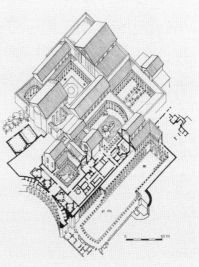

The palace reconstructed.

The Hippodrome: a garden in the shape of a stadium.

A wall belonging to the state rooms shown on page 36, showing the holes for the builders' scaffolding. The builders constructed two brick walls and filled the gap between with mortar and rubble, i.e. concrete. The scaffolding holes would have been hidden by marble facing or stucco rendering.

Vocabulary checklist 39

arbor, arboris, f.	*tree*
aut	*or*
cadō, cadere, cecidī	*fall*
campus, campī, m.	*plain*
capillī, capillōrum, m. pl.	*hair*
discrīmen, discrīminis, n.	*dividing line; crisis*
ergō	*therefore*
fallō, fallere, fefellī, falsus	*deceive, escape notice of, slip by*
fragor, fragōris, m.	*crash*
genus, generis, n.	*race*
hinc	*from here; then, next*
iuvō, iuvāre, iūvī, iūtus	*help, assist*
littera, litterae, f.	*letter (of the alphabet)*
litterae, litterārum, f. pl.	*letter, letters (correspondence), literature*
mēnsis, mēnsis, m.	*month*
simulō, simulāre, simulāvī, simulātus	*pretend*
spargō, spargere, sparsī, sparsus	*scatter*
stilus, stilī, m.	*pen (pointed stick for writing on wax tablet)*
studium, studiī, n.	*enthusiasm; study*
ūllus, ūlla, ūllum	*any*

*Domitian's palace: connecting rooms
leading to the Hippodrome.*

IUDICIUM

Stage 40

ingēns senātōrum multitūdō in cūriā convēnerat, ubi Gāius
Salvius Līberālis accūsābātur.

1 "multa scelera ā Salviō in Britanniā
commissa sunt."

prīmus accūsātor affirmāvit multa scelera ā
Salviō in Britanniā commissa esse.

2 "Salvius testāmentum rēgis fīnxit."

secundus accūsātor dīxit Salvium
testāmentum rēgis fīnxisse.

3 "innocēns sum."

Salvius respondit sē innocentem esse.

accūsātiō

accūsātiō *accusation*

I

septimō annō Domitiānī prīncipātūs, C. Salvius Līberālis, quī
priōre annō fuerat cōnsul, ab Acīliō Glabriōne falsī accūsātus est.
quā rē imprōvīsā perturbātus, amīcōs statim cōnsuluit utrum
accūsātiōnem sperneret an dēfēnsiōnem susciperet.

Salviō rogantī quid esset agendum, aliī alia suādēbant. aliī
affirmāvērunt nūllum perīculum īnstāre quod Salvius vir
magnae auctōritātis esset. aliī exīstimābant Domitiānī īram
magis timendam esse quam minās accūsantium; Salvium
hortābantur ut ad Imperātōrem īret veniamque peteret. amīcīs
dīversa monentibus, Salvius exspectāre cōnstituit, dum
cognōsceret quid Domitiānus sentīret.

intereā Glabriō et aliī accūsātōrēs causam parābant. eīs
magnō auxiliō erat L. Mārcius Memor, haruspex et Salviī cliēns,
quī, socius quondam scelerum Salviī, nunc ad eum prōdendum
adductus est, spē praemiī vel metū poenārum. quō testimōniō
ūsī, accūsātōrēs rem ad Imperātōrem rettulērunt.

Domitiānus, ubi verba accūsātōrum audīvit, cautē sē gessit;
bene enim sciēbat sē ipsum sceleribus Salviī implicārī. intereā, ut
speciem amīcitiae praebēret, Salvium dōnīs honōrāvit, ad cēnam
invītāvit, cōmiter excēpit.

prīncipātūs: prīncipātus
         principate, reign
falsī: falsum *forgery*
imprōvīsā: imprōvīsus
         unexpected, unforeseen
sperneret: spernere *ignore*
5 dēfēnsiōnem: dēfēnsiō *defense*
aliī alia ... *some ... one thing,*
         some ... another
īnstāre *be pressing, threaten*
minās: minae *threats*
10 dīversa: dīversus *different*
accūsātōrēs: accūsātor
         accuser, prosecutor
socius *companion, partner*
ad eum prōdendum *to betray*
         him
15 testimōniō: testimōnium
         evidence
implicārī: implicāre *implicate,*
         involve
20 speciem: speciēs *appearance*

II

Domitia autem, iam ab exiliō revocāta atque in favōrem
Domitiānī restitūta, intentē ultiōnem adversus Salvium
meditābātur. patefēcerat enim Myropnous pūmiliō Salvium
auctōrem fuisse exiliī Domitiae, Paridis mortis; Salvium domum
Hateriī falsīs litterīs Domitiam Paridemque invītāvisse; Salviō
auctōre, Domitiam in īnsulam duōs annōs relēgātam esse,
Paridem occīsum esse.

    accūsātōrēs igitur, ā Domitiā incitātī, cognitiōnem senātūs
poposcērunt et impetrāvērunt. invidia Salviī aucta est
suspīciōne Cogidubnum venēnō necātum esse. praetereā
nōnnūllī dīxērunt reliquiās corporum in thermīs Aquārum Sūlis
inventās esse, dēfīxiōnēs quoque nōmine Cogidubnī īnscrīptās.
quibus audītīs, multī crēdēbant Salvium dīs īnferīs inimīcōs
cōnsecrāvisse.

    tum dēmum Salvius intellēxit quantō in perīculō esset. veste
ergō mūtātā, domōs circumiit amīcōrum, quī sibi auxiliō essent.
omnibus autem recūsantibus, domum rediit, spē omnī dēiectus.

restitūta: restituere *restore*	
adversus *against*	
domum Hateriī *to Haterius'*	
	house (line 5)
cognitiōnem senātūs: cognitiō	
senātūs *trial by the senate*	
impetrāvērunt: impetrāre *obtain* (line 10)	
invidia *unpopularity*	
reliquiās: reliquiae *remains*	
dēfīxiōnēs: dēfīxiō *curse*	
dīs īnferīs: dī īnferī *gods of the*	
	underworld
cōnsecrāvisse: cōnsecrāre	
	consecrate
veste … mūtātā: vestem	
mūtāre *change clothing, i.e.* (line 15)	
	put on mourning
	clothes
circumiit: circumīre *go around*	

cognitiō

diē dictā, magna senātōrum multitūdō ad causam audiendam in
cūriā convēnit. Salvius, iam metū cōnfectus, ad cūriam lectīcā
vectus est; fīliō comitante, manibus extentīs, Domitiānō lentē ac
suppliciter appropinquāvit. quī Salvium vultū compositō
excēpit; crīminibus recitātīs, pauca dē Salviō ipsō addidit: eum
Vespasiānī patris amīcum fuisse, adiūtōremque Agricolae ā sē
missum esse ad Britanniam administrandam. dēnique L. Ursum
Serviānum, senātōrem clārissimum, ēlēgit quī cognitiōnī
praeesset.

dictā: dictus *appointed*	
ad causam audiendam	
to hear the case, for the	
purpose of the case being heard	
cōnfectus *exhausted* (line 5)	
suppliciter *like a suppliant,*	
humbly	
crīminibus: crīmen *charge*	
adiūtōrem: adiūtor *assistant*	

primō diē cognitiōnis Glabriō crīmina levia et inānia
exposuit. dīxit Salvium domī statuam suam in locō altiōre quam
statuam prīncipis posuisse; imāginem dīvī Vespasiānī quae
aulam rēgis Cogidubnī ōrnāvisset ā Salviō vīlī pretiō vēnditam
esse; et multa similia. quibus audītīs, Salvius spērāre coepit sē ē
manibus accūsātōrum ēlāpsūrum esse.

postrīdiē tamen appāruit accūsātor novus, Quīntus Caecilius
Iūcundus. vōce ferōcī, vultū minantī, oculīs ardentibus, verbīs
īnfestissimīs Salvium vehementer oppugnāvit. affirmāvit
Salvium superbē ac crūdēliter sē in Britanniā gessisse; cōnātum
esse venēnō necāre Ti. Claudium Cogidubnum, rēgem populō
Rōmānō fidēlissimum et amīcissimum; rēge mortuō, Salvium
testāmentum finxisse; poenās maximās meruisse.

Quīntō haec crīmina expōnentī ācriter respondit Salvius: "id
quod dīcis absurdum est. quō modō venēnum Cogidubnō darī
potuit, tot spectātōribus adstantibus? quis tam stultus est ut
crēdat mē mortem rēgis octōgintā annōrum efficere voluisse?
etiam rēgēs mortālēs sunt." dē testāmentō nihil explicāvit.

subitō extrā cūriam īnfestae vōcēs sunt audītae clāmantium
sē ipsōs Salvium interfectūrōs esse sī poenam scelerum
effūgisset. aliī effigiem Salviī dēreptam multīs contumēliīs in
Tiberim iēcērunt; aliī domum eius circumventam secūribus
saxīsque pulsāre coepērunt. tantus erat strepitus ut ēmitteret
prīnceps per urbem mīlitēs praetōriānōs quī tumultum sēdārent.

intereā Salvius, lectīcā vectus, ā tribūnō domum dēductus est;
utrum tribūnus custōs esset an carnifex, nēmō sciēbat.

10 **levia: levis** *trivial*
    exposuit: expōnere *set out, explain*
    imāginem: imāgō *image, bust*

15

    crūdēliter *cruelly*

20 **amīcissimum: amīcus** *friendly*
    finxisse: fingere *forge*
    meruisse: merēre *deserve*
    ācriter *keenly, fiercely*

25

30 **dēreptam: dēripere** *tear down*

    sēdārent: sēdāre *quell, calm down*

35

1   From Stage 35 on, you have met sentences in which indirect statements are introduced by a verb in the present tense, such as **dīcit**, **spērant**, **audiō**, etc.:

direct statements	*indirect statements*
"custōs revenit."	puer dīcit custōdem revenīre.
"The guard is returning."	*The boy says that the guard is returning.*
"puella recitābit."	spērant puellam recitātūram esse.
"The girl will recite."	*They hope that the girl will recite.*
"vīllae dēlētae sunt."	audiō vīllās dēlētās esse.
"The villas have been destroyed."	*I hear that the villas have been destroyed.*

2   In Stage 40, you have met sentences in which indirect statements are introduced by a verb in the perfect or imperfect tense, such as **dīxit**, **spērābant**, **audīvī**, etc.

direct statements	*indirect statements*
"custōs revenit."	puer dīxit custōdem revenīre.
"The guard is returning."	*The boy said that the guard was returning.*
"puella recitābit."	spērābant puellam recitātūram esse.
"The girl will recite."	*They hoped that the girl would recite.*
"vīllae dēlētae sunt."	audīvī vīllās dēlētās esse.
"The villas have been destroyed."	*I heard that the villas had been destroyed.*

Compare the indirect statements in paragraph 1 with the indirect statements in paragraph 2. How do they differ?

3   Further examples:

   a   "Salvius multa scelera commīsit."

   b   accūsātōrēs affirmāvērunt Salvium multa scelera commīsisse.

   c   "mīlitēs urbem facile capient."

   d   centuriō crēdēbat mīlitēs facile urbem captūrōs esse.

   e   "Agricola iniūstē revocātus est."

   f   multī senātōrēs putābant Agricolam iniūstē revocātum esse.

   g   "frāter tuus in Britanniā iam habitat."

   h   nūntius dīxit frātrem meum in Britanniā illō tempore habitāre.

   i   "Domitiānus timōre coniūrātiōnis saepe perturbātur."

   j   cīvēs sciēbant Domitiānum timōre coniūrātiōnis saepe perturbārī.

dēspērātiō

dēspērātiō *despair*

I

When you have read this part of the story, answer the questions at the end.

intereā Rūfilla, Salviī uxor, dum spēs eius firma manēbat, pollicēbātur sē sociam cuiuscumque fortūnae futūram esse. cum autem sēcrētīs Domitiae precibus veniam ā prīncipe impetrāvisset, Salvium dēserere cōnstituit; dēnique mediā nocte ē marītī cubiculō ēgressa domum patris suī rediit.

tum dēmum Salvius dēspērābat. fīlius Vitelliānus identidem affirmāvit senātōrēs numquam eum damnātūrōs esse; Salvium hortābātur ut animō firmō dēfēnsiōnem postrīdiē renovāret. Salvius autem respondit nūllam iam spem manēre: īnfestōs esse senātōrēs, prīncipem nūllō modō lēnīrī posse.

postulāvit tabulās testāmentī. quās signātās lībertō trādidit. tum frēgit ānulum suum, nē posteā ad aliōs accūsandōs ūsuī esset. postrēmō litterās in hunc modum compositās ad prīncipem mīsit:

"opprimor, domine, inimīcōrum coniūrātiōne mendācibusque testibus, nec mihi licet innocentiam meam probāre. deōs immortālēs testor mē semper in fidē mānsisse. hoc ūnum ōrō ut fīliō meō innocentī parcās. nec quicquam aliud precor."

dē Rūfillā nihil scrīpsit.

dum *so long as*
firma: firmus *firm*
sociam: socia *companion, partner*
5   cuiuscumque: quīcumque *any, any whatever*

10

ūsuī esset: ūsuī esse *be of use*

15   mendācibus: mendāx *lying, deceitful*
mihi licet *I am allowed*
innocentiam: innocentia *innocence*
in fidē mānsisse: in fidē manēre *remain loyal*

Questions

1   What did Rufilla at first promise?

2   Explain why she broke her promise (lines 2–4). Who was Domitia?

3   What suggests that Rufilla did not tell Salvius about her decision (lines 4–5)?

4   What effect did Rufilla's behavior have on Salvius?

5   How did his son try to reassure him? What did he encourage him to do (lines 7–8)?

6   **Salvius … manēre** (line 9). Why did Salvius think this?

7   What did Salvius do after sealing and handing over his will? Explain why he did this (lines 11–13).

8   In his letter to the emperor, Salvius explains the reasons for his downfall (lines 15–16). What were they?

9   What request did Salvius make to the emperor in his letter (lines 17–18)? What did he say about his wife?

10   Does this story change your previous opinion of Salvius? Give a reason.

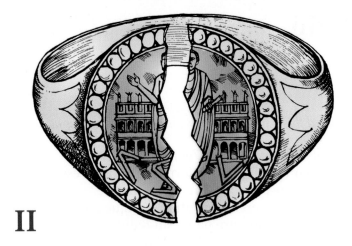

II

cum advesperāsceret, Salvius aliīs servīs pecūniam, aliīs lībertātem dedit. deinde mortem sibi cōnscīscere parāvit. venēnō ūtī nōn potuit; nam corpus iam diū antidotīs mūniēbātur. cōnstituit ergō vēnās pugiōne incīdere. quō factō, in balneum inlātus mox exanimātus est.

    at prīnceps, simulac mortem ā Salviō cōgitārī per ministrōs cognōvit, tribūnum mīlitēsque domum eius ēmīsit. mandāvit eīs ut Salviī mortem prohibērent; ipse enim crūdēlis vidērī nōlēbat. mīlitēs igitur, ā tribūnō iussī, Salvium ē balneō extrāxērunt, dēligāvērunt bracchia vulnerāta, sanguinem suppressērunt.

mortem sibi cōnscīscere *commit suicide*
antidotīs: antidotum *antidote, remedy*
5
mūniēbātur: mūnīre *protect, immunize*
vēnās: vēna *vein*
incīdere *cut open*
10   **suppressērunt: supprimere** *staunch, stop the flow of*

damnātiō

damnātiō *condemnation*

postrīdiē Ursus Serviānus, quī cognitiōnī praefuerat, sententiam prōnūntiāvit: nōmen Salviī Fāstīs ērādendum esse; bonōrum eius partem pūblicandam, partem fīliō trādendam; Salvium ipsum quīnque annōs relēgandum.

    ille igitur, vulneribus sānātīs, Rōmā discessit. eōdem diē mīrum fideī exemplum oculīs populī Rōmānī obiectum est. Q. Haterius Latrōniānus, quī favōrem Salviī flōrentis semper quaerēbat, eum rēbus adversīs oppressum nōn dēseruit, sed in exilium comitātus est.

    paucīs post diēbus Domitiānus accūsātōribus honōrēs ac praemia distribuit. Glabriōnī sacerdōtium dedit; plūrimī autem exīstimābant Glabriōnem rē vērā Domitiānum hāc accūsātiōne graviter offendisse. Quīntō Caeciliō prīnceps favōrem suum ad honōrēs petendōs pollicitus est; simul autem eum monuit nē nimis ēlātus vel superbus fieret. pūmiliōnī Myropnoō, quī Salviī scelera Domitiae patefēcerat, lībertātem obtulit; quam tamen ille recūsāvit. "quid mihi cum lībertāte?" rogāvit; "satis est mihi amīcum mortuum vindicāvisse." et tībiīs dēmum resūmptīs, exsultāns cantāre coepit.

sententiam: sententia *sentence*
prōnūntiāvit: prōnūntiāre *announce*
Fāstīs: Fāstī *the list of consuls*
5   **bonōrum: bona** *goods, property*
pūblicandam: pūblicāre *confiscate*
flōrentis: flōrēre *flourish*

10

15

About the language 2: more about gerundives

1 In Stage 32, you met sentences like these:

> mihi fābula nārranda est.   Haterius laudandus est.
> *I must tell a story.*   *Haterius should be praised.*

In these examples, the gerundives **nārranda** and **laudandus** are being used with **est** to indicate that something *ought* to be done ("the story *ought* to be told," "Haterius *ought* to be praised").

2 In Stage 40, you have met the gerundive used with **ad**, meaning *for the purpose of...*:

> deinde Quīntus ad Salvium accūsandum surrēxit.
> *Then Quintus stood up for the purpose of Salvius being accused.*

Or, in more natural English:
> *Then Quintus stood up to accuse Salvius.*

> mercātōrēs in portū ad nāvem reficiendam manēbant.
> *The merchants stayed in port for the purpose of their ship being repaired.*

Or, in more natural English:
> *The merchants stayed in port to repair their ship.*

3 Further examples:

  a Calēdoniī nūntiōs ad pācem petendam mīsērunt.
  b sculptor ingentem marmoris massam ad statuās faciendās comparāvit.
  c poēta ad versūs recitandōs scaenam ascendit.
  d Memor ad scelera Salviī patefacienda adductus est.
  e servōs in agrōs ad frūmentum colligendum ēmīsī.

dē tribus capellīs

The following poem by Martial is about a court case over the theft of three she-goats. However, the lawyer for the prosecution, Postumus, treats it as though it were a very important case requiring all his powers of oratory.

nōn dē vī neque caede nec venēnō,
sed līs est mihi dē tribus capellīs.
vīcīnī queror hās abesse fūrtō.
hoc iūdex sibi postulat probārī;
tū Cannās Mithridāticumque bellum   5
et periūria Pūnicī furōris
et Sullās Mariōsque Mūciōsque
magnā vōce sonās manūque tōtā.
iam dīc, Postume, dē tribus capellīs.

caede: caedēs *murder*
līs *court case*
fūrtō: fūrtum *theft*
Cannās: Cannae *Cannae, the site of a famous battle*
Mithridāticum ... bellum *the war with Mithridates*
periūria Pūnicī furōris *the frenzied treachery of Carthage (literally the false oaths of Carthaginian frenzy)*
Sullās, Mariōs ... Mūciōs *people like Sulla, Marius, and Mucius (famous Roman leaders)*
sonās: sonāre *sound off*
manū ... tōtā *with every kind of gesture, literally, with the whole hand*

Questions for discussion

1 How does Martial emphasize that the court case is about a trivial theft?

2 What kind of speech does the lawyer make (lines 5–8)? Why?

3 Why do you think Martial repeats the phrase **dē tribus capellīs** at the end of the poem?

Word patterns: inceptives

1 Study the following forms:

calēre	*to be warm*	calēscere	*to grow warm*
concupere	*to long for*	concupīscere	*to develop a longing for*
senex	*old man*	senēscere	*to grow old*
īrātus	*angry*	īrāscī	*to become angry*

The verbs in the second column are called **inceptives** or **inchoatives** (from **incipere** and **inchoāre**, both meaning *to begin*) because they indicate an action which is beginning or developing.

2 Give a meaning for each of the following verbs:

advesperāscere, ascīscere, cognōscere, convalēscere, ērubēscere, ēvānēscere, ignōscere, ingravēscere, nāscī, oblīvīscī, pallēscere, ulcīscī.

A goat balanced improbably on a branch – a wall decoration from a villa near Pompeii.

Practicing the language

1 Translate each sentence into Latin by selecting correctly from the list of Latin words.

   a *I was being looked after by a very experienced doctor.*

ā medicō	perītiōre	cūrābam
prope medicum	perītissimō	cūrābar

   b *The commander hopes that the messengers will return soon.*

lēgātus	spērō	nūntiī	mox	revenīre
lēgātī	spērat	nūntiōs	nūper	reventūrōs esse

   c *We hear that a new house is being built.*

audīmus	domus	nova	aedificāre
audīvimus	domum	novam	aedificārī

   d *After the conspiracy had been revealed* (two words only), *very many senators were condemned.*

coniūrātiōnem	patefactā	plūrimī	senātōrī	damnātī sunt
coniūrātiōne	patefactam	maximī	senātōrēs	damnātus est

   e *The soothsayer advises you not to leave the city.*

haruspex	tū	monet	ut	urbī	discēdās
haruspicem	tē	monēbat	nē	ex urbe	discessissēs

2 With the help of paragraph 1 on page 267, turn each of the following pairs of sentences into one sentence by replacing the word in **boldface** with the correct form of the relative pronoun **quī**, **quae**, **quod**. Then move the relative pronoun to the *beginning* of the relative clause. Finally, translate the sentence. You may need to check the gender of the noun in the Vocabulary.

For example:	intrāvit medicus. senex **medicum** arcessīverat.
This becomes:	intrāvit medicus, **quem** senex arcessīverat.
	*In came the doctor, **whom** the old man had sent for.*

   a templum nōtissimum vīsitāvimus. Domitiānus ipse **templum** exstrūxerat.

   b prō domō cōnsulis stābat pauper. praecō **pauperī** sportulam trādēbat.

   c ille vir est Quīntus. pater **Quīntī** mēcum negōtium agere solēbat.

   d servī flammās exstīnxērunt. vīlla **flammīs** cōnsūmēbātur.

   e praemium illīs puellīs dabitur. auxiliō **puellārum** fūr herī comprehēnsus est.

3 Complete each sentence with the correct verb. Then translate the sentence.
Finally write down whether the sentence expresses a purpose, a result, or an
indirect command.

a iuvenis puellae persuādēre nōn poterat ut sēcum . . . . (fugeret, sperneret)
b senātōrēs tacēre cōnstituērunt nē Imperātōrem . . . . (offenderent, incēderent)
c tam fortis erās ut vērum dīcere nōn . . . . (funderēs, timērēs)
d tālis erat ille homō ut nēmō eī . . . . (crēderet, spērāret)
e uxōrēs ducem ōrābant nē captīvōs . . . . (interficeret, dēcideret)
f tam diū in vīllā rūsticā manēbam ut ad urbem regredī . . . . (sentīrem, nōllem)
g Domitiānus vōbīs imperat ut ad aulam statim . . . . (vincātis, conveniātis)
h vīsne mēcum ad theātrum venīre ut pantomīmum nōtissimum . . . . ?
(spectēmus, moveāmus)

Domitian

In this picture, Domitian is shown as a young man at the start of the principate of his father, Vespasian. Domitian is in the center, welcoming Vespasian (right) to Rome.

When Vespasian became emperor he was campaigning overseas, and Domitian looked after affairs in Rome until his father could get back to the capital and take control himself. His critics said this experience gave Domitian a lust for power. When eventually he became emperor himself, he was a tyrant. He ignored the senate much of the time, relying on his inner circle of amici. Conspiracies against him were ruthlessly suppressed. Eventually he was assassinated by plotters including his wife, Domitia.

Roman law courts

At the beginning of the first century AD, there were several different law courts in Rome, for handling different sorts of cases. If a Roman was charged with a criminal offense, he or she might find themselves in one of a group of jury courts known as **quaestiōnēs** (commissions of inquiry), each responsible for judging a particular crime, such as treason, murder, adultery, misconduct by governors of provinces, forgery, and election bribery. If he or she was involved in a civil (that is, non-criminal) case, such as a dispute over a legacy or an attempt to gain compensation from a next-door neighbor for damage to property, he or she would go first of all to a **praetor**. The praetor would inquire into the cause and nature of the dispute, then either appoint an individual judge (**iūdex**) to hear the case or refer it to an appropriate court. Cases involving inheritance or property claims, for example, usually went to the court of the **centumvirī**.

By the time of Domitian, some further ways of handling law cases had been added. For example, a senator charged with a crime could be tried in the senate by his fellow-senators, like Salvius in the story on pages 85–90; and the emperor himself took an increasingly large part in administering the law (see page 43). But the courts described in the previous paragraph continued to operate alongside these new arrangements.

In modern times, someone who has committed an offense is liable to be charged by the police and prosecuted by a lawyer who acts on behalf of the state; the system is supervised by a government department. In Rome, however, there were no charges by the police, no state lawyers, and no government department responsible for prosecutions. If a man committed a crime, he could be prosecuted only by a private individual, not by a public official. A man who held citizenship could bring a prosecution, and if the accused was found guilty, there was sometimes a reward for the prosecutor. A woman who was not under the authority of her father or husband was allowed to bring a criminal charge, but only if she had a personal interest in the case (that is, if an offense had been committed against herself or a close relative). She was also allowed to bring a civil suit on her own behalf but not to represent others in such cases, and it may in fact have been more usual for a woman to be represented in court by a male advocate.

The courts played an important part in the lives of many Romans, especially senators and their sons. Success as a speaker in court was one of the aims of the long training which they had received from the rhetor. In the courts, a Roman could make a name for himself with the general public, play his part as a patron by looking after any clients who had gotten involved with the law, and catch the eye of people (such as the emperor and his advisers) whose support might help him gain promotion in the cursus honorum. One such success story concerns

This coin illustrates voting in the senate: in the center, under a canopy, the presiding magistrate's chair; on the right, the tablets used by the jurors (A and C); and on the left the urn into which they were cast.

Cicero, a young, unknown lawyer with no family influence. A case with political ramifications attracted attention to this **novus homō**. In only a few days the extraordinary eloquence of his defense made him a leading figure in the courts and laid the foundation for his future political success.

Fame and prestige usually mattered more than financial reward to the men who conducted cases in the courts. For a long time, they were forbidden to receive payment at all from their clients. Later, they were permitted to accept a fee for their services, but this fee was regarded as an unofficial "present," or donation, which the client was not obliged to pay and the lawyer was not supposed to ask for.

Roman courts were probably at their liveliest in the first century BC, when rival politicians fought each other fiercely in the courts as part of their struggle for power. By the time of Domitian, some of the glamor had faded; now that Rome was ruled by an emperor, there was less political power to be fought for. Nevertheless, the contests in court still mattered to the speakers and their clients and attracted enthusiastic audiences. When a well-known orator was to speak, the news spread and a large audience gathered, often taking sides vocally. Pliny gives a vivid description of a case that aroused particularly lively interest:

> **There they were, one hundred and eighty jurors, a great crowd of lawyers for both plaintiff and defendant, dozens of supporters sitting on the benches, and an enormous circle of listeners, several rows deep, standing around the whole courtroom. The platform was packed solid with people, and in the upper galleries of the basilica men and women were leaning over in an effort to hear, which was difficult, and see, which was rather easier.**

The writings of Martial, Pliny, and Quintilian are full of casual details which convey the liveliness and excitement of the courts: the gimmicky lawyer who always wears an eye-patch while pleading a case; the claque of spectators who applaud at the right moments in return for payment; the successful speaker who wins a standing ovation from the jury; the careful allocation of time for each side, measured by the water clock; the lawyer with the booming voice, whose speech is greeted by applause not only in his own court but also from the court next door; the windbag who is supposed to be talking about the theft of three she-goats, but goes off into long irrelevant ramblings about Rome's wars with Carthage three hundred years earlier (see the poem on page 92); and the anxious wife who sends messengers to court every hour to find out how her husband is doing.

It is difficult to say how fair Roman justice was. Some of the tactics used in Roman law courts had very little to do with the rights and wrongs of the case. An accused man might dress up in mourning or hold up his little children to the jury to arouse their pity. A speaker whose client was in the wrong might ignore the facts altogether, and

Statue of a Roman making a speech.

try to win his case by appealing to the jury's emotions or prejudices, or by using irrelevant arguments. Sometimes a man might be accused and found guilty for political reasons; there were a number of "treason trials" under Domitian, in which innocent men were condemned. However, the writings of such men as Pliny and Quintilian show that at least some Roman judges made an honest effort to be fair and just.

Fairness in a Roman court was partly the result of the **lēgēs** (the laws) themselves. In the middle of the fifth century BC the Romans had set up a ten-man board (**decemvirī lēgibus scrībendīs**) to write down the important points of law on bronze tablets for all to see and use. These Twelve Tables (**duodecim tabulae**), since they were written and publicly displayed, eliminated arbitrary decisions by magistrates. Over the centuries the laws evolved, accumulating legal interpretations and precedents. At its best Roman law was careful, practical, and immensely detailed; it became the basis of many present-day legal systems in North America and Europe.

Remains of the Basilica Iulia in the Forum, an important law court. The case described by Pliny took place here. This is the building seen in the background on page 42.

Vocabulary checklist 40

affirmō, affirmāre, affirmāvī	*declare*
amīcitia, amīcitiae, f.	*friendship*
augeō, augēre, auxī, auctus	*increase*
cōnsul, cōnsulis, m.	*consul (senior magistrate)*
crīmen, crīminis, n.	*charge*
cūria, cūriae, f.	*senate-house*
dēmum	*at last*
tum dēmum	*then at last, only then*
exīstimō, exīstimāre, exīstimāvī, exīstimātus	*think, consider*
inānis, ināne	*empty, meaningless*
invidia, invidiae, f.	*jealousy, envy, unpopularity*
levis, leve	*light, slight, trivial*
minor, minārī, minātus sum	*threaten*
mūtō, mūtāre, mūtāvī, mūtātus	*change*
obiciō, obicere, obiēcī, obiectus	*present, put in the way of, expose to*
probō, probāre, probāvī, probātus	*prove*
prōdō, prōdere, prōdidī, prōditus	*betray*
similis, simile	*similar*
socius, sociī, m.	*companion, partner*
suādeō, suādēre, suāsī	*advise, suggest*
ūtor, ūtī, ūsus sum	*use*
videor, vidērī, vīsus sum	*seem*

One of the boards for various games scratched on the steps of the Basilica Julia.

BITHYNIA

Governing an empire

For about four hundred and fifty years, the Romans controlled an empire that, at its height, stretched from the Atlantic Ocean to the edge of Russia and from Scotland to the Sahara Desert. The empire's provinces were ruled by an enormous and complicated organization of governors and their staffs.

As a rule, we know very little about the day-to-day running of this vast network; but in one case we have an unusually large amount of information because the provincial governor's letters to the emperor have survived, together with the emperor's replies. In about AD 110, Gaius Plinius Caecilius Secundus (Pliny) was appointed by the Emperor Trajan to govern the province of Bithynia et Pontus (roughly equivalent to northern Turkey). It was an abnormal governorship: Pliny had been personally chosen by the emperor himself; he was given special authority and status, and he had a special job to do. Stage 41 contains five of Pliny's official letters to Trajan, together with Trajan's replies.

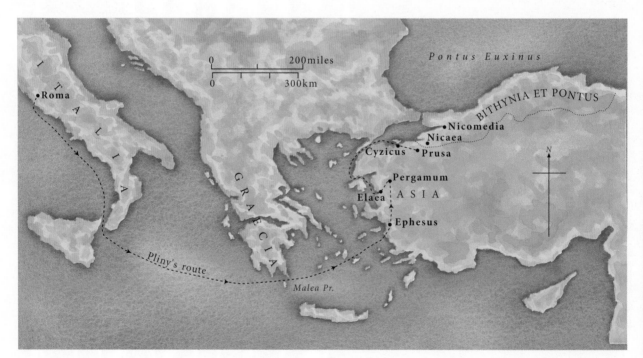

Pliny's route.

adventus

I

Gāius Plīnius Trāiānō Imperātōrī

nāvigātiō mea, domine, usque Ephesum salūberrima erat; inde, postquam vehiculīs iter facere coepī, gravissimīs aestibus atque etiam febriculīs afflīgēbar; Pergamī igitur ad convalēscendum substitī. deinde, cum nāvem iterum cōnscendissem, contrāriīs ventīs retentus sum; itaque Bīthȳniam intrāvī aliquantō tardius quam spērāveram, id est XV Kal. Octōbrēs.

   nunc ratiōnēs Prūsēnsium excutiō; quod mihi magis ac magis necessārium vidētur. multae enim pecūniae, variīs ex causīs, ā prīvātīs cīvibus retinentur; praetereā quaedam pecūniae sine iūstā causā impenduntur. dispice, domine, num necessārium putēs mittere hūc mēnsōrem, ad opera pūblica īnspicienda; crēdō enim multās pecūniās posse revocārī ā cūrātōribus pūblicōrum operum, sī mēnsūrae fidēliter agantur. hanc epistulam tibi, domine, in ipsō adventū meō scrīpsī.

5

10

15

nāvigātiō *voyage*
usque Ephesum *as far as Ephesus*
salūberrima: salūbris *comfortable*
vehiculīs: vehiculum *carriage*
gravissimīs: gravis *severe*
aestibus: aestus *heat*
febriculīs: febricula *slight fever*
Pergamī *at Pergamum*
ad convalēscendum *for the purpose of getting better, in order to get better*
substitī: subsistere *halt, stop*
aliquantō *somewhat, rather*
XV Kal. Octōbrēs *September 17* (literally *fifteen days before October 1*)
Prūsēnsium: Prūsēnsēs *people of Prusa*
excutiō: excutere *examine, investigate*
necessārium: necessārius *necessary*
pecūniae: pecūnia *sum of money*
iūstā: iūstus *proper, right*
impenduntur: impendere *spend*
dispice: dispicere *consider*
mēnsōrem: mēnsor *surveyor*
opera: opus *work, building*
revocārī: revocāre *recover*
ā *from*
cūrātōribus: cūrātor *supervisor, superintendent*
mēnsūrae: mēnsūra *measurement*
fidēliter *faithfully, reliably*

Questions

1 How did Pliny travel to Ephesus?
2 What change in his method of traveling did he make when he got there?
3 Why was he forced to stop at Pergamum?
4 What method of travel did he use for the final stage of his journey? What delayed him?
5 What is Pliny doing at Prusa? From lines 9–11 find two reasons why Prusa is short of public money.
6 What kind of assistant does Pliny ask Trajan for?
7 What job does Pliny want this assistant to do?
8 What impression does Pliny give by the words **nunc** (line 8) and **in ipsō adventū** (lines 14–15)? Can you suggest why Pliny is so anxious to impress Trajan in this way – is it, for example, to make up for any failure on his part?

II

Trāiānus Plīniō

cognōvī litterīs tuīs, Secunde cārissime, quō diē in Bīthȳniam
pervēnissēs. brevī tempore, crēdō, Bīthȳnī intellegent
prōvinciam mihi esse cūrae: nam ego tē ēlēgī quī ad eōs meī locō
mittāris; tū efficiēs ut benignitās mea sit manifesta illīs.   5

   prīmum autem tibi ratiōnēs pūblicae sunt excutiendae; nam
satis cōnstat et eās vexātās esse.

   mēnsōrēs vix sufficientēs habeō etiam eīs operibus quae aut
Rōmae aut in proximō fiunt. sed in omnī prōvinciā inveniuntur
mēnsōrēs quibus crēdere possīmus; et ideō nōn vereor nē tibi   10
dēsint. sī tū dīligenter excutiēs, inveniēs.

Bīthȳnī *Bithynians*
meī locō *in my place*
efficiēs ut: efficere ut *bring it
     about that, see to it that*
benignitās *concern, kindly interest*
manifesta: manifestus *clear*
satis cōnstat *it is generally agreed*
vexātās: vexātus *confused, in chaos*
sufficientēs: sufficiēns *enough,
                    sufficient*
aut … aut *either … or*
in proximō *nearby*
omnī: omnis *every*
dēsint: dēesse *be lacking, be
                unavailable*

*mēnsōrēs vix sufficientēs habeō etiam eīs operibus quae aut Rōmae
aut in proximō fiunt.*

Questions

1   What phrase does Trajan use to emphasize that Pliny's job in
    Bithynia is an important one?

2   What impression of himself does Trajan want the Bithynians
    to have?

3   Why is Trajan unable to agree to Pliny's request for a surveyor?
    What steps does he suggest Pliny should take instead?

4   On the evidence of this pair of letters, what special task has
    Pliny been sent to Bithynia to perform? Can you suggest
    reasons why Trajan should have chosen Pliny for this task?

carcer

I

Gāius Plīnius Trāiānō Imperātōrī

rogō, domine, ut mē tuō cōnsiliō adiuvēs: incertus enim sum
utrum carcerem custōdīre dēbeam per pūblicōs servōs (quod
usque adhūc factum est) an per mīlitēs. sī enim servīs pūblicīs
ūtar, vereor nē parum fidēlēs sint; sī mīlitibus ūtar, vereor nē hoc
officium magnum numerum mīlitum distringat. interim pūblicīs
servīs paucōs mīlitēs addidī. videō tamen in hōc cōnsiliō
perīculum esse nē utrīque neglegentiōrēs fīant; nam sī quid
adversī acciderit, culpam mīlitēs in servōs, servī in mīlitēs
trānsferre poterunt.

usque adhūc *up till now, until now*
parum *too little, not … enough*
fidēlēs: fidēlis *reliable, trustworthy*
officium *task, duty*
distringat: distringere *distract, divert*
interim *meanwhile*
utrīque *both groups of people*
sī quid *if anything*
adversī: adversus *unfortunate, undesirable*
culpam: culpa *blame*
trānsferre *transfer, put*

Questions

1 What problem is causing Pliny difficulty? What disadvantage
  does each of his two alternatives have?

2 What step has Pliny taken for the moment?

3 Is Pliny satisfied with his present solution? If not, why not?

4 What reply would you expect from Trajan? Would you expect
  him to agree with what Pliny has done? or to prefer another
  solution? or to snap at Pliny for bothering him with trivialities?

Trajan addressing the army.

II

Trāiānus Plīniō

nihil opus est, mī Secunde cārissime, mīlitēs ad carcerem
custōdiendum convertere. melius est persevērāre in istīus
prōvinciae cōnsuētūdine, et pūblicīs servīs ad vigilandum in
carcere ūtī; tū enim, sevēritāte ac dīligentiā tuā, potes efficere ut   5
servī fidēliter hoc faciant. nam, sī mīlitēs servīs pūblicīs
permiscentur, rēctē verēris nē utrīque neglegentiōrēs sint; sed
nōs semper oportet hoc meminisse: mīlitēs Rōmānōs in
prōvinciīs nostrīs positōs esse nōn ad carcerēs custōdiendōs, sed
ad pugnandum.   10

nihil opus est *there is no need*
convertere *divert*
persevērāre *continue*
cōnsuētūdine: cōnsuētūdō *custom*
ad vigilandum *for keeping watch*
sevēritāte: sevēritās *strictness,
severity*
permiscentur: permiscēre
mix with
meminisse *remember*

Questions

1 In Trajan's view, who ought to guard the prisoners?
2 Why had Pliny been reluctant to adopt this solution, and how
   does Trajan answer his objection?
3 Which of Pliny's fears does Trajan agree with?
4 What aspect of the problem does Trajan seem to feel most
   strongly about? Is it the unreliability of the public slaves, the
   disadvantage of sharing the work, or some other aspect?

About the language 1: gerunds

1 In Stage 40, you met the gerundive used with **ad**, meaning "for the purpose of...":

> Quīntus ad Salvium accūsandum surrēxit.
> *Quintus stood up for the purpose of Salvius being accused.*
> Or, in more natural English:
> *Quintus stood up in order to accuse Salvius.*

> iuvenēs ad pompam spectandam advēnērunt.
> *The young men arrived for the purpose of the procession being watched.*
> Or, in more natural English:
> *The young men arrived to watch the procession.*

2 In Stage 41, you have met sentences like these:

> pontifex ad **sacrificandum** aderat.
> *The priest was present for the purpose of sacrificing.*
> Or, in more natural English:
> *The priest was present in order to sacrifice.*

> līberī ad **lūdendum** exiērunt.
> *The children went out for the purpose of playing.*
> Or, in more natural English:
> *The children went out to play.*

The word in **boldface** is known as a **gerund**.

Further examples:

a puer in fossam ad latendum dēsiluit.
b senex ad cēnandum recumbēbat.

3 Further examples of sentences containing gerunds and gerundives:

a mīlitēs ad imperātōrem **salūtandum** īnstrūctī erant. (*gerundive*)
b mīlitēs ad **pugnandum** īnstrūctī erant. (*gerund*)
c Plīnius ad **convalēscendum** in oppidō manēbat. (*gerund*)
d haruspicēs ad victimās **īnspiciendās** prōcessērunt. (*gerundive*)
e servus ad **labōrandum** ē lectō surrēxit. (*gerund*)
f dominus ad pecūniam **numerandam** in tablīnō sedēbat. (*gerundive*)
g clientēs ad patrōnōs **vīsitandōs** per viās contendēbant.
h amīcus meus ad **dormiendum** abiit.
i multī āthlētae ad **certandum** aderant.
j cīvēs aquam ad incendium **exstinguendum** quaerēbant.

In sentences **g–j**, which of the words in **boldface** are gerundives, and which are gerunds?

aquaeductus

I

Gāius Plīnius Trāiānō Imperātōrī

in aquaeductum, domine, Nīcomēdēnsēs impendērunt sestertium
XXX CCCXVIII, quī, imperfectus adhūc, nōn modo omissus
sed etiam dēstrūctus est; deinde in alium aquaeductum impēnsa
sunt CC. hōc quoque relictō, novō impendiō opus est, ut aquam   5
habeant, postquam tantam pecūniam perdidērunt. ipse pervēnī ad
fontem pūrissimum, ex quō vidētur aqua dēbēre perdūcī (sīcut
initiō temptātum erat), arcuātō opere, nē tantum ad humilēs
regiōnēs oppidī perveniat. manent adhūc paucissimī arcūs;
possunt etiam exstruī arcūs complūrēs lapide quadrātō quī ex   10
priōre opere dētractus est; aliqua pars, ut mihi vidētur, testāceō
opere agenda erit (id enim et facilius et vīlius est). sed in prīmīs
necessārium est mittī ā tē vel aquilegem vel architectum, nē id
quod prius accidit rūrsus ēveniat. ego quidem cōnfīdō et
ūtilitātem operis et pulchritūdinem prīncipātū tuō esse   15
dignissimam.

aquaeductus *aqueduct*
Nīcomēdēnsēs *people of*
        Nicomedia
XXX CCCXVIII *3,318,000:*
   ☐ = *multiply by 100,000;*
   = *multiply by 1,000*
imperfectus *unfinished*
adhūc *still*
omissus = omissus est: omittere
              abandon
dēstrūctus est: dēstruere
            pull down, demolish
CC *200,000*
impendiō: impendium
       expense, expenditure
opus est *there is need of (literally*
     there is work (to be done)
     with)
perdidērunt: perdere *waste, lose*
perdūcī: perdūcere *bring, carry*
arcuātō: arcuātus *arched*
humilēs: humilis *low-lying*
lapide: lapis *stone*
quadrātō: quadrātus *squared, in*
          blocks
testāceō opere: testāceum
   opus *brickwork*
in prīmīs *in the first place*
vel ... vel *either ... or*
aquilegem: aquilex *water engineer,*
          hydraulic
          engineer
ēveniat: ēvenīre *occur*
ūtilitātem: ūtilitās *usefulness*
pulchritūdinem: pulchritūdō
          beauty

Questions

1 What happened to the Nicomedians' first aqueduct?

2 What has happened to their second attempt?

3 Why does the aqueduct have to be carried on arches?

4 **manent ... agenda erit** (lines 9–12). What three suggestions
   does Pliny make for the providing of arches?

5 What request does he make of Trajan?

6 How does Pliny attempt to make his idea more persuasive to
   Trajan?

II

Trāiānus Plīniō

cūrandum est, ut aqua in oppidum Nīcomēdīam perdūcātur.
cōnfīdō tē summā dīligentiā hoc opus effectūrum esse. sed
medius fidius! necesse est tibi eādem dīligentiā ūtī ad
cognōscendum quōrum vitiō tantam pecūniam Nīcomēdēnsēs   5
perdiderint; suspicor eōs ideō tot aquaeductūs incohāvisse et
relīquisse, ut inter sē grātificentur. quicquid cognōveris, perfer in
nōtitiam meam.

cūrandum est *steps must be taken*
medius fidius! *for goodness sake!*
vitiō: vitium *fault, failure*
incohāvisse: incohāre *begin*
grātificentur: grātificārī *do favors*
quicquid: quisquis *whoever, whatever*
perfer: perferre *bring*
nōtitiam: nōtitia *notice*

Questions

1 Does Trajan give permission for the new aqueduct?
2 What is Trajan especially concerned about? What does he suspect?
3 What does Trajan do about Pliny's request for a water engineer?

lapis quadrātus.

testāceum opus.

supplicium

I

Gāius Plīnius Trāiānō Imperātōrī

Semprōnius Caeliānus, ēgregius iuvenis, duōs servōs inter tīrōnēs
repertōs mīsit ad mē; quōrum ego supplicium distulī, ut tē
cōnsulerem dē modō poenae. ipse enim ideō maximē dubitō,
quod hī servī, quamquam iam sacrāmentum dīxērunt, nōndum in
numerōs distribūtī sunt. rogō igitur, domine, ut scrībās quid facere
dēbeam, praesertim cum pertineat ad exemplum.

ēgregius *excellent, outstanding*
tīrōnēs: tīrō *recruit*
repertōs: reperīre *find*
distulī: differre *postpone*
sacrāmentum dīxērunt:
    sacrāmentum dīcere
        take the military oath
numerōs: numerī *military units*
cum *since, because*
pertineat ad exemplum:
    pertinēre ad exemplum
        involve a precedent

Legionaries on the march.

Questions

1 What has Sempronius Caelianus discovered? What action has
   he taken?
2 What does Pliny want Trajan to decide?
3 Why is Pliny particularly hesitant?
4 Why does he think the case is important?

II

Trāiānus Plīniō

rēctē mīsit Semprōnius Caeliānus ad tē eōs servōs, quī inter
tīrōnēs repertī sunt. nunc tē oportet cognōscere num supplicium
ultimum meruisse videantur. rēfert autem utrum voluntāriī
vēnerint an lēctī sint vel etiam vicāriī ab aliīs datī. sī lēctī sunt,   5
illī peccāvērunt quī ad mīlitandum eōs ēlēgērunt; sī vicāriī datī
sunt, culpa est penes eōs quī dedērunt; sī ipsī, cum habērent
condiciōnis suae cōnscientiam, nihilōminus vēnērunt, sevērē
pūniendī erunt. neque multum rēfert, quod nōndum in numerōs
distribūtī sunt. illō enim diē, quō prīmum probātī sunt, vēritās   10
condiciōnis eōrum patefacienda erat.

rēfert: rēferre *make a
                    difference*
voluntāriī: voluntārius *volunteer*
vēnerint: venīre *come forward*
lēctī sint: legere *recruit,
                    conscript*
vicāriī: vicārius *substitute*
datī: dare *put forward*
peccāvērunt: peccāre
       do wrong, be to blame
penes *with*
cum *although*
condiciōnis: condiciō *status*
cōnscientiam: cōnscientia
       awareness, knowledge
probātī sunt: probāre
       *examine (at time of
       enrollment)*
vēritās *truth*

Marble bust of Trajan.

Questions

1 What punishment are the slaves liable to suffer if they are
   found guilty?
2 Trajan refers to three possible explanations for the situation.
   What are they? What action does he think should be taken in
   each case?
3 When should the status of the recruits have been discovered?
4 Who seems to have a better grasp of the problem, Pliny or
   Trajan?

About the language 2: present subjunctive passive

1 Study the following examples:

> tam stultus est ille puer ut ā cēterīs discipulīs semper **dērīdeātur**.
> *That boy is so stupid that he is always laughed at by the other pupils.*

> medicus ignōrat quārē hōc morbō **afflīgāris**, mī amīce.
> *The doctor does not know why you are stricken with this illness, my friend.*

The form of the verb in **boldface** is the **present subjunctive passive**.

Further examples:

a scīre velim quot captīvī in illō carcere retineantur.
b tot clientēs habēmus ut in viās semper salūtēmur.
c arma semper gerō nē ā latrōnibus interficiar.

2 Compare the active and passive forms of the present subjunctive of **portō**:

present subjunctive active	*present subjunctive passive*
portem	porter
portēs	portēris
portet	portētur
portēmus	portēmur
portētis	portēminī
portent	portentur

The present subjuntive passive of all four conjugations is set out in full on page 273 of the Language information section.

3 Study the following examples:

> nescio quid iuvenis efficere **cōnētur**.
> *I do not know what the young man is trying to achieve.*

> crās equōs cōnscendēmus ut **proficīscāmur**.
> *Tomorrow we will mount our horses in order to set out.*

The verbs in **boldface** are present subjunctive forms of deponent verbs.

Further examples:

a tam timidī sunt servī meī ut etiam umbrās vereantur.
b dīcite mihi quārē illōs senēs sequāminī.

The present subjunctive of deponent verbs is set out in full on page 278.

incendium

I

Gāius Plīnius Trāiānō Imperātōrī

cum dīversam partem prōvinciae circumīrem, vāstissimum incendium Nīcomēdīae coortum est. nōn modo multās cīvium prīvātōrum domōs dēlēvit, sed etiam duo pūblica opera, Gerūsiān et templum Īsidis. flammae autem lātius sparsae sunt, prīmum violentiā ventī, deinde inertiā hominum, quī ōtiōsī et immōtī adstābant, neque quicquam ad adiuvandum fēcērunt. praetereā, nūllus est usquam pūblicus sīpō, nūlla hama, nūllum omnīnō īnstrūmentum ad incendia exstinguenda. et haec quidem īnstrūmenta, ut iam praecēpī, parābuntur; tū, domine, dispice num putēs collēgium fabrōrum esse īnstituendum, dumtaxat hominum CL. ego efficiam nē quis nisi faber in hoc collēgium admittātur, nēve fabrī hōc iūre in aliud ūtantur; nec erit difficile custōdīre tam paucōs.

5

10

vāstissimum: **vāstus** *great, large*
Nīcomēdīae *at Nicomedia*
coortum est: **coorīrī** *break out*
Gerūsiān: *Greek accusative of* **Gerūsia** *the Gerusia (club for wealthy elderly men)*
lātius: **lātē** *widely*
sparsae sunt: **spargere** *spread*
violentiā: **violentia** *violence*
inertiā: **inertia** *laziness, idleness*
sīpō *fire pump*
hama *fire bucket*
īnstrūmentum *equipment*
praecēpī: **praecipere** *instruct, order*
collēgium *brigade*
fabrōrum: **faber** *fireman*
īnstituendum: **īnstituere** *set up*
dumtaxat *not exceeding*
nē quis *that nobody*
nēve *and that … not*
iūre: **iūs** *right, privilege*
in aliud *for any other purpose*

Questions

A 1 What has happened in Nicomedia?

2 Where was Pliny at the time?

3 How extensive was the damage?

4 What was the attitude of the bystanders?

5 In what way was the city ill-prepared for such a disaster?

6 What preventive measure is Pliny taking?

7 What further suggestion does he make to the emperor?

B 1 Why does Pliny mention his whereabouts at the time of the disaster?

2 Do the words **ōtiōsī et immōtī adstābant** (lines 6–7) merely describe the scene, or do they also convey Pliny's attitude toward the bystanders? If so, what *is* his attitude?

3 Does Pliny's suggestion to the emperor seem to you reasonable? What reply would you expect to this letter?

4 Do lines 11–14 (from **dumtaxat hominum** to the end) indicate Pliny's confidence that the emperor will agree to his suggestion, or does he think the emperor may disapprove?

admonendī quoque sunt dominī praediōrum ut ipsī flammās exstinguere cōnentur.

II

Trāiānus Plīniō

tibi in mentem vēnit collēgium fabrōrum apud
Nīcomēdēnsēs īnstituere, sīcut in aliīs prōvinciīs factum est.
sed nōs oportet meminisse prōvinciam istam et praecipuē urbēs
factiōnibus eius modī saepe vexātās esse. quodcumque nōmen   5
dederimus eīs quī in idem contractī erunt, hetaeriae brevī tempore
fient. melius igitur est comparāre ea quae ad incendia exstinguenda
auxiliō esse possint; admonendī quoque sunt dominī
praediōrum ut ipsī flammās exstinguere cōnentur; dēnique, sī
opus est, auxilium ā spectantibus est petendum.   10

**in mentem vēnit: in mentem
    venīre** *occur, come to mind*
praecipuē *especially*
factiōnibus: factiō *organized
          group*
quodcumque *whatever*
in idem *for a common purpose,
    for the same purpose*
contractī erunt: contrahere
      bring together, assemble
hetaeriae: hetaeria *political club*
dominī: dominus *owner*
praediōrum: praedium *property*

Questions

1 What decision does Trajan give?
2 How has the previous history of Bithynia affected Trajan's
   decision?
3 What three suggestions does Trajan make?
4 To what extent do you agree with the following opinion?
   "Trajan seems more concerned with politics than with the
   safety of his subjects; his advice to Pliny is vague and unhelpful.
   He appears not to realize the seriousness of fires in large towns."

Bronze water pump.

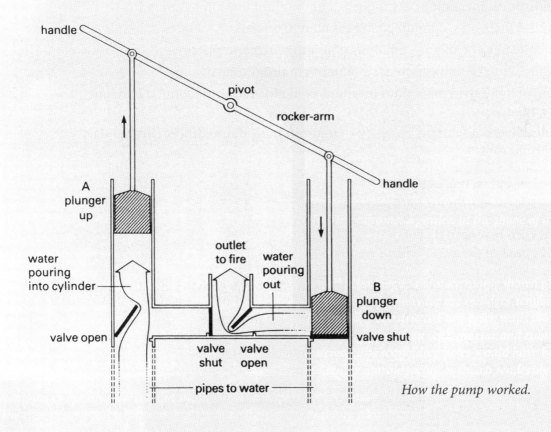

handle

pivot

rocker-arm

handle

A
plunger
up

water
pouring
into cylinder

outlet
to fire

water
pouring
out

B
plunger
down

valve open

valve shut

valve
shut

valve
open

pipes to water

How the pump worked.

1 Study the following examples:

cum nāvem iterum cōnscendissem, contrāriīs ventīs retentus sum.
When I had boarded a ship again, I was held back by headwinds.

rogō quid facere dēbeam, praesertim **cum pertineat ad exemplum**.
I ask what I should do, especially since it involves a precedent.

sī ipsī, **cum habērent condiciōnis suae cōnscientiam**, vēnērunt, pūniendī erunt.
If they came themselves, although they were aware of their status, they will have to be punished.

In Unit 3, we met the conjunction **cum** meaning *when* as in the first sentence above. While *when* is also a possible equivalent for **cum** in the second and third sentences, *since* and *although* are more satisfactory meanings. You will need to check all three meanings, to see which makes the best sense in any particular sentence.

2 Further examples:

a difficile est incendium exstinguere, cum nūllum īnstrūmentum adsit.
b nūllōs mēnsōrēs, cum dīligenter excuterem, invēnī.
c architectus pecūniam, cum opus nōndum perfēcerit, poscit.
d iūdex, cum crīmina audīvisset, sententiam prōnūntiāvit.
e Imperātor Salviō praemium meritum pollicitus est, cum Domitia Parisque pūnītī essent.
f cum dīversam partem prōvinciae circumīrēmus, duo aedificia Nīcomēdīae perdita sunt.

3 **cum fēlēs abest**, mūrēs lūdunt.
When the cat's away, the mice play.

servīs **cum revēnerō** dīcam.
I shall speak to the slaves when I return.

cum meaning *when* can introduce clauses in which the verb is indicative mood.
cum meaning *since* or *although* cannot.

Practicing the language

1 The following list contains the 3rd person singular present and perfect forms of seven verbs, jumbled together. Sort them into pairs, writing the present form first and then the perfect, and give the meaning of each form.

For example: **portat** *he carries*   **portāvit** *he carried*

portat, facit, tulit, est, cōgit, fēcit, fert, ēgit, fuit, vēnit, coēgit, venit, agit, portāvit.

2 Complete each sentence with the correct word and then translate.

a ego vōs servāvī, ubi ab inimīcīs . . . . (accūsābāminī, fingēbāminī)

b difficile erat nōbīs prōcēdere, quod ā turbā . . . . (dīcēbāmur, impediēbāmur)

c audīte, meī amīcī! nōs ad aulam contendere . . . . (regimur, iubēmur)

d rēctē nunc . . . . , quod ā proeliō herī fūgistis. (culpāminī, agnōscīminī)

e epistulam ad prīncipem hodiē mittam, mīlitēs, ut facta nostra nūntiem; sine dubiō ab illō . . . . (rogābimur, laudābimur)

f iūdex "facinus dīrum commīsistis" inquit. "crās . . . . " (amābiminī, necābiminī)

3 Referring to the letters on pages 106–109, complete each of the sentences below with one of the following groups of words. Then translate the sentence. Use each group of words once only.

> Plīnium rem dīligenter effectūrum esse
> quamquam multam pecūniam impenderant
> quod servī erant
> num servī supplicium ultimum meruissent
> ut architectum ad Bīthȳniam mitteret

a Nīcomēdēnsēs, ... , nūllam aquam habēbant.

b Plīnius Imperātōrī persuādēre cōnābātur . . . .

c Trāiānus cōnfīdēbat . . . .

d Semprōnius duōs tīrōnēs ad Plīnium mīsit . . . .

e Plīnius incertus erat . . . .

The provinces of the Roman empire during the reign of Trajan.

The government of the Roman provinces

The map on page 116 shows the provinces of the Roman empire at the time of its greatest extent, during the reign of the Emperor Trajan. The Romans obtained these territories gradually during several centuries, starting with the island of Sicily in the third century BC, and ending with Trajan's conquests in Dacia (modern Romania) and the east. Some provinces, such as Britain, became part of the empire as a result of a successful Roman invasion. Others were given to the Romans by their previous rulers; Bithynia, for example, was bequeathed to Rome by its king in his will.

A number of provinces (which were generally the more dangerous frontier provinces and whose names are marked on the map in *italics*) were known as "imperial provinces." Their governor was chosen by the emperor, he usually ruled for three years, and his official title was **lēgātus Augustī** (emperor's deputy). The other provinces (which were generally the more peaceful provinces and whose names are in **boldface** on the map) were known as "senatorial provinces." Their governor was appointed by the senate, he generally governed for one year, and his official title was **prōcōnsul**. Occasionally the emperor stepped in and picked the governor of a senatorial province himself, as Trajan did when he appointed Pliny as governor of Bithynia, instead of leaving the choice to the senate.

Both the senate and the emperor took trouble to select suitable people for governorships. No senator could become the governor of a province unless he had previously held the praetorship, and some important provinces could be governed only by men who had been consul. The senate and emperor kept a lookout for men who had shown special skill or talent during the earlier part of their career. For example, both Agricola and Pliny were sent to provinces where they could put their particular qualities and experience to good use; Agricola had already served in Britain as a military tribune and as a legionary commander, and Pliny had served in two treasury offices. (See page 45 for the cursus honorum of each man.)

A small group of imperial provinces were governed by members of the equestrian class, who were known as **praefectī**. The most important of these provinces was Egypt, whose governorship was one of the highest honors that an **eques** could hope for. No senator was allowed to enter Egypt without the emperor's permission, for fear that an ambitious senator would cut off the grain supply to Rome. Another province with an equestrian governor was Judea, one of whose praefecti was the best known of all Roman governors, Pontius Pilatus (Pilate), who offended the Jews with his harshness and tactlessness and became notorious among Christians for the crucifixion of Jesus.

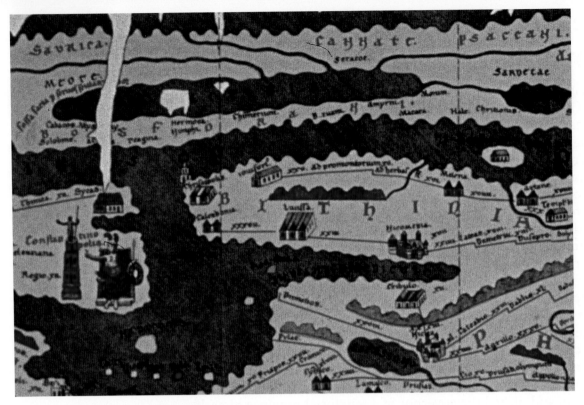

Peutinger Table showing Bithynia.

A governor's first and most important duty was a military one, to protect his province against attack from outside and rebellion from inside. Under his command were one or more **legiōnēs** or **auxilia**. He might, like Agricola in Scotland, use these troops to conquer further territory; he could also use them, if necessary, to deal with problems such as bandits or pirates. A small number of soldiers were taken away from their military duties to serve as officials on the governor's staff, but the governor was not supposed to use soldiers for jobs that could be done by civilians. Trajan reminded Pliny firmly about this when Pliny thought of using soldiers as prison guards. (See **carcer**, pages 103–104.) Whoever the governor was, he would not be completely inexperienced in army matters, because normally he would have served as a military tribune in the early part of his career and, in most cases, he would have commanded a legion after his praetorship.

The governor's other main task was to administer the law, by traveling around his province and acting as judge in the towns' law courts. He had supreme power, and his decisions could not be challenged, with one exception: any Roman citizen who was sentenced to death or flogging had the right to appeal to the emperor against the governor's decision. One man who appealed in this way was St Paul, who was arrested in the province of Judea. The Jews wished to try him in their own court. Paul, however, not only insisted on being tried in a Roman court but also appealed to the emperor. The following extract from the *Acts of the Apostles* describes the confrontation between Paul and the Roman governor Festus:

> But Paul said to Festus, "Against the Jews I have committed no offense, as you very well know. If I am guilty of any capital crime, I do not ask to escape the death penalty; but if there is no truth in the charges which these men bring against me, no one has any right to hand me over to them. I appeal to Caesar!" Then Festus, after consulting his council of advisers, replied, "You have appealed to Caesar; to Caesar you shall go."

Sometimes, especially in imperial provinces, the governor was too busy with his military tasks to carry out his other duty of administering the law. When this happened, the emperor could send out another official, known as a **iūridicus**, to take charge in the law courts while the governor carried on with the fighting. For example, Salvius acted as a iuridicus in the south of Britain while Agricola was busy campaigning in Scotland.

A governor appointed by the emperor was normally given instructions or **mandāta** about the work he was to do in the province. Pliny, for example, was instructed in his mandata to make a public announcement banning political clubs. It is likely that he was also under Trajan's orders to investigate the financing and construction of public

The Pont du Gard, an aqueduct built by the Romans in Gaul.

buildings in his province. The Bithynians had been spending large sums of money on schemes of this kind, often with disastrous results. Several of Pliny's letters deal with building projects; for example, he writes to Trajan about an aqueduct in Nicomedia, public baths at Prusa, a theater at Nicaea, and a smelly and unhygienic sewer at Amastris.

In the first century BC, Roman governors were often feared and hated for their greed and cruelty. This was, in part, due to the Roman system of taxation in the provinces. Tax collection was contracted out to the highest bidder. The **pūblicānus** (tax collector or publican) was required to make up, himself, any deficit to what his tax contract called for. On the other hand, he was allowed to keep for himself any surplus monies. The very system encouraged abuse: most publicans demanded high taxes from the provincials to ensure a surplus for themselves. No wonder the people of the provinces believed that the Romans were interested in their empire only for what they could get out of it.

A fair analysis of provincial government is difficult, since most of our information comes from the Romans themselves, rather than from the people being governed. By the time of Trajan, however, there seems to have been some improvement. The correspondence of Pliny and Trajan testifies to an interest in the health, safety, and financial accountability of the people of Bithynia. Pliny's letters often express concern for the Bithynians' well-being (e.g. in **incendium**, pages 111–112). Tacitus, in his account of Agricola's life, claims that a deliberate attempt was made to introduce the Britons to some benefits of the Roman way of life:

> **Agricola encouraged individuals and gave help to local communities for the building of temples, forums, and houses. He also provided an education for the sons of the chieftains. Those who had recently refused to use the Roman language were now eager to make speeches in it. Roman clothing became a sign of status, and togas were often to be seen.**

Roman governors may have behaved in this way partly from kindness, partly from self-interest; if people are comfortable and contented, they are less likely to make trouble for their rulers. Tacitus follows his description of Agricola's policy with a cynical comment:

> **The Britons were gradually led astray by the temptations of idleness and luxury: colonnades, baths, and elegant dinner parties. In their innocence, the Britons referred to this as "civilization;" in fact it was part of their slavery.**

Many people, however, were bitterly hostile to the Romans and their empire. In the following extract, Tacitus imagines the speech which might have been made by a Scottish chieftain whose homeland was being invaded:

The Romans plunder the whole world; when there is no land left for them to devastate, they search the sea as well. If their enemy is rich, they are greedy for wealth; if he is poor, they are eager for glory. They describe robbery and slaughter with the deceptive name of "empire;" they make a desert and call it "peace."

Coins of Nicomedes III of Bithynia (above) *and of Mithridates VI Eupator Dionysus of Pontus* (below).

Vocabulary checklist 41

dīversus, dīversa, dīversum	*different*
factum, factī, n.	*deed, achievement*
glōria, glōriae, f.	*glory*
incendium, incendiī, n.	*fire*
lūdō, lūdere, lūsī, lūsus	*play*
mereō, merēre, meruī	*deserve*
nōndum	*not yet*
opus est (+ABL)	*there is need of*
peditēs, peditum, m. pl.	*foot soldiers, infantry*
perdō, perdere, perdidī, perditus	*waste, lose*
sī quis	*if anyone*
sī quid	*if anything*
vīlis, vīle	*cheap*
vitium, vitiī, n.	*sin, fault, vice*

Aureus of Trajan.

CARMINA

Stage 42

Phaedrus

Phaedrus, who lived in the first half of the first century AD, was originally a slave of the emperor, and became a **lībertus Augustī**. He composed five books of verse mainly based on the animal fables of Aesop, such as the following fable of the wolf and the lamb:

<table>
<tr><td>

ad rīvum eundem lupus et agnus vēnerant
sitī compulsī; superior stābat lupus
longēque īnferior agnus. tunc fauce improbā
latrō incitātus iūrgiī causam intulit.
"quārē" inquit "**turbulentam** fēcistī mihi
aquam* bibentī?" lāniger contrā timēns:
"quī possum, quaesō, facere quod quereris, lupe?
ā tē dēcurrit ad meōs haustūs liquor."
repulsus ille vēritātis vīribus:
"ante hōs sex mēnsēs male" ait "dīxistī mihi."
respondit agnus: "equidem nātus nōn eram."
"pater hercle tuus" ille inquit "male dīxit mihi;"
atque ita correptum lacerat, iniūstā nece.

</td><td>

5

10

</td></tr>
</table>

rīvum: rīvus *stream*
sitī: sitis *thirst*
compulsī: compellere *drive, compel*
superior *higher, farther upstream*
īnferior *lower, farther downstream*
tunc *then*
fauce (ablative singular)
        hunger (literally *throat*)
improbā: improbus *wicked, relentless*
latrō *the robber, i.e. the wolf*
iūrgiī: iūrgium *argument, dispute*
causam intulit: causam īnferre
   make an excuse, invent an excuse
turbulentam: turbulentus *disturbed,*
            muddy
lāniger *the woolly one, i.e. the lamb*
contrā *in reply*
quī? *how?*
dēcurrit: dēcurrere *run down*
haustūs: haustus *drinking, drinking-*
         place
liquor *water*
repulsus *repelled, taken aback*
vīribus: vīrēs *strength*
male ... dīxistī: male dīcere *insult*
ait *said*
correptum: corripere *seize*
lacerat: lacerāre *tear apart*
iniūstā: iniūstus *unjust*
nece: nex *slaughter*

* Some noun-and-adjective phrases, in which an adjective is separated by one word or more from the noun which it describes, are shown in **boldface**.

Aesop's Fables.

Questions

1 Where had the wolf and lamb come to, and why? Where did they stand?
2 Who started the argument? What excuse did he invent?
3 What reason did the lamb give for saying that the wolf must be wrong?
4 What accusation did the wolf then make? What was the lamb's reply?
5 How did the wolf then change his accusation? What did he do next?
6 Suggest a moral (or a title) for this fable. Then compare your moral with the one which Phaedrus wrote:

> **haec** propter illōs scrīpta est hominēs **fābula**
> quī fictīs causīs innocentēs opprimunt.

Catullus

Gaius Valerius Catullus came from Verona in the north of Italy. He was born in about 84 BC and died not long after 54 BC. His poems, mostly short, vary from tender and loving to insulting and obscene. Stage 42 contains two poems by Catullus in very contrasting styles.

I

Egnātius, quod **candidōs** habet **dentēs**,
renīdet usque quāque. sī ad reī ventum est
subsellium, cum ōrātor excitat flētum,
renīdet ille; sī ad **piī** rogum **fīlī**
lūgētur, **orba** cum flet ūnicum **māter**, 5
renīdet ille. quidquid est, ubicumque est,
quodcumque agit, renīdet: hunc habet morbum,
neque ēlegantem, ut arbitror, neque urbānum.
quārē monendum est tē mihi, bone Egnātī.
sī urbānus essēs aut Sabīnus aut Tīburs 10
aut pinguis Umber aut obēsus Etruscus
aut quīlibet, quī pūriter lavit dentēs,
tamen renīdēre usque quāque tē nōllem:
nam rīsū ineptō **rēs** ineptior **nūlla** est.

candidōs: candidus *bright, gleaming white*
renīdet: renīdēre *grin, smirk*
usque quāque *on every possible occasion*
reī: reus *defendant*
ventum est *people have come (literally there has been an arrival)*
subsellium *bench (for prisoner in court)*
ōrātor *speaker (in court), pleader*
flētum: flētus *weeping, tears*
piī: pius *good, pious*
lūgētur *mourning is taking place, mourning is in progress*
orba: orbus *bereaved*
flet: flēre *weep for*
ūnicum: ūnicus (fīlius) *one and only (son)*
quidquid est *whatever is happening*
ubicumque *wherever*
arbitror: arbitrārī *think*
urbānum: urbānus (line 8) *refined*
quārē *therefore*
urbānus (line 10) *a city-dweller, a man from Rome*
Sabīnus *a Sabine*
Tīburs *a man from Tibur*
pinguis *plump*
Umber *an Umbrian*
Etruscus *an Etruscan*
quīlibet *anyone at all*
pūriter *decently, with clean water*
nōllem *I would not want*
ineptō: ineptus *silly*

sī ad reī ventum est subsellium, cum ōrātor excitat flētum, renīdet ille.

Questions

1 Why, according to Catullus, does Egnatius grin so continually?

2 What is happening in lines 2–5 (a) in court and (b) at the funeral pyre? What does Egnatius do on each occasion? Suggest reasons why Catullus includes the words **cum ōrātor excitat flētum** (line 3) and **orba cum flet ūnicum māter** (line 5) in his description of the scenes.

3 Suggest a reason why the verb **renīdet** is repeated so often (lines 2, 4, 6, 7, and **renīdēre** in line 13).

4 How does Catullus describe Egnatius' habit in lines 7–8?

5 What does Catullus say he must do to Egnatius in line 9?

6 Study the long sentence in lines 10–13. Does Catullus imply that Egnatius in fact comes from any of these places? Does he imply that Egnatius cleans his teeth **pūriter**?

7 According to line 14, why would Catullus still object to Egnatius' smile, no matter where he came from?

II

multās per gentēs et multa per aequora vectus,
    adveniō **hās miserās**, frāter, ad **īnferiās**,
ut tē postrēmō dōnārem mūnere mortis
    et **mūtam** nēquīquam adloquerer **cinerem**.
quandoquidem fortūna mihī tētē abstulit ipsum,   5
    heu miser indignē frāter adēmpte mihī,
nunc tamen intereā haec*, **prīscō** quae **mōre** parentum
    trādita sunt trīstī mūnere ad īnferiās,
accipe* **frāternō** multum mānantia **flētū**,
    atque in perpetuum, frāter, avē atque valē.   10

aequora: aequor *sea*
vectus: vehī *be carried* (e.g. by horse or ship), *travel*
īnferiās: īnferiae *tribute to the dead*
postrēmō: postrēmus *last*
mūnere: mūnus *gift*
mūtam: mūtus *silent*
nēquīquam *in vain*
(ut) adloquerer *(so that) I might speak to*
quandoquidem *seeing that, since*
mihī *from me*
tētē = tē
heu = ēheu
indignē *unfairly*
adēmpte: adēmptus *taken away*
haec *these things, these gifts*
prīscō … mōre *by the ancient custom*
parentum: parentēs *ancestors, forefathers*
trīstī mūnere *as a sad gift, by way of a sad gift*
frāternō: frāternus *of a brother, fraternal*
multum mānantia *drenched*
avē atque valē *hail and farewell*

Questions

1 How does Catullus emphasize the distance he has traveled?

2 Why has he made this journey? Why do you think he emphasizes its length?

3 Explain **nēquīquam** in line 4. How is your explanation supported by other words in the same line?

4 What indications are there in the poem that Catullus believes or disbelieves in an afterlife?

5 Where in the poem does the emotion seem to be most intense? What, in your opinion, is the mood of the final line?

* These two words go closely together.

Mārtiālis

A number of Martial's epigrams were included in Stage 36. Martial (Marcus Valerius Martialis) was originally a native of Spain, and lived from about AD 40 to about AD 104. Pliny said of him: "He was a talented man, sharp and shrewd, whose epigrams had plenty of salt and vinegar in them."

I

tū Sētīna quidem semper vel Massica pōnis,
  Pāpyle, sed rūmor tam bona vīna negat:
dīceris **hāc** factus caelebs quater esse **lagōnā**.
  nec putō nec crēdō, Pāpyle, nec sitiō.

Sētīna = vīna Sētīna *Setian wine*
                            (a good wine)
Massica = vīna Massica
    Massic wine (another good wine)
pōnis: pōnere *serve*
rūmor *rumor*
negat: negāre *deny, say that … not*
tam bona vīna negat = negat ea esse
    tam bona vīna
caelebs *widower*
quater *four times*
lagōnā: lagōna *bottle*
sitiō: sitīre *be thirsty*

II

Eutrapelus tōnsor dum circuit ōra Lupercī
expingitque genās, altera barba subit.

Eutrapelus tōnsor dum = dum
    Eutrapelus tōnsor
circuit = circumit
expingit: expingere *paint, put paint
                            onto*
genās: genās *cheek*
subit: subīre *come up*

III

nūbere Paula cupit nōbīs, ego dūcere Paulam
nōlō: anus est. vellem, sī magis esset anus.

nōbīs = mihi
dūcere *marry*
vellem *I would be willing*

About the language 1: conditional sentences

1 From Unit 2 on, you have met sentences like these:

> **sī illud dīxistī**, errāvistī.
> *If you said that, you were wrong.*

> **sī fīlius meus mortuus est**, fundum lībertīs lēgō.
> *If my son is dead, I leave the farm to the freedmen.*

The group of words in **boldface** is known as a **conditional clause**, and sentences which contain a conditional clause are known as **conditional sentences**.

2 Translate the following examples, and pick out the conditional clause in each sentence:

a sī Marcō crēdis, īnsānus es.

b sī Salvius tālia facinora commīsit, pūniendus est.

c sī illam ancillam magnō pretiō ēmistī, vēnālīcius tē dēcēpit.

3 From Stage 33 on, you have met sentences in which a conditional clause refers to the future:

> sī **respexerit**, aliquid mīrī **vidēbit**.
> *If he looks back, he will see something amazing.*

> sī tū dīligenter **excutiēs**, mēnsōrēs **inveniēs**.
> *If you investigate carefully, you will find surveyors.*

Notice again how the verb in the Latin conditional clause is put into either the future perfect tense (as in the first example, **respexerit**) or the future tense (as in the second example, **excutiēs**). English, however, normally uses a present tense (*looks back, investigate*).

4 Further examples:

a sī pecūniam meam reppereritis, vōbīs praemium ingēns dabō.

b sī pompam spectābis, dēlectāberis.

c sī Virginēs Vestālēs ignem sacrum neglēxerint, dī populum Rōmānum pūnient.

d sī tū mihi nocueris, ego tibi nocēbō.

5 Notice how the word **nisi** ("unless" or "if… not") is used in conditional clauses:

> nisi tacueritis, ē tabernā ēiciēminī.
> *Unless you are quiet, you will be thrown out of the inn.*
> Or, in more natural English:
> *If you aren't quiet, you'll be thrown out of the inn.*

Further examples:

a nisi prīnceps mē līberābit, in exiliō reliquam vītam manēbō.

b nisi cāveris, custōdēs tē invenient.

6 In Stage 42, you have met a slightly different type of conditional sentence:

> sī urbānus essēs, tamen renīdēre usque quāque tē nōllem.
> *If you were a city-dweller, I still wouldn't want you to be forever grinning.*

> sī magis esset anus, Mārtiālis eam dūcere vellet.
> *If she were older, Martial would be willing to marry her.*

Notice that in these sentences, Latin uses the subjunctive and English uses the word "would."

Horātius

Quintus Horatius Flaccus, the son of a freedman auctioneer, was a native of Venusia in southern Italy. He went to Athens to continue his education. Once he arrived in Rome, he became a literary success almost immediately, enjoying the patronage of Maecenas and the friendship of Virgil and the Emperor Augustus. Horace's poems cover a wide range of topics. The following has a philosophical theme.

> tū nē quaesierīs, scīre nefas, **quem** mihi, **quem** tibi
> **fīnem** dī dederint, Leuconoē, nec **Babylōniōs**
> temptāris **numerōs**. ut melius quidquid erit patī,
> seu plūrēs hiemēs seu tribuit Iuppiter ultimam,
> quae nunc oppositīs dēbilitat pūmicibus mare   5
> Tyrrhēnum: sapiās, vīna liquēs, et spatiō brevī
> spem longam resecēs. dum loquimur, fūgerit invida
> aetās: carpe diem, quam minimum crēdula posterō.

nē quaesierīs *do not ask* (**nē** + perfect subjunctive for a more polite form of command than **nōlī quaerere**)
nefas (est) *(it is) forbidden*
dī = deī
Leuconoē: Leuconoē *Leuconoe* (Her name may mean *clear-minded*.)
Babylōniōs . . . numerōs: Babylōniī numerī *Babylonian calculations* (This is an allusion to the mathematical calculations of Babylonian astrologers.)
nec . . . temptāris = et nōlī temptāre   *and do not meddle with*
ut melius (est) *how much better (it is)*
seu ... seu *whether ... or, if ... or if*
tribuit: tribuere *grant, allot, assign*
ultimam (hanc hiemem) *(this) final (winter)*
oppositīs: oppōnō *oppose*
dēbilitat: dēbilitāre *weaken, exhaust, cripple*
pūmicibus: pūmex *cliff, volcanic stone*
mare Tyrrhēnum *the Tyrrhenian sea* (the sea between Sicily and Italy)
sapiās, liquēs, resecēs (present subjunctives for polite commands)
sapiās: sapere *be wise*
liquēs: liquāre *strain*
spatiō: spatium *space of time*
resecēs: resecāre *cut back, prune*
invida: invidus *envious*
aetās *time*
carpe: carpere *seize, pluck*
crēdula: crēdulus *trusting*
posterō (diē) *tomorrow*

Questions

A 1 In lines 1–3, what two things does Horace warn Leuconoe not to do?

   2 What advice does the poet give at the end of line 3?

   3 In line 4, what image marks the passage of years? Who is seen as responsible for the granting of these years?

   4 In the seasonal battle between the sea and its shoreline, which would be the expected winner? In lines 5–6, how does Horace reverse this image?

   5 **liquēs**, **resecēs** (lines 6–7): what advantage is gained by straining the wine? by pruning a shrub?

   6 What is happening even while Leuconoe and Horace speak (lines 7–8)?

B 1 Write down and examine all the verbs with which Horace gives advice to Leuconoe. What philosophical school would applaud this advice?

   2 In line 4, Horace uses the word **hiemēs** rather than **annōs** or **aestātēs**. Suggest why.

   3 How do the images from nature in lines 4–7 prepare for the **carpe diem** image in the last line?

   4 In lines 5–6, Horace uses the phrase **mare Tyrrhēnum** rather than just **mare**. Suggest why.

   5 How does the rapid movement of the poem reinforce the theme of the poem?

1 Study the following pairs of sentences:

puerī clāmōrem faciunt.   clāmor **fit**.
The boys are making a noise.   *A noise is being made.*

Nerō multa et dīra faciēbat.   multa et dīra **fiēbant**.
Nero was doing many terrible things. *Many terrible things were being done.*

The words in **boldface** are forms of the irregular verb **fiō** ("I am made").

2 The verb **faciō** ("I make, I do") has no passive forms in the present, future, and imperfect tenses. Instead, Latin uses the following forms of **fiō**:

present indicative
fiō   *I am made*
fīs   *you (sing.) are made*
fit   *s/he is made*
fīunt   *they are made*

future indicative
fīam   *I shall be made*
fīēs   *you (sing.) shall be made*
etc.

imperfect indicative
fīēbam   *I was being made*
fīēbās   *you (sing.) were being made*

For complete tables of the forms of **fiō**, see page 286 of the Language information section.

Translate the following pairs of sentences:

a mīlitēs impetum mox facient.
   impetus mox fīet.

b servus nihil in culīnā faciēbat.
   nihil in culīnā fīēbat.

c ignōrābāmus quid senātōrēs in cūriā facerent.
   ignōrābāmus quid in cūriā fieret.

3 Notice some of the different ways in which **fīō** can be translated:

> aliquid mīrī fīēbat.
> *Something strange was being done.*
> Or, *Something strange was happening.*

> ecce! deus fīō.
> *Look! I'm being made into a god.*
> Or, *Look! I'm becoming a god.*

Further examples:

a crās nōs cōnsulēs fīēmus.

b salvē, Marce! quid in fundō tuō hodiē fit?

c tam timidē hostēs resistēbant ut peditēs nostrī audāciōrēs fierent.

> **peditēs**   *foot soldiers, infantry*

4 The perfect, future perfect, and pluperfect tenses of the passive of **faciō** are formed in the normal way. Study the following pairs of sentences and notice some of the different ways of translating **factus est**, etc.:

a mīlitēs Claudium imperātōrem fēcērunt.
   The soldiers made Claudius emperor.

b Claudius imperātor factus est.
   Claudius was made emperor.
   Or, *Claudius became emperor.*

c haruspex rem rīdiculam fēcerat.
   The soothsayer had done a silly thing.

d rēs rīdicula facta erat.
   A silly thing had been done.
   Or, *A silly thing had happened.*

Ovidius

Stage 39 included a short extract from the *Metamorphoses* of Ovid (Publius Ovidius Naso, 43 BC–AD 17). The following lines are taken from Ovid's *Ars Amatoria* or *Art of Love*, of which the first two sections (or "books") give advice to young men on how to find, win, and keep a girlfriend. Here, Ovid is telling his reader what to do if a girl ignores him and sends his love messages back without reading them:

sī nōn accipiet scrīptum inlēctumque remittet,
　　lēctūram spērā prōpositumque tenē.
tempore **difficilēs** veniunt ad arātra **iuvencī**,
　　tempore **lenta** patī **frēna** docentur equī.
ferreus assiduō cōnsūmitur **ānulus** ūsū,　　　　　　　5
　　interit assiduā vōmer aduncus humō.
quid magis est saxō dūrum, quid mollius undā?
　　dūra tamen mollī **saxa** cavantur aquā.
Pēnelopēn ipsam, perstā modo, tempore vincēs:
　　capta vidēs sērō **Pergama**, capta tamen.　　　　　　10

inlēctum: inlēctus　*unread*
lēctūram spērā = **spērā eam id**
　　lēctūram esse
prōpositum: prōpositum　*intention, resolution*
tenē: tenēre　*keep to, hold on to*
difficilēs: difficilis　*obstinate*
arātra: arātrum　*plow*
iuvencī: iuvencus　*bullock, young ox*
lenta: lentus　*supple*
frēna　*reins*
ferreus　*iron, made of iron*
assiduō: assiduus　*continual*
interit: interīre　*wear away, wear out*
vōmer　*plowshare*
cavantur: cavāre　*hollow out*
Pēnelopēn　(Greek accusative) *Penelope*
sērō　*late, after a long time*

Questions

1　What is Ovid's advice to the young man? What arguments does he use to support his advice? Do these arguments actually prove Ovid's point? If not, why does he include them?

2　Using a classical dictionary or the Internet if necessary, find out what or where **Pergama** (line 10) was, and how long a time is referred to by **sērō** (line 10). Then (using the dictionary again if needed) find out who Penelope was, and suggest reasons why Ovid uses her as his example in line 9.

Illustration from a medieval manuscript showing Doctor Ovid lecturing in a Garden of Lovers.

Vergilius

Writing exercise on papyrus, containing a line from Virgil.

Publius Vergilius Maro (70–19 BC) was born in northern Italy near Mantua. His chief work was the *Aeneid*, an epic poem in nearly ten thousand lines, which related the adventures of Aeneas, the legendary ancestor of the Romans. The following lines form a tiny but complete episode in this huge poem; Aeneas, who is describing his earlier wanderings to Dido, Queen of Carthage, tells of a storm that hit him and his Trojan companions as they sailed westwards from the island of Crete.

altum	*deep sea, open sea*
tenuēre = tenuērunt: tenēre	*occupy, be upon*
ratēs: ratis	*boat*
amplius	*any more*
caeruleus	*dark*
adstitit: adstāre	*stand*
imber	*storm cloud*
noctem: nox	*darkness*
hiemem: hiems	*storm*
inhorruit: inhorrēscere	*shudder*
continuō	*immediately*
volvunt: volvere	(line 5) *set rolling, turn to billows*
dispersī: dispergere	*scatter*
gurgite: gurges	*whirlpool, swirling water*
involvēre = involvērunt: involvere	*envelop, swallow up*
ūmida: ūmidus	*rainy, stormy*
ingeminant: ingemināre	*redouble*
abruptīs: abrumpere	*split, tear apart*
ignēs: ignis	*lightning*
excutimur: excutere	*shake off, drive violently off*
caecīs: caecus	(line 9) *unseen* (literally *blind*)
negat = negat sē posse	
discernere	*distinguish*
Palinūrus	*Palinurus* (the Trojans' helmsman)
trēs adeō	*as many as three, three entire*
caecā: caecus	(line 12) *impenetrable*
cālīgine: cālīgō	*darkness, gloom*
sōlēs: sōl	*day*
pelagō: pelagus	*sea*
totidem	*the same number*
prīmum	*for the first time*
sē attollere	*raise itself, rise up*
aperīre	*reveal*
volvere	(line 15) *send rolling upwards*

postquam altum tenuēre ratēs nec iam amplius ūllae
appārent terrae, caelum undique et undique pontus,
tum mihi **caeruleus** suprā caput adstitit **imber**
noctem hiememque ferēns, et inhorruit unda tenebrīs.
continuō ventī volvunt mare magnaque surgunt   5
aequora, dispersī iactāmur gurgite vāstō;
involvēre diem nimbī et nox ūmida caelum
abstulit, ingeminant abruptīs nūbibus ignēs.
excutimur cursū et **caecīs** errāmus in **undīs**.
ipse* diem noctemque negat discernere caelō   10
nec meminisse viae **mediā** Palinūrus* in **undā**.
trēs adeō incertōs caecā cālīgine **sōlēs**
errāmus pelagō, totidem sine sīdere noctēs.
quārtō terra **diē** prīmum sē attollere tandem
vīsa, aperīre procul montēs ac volvere fūmum.   15

* These two words go closely together.

Questions

A 1 Where were the boats when the storm broke? What surrounded them?

   2 What was the first sign of trouble? Where was it? What did it bring with it?

   3 What did the winds do to the ocean (line 5)? What happened to the Trojans?

   4 What was the effect of the rain clouds (line 7)? What further detail of the storm does Virgil give in line 8?

   5 What was the next thing that happened to the Trojans?

   6 What did Palinurus say he could not do (line 10)? What other difficulty was he having?

   7 For how long did the Trojans wander? What was unusual about the **noctēs** (line 13)?

   8 When did the Trojans finally catch sight of land?

   9 List the three stages in which they got an increasingly detailed view of land in lines 14–15.

Mosaic of ships.

B 1 What idea is most strongly emphasized in lines 1–2? In what way is it relevant to the storm that follows?

2 What does Virgil suggest in line 4 about the appearance of the sea?

3 Compare the following translations of **continuō ventī volvunt mare magnaque surgunt aequora** (lines 5–6):

(a) "The ruffling winds the foamy billows raise."

(John Dryden, 1697)

(b) "The winds quickly set the sea-surface rolling and lifted it in great waves."

(W.F. Jackson Knight, 1956)

(c) "Winds billowed the sea at once, the seas were running high."

(C. Day Lewis, 1952)

(d) "The winds roll up the sea, great waters heave."

(Allen Mandelbaum, 1981)

(e) "Soon the winds
Made the sea rise and big waves came against us."

(Robert Fitzgerald, 1983)

Which of the translations is most successful in conveying the feeling of Virgil's words? Which gives the most vivid picture?

4 What is the point of **ipse** (line 10)?

5 Compare the following translations of lines 12–13:

(a) "Three starless nights the doubtful navy strays
Without distinction, and three sunless days."

(Dryden)

(b) "For three whole days, hard though they were to reckon, and as many starless nights, we wandered in the sightless murk over the ocean."

(Jackson Knight)

(c) "Three days, three days befogged and unsighted by the darkness,
We wandered upon the sea, three starless nights we wandered."

(Day Lewis)

(d) "We wander for three days in sightless darkness and for as many nights without a star."

(Mandelbaum)

(e) "Three days on the deep sea muffled in fog,
Three starless nights we wandered blind."

(Fitzgerald)

The storm.

About the language 3: more about word order

1 In Stage 39, you met sentences in which one noun-and-adjective phrase is placed inside another one:

> cōnstitit ante *oculōs* **pulchra puella** *meōs*.
> *A beautiful girl stood before my eyes.*

2 In Stage 42, you have met sentences like this, in which two noun-and-adjective phrases are intertwined with each other:

> *dūra* tamen **mollī** *saxa* cavantur **aquā**.
> *Nevertheless, hard stones are hollowed out by soft water.*

Further examples:

a **parva** necat morsū *spatiōsum* **vīpera** *taurum*. (*Ovid*)
b *frīgidus* **ingentēs** irrigat *imber* **agrōs**.

> **morsū: morsus** *bite, fangs*
> **spatiōsum: spatiōsus** *huge*
> **vīpera** *viper*
> **frīgidus** *cold*
> **irrigat: irrigāre** *to water*

3 In each of the following examples, pick out the Latin adjectives and say which nouns they are describing:

a impiaque aeternam timuērunt saecula noctem. (*Virgil*)
  The evil generations were in fear of endless night.

b molliaque immītēs fīxit in ōra manūs. (*Propertius*)
  And it fastened its cruel hands on her soft face.

4 Translate the following examples:

a *Poets and poverty:*
  Maeonidēs nūllās ipse relīquit opēs. (*Ovid*)

b *A poet's epitaph on himself:*
  hīc iacet immītī cōnsūmptus morte Tibullus. (*Tibullus*)

c *Ovid congratulates Cupid on his forthcoming victory procession:*
  haec tibi magnificus pompa triumphus erit. (*Ovid*)

> **Maeonidēs** *Homer (the greatest of Greek poets)*

Practicing the language

1 Notice again that there are often several different ways of translating a Latin word, and that you always have to choose the most suitable translation for the particular sentence you are working on.

For example, the Vocabulary section at the end of the book gives the following meanings for **ēmittō**, **petō**, and **referō**:

ēmittō	*throw, send out*
petō	*head for, attack; seek, beg for, ask for*
referō	*bring back, carry, deliver, tell, report*

Translate the following sentences, using suitable translations of **ēmittō**, **petō**, and **referō** chosen from the above list:

a dux trīgintā equitēs ēmīsit.
b duo latrōnēs, fūstibus armātī, senem petīvērunt.
c uxor tōtam rem rettulit.
d nautae, tempestāte perterritī, portum petēbant.
e subitō mīlitēs hastās ēmittere coepērunt.
f mercātor nihil ex Āfricā rettulit.
g captīvus, genibus ducis haerēns, lībertātem petīvit.

2 Complete each sentence with the correct word and then translate.

a corpora mīlitum mortuōrum crās . . . . (sepeliētur, sepelientur)
b nōlīte timēre, cīvēs! ā vestrīs equitibus . . . . (dēfendēris, dēfendēminī)
c sī custōdēs mē cēperint, ego sine dubiō . . . . (interficiar, interficiēmur)
d fābula nōtissima in theātrō . . . . (agētur, agentur)
e difficile erit tibi nāvigāre; nam ventīs et tempestātibus . . . . (impediēris, impediēminī)
f nisi fortiter pugnābimus, ab hostibus . . . . (vincar, vincēmur)

3 Translate the first sentence. Then change it from a direct statement to an indirect statement by completing the second sentence. Finally, translate the second sentence.

For example: equī hodiē exercentur.
                        audiō equ... hodiē exerc... .

Translated and completed, this becomes:
                        equī hodiē exercentur.
                        The horses are being exercised today.

                        audiō equōs hodiē exercērī.
                        I hear that the horses are being exercised today.

In sentences **a–c**, a *present passive* infinitive is required. For examples of the way in which this infinitive is formed, see page 294, paragraph 1.

a patrōnus ā clientibus cotīdiē salūtātur.
scio patrōn... ā clientibus cotīdiē salūt.... .

b duae puellae in hōc carcere retinentur.
centuriō putat du... puell... in hōc carcere retin.... .

c vīlla nova prope montem aedificātur.
agricola dīcit . . . . prope montem . . . .

In sentences **d–f**, a *future active* infinitive is required. For examples of the way in which it is formed, see page 295, paragraph 1. Note that the first part of this infinitive (e.g. **parātūrus** in **parātūrus esse**) changes its ending to agree with the noun it describes.

For example: puella ad nōs scrībet.
                 spērō puell... ad nōs scrīp.... .

Translated and completed, this becomes:
                 puella ad nōs scrībet
                 The girl will write to us.

                 spērō puellam ad nōs scrīptūram esse.
                 I hope that the girl will write to us.

d gladiātor crās pugnābit.
exīstimō gladiāt... crās pugnā... . . . .

e nostrī mīlitēs vincent.
dux crēdit nostr... mīl... vic... . . . .

f discipulī crās recitābunt.
rhētor pollicētur . . . . crās . . . .

Latin poetry

Quintilian, the instructor engaged by Domitian to teach his adopted sons (Stage 39), had them learning poetry. This was not unusual. In his book, *Institutio Oratoria (The Training of an Orator)*, Quintilian rated poetry above all other forms of literature as being suitable for future Roman leaders to study.

> **It is to the poets that we must turn for inspiration, for elevation of language, for stirring all our emotions, and for appropriateness in delineating character.**

However, Quintilian was writing as a teacher of rhetoric, and he felt that poetry, with (in his opinion) its emphasis only on entertainment, its many unrealistic images, and the constraining effect of its rules for rhythm and structure, was at best an imperfect model for the courtroom. For a poet's view of poetry, we could turn to Horace, whose lyric poetry, written a century before Quintilian's time, won justified praise from the rhetor. In a long poem which has come to be known as the *Ars Poetica (The Art of Poetry)*, he wrote,

> **Poets want either to be of use or to give pleasure or to say things which are both pleasing and useful for life at the same time ... . The poet who has mixed the useful (ūtile) with the pleasurable (dulce) is superior, because he delights and advises the reader at one and the same time.**

But what of the average Roman? Where did poetry rate in his or her life? Consider this famous graffito from Pompeii:

ADMIROR, O PARIES, TE NON CECIDISSE (RVINIS), QVI TOT SCRIPTORVM TAEDIA SVSTINEAS.

> **I wonder, o wall, that you have not collapsed (in ruins), since you bear the boring weight of so many writers.**

This commentary, scratched on the walls of Pompeii, is, in fact, in Latin verse. Its structure and rhythm are those of an elegiac couplet, the same form that Martial used for the epigrams we read in Stage 36. (For basic meters and rhythmical patterns, see the Language information, pages 303–306.) Latin poets also deliberately used stylistic or rhetorical devices. In the two lines of the graffito, the writer personifies the wall, chooses the word **taedia** to refer to the scrawlings on the walls and metaphorically to compare them to heavy and boring items of baggage, and uses humor to condemn the habit of writing on walls while self-deprecatingly adding to the "baggage." This average Roman, in short, was well aware of the characteristics of Latin poetry and able to use them effectively.

Let us examine some of these characteristics in more detail.

A line of Latin poetry is distinguished by its meter or repetitive pattern of sound. Prose normally has no such regular rhythm. The repetition of rhythmic patterns takes various forms in different literary traditions. English metrical poetry relies on the natural word accent to give stressed and unstressed syllables. Latin meter, unlike English poetry, does not rely on accent but on quantity, that is, on the number of long and short syllables in a line.

The Romans initially considered Greek as the language of literature. Greek poetry was originally closely allied to music and the long or short quantity of a syllable represented the musical time allowed (like half notes and quarter notes) for the pronunciation of the syllable. Latin poets very early borrowed the Greek system of quantitative meter as part of their general imitation of Greek literary forms and techniques, even though Latin poetry was not meant to be sung. By the time of Augustus, Latin poets had adapted Greek meters to Latin and had vindicated Latin as a great literary language in itself.

It is not only meter, however, that characterizes Latin poetry. It is in poetry that the effects of rhetorical training and the striving for originality and style are most strongly felt. Roman poets make an abundant use of rhetorical devices such as connotations, antithesis, parallelism, sound effects, word choices, imagery, figures of speech, effective use of proper names, and many other stylistic features. (See pages 301–302 for examples and definitions of these stylistic terms.)

Among the stylistic devices used in Latin poetry, word order is a distinctive feature. Latin is an inflected language: it is the ending of the word not the order of the words that provides the meaning. This fact enables the poet to vary the order of his words. For example, an important word may be placed in the emphatic first word or last word position in a line of verse, a word may be placed out of its usual order and framed by a pair of related words, words of one noun-and-adjective phrase may interlock with those of another, one word may be juxtaposed with another, and so on. From their position and their relation, the poet's words take on added point and significance.

Roman poets frequently use allusions, brief references to details the writers expect their readers to recognize. Through the fabric of Latin poetry runs the thread of classical mythology. A knowledge of the myths is part of the equipment of the Roman poet. Sometimes he (or – very occasionally perhaps – she) uses a passing reference to a myth, sometimes he bases a whole work on a familiar story. Besides mythological allusions, Roman poets often use historical or geographical references which the readers must know if they are to participate fully in the poem.

A scrupulous and detailed examination of a poem or a passage ideally will allow you to say what elements give a work its peculiar quality, to analyze the poetic craftsmanship or artistic expression, and to explain clearly your considered reaction to it. There are various stylistic terms which are the common currency of literary criticism. It is not enough, however, merely to recognize and label poetic devices. It is more important to examine how the poet uses each stylistic device and what effect is achieved by its use in its context, and to consider the blending of the different elements in the creation of the poetic whole.

This time chart shows the dates of the six Roman poets represented in Stage 42, together with some events in Roman history.

Time chart

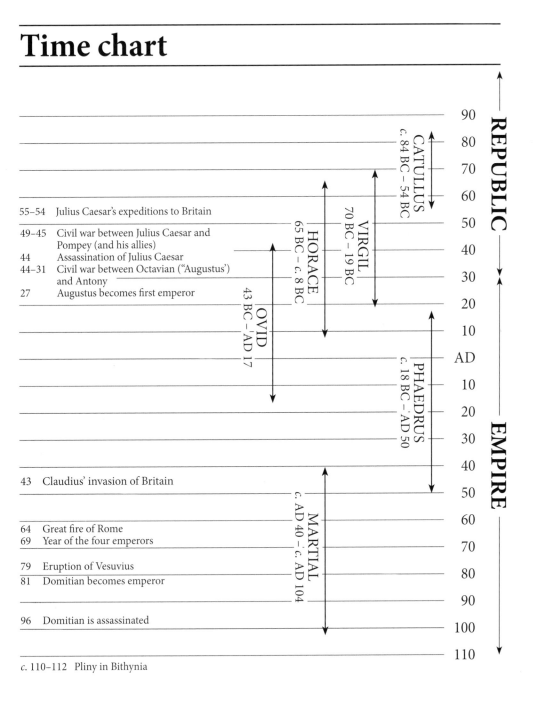

55–54   Julius Caesar's expeditions to Britain

49–45   Civil war between Julius Caesar and Pompey (and his allies)
44   Assassination of Julius Caesar
44–31   Civil war between Octavian ("Augustus") and Antony
27   Augustus becomes first emperor

43   Claudius' invasion of Britain

64   Great fire of Rome
69   Year of the four emperors

79   Eruption of Vesuvius
81   Domitian becomes emperor

96   Domitian is assassinated

c. 110–112   Pliny in Bithynia

CATULLUS c. 84 BC – 54 BC
VIRGIL 70 BC – 19 BC
HORACE 65 BC – c. 8 BC
OVID 43 BC – AD 17
PHAEDRUS c. 18 BC – AD 50
MARTIAL c. AD 40 – c. AD 104

REPUBLIC
EMPIRE

90
80
70
60
50
40
30
20
10
AD
10
20
30
40
50
60
70
80
90
100
110

Vocabulary checklist 42

adloquor, adloquī, adlocūtus sum	*speak to, address*
caecus, caeca, caecum	*blind; invisible, unseen*
genū, genūs, n.	*knee*
longē	*far, a long way*
lūgeō, lūgēre, lūxī	*lament, mourn*
meminī, meminisse	*remember*
mollis, molle	*soft*
neque	*and not, nor*
quīcumque, quaecumque, quodcumque	*whoever, whatever*
reperiō, reperīre, repperī, repertus	*find*
sepeliō, sepelīre, sepelīvī, sepultus	*bury*
sīdus, sīderis, n.	*star*

"ut … mūtam nēquīquam adloquerer cinerem." A cinerary urn.

UNIVIRA

Stage 43

mātrōna Ephesia

Versions of the following story have been found all over the world. Its first appearance in Latin is in the fables of Phaedrus, and it was particularly popular in the Middle Ages; numerous versions exist in Latin, French, Italian, English, German, Russian, Chinese, and Hebrew; and it was turned into a stage play *(A Phoenix Too Frequent)* by twentieth-century writer Christopher Fry. The following version is based closely on the *Satyrica* by Petronius, who is probably the same man as Gaius Petronius Arbiter, Nero's **arbiter ēlegantiae** (adviser on taste and fashion) who was eventually ordered by Nero to commit suicide in AD 66.

Facades of Roman "house" tombs.

I

mātrōna quaedam, quae Ephesī habitābat, ita nōta erat propter pudīcitiam ut ab omnibus fēminīs illīus locī laudārētur. haec ergō, marītō mortuō, tantō dolōre affecta est ut sine eō vīvere nōllet; nōn modo fūnus eius, ut mōs erat, passīs crīnibus et veste scissā prōsecūta est, sed etiam servīs imperāvit ut ipsa in sepulcrō eōdem   5
ūnā cum corpore marītī clauderētur. ibi corpus eius custōdīre ac flēre tōtās noctēs diēsque coepit; neque cibum neque vīnum accipere volēbat; precēs parentum, propinquōrum, etiam magistrātuum, repudiāvit; cōnstituerat enim mortem inediā iuxtā corpus marītī obīre.   10

Ephesī: Ephesus
   Ephesus (city in Asia Minor)
ita *so*
pudīcitiam: pudīcitia
   chastity, virtue, purity
fūnus *funeral procession*
passīs: passus *loose, disheveled*
prōsecūta est: prōsequī *follow, escort*
propinquōrum: propinquus *relative*
repudiāvit: repudiāre *reject*
inediā: inedia *starvation*

quīntum iam diem mātrōna sine cibō agēbat, cīvibus
affirmantibus eam vērum pudīcitiae amōrisque exemplum
omnibus uxōribus praestitisse.

interim lēgātus prōvinciae trēs latrōnēs iussit crucibus affīgī
prope illud sepulcrum ubi mātrōna lūgēbat. proximā ergō nocte, 15
mīles quīdam, ad crucēs custōdiendās ēlēctus, nē corpora ad
sepultūram ā propinquīs latrōnum dētraherentur, lūmine inter
sepulcra cōnspectō et gemitū lūgentis audītō, statim contendit ad
cognōscendum quid ibi fieret. sepulcrum ingressus, vīsāque
mātrōnā pulcherrimā, attonitus cōnstitit; deinde, cum corpus marītī 20
vīdisset lacrimāsque mātrōnae, intellēxit eam dēsīderium mortuī
nōn posse patī; ad sepulcrum igitur cēnulam suam attulit, coepitque
hortārī lūgentem nē in dolōre inānī persevērāret; omnibus enim
mortālibus tandem pereundum esse. "quid tibi prōderit" inquit "sī
inediā perieris, sī tē vīvam sepelīveris?" et cibum vīnumque 25
mātrōnae obtulit. quae, inediā paene cōnfecta, tandem passa est
superārī pertināciam suam.

at mīles, quī mātrōnam esse pulcherrimam prius animadverterat,
in sepulcrō multās hōrās manēbat, et eīsdem blanditiīs pudīcitiam
eius aggredī coepit, quibus eam anteā incitāverat ut cibum acciperet. 30
multa dē pulchritūdine eius locūtus est, multa dē amōre suō.
postrēmō mīles mātrōnae persuāsit ut illam noctem ibi in sepulcrō
sēcum iacēret.

crucibus: crux *cross*
crucibus affīgī: crucī
    affīgere *nail to a cross,*
        crucify
sepultūram: sepultūra *burial*
lūmine: lūmen *light*

dēsīderium *loss*
cēnulam: cēnula *snack,*
        little supper
quid ... prōderit? *what good*
        will it do?
passa est: patī *allow*
pertināciam: pertinācia
    obstinacy, determination

aggredī *assail, make an*
    attempt on

II

mātrōnae quid accidisset exposuit. (line 7)

mediā autem nocte, cum mīles et fēmina in sepulcrō ūnā
iacērent, parentēs ūnīus latrōnum crucibus affīxōrum, ubi vīdērunt
nēminem crucēs custōdīre, corpus clam dē cruce dētractum ad
rīte sepeliendum abstulērunt.

    postrīdiē māne mīles, ē sepulcrō ēgressus, ubi vīdit ūnam sine   5
corpore crucem esse, supplicium ultimum sibi verēbātur.
mātrōnae quid accidisset exposuit; negāvit sē iūdicis sententiam
exspectātūrum esse; potius sē ipsum neglegentiam suam
pūnitūrum esse. "trāde mihi pugiōnem" inquit "ut ego hīc in marītī
tuī sepulcrō moriar atque sepeliar." mātrōna tamen, quae nōn minus   10
misericors quam pudīca erat, "nē illud deī sinant" inquit "ut eōdem
tempore corpora duōrum mihi cārissimōrum hominum spectem.
mālō mortuum impendere quam vīvum occīdere." quibus verbīs
dictīs, imperāvit ut ex arcā corpus marītī suī tollerētur atque illī
quae vacābat crucī affīgerētur. itaque mīles cōnsiliō prūdentissimae   15
mātrōnae libenter ūsus est, et postrīdiē populus mīrābātur quō modō
mortuus in crucem ascendisset.

rīte *properly*	
neglegentiam: neglegentia	
	carelessness
minus *less*	
misericors *tender-hearted, full*	
	of pity
pudīca: pudīcus *chaste,*	
	virtuous
nē illud deī sinant! *heaven*	
	forbid! (literally *may the*
	gods not allow it!)
impendere *make use of*	
arcā: arca *coffin*	
vacābat: vacāre *be empty, be*	
	unoccupied

Questions

1 What happened outside the tomb in the middle of the night?

2 What did the soldier see next morning when he came out of the tomb? What did he fear would happen to him? Rather than wait for this fate, what did he say he would do?

3 What did he ask the lady to do? What were his intentions?

4 What reason did the lady give for objecting violently to the soldier's request?

5 Whom did she mean by **mortuum** and **vīvum** (line 13)?

6 What did she tell the soldier to do?

7 Why were the people puzzled next day?

8 Do you approve of the lady's decision?

9 Why do you think this story has been so popular and been retold so often?

About the language 1: imperfect subjunctive (passive and deponent)

1 Study the following examples:

> lēgātus prōvinciam tam bene regēbat ut ab omnibus **dīligerētur**.
> *The governor ruled the province so well that he was loved by everybody.*

> nesciēbāmus utrum ā sociīs nostrīs **adiuvārēmur** an **impedīrēmur**.
> *We did not know whether we were being helped or hindered by our companions.*

The form of the verb in **boldface** is the **imperfect subjunctive passive**.

Further examples:

a intellegere nōn poteram quārē fēminae līberīque in oppidō relinquerentur.
b tam ignāvus erat coquus ut ā cēterīs servīs contemnerētur.
c ferōciter resistēbāmus nē ā barbarīs superārēmur.

2 Compare the active and passive forms of the imperfect subjunctive of **portō**:

imperfect subjunctive active	imperfect subjunctive passive
portārem	portārer
portārēs	portārēris
portāret	portārētur
portārēmus	portārēmur
portārētis	portārēminī
portārent	portārentur

The imperfect subjunctive passive of all four conjugations is set out in full on page 273 of the Language information section.

3 Study the following examples:

> tantus erat fragor ut omnēs nautae **verērentur**.
> *So great was the crash that all the sailors were afraid.*

> iūdex mē rogāvit num **mentīrer**.
> *The judge asked me whether I was lying.*

The verbs in **boldface** are imperfect subjunctive forms of deponent verbs.

Further examples:

a cum ēgrederēmur, amīcus meus subitō cōnstitit.
b pontifex cīvibus imperāvit ut deōs immortālēs precārentur.

Imperfect subjunctive forms of deponent verbs are set out in full on page 278.

Tūria

The funeral ceremony of a Roman noble often included a **laudātiō** or speech in praise of the dead person, which might later be inscribed on the tomb. The following passages are based on one of these speeches, which survives (in an incomplete form) on a number of stone fragments. It is not known who the speaker was but we refer to him in this Stage as "Vespillo," and to his wife (the subject of the inscription) as "Turia." As often in such speeches, the dead woman is addressed directly by her husband as "you," as if her **mānēs** (departed spirit) could hear the speech or read it on the inscription.

Woman using a drop spindle.

I

Vespillo and Turia lived through a time of great violence, when the Romans' system of Republican government was collapsing in ruins, and Italy was torn by a series of horrific civil wars. The laudatio mentions three separate incidents which reflect the violence of the period. The first occurred on the eve of Vespillo and Turia's wedding:

orba repente facta es ante nūptiārum diem, utrōque parente
in rūsticā sōlitūdine occīsīs. per tē maximē (quod ego in
Macedoniam abieram) mors parentum nōn inulta mānsit. tū
officium tuum tantā dīligentiā et tantā pietāte ēgistī, efflāgitandō
et investīgandō et ulcīscendō, ut ego ipse, sī adfuissem, nōn   5
amplius efficere potuissem.

orba *orphan*
sōlitūdine: sōlitūdō *lonely place*
inulta: inultus *unavenged*
pietāte: pietās *piety, family feeling*
efflāgitandō: efflāgitāre *demand
                             justice*
investīgandō: investīgāre *investigate*
ulcīscendō: ulcīscī *take vengeance*
nōn ... potuissem *would not have
                    been able*

In 49 BC, civil war broke out between Julius Caesar and Pompey the Great. Vespillo had to flee for his life, and he describes the help he received from Turia on that occasion:

mihi fugientī tū maximō auxiliō fuistī; omne aurum
margarītaque corporī tuō dētracta trādidistī quae ferrem mēcum;
callidē dēceptīs inimīcīs nostrīs, mihi absentī servōs et pecūniam
et alia bona subinde praebuistī.   10

margarīta: margarītum *pearl*
dētracta: dētrahere *take off*
callidē *cleverly*
subinde *regularly*

In 43 BC, civil war was again raging and Vespillo was in still greater danger; his name was published in a list of "public enemies," and a reward was offered for killing him. Vespillo evidently wanted to make a bold dash for escape, but Turia persuaded him otherwise:

ubi amīcī nostrī mē ad imminentia perīcula vītanda excitābant,
tuō cōnsiliō servātus sum. tū enim mē audāciā meā efferrī nōn
passa es, sed latebrās tūtās parāvistī; mē inter cameram et tēctum
cubiculī cēlātum ab exitiō servāvistī. tanta erat virtūs tua ut mē
dēfendere assiduē cōnārēris, nōn sine magnō perīculō tuō.   15

efferrī: efferre *carry away*
cameram: camera *ceiling*

tanta erat virtūs tua ut mē dēfendere assiduē cōnārēris.

II

After the civil wars were over, Vespillo and Turia could at last enjoy peace and prosperity. But in their private life, they had one cause of great unhappiness:

pācātō orbe terrārum, restitūtā rēpūblicā, tandem contigit nōbīs
ut temporibus quiētīs fruerēmur. magis ac magis līberōs optābāmus,
quōs diū sors nōbīs invīderat. sī precibus nostrīs fortūna fāvisset,
quid ultrā cupīvissēmus? annīs tamen lābentibus, spēs nostrae
ēvānēscēbant.   5

    diffīdēns fēcunditātī tuae et dolēns orbitāte meā, timēbās nē ego,
tenendō tē in mātrimōniō, spem habendī līberōs dēpōnerem atque
ideō fierem īnfēlīx; dīvortium igitur prōpōnere ausa es. dīxistī tē
vacuam domum nostram alicui fēminae fēcundiōrī trāditūram esse;
tē ipsam mihi dignam uxōrem quaesītūram, ac futūrōs līberōs prō   10
tuīs habitūram esse.

    quibus verbīs audītīs, adeō cōnsiliō tuō incēnsus sum ut vix
redderer mihi. num mihi erat tanta mihi cupiditās aut necessitās
habendī līberōs, ut proptereā fidem fallerem, mūtārem certa dubiīs?
sed quid plūra? mānsistī apud mē; nōn enim cēdere tibi sine   15
dēdecore meō et commūnī dolōre poteram.

pācātō: pācāre *make peaceful*
rēpūblicā: rēspūblica
    *the republic (i.e. republican
    government, which Augustus,
    the first Roman emperor,
    claimed to have restored)*
contigit nōbīs ut
    *it was our good fortune
    that…, we had the good
    fortune that…*
fruerēmur: fruī *enjoy*
optābāmus: optāre *pray for,
               long for*
sors *fate, one's lot*
invīderat: invidēre *begrudge*
ultrā *more, further*
cupīvissēmus *would have
           wanted*
lābentibus: lābī *pass by, slide by*
ēvānēscēbant: ēvānēscere
           die away, vanish
diffīdēns: diffīdere *distrust*
fēcunditātī: fēcunditās *fertility*
orbitāte: orbitās *childlessness*
dēpōnerem: dēpōnere *give up,
            abandon*
dīvortium *divorce*
fēcundiōrī: fēcundus *fertile*
futūrōs: futūrus *future*
prō *as*
habitūram esse: habēre
           regard, consider
redderer mihi: sibi reddī
    *be restored to one's senses, be
    restored to oneself*
cupiditās *desire*
necessitās *need*
proptereā *for that reason*
fidem fallerem: fidem
    fallere *break one's word*
dubiīs: dubius *uncertain*
quid plūra? *why say more?*
dēdecore: dēdecus *disgrace*
commūnī: commūnis
    shared (by both of us)

III

Vespillo praises Turia for being faithful, obedient, and loving; he says she was conscientious in her weaving and spinning (two traditional tasks of Roman wives, see page 154), elegant without being showy, and religious without being superstitious. Finally, he speaks of Turia's death and his own bereavement:

contigit nōbīs ut ad annum XXXXI sine ūllā discordiā
mātrimōnium nostrum perdūcerētur. iūstius erat mihi, ut maiōrī
annīs, priōrī mortem obīre. tū tamen praecucurristī; mihi dolōrem
dēsīderiumque lēgāvistī. aliquandō dēspērō; sed exemplō tuō
doctus, dolōrī resistere cōnor. fortūna mihi nōn omnia ēripuit;   5
adhūc enim est mihi memoria tuī.
     optō ut dī mānēs tē quiētam iacēre patiantur atque tueantur.

perdūcerētur: perdūcere
          continue
iūstius erat *it would have been*
       fairer, more proper
praecucurristī: praecurrere
      go on ahead, run ahead
dī mānēs *the spirits of the dead*
tueantur: tuērī *watch over,*
           protect

Part of the inscription on which the story of Vespillo and Turia is based.

About the language 2: more about gerunds

1 In Stage 41, you met the gerund used with **ad** meaning "for the purpose of ..." in sentences like this:

> ego et frāter meus ad **certandum** missī sumus.
> *My brother and I were sent for the purpose of competing.*
> Or, in more natural English:
> *My brother and I were sent to compete.*

In this example, the gerund is in the **accusative** case, because it is being used with the preposition **ad**.

2 In Stage 43, you have met the **genitive** and **ablative** cases of the gerund, used in sentences like these:

> *genitive* nūlla spēs **habendī** līberōs iam manet.
> *No hope of having children remains now.*
>
> in omnibus āthlētīs ingēns cupīdō **vincendī** inest.
> *In all athletes, there is an immense love of winning.*

> *ablative* **investīgandō**, Tūria cognōvit quid accidisset.
> *By investigating, Turia found out what had happened.*
>
> nūntius, celerrimē **currendō**, Rōmam prīmā lūce pervēnit.
> *The messenger, by running very fast, reached Rome at dawn.*

The cases of the gerund are listed in full on page 275.

3 Further examples of the gerund used in the accusative, genitive, and ablative cases:

   a cōnsul ōs ad respondendum aperuit; nihil tamen dīcere poterat.

   b optimam occāsiōnem effugiendī nunc habēmus.

   c ad bene vīvendum, necesse est magnās opēs possidēre.

   d cantandō et saltandō, puellae hospitēs dēlectāvērunt.

   e poētae nihil dē arte nāvigandī sciunt.

   f et Agricola et mīlitēs magnam glōriam adeptī sunt, ille imperandō, hī pārendō.

Practicing the language

1 Match each word in the top list with a word of similar meaning taken from the bottom list.

For example: aedificāre   exstruere

aedificāre, epistula, festīnāre, fīdus, igitur, metus, nihilōminus, occīdere, poena, rūrsus, sermō, uxor

ergō, supplicium, autem, colloquium, interficere, litterae, exstruere, iterum, contendere, coniūnx, timor, fidēlis

2 Complete each sentence with the most suitable word from the box below, and then translate.

> erit   reperiēmus   necābunt   gaudēbit   poteritis   dabit

   a sī mēcum domum revēneris, frāter meus . . . .
   b sī dīligenter quaesīverimus, equum āmissum mox . . . .
   c sī mea fīlia huic senī nūpserit, semper miserrima . . . .
   d mīlitēs sī urbem oppugnāvērunt, multōs cīvēs . . . .
   e sī patrōnus meus tē ad cēnam invītāverit, vīnum optimum tibi . . . .
   f sī ad forum hodiē ieritis, pompam spectāre . . . .

3 Translate each sentence into Latin by selecting correctly from the list of Latin words.

   a *We were being hindered by shortage of water.*
   inopiae   aquae   impediēmur
   inopiā   aquā   impediēbāmur

   b *They were afraid that the robbers would return next day.*
   timēbant   nōn   latrōnī   postrīdiē   revenīrent
   timēbunt   nē   latrōnēs   cotīdiē   reveniēbant

   c *As the enemy approached, I heard strange noises.*
   hostibus   appropinquantibus   sonitum   mīrōs   audītī
   hostēs   appropinquantēs   sonitūs   mīrum   audīvī

   d *We tried to set out at first light.*
   prīmam   lūcem   proficīscī   cōnātus   erāmus
   prīmā   lūce   proficīscimur   cōnātī   sumus

   e *Why do you promise what you cannot carry out?*
   cūr   pollicēmur   id quod   suscipere   nōn   vultis?
   ubi   pollicēminī   is quī   efficere   nusquam   potestis?

About the language 3: more about indirect speech

1 Study the following examples:

> **dīcō** testem mentīrī.
> *I say that the witness is lying.*

> **rogāvimus** quis cibum reliquum cōnsūmpsisset.
> *We asked who had eaten the rest of the food.*

> dux **nūntiāvit** sociōs nōbīs mox subventūrōs esse.
> *The leader announced that our companions would soon come to our aid.*

Each sentence contains

a a verb of speaking, asking, etc., e.g. **dīcō**, **rogāvimus**;
b an indirect statement or indirect question.

Notice that in each example, the verb of speaking, asking, etc. is placed at the *beginning* of the sentence.

2 Compare the examples in paragraph 1 with the following sentences:

> multōs barbarōs **dīcimus** in proeliō cecidisse.
> *We say that many barbarians fell in the battle.*

> quid prīnceps cupiat, numquam **scio**.
> *I never know what the emperor wants.*

> haruspex deōs nōbīs favēre **affirmāvit**.
> *The soothsayer declared that the gods favored us.*

In these examples, the verb of speaking, asking, knowing, etc. is placed in the *middle* or at the *end* of the sentence.

3 Read through each of the following sentences, noticing the position of the verb of speaking, asking, etc.; then translate the sentence.

a nūntius hostēs in eōdem locō manēre dīcit.
b quārē familiam convocāverīs, omnīnō ignōrō.
c togam tuam vīdī scissam esse.
d fabrōs opus iam perfēcisse audīvimus.
e ubi rēx exercitum suum collocāvisset, incertum erat.
f ego vērō et gaudeō et gaudēre mē dīcō. (*Pliny*)

convocāverīs: convocāre *call together*

Divorce and remarriage

The Romans believed that the first divorce in Rome took place in about 230 BC, when the senator Spurius Carvilius, although he loved his wife deeply, divorced her because she was unable to have children.

The story of Carvilius' divorce may be partly or entirely fiction; it certainly cannot have happened in 230 BC, because laws about divorce appear as early as the Twelve Tables of 451 BC (see page 97). But the reason for Carvilius' divorce is a very typical one; it is the same reason as the one put forward by Turia on page 155. Roman marriage was supposed to produce children. When a marriage ended in divorce, childlessness was the reason in many cases.

There were, of course, many other reasons why a husband or wife, or both, might decide to end a marriage. Continual bickering and disagreement, or objectionable behavior such as unfaithfulness or brutality, could all lead to divorce. Divorces were sometimes arranged for political reasons, especially in the first century BC; for example, an ambitious man might divorce his wife in order to remarry into a wealthier or more powerful family. In fact, however, no cause had to be given by either party for a marriage to be dissolved.

If a wife was under the legal control (**manus**) of her husband, he could divorce her but she could not divorce him. But if the marriage had taken place **sine manū** (see pages 60–61), the wife was free from her husband's legal control, and husband and wife each had the power to divorce the other (although if either of their fathers was alive they may have required his consent). In law, the child of a marriage belonged to the father and after divorce children remained in the household of the father.

There was no religious ban on divorce and no social stigma was attached to a divorced spouse. The only thing necessary for divorce, in the eyes of the law, was that the husband or wife, or both, had to demonstrate that they regarded the marriage as finished and intended to live separately in future; if one partner moved out of the marital house and began to live somewhere else, nothing else was legally required. But the husband and wife could also follow certain procedures, in action or in writing, to emphasize that they intended their separation to be permanent. In the early years of Rome's history, a husband could divorce his wife by addressing her, in front of witnesses, with the phrase **tuās rēs tibi habētō** (take your things and go)

A Roman couple.

or by demanding the return of the keys of the house. By the first century AD, these picturesque customs were no longer in common use; instead, one partner might send the other a written notification of divorce, or the husband and wife might make a joint declaration, either spoken before witnesses or put in writing, as in the following agreement, which was discovered on an Egyptian papyrus:

> **Zois, daughter of Heraclides, and Antipater, son of Zeno, agree that they have separated from each other, ending the marriage which they made in the seventeenth year of Augustus Caesar, and Zois acknowledges that she has received from Antipater by hand the goods which he was previously given as dowry, namely clothes to the value of 120 drachmas and a pair of gold earrings. Hereafter it shall be lawful both for Zois to marry another man and for Antipater to marry another woman without either of them being answerable.**

It is difficult to discover how common divorce was in Rome. Among the richer classes, it may perhaps have reached a peak in the first century BC, and then declined during the following century. (Nothing is known about the divorce rate of Rome's poor.) Some Roman writers speak as if divorce was rare in early Roman history but common in their own times. Juvenal says of one woman that she "wears out her wedding veil as she flits from husband to husband, getting through eight men in five years." But it is impossible to tell how much truth there is in Juvenal's description and how much is satirical exaggeration; nor do we know how typical such women were.

Any husband who was thinking of divorcing his wife had to bear in mind that he would have to return all or part of her **dōs**, or dowry, as in the papyrus document quoted above. This may have made some husbands have second thoughts about going ahead with a divorce.

Remarriage after divorce was frequent. "They marry in order to divorce; they divorce in order to marry," said one Roman writer. Remarriage was also common after the death of a husband or wife, especially if the surviving partner was still young. For example, a twelve-year-old girl who married an elderly husband might find herself widowed in her late teens, and if a wife died in childbirth, a man might become a widower within a year or two of the marriage, perhaps while he himself was still in his early twenties; in this situation, the idea of remarriage was often attractive and sensible for the surviving partner.

Nevertheless, the Romans had a special respect for women who married only once. They were known as **ūnivirae** and had certain religious privileges; for a long time, they were the only people allowed to worship at the temple of Pudicitia (*Chastity*) and it was a Roman tradition for a bride to be undressed by univirae on her wedding night. Some women took great pride in the idea that they were remaining faithful to a dead husband, and the description univira is often found on tombstones.

The idea of being univira is sometimes used by Roman authors for the purposes of a story or poem. For example, the lady in the story on pages 150–151 is so determined to remain loyal to her dead husband that she refuses to go on living after his death, until a twist in the story persuades her to change her mind. A similar idea provides the starting point of Book Four of Virgil's poem, the *Aeneid*. In an earlier part of the poem, the Trojan prince Aeneas had landed in Africa and been hospitably received by Dido, Queen of Carthage. The two are strongly attracted to each other, and Dido is very much moved by Aeneas' account of his adventures. Aeneas, however,

The death of Dido.

is under orders from the gods to seek a new home in Italy, while Dido has sworn an oath of loyalty to her dead husband, binding herself like a Roman univira never to marry again; and so, although a love affair quickly develops between Dido and Aeneas, it ends in disaster and death.

Vocabulary checklist 43

aggredior, aggredī, aggressus sum	*attack, make an attempt on*
bona, bonōrum, n. pl.	*goods, property*
contemnō, contemnere, contempsī, contemptus	*despise, disregard*
efferō, efferre, extulī, ēlātus	*carry out, carry away*
fīdus, fīda, fīdum	*loyal, trustworthy*
inopia, inopiae, f.	*shortage, scarcity, poverty*
iuxtā (+ACC)	*next to*
magistrātus, magistrātūs, m.	*elected government official*
negō, negāre, negāvī, negātus	*deny, say . . . not*
possideō, possidēre, possēdī, possessus	*possess*
propter (+ACC)	*because of*
repente	*suddenly*
ulcīscor, ulcīscī, ultus sum	*avenge, take revenge on*

Statue of a mourning woman.

DAEDALUS ET
ICARUS

The following story is taken from Ovid's poem, the *Metamorphoses*, an immense collection of myths, legends, and folktales which begins with the creation of the world and ends in Ovid's own day.

I

Daedalus, who was famous as a craftsman and inventor, came from Athens to the island of Crete at the invitation of King Minos. The king, however, quarreled with him and refused to allow him and his son Icarus to leave the island.

Daedalus intereā Crētēn longumque perōsus
exilium, tāctusque locī nātālis amōre,
clausus erat pelagō. "terrās licet" inquit "et undās
obstruat, at caelum certē patet; ībimus illāc!
omnia possideat, nōn possidet āera Mīnōs."   5
dīxit et **ignōtās*** animum dīmittit in **artēs**,
nātūramque novat. nam pōnit in ōrdine pennās,
ut clīvō crēvisse putēs; sīc **rūstica** quondam
fistula disparibus paulātim surgit avēnīs.

Crētēn (Greek accusative) *Crete*
perōsus *hating*
tāctus: tangere *touch, move*
locī nātālis: locus nātālis
       place of birth, native land
clausus erat: claudere *cut off*
licet *although*
obstruat *he (i.e. Minos) may block my*
      way through
at *yet*
certē *at least*
patet: patēre *lie open*
illāc *by that way*
omnia possideat *he may possess*
      everything (else)
āera (accusative of āēr) *air*
dīmittit: dīmittere *turn, direct*
novat: novāre *change, revolutionize*
pennās: penna *feather*
clīvō: clīvus *slope*
crēvisse: crēscere *grow*
crēvisse = pennās crēvisse
putēs *you would think*
sīc *in the same way*
rūstica: rūsticus *of a countryman*
quondam *sometimes*
fistula *pipe*
disparibus: dispār *of different length*
surgit: surgere *grow up, be built up*
avēnīs: avēna *reed*

*Some noun-and-adjective phrases, in which an adjective is separated by one word or more from the noun which it describes, are shown in **boldface**.

Questions

1 Why was Daedalus eager to leave Crete?
2 Why was it difficult for him to get away?
3 What method of escape did he choose?
4 How did he set about preparing his escape?
5 What did the arrangement of feathers resemble?

Crete and the Greek Islands.

II

tum līnō mediās et cērīs adligat īmās,
atque ita compositās parvō curvāmine flectit,
ut vērās imitētur avēs. puer Īcarus ūnā
stābat et, ignārus **sua** sē tractāre **perīcla**,
ōre renīdentī modo, quās vaga mōverat aura,   5
captābat plūmās, flāvam modo pollice cēram
mollībat, lūsūque suō mīrābile patris
impediēbat opus. postquam manus ultima coeptō
imposita est, geminās **opifex** lībrāvit in ālās
ipse suum corpus mōtāque pependit in aurā.   10

līnō: līnum *thread*
mediās (pennās) *the middle (of the feathers)*
īmās (pennās) *the bottom (of the feathers)*
curvāmine: curvāmen *curve*
flectit: flectere *bend*
ūnā *with him*
sua … perīcla *cause of danger for himself* (literally *his own danger*)
tractāre *handle, touch*
ōre renīdentī *with smiling face*
modo … modo *now … now, sometimes … sometimes*
aura *breeze*
captābat: captāre *try to catch*
plūmās: plūma *feather*
flāvam: flāvus *yellow, golden*
mollībat = molliēbat: mollīre *soften*
lūsū: lūsus *play, games*
manus ultima *final touch*
coeptō: coeptum *work, undertaking*
geminās … ālās *the two wings*
opifex *inventor, craftsman*
lībrāvit: lībrāre *balance*
mōtā: mōtus *moving* (literally *moved, i.e. by the wings*)

Questions

1 What materials did Daedalus use to fasten the feathers together? Where did he fasten them? What did he then do to the wings?

2 In line 4, what was Icarus failing to realize?

3 How did Icarus amuse himself while his father was working? Judging from lines 5–8, what age would you imagine Icarus to be?

4 What actions of Daedalus are described in lines 9–10? Has the journey begun at this point?

"Daedalus Winged" by Michael Ayrton.

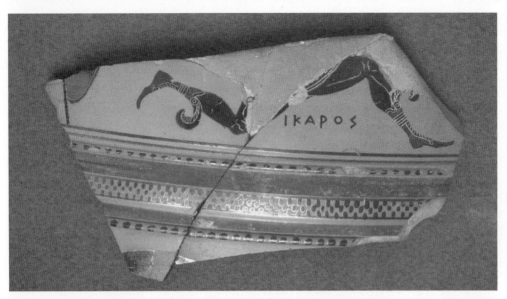

Fragment of a Greek painted vase.

III

īnstruit et nātum, "mediō" que "ut līmite currās,
Īcare," ait "moneō, nē, sī dēmissior ībis,
unda gravet pennās, sī celsior, ignis adūrat.
inter utrumque volā! nec tē spectāre Boōtēn
aut Helicēn iubeō strictumque Ōrīonis ēnsem:
mē duce carpe viam!" pariter praecepta volandī
trādit et ignōtās umerīs accommodat ālās.

5

īnstruit: īnstruere *equip, fit (with wings)*
nātum: nātus *son*
īnstruit et nātum = et īnstruit nātum
mediō … līmite *middle course*
currās: currere *go, fly*
ait *says*
dēmissior *lower, too low*
pennās: penna *wing*
celsior *higher, too high*
ignis *fire, heat of sun*
adūrat: adūrere *burn*
volā: volāre *fly*
Boōtēn (accusative of **Boōtēs**) *Herdsman* (constellation)
Helicēn (accusative of **Helicē**) *Great Bear*
strictum: stringere *draw, unsheathe*
Ōrīonis: Ōrīōn *Orion, the Hunter*
ēnsem: ēnsis *sword*
carpe: carpere *hasten upon*
pariter *at the same time*
praecepta: praeceptum *instruction*
accommodat: accommodāre *fasten*

About the language 1: historical present

1 Study the following example:

> fūr per fenestram intrāvit. circumspectāvit; sed omnia tacita erant. subitō sonitum **audit**; ē tablīnō canis **sē praecipitat**. fūr effugere **cōnātur**; **lātrat** canis; **irrumpunt** servī et fūrem **comprehendunt**.

> *A thief entered through the window. He looked around; but all was silent. Suddenly he **hears** a noise; a dog **hurtles** out of the study. The thief **tries** to escape; the dog **barks**; the slaves **rush in** and **seize** the thief.*

2 Notice that all the verbs in the above example, after the first two sentences, are in the *present* tense, even though the event obviously happened in the past. This is known as the historical use of the present tense (**historical present** for short); it is often used by Roman writers to make the narration rather more lively and vivid, as if the action were happening before the reader's (or listener's) eyes.

3 The historical present in Latin can be translated *either* by an English present tense (as in the example in paragraph 1), *or* by a past tense.

4 Look again at lines 6–7 of Part 1 on page 166. Which verbs in these two lines are in the historical present tense, and which in the perfect tense?

5 You have already met examples of the historical present in sentences containing the word **dum** (meaning *while*):

> dum equitēs **morantur**, nūntius prīncipia irrūpit.
> *While the cavalry were delaying, a messenger burst into headquarters.*

IV

inter opus monitūsque genae maduēre senīlēs,
et patriae tremuēre manūs. dedit ōscula nātō
nōn iterum repetenda suō pennīsque levātus
ante volat, comitīque timet, velut āles, ab **altō**
quae teneram prōlem prōdūxit in āera **nīdō**;   5
hortāturque sequī, damnōsāsque ērudit artēs,
et movet ipse **suās** et nātī respicit **ālās**.
hōs* aliquis, **tremulā** dum captat **harundine** piscēs,
aut pāstor baculō stīvāve innīxus arātor
vīdit* et obstipuit, quīque aethera carpere possent   10
crēdidit esse deōs.

inter *during*
monitūs: monitus *warning, advice*
genae: gena *cheek*
maduēre = maduērunt:
    madēscere *become wet*
senīlēs: senīlis *old*
patriae: patrius *of the father*
tremuēre = tremuērunt
nōn iterum repetenda *never to be repeated, never to be sought again*
levātus: levāre *raise, lift up*
ante *in front*
velut *like*
āles *bird*
teneram: tener *tender, helpless*
prōlem: prōlēs *offspring, brood*
prōdūxit: prōdūcere *bring forward, bring out*
nīdo: nīdus *nest*
damnōsās: damnōsus *ruinous, fatal*
ērudit: ērudīre *teach*
tremulā: tremulus *quivering*
harundine: harundō *rod*
baculō: baculum *stick, staff*
stīvā: stīva *plow handle*
-ve *or*
innīxus: innītī *lean on*
obstipuit: obstipēscere *gape in amazement*
carpere *hasten through, fly through*

*These two words go closely together.

Wall painting of Daedalus and Icarus from Pompeii.

Questions

A 1 What signs of emotion did Daedalus show while speaking to Icarus?

2 What was his last action before the journey began?

3 What is Daedalus compared to as he sets out on his flight?

4 Who witnessed the flight? What did they think of Daedalus and Icarus, and why?

B 1 What do you think caused Daedalus' agitation in lines 1–2?

2 In what ways is the comparison in lines 4–5 appropriate?

3 Does Ovid suggest in any way that the journey will end in disaster?

V

et iam Iūnōnia laevā
parte Samos (fuerant Dēlosque Parosque relictae),
dextra Lebinthos erat fēcundaque melle Calymne,
cum puer audācī coepit gaudēre volātū
dēseruitque ducem, caelīque cupīdine tractus   5
altius ēgit iter. rapidī vīcīnia sōlis
mollit **odōrātās**, pennārum vincula, **cērās**.
tābuerant cērae; nūdōs quatit ille lacertōs,
rēmigiōque carēns nōn ūllās percipit aurās.
ōraque **caeruleā** patrium clāmantia nōmen   10
excipiuntur **aquā**, quae nōmen trāxit ab illō.
at pater īnfēlīx nec iam pater "Īcare," dīxit;
"Īcare," dīxit, "ubi es? quā tē regiōne requīram?
Īcare," dīcēbat; pennās aspexit in undīs,
dēvōvitque suās artēs corpusque sepulcrō   15
condidit, et tellūs ā nōmine dicta sepultī.

Iūnōnia: Iūnōnius *sacred to Juno*
laevā parte *on the left hand*
-que ... -que *both ... and*
dextra: dexter *on the right*
fēcunda ... melle *rich in honey*
gaudēre *be delighted*
volātū: volātus *flying, flight*
tractus: trahere *draw on, urge on*
altius *higher, too high*
ēgit iter: iter agere *make one's way,
travel*
rapidī: rapidus *blazing, consuming*
vīcīnia *nearness*
odōrātās: odōrātus *sweet-smelling*
vincula: vincula *fastenings*
tābuerant: tābēscere *melt*
nūdōs: nūdus *bare*
quatit: quatere *shake, flap*
lacertōs: lacertus *arm*
rēmigiō: rēmigium *wings* (literally
oars)
carēns: carēre *lack, be without*
percipit: percipere *take hold of, get a
grip on*
ōra: ōs *mouth*
caeruleā: caeruleus *dark blue, dark
green*
trāxit: trahere *draw, derive*
nec iam *no longer*
requīram: requīrere *search for*
aspexit: aspicere *catch sight of*
dēvōvit: dēvovēre *curse*
condidit: condere *bury*
dicta = dicta est: dīcere *call, name*
sepultī: sepultus *the one who was
buried*

"The Fall of Icarus" by Allegrini.

Questions

A 1 On the map on page 167, find the point reached by Daedalus and Icarus in lines 1–3.

   2 What mistake did Icarus make?

   3 What effect did this have on his wings?

   4 Where did he fall? What was he doing as he fell?

   5 How did Daedalus learn of his son's fate? What did he do then?

B 1 Why did Icarus not obey his father's instructions?

   2 What effect is gained by describing Daedalus as **pater… nec iam pater** in line 12?

   3 After reading this story, what impression do you have of the different personalities of Daedalus and Icarus?

About the language 2: ellipsis

1 From Stage 13 on, you have met sentences like this:

> Britannī cibum laudāvērunt, Rōmānī vīnum.
> *The Britons praised the food, the Romans (praised) the wine.*

2 From Stage 15 on, you met a slightly different type of sentence:

> Britannī cibum, Rōmānī vīnum laudāvērunt.

3 Compare the examples in paragraphs 1 and 2 with a longer way of expressing the same idea:

> Britannī cibum laudāvērunt, Rōmānī vīnum laudāvērunt.

This kind of sentence is grammatically correct, but is not often used in Latin; the Romans would normally prefer the shorter versions in paragraphs 1 and 2, to avoid repeating the word **laudāvērunt**.

4 Sentences similar to the ones in paragraphs 1 and 2 are very common in Latin. Study the following examples, which you have met in Stages 36 and 44:

> Thāis habet nigrōs, niveōs Laecānia dentēs.
> *Thais has black teeth, Laecania has white ones.*

(Compare this with a longer way of expressing the same idea:
Thāis dentēs nigrōs habet, Laecānia dentēs niveōs habet.)

> et movet ipse suās et nātī respicit ālās.
> *He both moves his own wings himself and looks back at the wings of his son.*

(Compare: et ipse suās ālās movet et ālās nātī respicit.)

The omission of words seen in the above examples is known as **ellipsis**.

5 Further examples:

a centuriō gladium, mīles hastam gerēbat.
(Compare: centuriō gladium gerēbat, mīles hastam gerēbat.)

b hic caupō vēndit optimum, ille vīnum pessimum.
(Compare: hic caupō vīnum optimum vēndit, ille caupō vīnum pessimum vēndit.)

c nōs in urbe, vōs prope mare habitātis.

d altera fēmina quīnque līberōs habēbat, altera nūllōs.

e dīvitiās quaerit senex, spernit iuvenis.

f ēnumerat mīles vulnera, pāstor ovēs. (*Propertius*)

g culpāvit dominus, laudāvit domina vīlicum.

h nōn semper viātōrēs ā latrōnibus, aliquandō latrōnēs ā viātōribus occīduntur.

ēnumerat: ēnumerāre *count*
viātōrēs: viātor *traveler*

Practicing the language

1 In Stage 42, the different ways of translating **ēmittere, petere,** and **referre** were practiced. Another verb with a wide variety of translations is **solvere**, which you have often met with the meaning "untie" but which can be translated in many other ways as well. Match each of the phrases in the left-hand column with the correct English translation from the right-hand column.

nāvem solvere	*relaxed by the wine*
catēnās ex aliquō solvere	*to discharge a promise made to the gods*
vīnō solūtus	*to set out on a voyage*
aenigma solvere	*to settle a debt*
margarītam in acētō solvere	*to free somebody from chains*
pecūniam solvere	*to solve a puzzle*
vōtum solvere	*to dissolve a pearl in vinegar*

Suggest reasons why the Romans used **solvere** in all these phrases: is there any connection in meaning between them?

2 In each pair of sentences, translate the first sentence; then with the help of pages 258–259 and 270 express the same idea in a passive form by completing the noun and verb in the second sentence in the correct way, and translate again.

For example: hostēs nōs circumveniēbant.
ab host. . . circumveni. . . .

Translated and completed, this becomes:
hostēs nōs circumveniēbant.
The enemy were surrounding us.
ab hostibus circumveniēbāmur.
We were being surrounded by the enemy.

a cūr artifex tē culpābat?
cūr ā artif... culp... ?

b optimē labōrāvistis, puerī; vīlicus vōs certē laudābit.
optimē labōrāvistis, puerī; ā vīlic... certē laud... .

c moritūrus sum; amīcī mē in hōc locō sepelient.
moritūrus sum; ab amīc... in hōc locō sepel... .

d soror mē cotīdiē vīsitat.
ā sorōr... cotīdiē vīsit... .

e barbarī nōs interficient.
ā barbar... interfici... .

3 Complete each sentence by describing the word in **boldface** with the correct form of a suitable adjective from the box below. Refer to pages 260–261 if necessary. Do not use any adjective more than once.

īrātus	ingēns	fortis	pulcher	magnus
fēlīx	longus	audāx	gravis	

   a dominus **ancillās** arcessīvit.

   b iuvenis pecūniam **senī** reddidit.

   c sacerdōtēs **templum** intrāvērunt.

   d dux virtūtem **mīlitum** laudāvit.

   e cīvēs **spectāculō** dēlectātī sunt.

   f centuriō, **hastā** armātus, extrā carcerem stābat.

4 Complete each sentence with the correct infinitive or group of words from the list below, and then translate.

nūllam pecūniam habēre
per hortum suum flūxisse
scrīptam esse
aedificārī
equum occīsūrōs esse

   a nūntius sciēbat epistulam ab Imperātōre . . . .

   b senex affirmāvit sē . . . .

   c rēx crēdēbat leōnēs . . . .

   d agricola querēbātur multam aquam . . . .

   e puer dīxit novum templum . . . .

About the language 3: syncope

1 In Stage 6, you met the 3rd person plural of the perfect tense:

cīvēs gladiātōrem **incitāvērunt**.
The citizens urged the gladiator on.

2 From Stage 36 on, you have met examples like this:

centum mē **tetigēre** manūs.　　clientēs patrōnum **salūtāvēre**.
A hundred hands touched me.　　*The clients greeted their patron.*

In these examples, the 3rd person plural of the perfect tense ends in **-ēre** instead of **-ērunt**. The meaning is unchanged. This way of forming the 3rd person plural is especially common in verse, and is called **syncope**.

3 Translate the following:

a　servī contrā dominum coniūrāvēre.
b　in illō proeliō multī barbarī periēre.
c　coniūnxēre; ēripuēre; perdidēre; respexēre; studuēre.

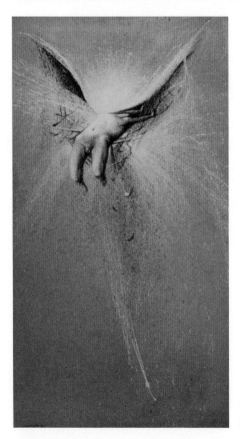

"Icarus at the Climax"
by Michael Ayrton.

Icarus in art

The story of Daedalus and Icarus has inspired many artists. The oldest surviving version of the story in picture form comes from Greece: a small fragment of a painted vase (see page 170) shows the lower edge of a tunic, two legs wearing winged boots, and the inscription Ι Κ Α Ρ Ο Σ (*Ikaros*). The vase was made in the middle of the sixth century BC, more than five hundred years earlier than Ovid's version of the story.

Daedalus and Icarus also appear in wall paintings excavated at Pompeii. One of these paintings is shown on page 173. The figure of Daedalus flying in the center has been almost entirely lost because of the hole in the painting, and only the wing tips are visible. Icarus, however, appears twice, once at the top near the sun, and again at the bottom where Daedalus is shown burying his son. The bystanders gaze skywards in wonder, as in Ovid's account (**Part IV**, line 10). The sun is shown not as a ball of fire but as a god driving his chariot and horses across the sky.

The works reproduced on pages 169 and 180 are by the twentieth-century artist Michael Ayrton. Ayrton was fascinated by the story of Daedalus and Icarus, and came back to it again and again during a period of several years. He created a large number of drawings, reliefs, and sculptures dealing not only with the making of the wings and the fall of Icarus, but also with other details of the Daedalus story, such as the maze that Daedalus built in Crete, and the monstrous half-man, half-bull known as the Minotaur, who lived at the center of the maze. Ayrton also retold the Daedalus story in his own words in two novels.

"The Fall of Icarus," reproduced on page 175, is by Allegrini (1491–1534), a Renaissance painter. Here, against a strong atmospheric sky, Daedalus looks back in horror at the sight of Icarus tumbling headlong. Like the onlookers in Ovid's version (**Part IV**, line 10), the people in the foreground gape in consternation, but, unlike the onlookers in Ovid's version, these people are witnesses of the tragedy and gesticulate in dread.

In the middle of the sixteenth century, Pieter Bruegel (1525–1569), a Flemish artist, painted the picture which is reproduced on page 183. Some of the details of Bruegel's "Landscape with the Fall of Icarus" are very close to Ovid's account; the plowman leaning on his plow, the shepherd with his staff, and the fisherman (**Part IV**, lines 8–9) are all there. In other ways, however, Bruegel's treatment of the story is unusual and at first sight surprising. Bruegel's bystanders, for example, are behaving very differently from those in Ovid's account. As the legs of Icarus disappear into the water, Bruegel's people are either unaware of or indifferent to the tragedy. In the face of the vastness of nature and the indifference of people, human aspirations are futile.

Just as the story of Daedalus and Icarus, as told by Ovid and other writers, became a subject for many artists, so Bruegel's painting, in turn, inspired the following poem by W. H. Auden. Auden's title, *Musée des Beaux Arts*, refers to the gallery in Brussels (Belgium) where Bruegel's painting is hung.

Musée des Beaux Arts

About suffering they were never wrong,
The Old Masters: how well they understood
Its human position; how it takes place
While someone else is eating or opening a window or just
    walking dully along;
How, when the aged are reverently, passionately waiting
For the miraculous birth, there always must be
Children who did not specially want it to happen, skating
On a pond at the edge of the wood:
They never forgot
That even the dreadful martyrdom must run its course
Anyhow in a corner, some untidy spot
Where the dogs go on with their doggy life and the
    torturer's horse
Scratches its innocent behind on a tree.

In Bruegel's Icarus, for instance: how everything turns away
Quite leisurely from the disaster; the ploughman may
Have heard the splash, the forsaken cry,
But for him it was not an important failure; the sun shone
As it had to on the white legs disappearing into the green
Water; and the expensive delicate ship that must have seen
Something amazing, a boy falling out of the sky,
Had somewhere to get to and sailed calmly on.

"Landscape with the Fall of Icarus" by Bruegel.

Vocabulary checklist 44

aspiciō, aspicere, aspexī, aspectus	*look towards, catch sight of*
coniungō, coniungere, coniūnxī, coniūnctus	*join*
coniūrō, coniūrāre, coniūrāvī	*plot*
crēscō, crēscere, crēvī	*grow*
cupīdō, cupīdinis, f.	*desire*
fēlīx, *gen.* fēlīcis	*lucky, happy*
licet, licēre	*be allowed*
mihi licet	*I am allowed*
paulātim	*gradually*
studeō, studēre, studuī	*study*
tellūs, tellūris, f.	*land, earth*
ūnā cum	*together with*
uterque, utraque, utrumque	*both, each of two*
vinculum, vinculī, n.	*fastening, chain*

A fisherman.

LESBIA

Stage 45

Some of Catullus' most famous poems are concerned with a woman to whom he gave the name "Lesbia." Stage 45 contains eight of the Lesbia poems.

I

ille mī pār esse deō vidētur,
ille, sī fās est, superāre dīvōs,
quī sedēns adversus identidem tē
    spectat et audit

dulce rīdentem, **miserō*** quod omnēs   5
ēripit sēnsūs **mihi**: nam simul tē,
Lesbia, aspexī, nihil est super mī
    vōcis in ōre,

lingua sed torpet, tenuis sub artūs
flamma dēmānat, sonitū suōpte   10
tintinant aurēs, **geminā** teguntur
    lūmina **nocte**.

ōtium, Catulle, tibi molestum est:
ōtiō exsultās nimiumque gestīs:
ōtium et rēgēs prius et beātās   15
    perdidit urbēs.

mī = mihi
fās *right*
superāre *surpass*
adversus *opposite*
dulce *sweetly*
quod *(a thing) which*
sēnsūs: sēnsus *sense*
simul = simulac
nihil ... vōcis *no voice*
est super = superest: superesse
               remain, be left
torpet: torpēre *be paralyzed*
tenuis *thin, subtle*
sub *to the depths of*
artūs: artus *limb*
dēmānat: dēmānāre *flow down*
suōpte = suō
tintinant: tintināre *ring*
geminā: geminus *twofold, double*
teguntur: tegere *cover*
lūmina *eyes*
exsultās: exsultāre *get excited*
gestīs: gestīre *become restless*
prius *before now*
beātās: beātus *prosperous, wealthy*

Questions

1 Why does Catullus regard **ille** (lines 1 and 2) as fortunate? Why does he regard himself as **miserō** (line 5)?

2 **omnēs ēripit sēnsūs** (lines 5–6): give an example of this from lines 7–12.

3 What warning does Catullus give himself in lines 13–16? Do you think these lines follow on naturally from lines 1–12, or are they a separate topic?

*Some noun-and-adjective phrases, in which an adjective is separated by one word or more from the noun which it describes, are shown in **boldface**.

A girl picking flowers.

II

vīvāmus, mea Lesbia, atque amēmus,
rūmōrēsque senum sevēriōrum
omnēs ūnius aestimēmus assis!
sōlēs occidere et redīre possunt:
nōbīs, cum semel occidit brevis lūx,   5
nox est perpetua ūna dormienda.
dā mī bāsia mīlle, deinde centum,
dein mīlle altera, dein secunda centum,
deinde usque altera mīlle, deinde centum,
dein, cum mīlia multa fēcerīmus,   10
conturbābimus illa, nē sciāmus,
aut nē quis malus invidēre possit,
cum tantum sciat esse bāsiōrum.

vīvāmus *let us live*
rūmōrēs *gossip*
sevēriōrum: sevērior *over-strict*
ūnius ... assis *at a single as* (smallest Roman coin)
aestimēmus: aestimāre *value*
semel *once*
est ... dormienda *must be slept through*
bāsia: bāsium *kiss*
dein = deinde
usque altera *yet another*
conturbābimus: conturbāre *mix up, lose count of*
nē quis *in case anyone*
invidēre *cast an evil eye*
tantum *so much, such a large number*

Questions

1 Who, according to Catullus, might be making comments about him and Lesbia? What does he think he and Lesbia should do about these comments?

2 What contrast does Catullus draw between **sōlēs** (line 4) and **nōs** (**nōbīs**, line 5)?

3 What have lines 7–9 got to do with lines 4–6?

4 Why does Catullus suggest in line 11 that he and Lesbia should deliberately lose count?

vīvāmus, mea Lesbia, atque amēmus!

About the language 1: more about the subjunctive

1 Study the following examples:

vīvāmus atque amēmus!	*Let us live and let us love!*
nē dēspērēmus!	*Let us not despair!*
aut vincāmus aut vincāmur!	*Let us either conquer or be conquered!*

In these sentences, the speaker is ordering or encouraging himself and one or more other people to do something. The 1st person plural form ("we") is used, and the verb is in the present tense of the subjunctive. This is known as the **hortatory** use of the subjunctive.

Further examples:

a in mediam pugnam ruāmus!
b nē haesitēmus!
c sociōs nostrōs adiuvēmus.
d opus perficiāmus.
e gaudeāmus igitur, iuvenēs dum sumus.
f flammās exstinguere cōnēmur!

2 The subjunctive can also be used in a 3rd person form of the verb ("he," "she," "it," or "they"):

omnēs captīvī interficiantur!	*Let all the prisoners be killed!* Or, *All the prisoners are to be killed.*
nē respiciat!	*Let him not look back!* Or, *He is not to look back.*

This is known as the **jussive subjunctive**.

Further examples:

a statim redeat!
b sit amīcitia inter nōs et vōs.
c prīmum taurus sacrificētur; deinde precēs Iovī adhibeantur.

3 Occasionally, the jussive subjunctive is used in a 2nd person command ("you"):

dēsinās querī.	*You should stop complaining.*

But it is far more common for Latin to use the imperative:

dēsine querī!	*Stop complaining!*

III

lūgēte, ō Venerēs Cupīdinēsque,
et quantum est hominum venustiōrum!
passer mortuus est meae puellae,
passer, dēliciae meae puellae,
quem plūs illa oculīs suīs amābat.   5
nam mellītus erat suamque nōrat
ipsam tam bene quam puella mātrem,
nec sēsē ā gremiō illius movēbat,
sed circumsiliēns modo hūc modo illūc
ad sōlam dominam usque pīpiābat;   10
quī nunc it per iter tenebricōsum
illūc, unde negant redīre quemquam.
at vōbīs male sit, malae tenebrae
Orcī, quae omnia bella dēvorātis:
tam bellum mihi passerem abstulistis.   15
ō factum male! ō miselle passer!
tuā nunc operā, meae puellae
flendō turgidulī rubent ocellī.

Venerēs Cupīdinēsque
   gods and goddesses of love,
      Venuses and Cupids
quantum est *all the company*
   (literally *as much as there is*)
venustiōrum: venustus *tender, loving*
passer *sparrow*
mellītus *sweet as honey*
nōrat = **nōverat**
ipsam: ipsa *mistress*
tam … quam *as … as*
sēsē = **sē**
gremiō: gremium *lap*
circumsiliēns: circumsilīre *hop*
                                    around
usque *continually*
tenebricōsum: tenebricōsus
                        dark, shadowy
quemquam: quisquam *anyone*
vōbīs male sit *curses on you*
Orcī: Orcus *the underworld, Hell*
ō factum male! *Oh dreadful deed!*
   (literally *Oh dreadfully done!*)
miselle: misellus *wretched little*
tuā … operā *by your doing, because*
                        of you
turgidulī: turgidulus *swollen*
rubent: rubēre *be red*
ocellī: ocellus *poor eye, little eye*

Questions

1 What has happened?
2 Who are asked to mourn in line 1? Why are they appropriate mourners on this occasion?
3 Is Catullus chiefly concerned about the death, or about something else?
4 Why does he speak as if he had been bereaved (**mihi**, line 15)?
5 Compare the two descriptions of the sparrow in (a) lines 8–10, (b) lines 11–12. Do they sound equally serious, or is one of the descriptions slightly comic? How serious is the poem as a whole?

IV

nūllī sē dīcit mulier mea nūbere mālle
    quam mihi, nōn sī sē Iuppiter ipse petat.
dīcit: sed mulier **cupidō** quod dīcit **amantī**,
    in ventō et rapidā scrībere oportet aquā.

nūllī *used as dative of* **nēmō**
mulier *woman*
nōn sī *not even if*
sed mulier … quod dīcit = **sed quod mulier … dīcit**
cupidō: cupidus *eager, passionate*
amantī: amāns *lover*
rapidā: rapidus *rushing, racing*

Questions

1 What does Lesbia say in lines 1–2? Why does the mention of Jupiter imply a compliment to Catullus?

2 What would be the best translation for the first **dīcit** in line 3?

  a "She says"

  b "She says so"

  c "That's what she *says*"

  d "*That's* what she says"

  or none of these?

3 What comment does Catullus then make about Lesbia's remark?

4 What does he mean? Does he mean, for example, that women can't be trusted? Or is he suggesting something more precise than that? Is he being cynical or fair-minded?

Wall painting of lovers.

V

dīcēbās quondam **sōlum** tē nōsse **Catullum**,
  Lesbia, nec prae mē velle tenēre Iovem.
dīlēxī tum tē nōn tantum ut vulgus amīcam,
  sed pater ut gnātōs dīligit et generōs.
nunc tē cognōvī: quārē etsī impēnsius ūror,   5
  multō mī tamen es vīlior et levior.
quī potis est, inquis? quod amantem iniūria tālis
  cōgit amāre magis, sed bene velle minus.

nōsse = nōvisse
prae *instead of, rather than*
tenēre *possess*
vulgus *the ordinary man, the*
       common man
amīcam: amīca *mistress, girlfriend*
gnātōs = nātōs
quārē *and so*
etsī *although, even if*
impēnsius: impēnsē *strongly, violently*
ūror: ūrere *burn (with passion)*
levior: levis *worthless*
quī potis est? *how is that possible?*
                how can that be?
bene velle *like, be friendly*

Questions

1 What statement by Lesbia does Catullus recall in lines
   1–2? What were his feelings about her at that time,
   according to lines 3–4?

2 What is the point of the comparison in line 4?

3 Explain what Catullus means by **nunc tē cognōvī** (line 5).
   In what way has his discovery affected his feelings for
   Lesbia? Why has it had this effect?

About the language 2: more about relative pronouns

1 From Unit 3 on, you have met sentences in which forms of the pronoun **is** are used as antecedents of the relative pronoun **quī**:

   is *quī nūper servus erat* nunc dīvitissimus est.
   He who was recently a slave is now extremely rich.

   id *quod mihi nārrāvistī* numquam patefaciam.
   That which you have told me I shall never reveal.
   Or, in more natural English:
   I shall never reveal what you have told me.

   dominus **eōs** pūniet *quī pecūniam āmīsērunt*.
   The master will punish those who lost the money.

   Notice that in these sentences the antecedent (in **boldface**) comes *before* the relative clause (*italicized*).

   Further examples:

   a id quod dīcis vērum est.
   b is quī rēgem vulnerāvit celeriter fūgit.
   c nūllum praemium dabitur eīs quī officium neglegunt.

2 You have also met sentences like these, in which the antecedent comes *after* the relative clause:

   quī auxilium mihi prōmīsērunt, **eī** mē iam dēserunt.
   Those who promised me help are now deserting me.

   quod potuimus, **id** fēcimus.
   That which we could do, we did.
   Or, in more natural English:
   We did what we could.

   Further examples:

   a quod saepe rogāvistī, ecce! id tibi dō.
   b quōs per tōtum orbem terrārum quaerēbam, eī in hāc urbe inventī sunt.

3 In Stages 41–45, you have met sentences in which the antecedent is omitted altogether:

> quod mulier dīcit amantī, in ventō scrībere oportet.
> *What a woman says to her lover should be written on the wind.*

> quī numquam timet stultus est.
> *He who is never frightened is a fool.*

> quī speciem amīcitiae praebent nōn semper fidēlēs sunt.
> *Those who put on an appearance of friendship are not always faithful.*

Further examples:

a quod suscēpī, effēcī.
b quae tū mihi heri dedistī, tibi crās reddam.
c quī multum habet plūs cupit.
d quod sentīmus loquāmur.
e quī rēs adversās fortiter patiuntur, maximam laudem merent.

laudem: laus *praise, fame*

VI

ōdī et amō. quārē id faciam, fortasse requīris.   **requīris: requīrere** *ask*
   nescio, sed fierī sentiō et excrucior.

Do the first three words of this poem make sense? Does Catullus mean that he hates at some times and loves at others, or that he hates and loves simultaneously?

VII

miser Catulle, dēsinās ineptīre,
et quod vidēs perīsse perditum dūcās.
fulsēre quondam candidī tibi sōlēs,
cum ventitābās quō puella dūcēbat
amāta nōbīs quantum amābitur nūlla.   5
ibi illa multa cum iocōsa fīēbant,
quae tū volēbās nec puella nōlēbat,
fulsēre vērē candidī tibi sōlēs.

nunc iam illa nōn volt: tū quoque impotēns nōlī,
nec quae fugit sectāre, nec miser vīve,   10
sed obstinātā mente perfer, obdūrā.

valē, puella. iam Catullus obdūrat,
nec tē requīret nec rogābit invītam.
at tū dolēbis, cum rogāberis nūlla.
scelesta, vae tē, quae tibi manet vīta?   15
quis nunc tē adībit? cui vidēberis bella?
quem nunc amābis? cuius esse dīcēris?
quem bāsiābis? cui labella mordēbis?
at tū, Catulle, dēstinātus obdūrā.

ineptīre *be a fool*
perditum: perditus *completely lost,*
gone forever
dūcās: dūcere *consider*
candidī: candidus *bright*
ventitābās: ventitāre *often go, go*
repeatedly

nōbīs = mihi *by me*
quantum *as, as much as*
ibi *then, in those days*
illa multa cum … fīēbant = cum illa
multa … fīēbant
iocōsa *moments of fun, moments of*
pleasure
vērē *truly*
nunc iam *now however, as things are*
now
volt = vult
impotēns *being helpless, being*
powerless
sectāre (imperative of **sectārī**) *chase*
after
perfer: perferre *endure*
obdūrā: obdūrāre *be firm*
requīret: requīrere *go looking for*
nūlla: nūllus *not at all*
scelesta: scelestus *wretched*
vae tē! *alas for you!*
bāsiābis: bāsiāre *kiss*
labella: labellum *lip*
mordēbis: mordēre *bite*
dēstinātus *determined*

Questions

1 Explain the advice which Catullus gives himself in lines 1–2. What English proverb corresponds to the idea expressed in line 2?

2 Does line 3 simply mean that it was fine weather?

3 Which word in line 9 contrasts with **quondam** (line 3)?

4 What future does Catullus foresee in lines 14–15?

5 On the evidence of lines 12–19, does Catullus seem capable of following his own advice? Give reasons for your view.

6 What is the mood of the poem? Sad, angry, bitter, determined, resigned? Does the mood change during the course of the poem? If so, where and in what way?

VIII

In the first four stanzas of this poem, given here in translation, Catullus describes the loyalty and friendship of Furius and Aurelius:

> Furius and Aurelius, comrades of Catullus,
> whether he journeys to furthest India,
> whose shores are pounded by far-resounding
>   Eastern waves,
>
> or whether he travels to soft Arabia,   5
> to Persia, Scythia, or the arrow-bearing Parthians,
> or the plains which are darkened by the seven mouths
>   of the river Nile,
>
> or whether he crosses the lofty Alps,
> visiting the scene of great Caesar's triumphs,   10
> over the Rhine and the ocean, to Britain on the
>   edge of the world,
>
> ready to join in any adventure,
> whatever the will of the gods may bring,
> carry a few bitter words   15
>   to my girl.

The poem's last two stanzas are Catullus' message:

> cum **suīs** vīvat valeatque **moechīs**,
> quōs simul complexa tenet trecentōs,
> nūllum amāns vērē, sed identidem omnium
>   īlia rumpēns;   20
>
> nec meum respectet, ut ante, amōrem,
> quī illius culpā cecidit velut prātī
> ultimī flōs, **praetereunte** postquam
>   tāctus **arātrō** est.

valeat: valēre *thrive, prosper*
moechīs: moechus *lover, adulterer*
complexa: complectī *embrace*
trecentōs: trecentī *three hundred*
īlia: īlia *groin*
rumpēns: rumpere *burst, rupture*
respectet: respectāre *look towards, count on*
illius culpā *through her fault, thanks to her*
cecidit: cadere *die*
prātī: prātum *meadow*
ultimī: ultimus *farthest, at the edge*

Questions

1 Why does Catullus spend so much of this poem describing Furius' and Aurelius' loyalty?

2 What is the gist of the message which he asks them to deliver?

3 What phrases or words in lines 17 and 19 remind you of other poems by Catullus that you have read?

4 "His final goodbye to Lesbia." Do you think this is an accurate description of the last two stanzas?

Practicing the language

1 Match each word in the top list with a word of opposite meaning taken from the bottom list.

For example: amor   odium

amor, celeriter, dare, dēmittere, hiems, impedīre, incipere, lūgēre, multō, poena, salūs, tenebrae

tollere, adiuvāre, gaudēre, paulō, odium, perīculum, lūx, dēsinere, aestās, accipere, lentē, praemium

2 Translate the first sentence of each pair. Then change it from a direct question to an indirect question by completing the second sentence with the correct form of the present subjunctive active or passive. Finally, translate the second sentence.

For example: cūr semper errātis?
                    dīcite nōbīs cūr semper.... .

Translated and completed, this becomes:

cūr semper errātis?
Why are you always wandering around?
dīcite nōbīs cūr semper errētis.
Tell us why you are always wandering around.

The active and passive forms of the present subjunctive are given on pages 272–273. You may also need to consult the Vocabulary at the end to find which conjugation a verb belongs to.

a   ubi habitās?
     dīc mihi ubi . . . .
b   quō captīvī illī dūcuntur?
     scīre volō quō captīvī illī . . . .
c   quot fundōs possideō?
     oblītus sum quot fundōs . . . .
d   quid quaerimus?
     tibi dīcere nōlumus quid . . . .
e   novumne templum aedificātur?
     incertus sum num novum templum . . . .
f   cūr in hōc locō sedētis?
     explicāte nōbīs cūr in hōc locō . . . .

3 Complete each sentence with the correct word or phrase and then translate.

a dēnique poēta . . . . surrēxit. (ad recitandum, ad dormiendum)
b nūntius, celeriter . . . . , mox ad castra pervēnit. (scrībendō, equitandō)
c captīvī, quī nūllam spem . . . . habēbant, dēspērābant. (coquendī, effugiendī)
d omnēs hospitēs in triclīnium . . . . contendērunt. (ad cēnandum, ad pugnandum)
e senex, quī procul ā marī habitābat, artem . . . . numquam didicerat. (nāvigandī, spectandī)
f pater meus, dīligenter . . . . , tandem magnās dīvitiās adeptus est. (labōrandō, bibendō)

About the language 3: more about the dative

1 In Stage 9, you met the dative case used in sentences like this:

> pater **nōbīs** dōnum ēmit.
> *Father bought a present **for us**.*

This use of the dative is sometimes described as the **dative of advantage**.

2 In Unit 4, you have met the dative used in sentences like these:

> Fortūna **mihi** frātrem ēripuit.
> *Fortune has snatched my brother away **from me**.*

> tenebrae Orcī **eī** passerem abstulērunt.
> *The shades of Hell stole the sparrow **from her**.*

This use of the dative is sometimes described as the **dative of disadvantage**.

Further examples:

a fūr mihi multam pecūniam abstulit.
b barbarī eīs cibum ēripuērunt.
c Rōmānī nōbīs lībertātem auferre cōnantur.

Catullus and Lesbia

The real identity of "Lesbia" is uncertain, but there are reasons for thinking that she was a woman named Clodia. Clodia came from the aristocratic family of the Claudii (who used a different spelling of their name), and was married to Metellus, a wealthy and distinguished noble. She was an attractive, highly educated woman, whose colorful lifestyle caused continual interest and gossip at Rome. Among the other rumors that circulated around her, she was said to have murdered her husband and committed incest with her brother.

One of Clodia's lovers was the lively and talented Marcus Caelius Rufus. Their relationship lasted for about two years, before being broken off by Caelius. There was a violent quarrel; and Clodia, furious and humiliated, was determined to revenge herself. She launched a prosecution against Caelius, alleging (among other things) that he had robbed her and attempted to poison her.

Mars and Venus.

Clodia, in spite of her doubtful reputation, was a powerful and dangerous enemy, with many influential friends, and the prosecution was a serious threat to Caelius. To defend himself against her charges, he turned to various friends, including Rome's leading orator, Cicero. Not only was Cicero a close friend of Caelius, but he had a bitter and long-running feud with Clodia's brother Clodius.

Some of the charges were dealt with by other speakers for the defense; Cicero's job was to deal with Clodia's allegations of theft and poisoning. It would not be enough to produce arguments and witnesses; Clodia herself had to be discredited and (if possible) made to look ridiculous, if a verdict of "not guilty" was to be achieved.

"Lesbia and her Sparrow" by Poynter. Which aspects of her character does the artist capture?

The following paragraphs are from Cicero's speech in defense of Caelius:

Two charges in particular have been made: theft and attempted murder, and both charges involve the same individual. It is alleged that the gold was stolen from Clodia, and that the poison was obtained for administering to Clodia. The rest of the chief prosecutor's speech was not a list of charges, but a string of insults, more suitable to a vulgar slanging-match than a court of law. When the prosecutor calls my client "adulterer, fornicator, swindler," these are not accusations, but mere abuse. Such charges have no foundation; they are wild mud-slinging, by an accuser who has lost his temper and has no one to back him up.

But when we come to the charges of theft and attempted murder, we have to deal not with the prosecutor but the person behind him. In speaking of these charges, gentlemen of the jury, my concern is wholly with Clodia, a lady who possesses not only nobility of birth but also a certain notoriety. However, I shall say nothing about her except in connection with the charges against my client. I should be more energetic and forceful in speaking about Clodia, but I do not wish to seem influenced by political dispute with her husband – I mean her *brother*, of course (I'm always making that mistake). I shall speak in moderate language, and will go no further than I am obliged by my duty to my client and the facts of the case: for I have never felt it right to argue with a woman, especially with one who has always been regarded not as any man's enemy but as *every* man's friend …

I shall name no names, but suppose there were a woman, unmarried, blatantly living the life of a harlot both here in the city and in the public gaze of the crowded resort of Baiae, flaunting her behavior not only by her attitude and her appearance, not only by her passionate glances and her insolent tongue, but by lustful embraces, drinking sessions, and beach parties, so that she seemed to be not merely a harlot, but a harlot of the lewdest and most lascivious description – suppose that a young man,

An interpretation of Lesbia by Weguelin in a statuesque pose with sparrows at her feet.

like my client, were to associate with such a woman; do you seriously claim that he would be seducing an innocent victim? …

I was present, gentlemen, and indeed it was perhaps the saddest and bitterest occasion of my whole life, when Quintus Metellus, who only two days previously had been playing a leading part in the political life of our city, a man in the prime of his years, in the best of health and at the peak of his physical strength, was violently, suddenly, shockingly taken from us. How can the woman, who comes from that house of crime, now dare to speak in court about the rapid effects of poison?

Caelius was acquitted. Nothing is known of Clodia's later fate.

Catullus' poems, whether about Lesbia or not, display an intensity of feeling and a mastery of different meters. These characteristics put Catullus' poetry firmly in the lyric genre. In Greek poetry this term applied originally to songs which were accompanied by music ("poetry sung to the lyre") and which expressed the personal sentiments of the poets, as distinct from the objectivity of, for example, epic or dramatic poetry. The adoption of the Greek lyric meters into Latin presented great difficulty. However, Catullus and, later, Horace were successful enough to become the two chief Roman lyric poets. Latin lyric poetry differed from Greek lyric in that it was written to be recited or read instead of sung to music. However, the Roman poets did continue the elements which still characterize lyric poetry in its wider meaning today: melodic poetry written in an intensely personal and direct style.

Statue from the second century AD. This respectable Roman matron's face and Flavian hairstyle contrast strikingly with her naked body and Venus-like pose.

Vocabulary checklist 45

aestās, aestātis, f.	*summer*
candidus, candida, candidum	*bright, shining*
culpa, culpae, f.	*blame*
fleō, flēre, flēvī	*weep*
modo … modo	*now … now, sometimes … sometimes*
mulier, mulieris, f.	*woman*
orbis, orbis, m.	*circle, globe*
orbis terrārum	*world*
ōtium, ōtiī, n.	*leisure*
quisquam, quicquam	*anyone, anything*
rumpō, rumpere, rūpī, ruptus	*break, split*
speciēs, speciēī, f.	*appearance*
tegō, tegere, tēxī, tēctus	*cover*
tenuis, tenuis, tenue	*thin*

Wall painting of cupids playing.

CLADES

Stage 46

Pliny wrote two letters to the historian Tacitus giving an eyewitness account of the eruption of Mount Vesuvius, which had taken place in the late summer or fall of AD 79 when Pliny was seventeen. In the first letter, he described the death of his uncle (Pliny the Elder), who went too near the danger zone on a rescue mission, and was choked to death by the fumes. In the second letter, on which the passages in this Stage are based, Pliny describes the adventures which he and his mother had at Misenum after Pliny the Elder had departed on his mission.

tremōrēs

I

profectō avunculō, ipse reliquum tempus studiīs impendī (ideō enim remānseram); deinde balneum, cēna, somnus inquiētus et brevis. per multōs diēs priōrēs, tremor terrae sentiēbātur, minus formīdolōsus quia Campāniae solitus; sed illā nocte ita invaluit, ut nōn movērī omnia sed ēvertī vidērentur. irrūpit cubiculum meum māter; surgēbam ipse, ad eam excitandam sī dormīret. cōnsēdimus in āreā domūs, quae mare ā tēctīs modicō spatiō dīvidēbat; ego, ut timōrem mātris meā sēcūritāte lēnīrem, poposcī librum et quasi per ōtium legere coepī. subitō advenit amīcus quīdam avunculī, quī ubi mē et mātrem sedentēs, mē vērō etiam legentem videt, vituperat illīus patientiam, sēcūritātem meam. ego nihilōminus intentus in librum manēbam.

  iam hōra diēī prīma; sed adhūc dubia lūx. iam quassātīs proximīs tēctīs, magnus et certus ruīnae metus. tum dēmum fugere cōnstituimus; nam sī diūtius morātī essēmus, sine dubiō periissēmus. ultrā tēcta prōgressī, ad respīrandum cōnsistimus. multa ibi mīrābilia vidēmus, multās formīdinēs patimur.

5

10

15

avunculō: avunculus *uncle*
remānseram: remānēre
        stay behind
somnus *sleep*
formīdolōsus *alarming*
Campāniae *in Campania*
solitus *common, usual*
invaluit: invalēscere *become strong*
tēctīs: tēctum *building*
spatiō: spatium *space, distance*
dīvidēbat: dīvidere *separate*
sēcūritāte: sēcūritās
    unconcern, lack of anxiety
per ōtium *at leisure, free from care*
quassātīs: quassāre *shake violently*
ruīnae: ruīna *collapse*
ultrā *beyond*
respīrandum: respīrāre
    recover one's breath, get one's breath back
formīdinēs: formīdō *fear, terror*

II

nam vehicula, quae prōdūcī iusserāmus, quamquam in plānissimō campō, in contrāriās partēs agēbantur, ac nē lapidibus quidem fulta in eōdem locō manēbant. praetereā mare in sē resorbērī vidēbāmus, quasi tremōre terrae repulsum esset. certē prōcesserat lītus, multaque maris animālia siccīs arēnīs dētinēbantur. ab alterō 5 latere nūbēs ātra et horrenda in longās flammārum figūrās dēhīscēbat; quae et similēs et maiōrēs fulguribus erant. tum vērō ille amīcus avunculī vehementius nōs hortātus est ut effugere cōnārēmur: "sī frāter" inquit "tuus, tuus avunculus, vīvit, salūtem vestram cupit; sī periit, superstitēs vōs esse voluit; cūr igitur 10 cūnctāminī?" respondimus nōs salūtī nostrae cōnsulere nōn posse, dum dē illō incertī essēmus. nōn morātus ultrā, sē convertit et quam celerrimē ē perīculō fūgit.

nec multō post, illa nūbēs ātra dēscendit in terrās, operuit maria; cēlāverat Capreās, Mīsēnī prōmunturium ē cōnspectū 15 abstulerat. tum māter mē ōrāre hortārī iubēre, ut quōquō modō fugerem; affirmāvit mē, quod iuvenis essem, ad salūtem pervenīre posse; sē, quae et annīs et corpore gravārētur, libenter moritūram esse, sī mihi causa mortis nōn fuisset. ego respondī mē nōlle incolumem esse nisi illa quoque effūgisset; deinde 20 manum eius amplexus, addere gradum cōgō. pāret invīta, castīgatque sē, quod mē morētur.

plānissimō: plānus *level, flat*
campō: campus *ground*
partēs: pars *direction*
agēbantur: agī *move, roll*
fulta: fulcīre *prop up, wedge*
resorbērī: resorbēre *suck back*
siccīs: siccus *dry*
arēnīs: arēna *sand*
dētinēbantur: dētinēre
        hold back, strand
latere: latus *side*
horrenda: horrendus *horrifying*
dēhīscēbat: dēhīscere *gape*
        open
fulguribus: fulgur *lightning*
cūnctāminī: cūnctārī *delay,*
        hesitate
cōnsulere *take thought for,*
    give consideration to
operuit: operīre *cover*
Capreās: Capreae *Capri*
Mīsēnī: Mīsēnum *Misenum*
prōmunturium *promontory*
ōrāre hortārī iubēre = ōrābat
    hortābātur iubēbat
quōquō: quisquis
    whatever (i.e. whatever
    possible)
incolumem: incolumis *safe*
amplexus: amplectī *grasp, clasp*
addere gradum *go forward step*
    by step (literally *add one*
    step (to another))

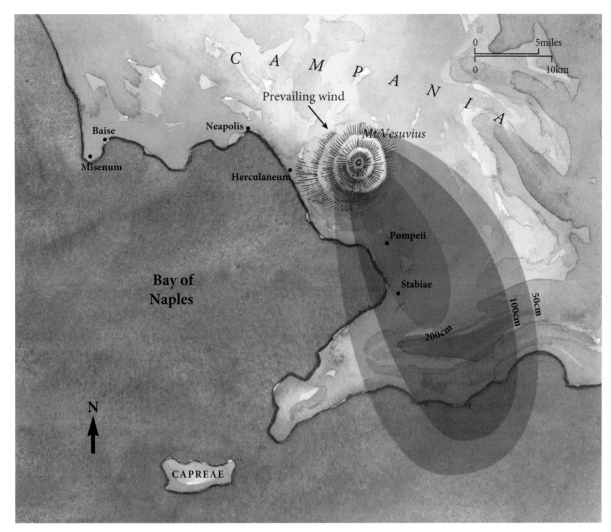

The area affected by ashfall after the eruption of Vesuvius in AD 79.

Questions

1 What strange things were happening to (a) Pliny's carriage, (b) the sea and shore, (c) the sea creatures?
2 Describe what Pliny saw in the sky (lines 5–7).
3 What did the friend of Pliny's uncle urge Pliny and his mother to do? What reason did they give for refusing? What did the friend then do?
4 What were the effects of the black cloud, as described in lines 14–16?
5 Why did Pliny's mother think they should separate? What action did Pliny take in response to her entreaties?
6 What impression do you have of the character of (a) the friend of Pliny's uncle, (b) Pliny and his mother, as shown by their behavior during the eruption?

About the language 1: pluperfect subjunctive passive

1 In Stage 30, you met the pluperfect indicative passive:

> omnēs servī **dīmissī erant**.
> *All the slaves had been sent away.*

2 In Stage 46, you have met sentences like these:

> cum omnēs servī **dīmissī essent,** ad āream rediimus.
> *When all the slaves had been sent away, we returned to the courtyard.*

> Plīnius scīre voluit num avunculus **servātus esset**.
> *Pliny wanted to know whether his uncle had been saved.*

The form of the verb in **boldface** is the **pluperfect subjunctive passive**.

Further examples:

a ancilla cognōvit quid in testāmentō dominī scrīptum esset.
b cum victimae sacrificātae essent, pontifex pauca verba dīxit.
c amīcī vestrī ignōrābant quārē comprehēnsī essētis.

3 Compare the indicative and subjunctive forms of the pluperfect passive of **portō**:

pluperfect passive indicative	*pluperfect passive subjunctive*
portātus eram	portātus essem
portātus erās	portātus essēs
portātus erat	portātus esset
portātī erāmus	portātī essēmus
portātī erātis	portātī essētis
portātī erant	portātī essent

Pluperfect subjunctive passive forms of all conjugations are given on page 273 of the Language information section.

4 Study the following examples:

> iūdex rogāvit quantam pecūniam mercātor mihi **pollicitus esset**.
> *The judge asked how much money the merchant had promised me.*

> cum Rōmam **regressus essem**, prīnceps mē arcessīvit.
> *When I had returned to Rome, the emperor sent for me.*

The words in **boldface** are pluperfect subjunctive forms of deponent verbs.

Further examples:

a cum multās gemmās adeptī essēmus, domum revēnimus.
b memineram quid māter mea locūta esset.

Pluperfect subjunctive forms of deponent verbs are given on page 278.

tenebrae

iam dēcidēbat cinis, adhūc tamen rārus. respiciō; dēnsa cālīgō,
tergīs nostrīs imminēns, nōs sequēbātur quasi ingēns flūmen ātrum
in terram effūsum esset. "dēflectāmus" inquam, "dum vidēmus, nē
in viā sternāmur et in tenebrīs ā multitūdine fugientum obterāmur."
vix cōnsēderāmus, cum dēscendit nox dēnsissima,   5
quasi omnia lūmina in conclāvī clausō exstīncta essent. sī
adfuissēs, audīvissēs ululātūs fēminārum, īnfantum vāgītūs,
clāmōrēs virōrum; aliī vōcibus parentēs requīrēbant, vōcibusque
nōscitābant, aliī līberōs, aliī coniugēs; hī suum cāsum, aliī suōrum
lūgēbant; nōnnūllī metū mortis mortem precābantur; multī ad deōs   10
manūs tollēbant, plūrēs nusquam iam deōs ūllōs esse affirmābant.
    paulum relūxit, quod nōn diēs nōbīs, sed appropinquantis ignis
indicium vidēbātur. ignis tamen procul substitit; deinde tenebrae
rūrsus, cinis rūrsus, multus et gravis. nisi identidem surrēxissēmus
et cinerem excussissēmus, sine dubiō opertī atque etiam oblīsī   15
pondere essēmus.
    tandem cālīgō tenuāta ac dissolūta est, sīcut fūmus vel nebula.
mox diēs rediit; sōl etiam fulgēbat, pallidus tamen. attonitī vīdimus
omnia mūtāta altōque cinere tamquam nive operta. regressī
Mīsēnum, noctem spē ac metū exēgimus. metus praevalēbat; nam 20
tremor terrae persevērābat. nōbīs tamen nūllum cōnsilium abeundī
erat, dōnec cognōscerēmus num avunculus servātus esset.

rārus *occasional*
dēflectāmus: dēflectāre
    *turn aside, turn off the
    road*
sternāmur: sternere *knock
                      over*
obterāmur: obterere *trample
                      to death*
ululātūs: ululātus *shriek*
vāgītūs: vāgītus *wailing, crying*
nōscitābant: nōscitāre
                      recognize
paulum *a little, to a slight
        extent*
relūxit: relūcēscere
        become light again
opertī = opertī essēmus:
    operīre *bury*
oblīsī … essēmus: oblīdere
                      crush
pondere: pondus *weight*
tenuāta: tenuāre *thin out*
dissolūta est: dissolvere
                disperse, dissolve
nebula *mist*
nive: nix *snow*
Mīsēnum *to Misenum*
exēgimus: exigere *spend*
praevalēbat: praevalēre
        prevail, be uppermost
dōnec *until*

Plaster casts of bodies from Pompeii.

About the language 2: more about conditionals

1 Study the following conditional sentences:

sī iuvenis respexisset, latrōnem vīdisset.
If the young man had looked back, he would have seen the robber.

sī mē vocāvissēs, statim vēnissem.
If you had called me, I would have come at once.

nisi canis lātrāvisset, servī effūgissent.
If the dog had not barked, the slaves would have escaped.

sī Imperātor ipse hanc rem iūdicāvisset, damnātī essētis.
If the emperor himself had judged this case, you would have been condemned.

Notice that:

a the Latin verbs are in the pluperfect tense of the subjunctive;
b the English translations contain the words *had...* , followed by *would have...* .

2 Further examples:

a sī nautae in portū mānsissent, tempestātem vītāvissent.
b sī satis pecūniae obtulissētis, agricola vōbīs equum vēndidisset.
c sī centuriō tergum vertisset, minus graviter vulnerātus esset.
d sī fīlia tua illī senī nūpsisset, miserrima fuisset.
e sī exercitus noster superātus esset, prīnceps novās cōpiās ēmīsisset.
f nisi pater mē prohibuisset, tibi subvēnissem.

Practicing the language

1 Translate each sentence; then, referring if necessary to the table of nouns on pages 258–259 and to the Vocabulary at the end of the book, change the *number* of the words in **boldface** (i.e. change singular words to plural, and plural words to singular) and translate again.

a centuriō barbarōs **catēnīs** vīnxit.
b fūr vestēs **amīcī tuī** abstulit.
c sacerdōs ad **templa** ambulābat.
d multitūdō artem **gladiātōris** mīrābātur.
e pāstōrēs strepitum **canum** audīvērunt.
f puer cum **ancillīs** et **iuvenibus** stābat.
g **mercātōrī** pecūniam trādidit.
h ego callidior **meīs inimīcīs** sum.

2 This exercise is based on lines 1–12 of **tremōrēs I** on page 207. Read the lines again, then translate the following sentences into Latin. All necessary vocabulary can be found on page 207 in lines 1–12, but you will need to make various alterations to the word-endings, e.g. by changing a verb from 1st person to 3rd person, or a noun from the nominative to the genitive. Refer to the appropriate pages in the Language information section where necessary.

a Plinius spent the remaining time *on dinner* (dative) and *sleep* (dative).
b Throughout those days, tremors were being felt.
c Plinius began to read a book, in order that he might calm *his* (omit) mother's fear.
d They *saw* (use either perfect or historical present) his uncle's friend arriving.
e Plinius, having been scolded *by the friend* (**ab** + ablative), was nevertheless remaining in the courtyard.

3 Translate each pair of sentences; then replace the word in **boldface** with the correct form of the relative pronoun **quī**, using the table in paragraph 1 on page 267 and adjusting the word order if necessary so that the relative pronoun comes at the beginning of the second sentence; then translate again. Do not join the two sentences together, but translate the relative pronoun as a *connecting relative*, i.e. as "he," "she," "it," "this," etc. If necessary, check the gender of the word in **boldface**.

For example: in mediā urbe stābat templum. simulatque **templum** intrāvī, attonitus cōnstitī.
*In the middle of the city stood a temple. As soon as I entered the **temple** I halted in amazement.*

This becomes: in mediā urbe stābat templum. **quod** simulatque intrāvī, attonitus cōnstitī.
*In the middle of the city stood a temple. As soon as I entered **it**, I halted in amazement.*

a subitō appāruērunt duo lupī. cum **lupōs** vīdissent, pāstōrēs clāmōrem sustulērunt.
b agricola uxōrem monuit ut fugeret. **uxor** tamen obstinātē recūsāvit.
c rēx epistulam celeriter dictāvit. cum servus **epistulam** scrīpsisset, nūntius ad Imperātōrem tulit.
d fūr ātrium tacitē intrāvit. **fūre** vīsō, canis lātrāvit.
e Quīntus "Salvium perfidiae accūsō," inquit. **verbīs** audītīs, Salvius tacuit.
f "ubi est pecūnia mea?" rogāvit mercātor. nēmō **mercātōrī** respondēre audēbat.
g hominēs clāmāre coepērunt. clāmōribus **hominum** excitātus, surrēxī.
h crās pontifex sacrificium faciet. ut **sacrificium** videās, tē ad templum dūcam.

About the language 3: more about ellipsis

1   From Unit 1 on, you have met sentences like these, containing various forms of the verb **esse** (*to be*):

> nihil tam ferōx est quam leō.
> *Nothing is as ferocious as a lion.*

> postrīdiē discessimus; sed iter longum et difficile erat.
> *We left the next day; but the journey was long and difficult.*

2   Sometimes, however, the various forms of **esse** are omitted, especially in verse or fast-moving narrative. In more recent Stages, you have met sentences like these:

> nam tam terribile quam incendium.
> *Nothing is as frightening as a fire.*

> caelum undique et pontus.
> *On every side was sky and sea.*

> subitō fragōrem audīvimus; deinde longum silentium.
> *Suddenly we heard a crash; then there was a long silence.*

3   Translate again lines 13–14 of **tremōrēs I** on page 207, from **iam** to **metus**. How many times does the Latin omit the word **erat** where the English translation contains the word "was"?

Roman letters

What the Romans called **ōtium** (free time), the freedom from **negōtium** (the business of life), was actually laborious leisure in which a great amount of time was devoted to reading and writing. Someone once expressed wonder at what Pliny the Elder had accomplished: he had performed important and time-consuming official duties, had practiced law, and had written many books. His nephew, Pliny the Younger, explained that **studia**, learning and studying, filled all his uncle's spare time. While he was resting after lunch, while dining, while traveling, while being carried through Rome in a litter, even while being rubbed down and dried after a bath, Pliny the Elder had books read aloud to him while he took notes, wrote extracts, or dictated to his secretary. Apparently Pliny the Younger practiced this routine as well. He tells us that, relaxing at his beloved Laurentine villa, he never wasted time even while hunting: "I was sitting by the hunting nets with stylus and writing tablets instead of hunting spears by my side, thinking and making notes, so that, even if I came home empty-handed, I should have my wax tablets filled at least."

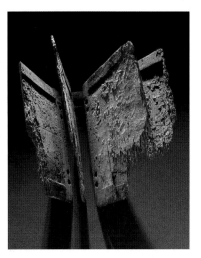

Roman writing tablet.

This inclination for reading and writing was widespread among cultivated Romans and letter writing accounted for a great amount of that time and devotion. In the small city-states of the Greek world, there had been relatively little need for written communication and the number of letters in classical Greek literature is small. But with Rome at the center of an expanding empire, written correspondence became absolutely essential. Landowners visiting their estates in Italy, bureaucrats on military or administrative service in the provinces, travelers, merchants, tax collectors, students, soldiers, and exiles, all needed to keep in touch with home or the capital.

Every traveler went laden with letters he had been asked to deliver, often in return for letters of introduction to influential persons (**epistulae commendāticiae**). A person about to send a messenger or who intended to go on a journey made it a point of courtesy to notify friends in time for them to prepare letters. There was a danger, of course, that letters sent in this way might fall into the wrong hands or be lost. It was customary, therefore, to send a copy of an important letter by another person and, if possible, by another route.

Notes, short letters, lists, receipts, and first drafts of literary works were written on wax tablets (**cērae**). A page of papyrus (**charta**) was expensive and was used only for important correspondence. Normally two parallel columns were written on each charta. A book was a long strip of papyrus, made from a number of chartae glued together. It was kept rolled in a scroll (**volūmen**) and was unrolled as it was read.

The sheer volume of correspondence carried on by most Romans of wealth made it impossible for them to write all their letters in their own hand, except for the most important or those to dear friends. It was, therefore, the practice to use **āmanuēnsēs** or secretaries. A slave employed in writing correspondence from dictation or copying was called a **notārius**, a **librārius**, or a **servus ab epistulīs**. If letters had been written by a secretary, the authors would often add a line or two in their own hand. Soon the personal letters of important men began to be collected. Cicero and Pliny, the most famous Roman letter writers, and their secretaries kept copies of letters they thought worth keeping and glued them together in **volūmina**.

Part of an epitaph praising a secretary.

Over nine hundred letters written by Cicero (106–43 BC), the famous orator and lawyer, have survived. Some of these, like newsletters, provide official and unofficial, public and private, views on current politics; others deal with personal and cultural matters. Some of Cicero's letters are private and were written without any thought of publication; others clearly have a wider circulation in mind. The letters discuss all that is in the writer's mind, in a lively, colloquial, and immediate style, much as in a modern journal. After Cicero no one could compose a letter without being conscious of the established epistolary form. It was to serve as a model for many Roman writers, including Pliny the Younger.

The letters of Pliny the Younger (*c.* AD 61 – *c.*112) resemble Cicero's in that they cover a wide range of topics and reflect the life, interests, and personality of their author. However, Pliny's letters, more so than Cicero's, were written self-consciously and selectively, with a view to future publication. The letters are fluent, elegant, and polished. From the hundreds of letters that have been preserved, we get an exceptionally vivid picture of the private lives of the Romans. The letters of both Cicero and Pliny show the results of a thorough education in rhetoric. Both men express themselves so well that their letters belong to the field of literature.

Distinct literary categories, or genres of literature, were established by the Greeks and had become traditional by Roman times – history, philosophy, oratory, comedy, tragedy, epic, pastoral, lyric, and didactic or instructive poetry. The Romans themselves claimed only one new invention, verse satire. Today, however, letter writing is also a recognized genre of Latin literature and, according to some critics, it is, next to satire, Rome's most distinctive literary legacy.

A Roman letter follows a conventional structure: it is expected to have a greeting, a body, and a valediction. The letter begins with the writer's name (in the nominative case) followed by the recipient's name (in the dative case). The next line generally reads **SAL**, **SD**, or **SPD** for **salūtem**, **salūtem dīcit**, or **salūtem plūrimam dīcit**. In the body of the letter the Romans often, although not always, put the verbs in the tense which would be the actual time when the letter was read, not the tense appropriate at the time of writing;

Cicero

for example, **scrībēbam** often means "I am writing." This is called the epistolary tense. After the message, the writer often uses formulaic phrases of courtesy or affection as a conclusion, for example **SVBE** (**sī valēs, bene est**), **valē**, or **cūrā ut valeās**. Since the sender's name has already appeared in the salutation, the letter is not signed at the end. The use of stylized opening and closing phrases injects a tone of formality even in personal letters.

As a genre, Roman letters often have certain stylistic characteristics in common, as well. Each letter is normally confined to a single theme. Consistency of literary style – the color and pattern of language and the tone or feeling – is also characteristic. Simplicity of language is combined with oratorical artifice in word order and structure. A young man once asked Pliny for a course of study. Pliny suggested that letter writing would be a valuable element in the proposed curriculum: "I know that your chief interest is law, but that is not a reason for advising you to limit yourself to this style … I should like you sometimes to take a passage of history or turn your attention to letter writing, for often history, in a speech, calls for a narrative or poetic description; and letters develop brevity and simplicity of style."

A publishing trade existed in Rome but, with duplication of works limited to the output of slaves copying by hand, publication was not on a great enough scale to provide authors with an income. The motive for publishing literary works, including letters, was not money but literary prestige, **dignitās**. However, whether for publication or not, Roman letters allowed both their writers and their readers to share in the enjoyment of well-written, entertaining correspondence.

Vocabulary checklist 46

clādēs, clādis, f.	*disaster*
iūdicō, iūdicāre, iūdicāvī, iūdicātus	*judge*
lapis, lapidis, m.	*stone*
lūmen, lūminis, n.	*light*
minus	*less*
paulum	*a little, slightly*
quisquis	*whoever*
quidquid (also spelled quicquid)	*whatever*
reliquus, reliqua, reliquum	*remaining, the rest*
requīrō, requīrere, requīsīvī	*ask, seek*
somnus, somnī, m.	*sleep*
sternō, sternere, strāvī, strātus	*lay low, knock over*
tēctum, tēctī, n.	*building*
ultrā	*further*

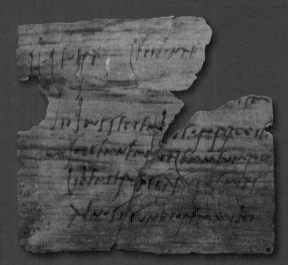

A letter found in a military camp in Britain.

LVDI

Stage 47

The following narrative, told partly in Latin and partly in translation, comes from Book Five of Virgil's *Aeneid*.

Map showing the voyage of Aeneas.

During their wanderings after the destruction of Troy, Aeneas and his Trojan followers have arrived at the island of Sicily, where Aeneas' father Anchises is buried. They decide to mark the anniversary of Anchises' death by holding a festival of games in his honor.

certāmen

I

First is the race between four ships,
Picked from the whole fleet, well-matched with heavy oars:
The speedy *Pristis*, with a keen crew led by Mnestheus;
Massive *Chimaera*, huge as a city, commanded by Gyas;
The large *Centaur*, which carries Sergestus,
And sea-blue *Scylla*, with Cloanthus as captain.

II

est procul in pelagō saxum spūmantia contrā
lītora, quod **tumidīs*** summersum tunditur ōlim

---

*Some noun-and-adjective phrases, in which an adjective is separated by one word or more from the noun which it describes, are shown in **boldface**.

spūmantia: spūmāre *foam*
contrā *opposite*
tumidīs: tumidus *swollen*
tunditur: tundere *beat, buffet*
ōlim *sometimes*
flūctibus: flūctus *wave*
hībernī: hībernus *wintry, of winter*
condunt: condere *hide*
hībernī condunt ubi = ubi hībernī ... condunt
Cōrī: Cōrus *Northwest wind*
tranquillō: tranquillum *calm weather*
attollitur: attollī *rise*
viridem: viridis *green*
frondentī: frondēns *leafy*
īlice: īlex *oak tree*
cōnstituit: cōnstituere *set up, place*
circumflectere cursūs: circumflectere cursum *turn one's course around*

flūctibus, hībernī condunt ubi sīdera Cōrī;
tranquillō silet immōtāque attollitur undā.
hīc viridem **Aenēās** frondentī ex īlice mētam   5
cōnstituit signum nautīs **pater**, unde revertī
scīrent et longōs ubi circumflectere cursūs.
   inde ubi clāra dedit sonitum tuba, **fīnibus** omnēs
(haud mora) prōsiluēre **suīs**; ferit aethera clāmor
nauticus, adductīs spūmant freta versa lacertīs.   10
   effugit ante aliōs prīmīsque ēlābitur undīs
turbam inter fremitumque Gyās; quem deinde Cloanthus
cōnsequitur, melior rēmīs, sed pondere pīnus
tarda tenet. post hōs aequō discrīmine Pristis
Centaurusque locum tendunt superāre priōrem;   15
et nunc Pristis habet, nunc victam praeterit ingēns
Centaurus, nunc ūnā ambae iūnctīsque feruntur
frontibus et longā sulcant vada salsa carīnā.

clāra: **clārus** *loud* (literally *clear*)
fīnibus: **fīnis** *starting place*
ferit: **ferīre** *strike*
nauticus *made by the sailors*
adductīs: **addūcere** *pull, draw up (to the chest)*
freta: **fretum** *water, sea*
versa: **vertere** *churn up*
fremitum: **fremitus** *noise, din*
cōnsequitur: **cōnsequī** *follow, chase*
pīnus *pine tree, i.e. boat (made from pine wood)*
tarda: **tardus** *slow*
tenet: **tenēre** *hold back*
aequō discrīmine *at an equal distance (from the leaders)*
tendunt: **tendere** *strain, strive*
superāre *achieve, win*
iūnctīs: **iūnctus** *side by side*
frontibus: **frōns** *prow*
sulcant: **sulcāre** *plow through*
vada: **vadum** *water*
salsa: **salsus** *salty*
carīnā: **carīna** *keel*

immōtā ... attollitur undā.

Questions

1 Where is the rock? What happens to it when the weather is stormy? What happens in calm weather?

2 What does Aeneas place on the rock? Why? Which noun in lines 5–7 emphasizes Aeneas' position of responsibility?

3 What is the starting signal? What do the words **haud mora** and **prōsiluēre** (line 9) indicate about the manner in which the competitors move off?

4 What does Virgil say in lines 9–10 about (a) the shouting of the sailors, (b) the appearance of the sea, (c) the movements of the oarsmen?

5 Who takes the lead?

6 Who comes next? What advantage does he have, and what disadvantage?

7 Which two ships are struggling for third place? What is happening at each of the three stages of the struggle, introduced by **nunc ... nunc ... nunc** (lines 16–17)?

8 The verb **sulcāre** (**sulcant**, line 18) literally means "to drive a furrow." In what way is it appropriate to the description of the ships' course?

Gyās et Cloanthus

I

    They were nearing the rock, close to the turning point,
When Gyas, leading at the halfway mark,
Cried out to his helmsman Menoetes: "What are you doing?
Don't wander so far to the right! Keep over this way!
Run close to the rock, let the oars on the port side graze it!
The rest can stay out to sea, if they want." But Menoetes,
Fearing a hidden reef, turned the prow to the open water.
"Where are you off to?" cried Gyas again. "Make for the rock!"
And looking round as he shouted, he saw Cloanthus,
Hard on his tail, cutting in between him and the rock.
Cloanthus, scraping through on the inside, took the lead
And reached safe water, leaving the turning post far behind.

II

tum vērō exarsit iuvenī dolor ossibus ingēns
nec lacrimīs caruēre genae, sēgnemque Menoetēn
in mare praecipitem puppī dēturbat ab altā;
ipse gubernāclō rēctor subit, ipse magister
hortāturque virōs clāvumque ad lītora torquet.   5
at **gravis*** ut fundō vix tandem redditus īmō est
iam senior madidāque fluēns in veste **Menoetēs**
summa petit scopulī siccāque in rūpe resēdit.
illum et lābentem Teucrī et rīsēre natantem
et salsōs rīdent revomentem pectore flūctūs.   10

exarsit: exardēre *blaze up*
ossibus: os *bone*
sēgnem: sēgnis *timid, unenterprising*
Menoetēn Greek accusative of **Menoetēs**
puppī: puppis *stern, poop*
dēturbat: dēturbāre *push, send flying*
gubernāclō = gubernāculō: gubernāclum *helm, steering oar*
rēctor *helmsman*
subit: subīre *take over*
magister *pilot*
clāvum: clāvus *tiller, helm*
torquet: torquēre *turn*
ut *when*
fundō: fundus *depth*
vix tandem *at long last*
īmō: īmus *lowest*
senior *elderly*
fluēns *dripping, streaming*
scopulī: scopulus *rock*
resēdit: resīdere *sit down, sink down*
Teucrī *Trojans*
revomentem: revomere *vomit up*
pectore: pectus *chest*

Questions

1 Who is the **iuvenis** (line 1)? What does he do to Menoetes in lines 2–3?

2 Who replaces Menoetes as helmsman? What are his first actions on taking over?

3 Which words and phrases in line 6 indicate that Menoetes (a) went a long way down, (b) did not resurface for some time, (c) could do nothing about getting to the surface himself but could only wait for the sea to buoy him up?

4 Why do you think Virgil includes the phrase **iam senior** (line 7) in his description of Menoetes? Which word in line 6 is partly explained by the phrase **madidāque fluēns in veste** in line 7?

5 What did Menoetes do as soon as he had resurfaced?

6 What three actions of Menoetes are described in lines 9–10? Do the Trojans show any sympathy for him? Does Virgil?

Competitors in a boat race.

*Some noun-and-adjective phrases, in which an adjective is separated by one word or more from the noun which it describes, are shown in **boldface**.

Sergestus et Mnēstheus

I

And now the two tailenders, Mnestheus and Sergestus,
Are fired with a joyful hope of catching Gyas.
As they reach the rock, Sergestus is in the lead,
Though not by as much as a boat-length; his bows are in front,
But his stern is overlapped by the eager *Pristis*.
And Mnestheus, pacing between his lines of rowers,
Is driving them on: "Now pull with your oars;
Once you were comrades of Hector, and when Troy fell
You became my chosen companions; now summon your strength,
Now summon the courage you showed on the African sandbanks,
The Ionian sea, the racing waves of Greece.
I can hope no longer now to finish first
(Though perhaps … but victory lies in the hand of Neptune) –
Yet to come in last, my friends, would be shameful;
Prevent the disgrace!" And his men, with a mighty heave,
Pulled hard on their oars; the whole ship shook with their efforts;
The sea raced by beneath them, their throats and limbs
Were gripped by breathless exertion, they streamed with sweat.

II

attulit ipse virīs optātum cāsus honōrem.
namque **furēns animī** dum prōram ad saxa suburget
interior spatiōque subit **Sergestus** inīquō,
īnfēlīx saxīs in prōcurrentibus haesit.
cōnsurgunt nautae et magnō clāmōre morantur   5
ferrātāsque trudēs et acūtā cuspide contōs
expediunt frāctōsque legunt in gurgite rēmōs.

cāsus *chance*
furēns animī
  furiously determined,
  with furious eagerness
prōram: prōra *prow*
suburget: suburgēre
  drive … up close
interior *in the inside*
subit: subīre *approach*
inīquō: inīquus *narrow,*
  dangerous
prōcurrentibus: prōcurrere
  project
cōnsurgunt: cōnsurgere
  jump up
morantur: morārī
  hold (the ship) steady
ferrātās: ferrātus *tipped*
  with iron
trudēs: trudis *pole*
acūtā: acūtus *sharp*
cuspide: cuspis *point*
contōs: contus *pole, rod*
expediunt: expedīre
  bring out, get out
legunt: legere *gather up*

About the language 1: more about the ablative

1 From Unit 1 on, you have met sentences like these:

> sacerdōs **ā templō** discessit.
> *The priest departed from the temple.*

> servī **in agrīs** labōrābant.
> *The slaves were working in the fields.*

In these sentences, "from" is expressed by one of the prepositions **ā**, **ab**, **ē**, or **ex**, while "in" is expressed by the preposition **in**. Each preposition is followed by a noun in the ablative case.

2 In verse, however, the idea of "in" and "from" is often expressed by the ablative case alone, without any preposition:

> ipse diem noctemque negat discernere **caelō**... Palinūrus.
> *Palinurus himself says he cannot distinguish day and night in the sky.*

> **fīnibus** omnēs ... prōsiluēre **suīs**.
> *They all leapt forward from their starting places.*

> ... **immōtā**que attollitur **undā**.
> *... and it rises up from the still water.*

Further examples:

a nōbīs tempus erat patriā discēdere cārā.
b flūmine nant piscēs, arbore cantat avis.
c iamque senex laetus nostrā proficīscitur urbe.
d dīcitur immēnsā Cyclōps habitāre cavernā.

victor

I

at laetus Mnēstheus successūque ācrior ipsō
prōna petit maria et pelagō dēcurrit apertō.
et prīmum in scopulō **lūctantem** dēserit altō
Sergestum brevibusque vadīs frūstrāque vocantem
auxilia et frāctīs discentem currere rēmīs.   5
inde Gyān ipsamque ingentī mōle Chimaeram
cōnsequitur; cēdit, quoniam spoliāta magistrō est.

successū: successus *success*
ācrior: ācer *eager, excited*
prōna: prōnus *easy*
lūctantem: lūctārī *struggle*
dēcurrit: dēcurrere *speed, race*
dēserit: dēserere *leave behind*
currere *race, row*
Gyān Greek accusative of **Gyās**
mōle: mōlēs *bulk*
quoniam *since*
spoliāta … est: spoliāre *deprive*

Questions

1 Why does Mnestheus feel encouraged at this point?

2 Who is the first competitor to be overtaken by Mnestheus? What is he doing, and trying to do?

3 Whom does Mnestheus overtake next? Why is he able to do so?

II

sōlus iamque **ipsō** superest in **fīne** Cloanthus:
quem petit et summīs adnīxus vīribus urget.
tum vērō ingeminat clāmor cūnctīque sequentem
īnstīgant studiīs, resonatque fragōribus aethēr.
hī proprium decus et partum indignantur honōrem   5
nī teneant, vītamque volunt prō laude pacīscī;
hōs successus alit: possunt, quia posse videntur.
et fors aequātīs cēpissent praemia rōstrīs,
nī palmās pontō tendēns utrāsque Cloanthus
fūdissetque precēs dīvōsque in vōta vocāsset: 10
"dī, quibus imperium est pelagī, quōrum aequora currō,
vōbīs laetus ego **hōc** candentem in **lītore** taurum
cōnstituam ante ārās vōtī reus, extaque salsōs
prōiciam in flūctūs et vīna liquentia fundam."
dīxit, eumque īmīs sub flūctibus audiit omnis   15
Nēreidum Phorcīque chorus Panopēaque virgō,
et pater ipse manū magnā Portūnus euntem
impulit: illa Notō citius volucrīque sagittā
ad terram fugit et portū sē condidit altō.

adnīxus: adnītī *strain, exert oneself*
urget: urgēre *pursue, press upon*
cūnctī: cūnctus *all*
īnstīgant: īnstīgāre *urge on*
studiīs: studium *shout of support, cheer*
resonat: resonāre *resound*
fragōribus: fragor *shout*
proprium: proprius *one's own, that belongs to one*
decus *glory*
partum: parere *gain, win*
indignantur: indignārī *feel shame, think it shameful*
nī = nisi
indignantur … nī teneant *think it shameful if they do not hold on to*
pacīscī *exchange, bargain*
alit: alere *encourage*
fors *perhaps*
aequātīs: aequātus *level, side by side*
rōstrīs: rōstrum *prow*
palmās: palma *hand (literally palm)*
tendēns: tendere *stretch out*
fūdisset: fundere *pour out*

in vōta *to (hear) his vow*
vocāsset = vocāvisset
candentem: candēns *gleaming white*
vōtī reus *bound by one's vow, in payment of one's vow*
prōiciam: prōicere *cast (as an offering)*
liquentia: liquēre *flow*
Nēreidum: Nēreis *sea nymph*
Phorcī: Phorcus *Phorcus (a sea god)*
Panopēa *Panopea (one of the sea nymphs)*
Portūnus *Portunus (god of harbors)*
citius: citō *quickly*
volucrī: volucer *winged, swift*
sagittā: sagitta *arrow*
sē condidit: sē condere *bring oneself to rest*

Questions

A 1 Which two captains are involved in the final dash for victory? Which of them has the better chance, and which phrase in line 1 emphasizes this?

  2 What happens in line 3 to the noise level? Suggest a reason for this. Which contestant do the spectators support?

  3 Why are Cloanthus' men especially anxious not to be beaten? How deeply (according to Virgil) do they care about winning?

  4 What psychological advantages do Mnestheus and his men have?

  5 What would the result have been, but for Cloanthus' prayer?

  6 Which gods does Cloanthus address? What three promises does he make? Does his prayer imply a request as well as a promise?

  7 Who heard the prayer? What help did Cloanthus receive?

  8 Which word in lines 17–18 has Virgil placed in an especially emphatic position, and why?

  9 What is the speed of Cloanthus' boat compared to? What is the result of Portunus' action?

B 1 To what extent (if any) do the *personalities* of the four captains influence the action and result of the race?

  2 Consider how **victor II** should be read aloud. At which point or points should the reading be liveliest? How should Cloanthus' prayer be read? Are there any points where the reading should be calm or quiet?

About the language 2: poetic plurals

1 Study the following quotations from Latin verse:

> ōraque caeruleā patrium clāmantia nōmen
> excipiuntur aquā. (*Ovid*)
> *And his mouth, shouting the name of his father,*
> *was received by the dark blue water.*

> per amīca **silentia** lūnae (*Virgil*)
> *through the friendly silence of the moonlight*

> cōnscendit furibunda **rogōs**. (*Virgil*)
> *She climbed the funeral pyre in a mad frenzy.*

In each of these phrases or sentences, the poet uses a **plural noun** (**ōra**, **silentia**, **rogōs**) with a **singular meaning** (*mouth, silence, pyre*). A similar use of the plural is sometimes found in English verse:

> And it is clear to my long-searching eyes
> That love at last has might upon the **skies**.

> While Shasta signals to Alaskan **seas**
> That watch old sluggish glaciers downwards creep.

2 From each of the following lines in Stage 47, pick out one example of a plural noun used with a singular meaning:

a **victor I** (page 226), line 5.
b **victor II** (page 226), line 14.

Practicing the language

1 Match each word in the top list with a word of similar meaning taken from the bottom list.

For example: aedificāre   exstruere

castīgāre, dēcipere, dīvitiae, dulcis, ignis, nocēre, nōn, ōlim, quia, scelus, spernere, superāre, timēre, tūtus, vērō

suāvis, quod, culpāre, laedere, quidem, vincere, fallere, contemnere, haud, opēs, verērī, incolumis, facinus, quondam, incendium

2 Complete each sentence with the correct word and then translate.

    a sī mē rogāvissēs, ... (dūxissem, respondissem)

    b sī Īcarus mandātīs patris pāruisset, nōn in mare . . . . (cecidisset, crēdidisset)

    c sī exercituī nostrō subvēnissētis, vōbīs magnum praemium . . . . (dedissēmus, exstrūxissēmus)

    d sī in Circō heri adfuissēs, spectāculō . . . . (dēlectātus essēs, dēpositus essēs)

    e nisi senex ā lībertīs dēfēnsus esset, latrōnēs eum . . . . (exiissent, occīdissent)

3 Translate each sentence, then replace the verb in **boldface** with the correct form of the verb in parentheses, keeping the same person, tense, etc. Refer if necessary to the Vocabulary at the end of the book, and to the tables of deponent verbs on pages 276–278.

    For example: cōnsul pauca verba **dīxit**. (loquī)
    This becomes: cōnsul pauca verba **locūtus est**.
                    The consul said a few words.

    a dux nautās **incitābat**. (hortārī)

    b captīvus quidem sum; sed effugere **temptābō**. (cōnārī)

    c crās ab hōc oppidō **discēdēmus**. (proficīscī)

    d **prōmīsī** mē pecūniam mox redditūrum esse. (pollicērī)

    e mīlitēs arma nova **comparāvērunt**. (adipīscī)

    f cognōscere volēbam num omnēs nūntiī **revēnissent**. (regredī)

4 Complete each sentence with the most suitable word from the box below, and then translate. Refer to the story on pages 220–227 where necessary.

ēiceret	taurum	tuba	relictō	parum

    a simulatque . . . . sonuit, omnēs nāvēs prōsiluērunt.

    b iuvenis adeō īrātus erat ut senem ē nāve . . . .

    c Sergestus, quī . . . . cautē nāvigābat, in scopulum incurrit.

    d saxō . . . . , nautae cursum ad lītus dīrigēbant.

    e Cloanthus pollicitus est sē . . . . deīs sacrificātūrum esse.

The chariot race in Homer's *Iliad*

When Virgil wrote the *Aeneid*, part of his inspiration came from two famous epic poems of ancient Greece, the *Iliad* and *Odyssey* of Homer. Throughout his poem, Virgil uses ideas, incidents, and phrases from Homer, but reshapes them, combines them with his own subject matter, and handles them in his own style, to produce a poem which in some ways is very similar to the *Iliad* and *Odyssey*, but in other ways is utterly different.

The following extracts from Book Twenty-three of Homer's *Iliad* describe the chariot race which took place during the funeral games held by the Achaians (Greeks) outside the walls of Troy during the Trojan War. Homer's account provided Virgil with some of the raw material for his description of the boat race. The chief characters involved are:

Achilleus (often known as Achilles), who had organized the games in honor of his dead friend Patroklos;

Antilochos son of Nestor and grandson of Neleus;

Diomedes son of Tydeus, hated by the god Phoibos Apollo but befriended and supported by the goddess Athene; he drives a team of horses which he has captured from the Trojans, and his companion is named Sthenelos;

Eumelos son of Admetos (sometimes described as son of Pheres);

Menelaos son of Atreus (Atreides), brother of the great king Agamemnon, whose mare Aithe he has borrowed for the chariot race.

The winner of the race is to receive as his prize a skilled slave woman and a huge tripod with ear-shaped handles.

They stood in line for the start, and Achilleus showed them the turn-post
far away on the level plain, and beside it he stationed
a judge, Phoinix the godlike, the follower of his father …
    Then all held their whips high-lifted above their horses,
then struck with the whip thongs and in words urged their horses onward   5
into speed. Rapidly they made their way over the flat land
and presently were far away from the ships. The dust lifting
clung beneath the horses' chests like a cloud or a stormwhirl.
Their manes streamed along the blast of the wind, …
                                                        … the drivers   10
stood in the chariots, with the spirit beating in each man
with the strain to win, and each was calling aloud upon his own
horses, and the horses flew through the dust of the flat land.
But as the rapid horses were running the last of the race-course
back, and toward the grey sea, then the mettle of each began to   15
show itself, and the field of horses strung out, and before long
out in front was the swift-stepping team of the son of Pheres,
Eumelos, and after him the stallions of Diomedes,

230   Stage 47

the Trojan horses, not far behind at all, but close on him,
for they seemed forever on the point of climbing his chariot   20
and the wind of them was hot on the back and on the broad shoulders
of Eumelos. They lowered their heads and flew close after him.

   And how he might have passed him or run to a doubtful decision,
had not Phoibos Apollo been angry with Diomedes,
Tydeus' son, and dashed the shining whip from his hands, so   25
that the tears began to stream from his eyes, for his anger
as he watched how the mares of Eumelos drew far ahead of him
while his own horses ran without the whip and were slowed. Yet
Athene did not fail to see the foul play of Apollo
on Tydeus' son. She swept in speed to the shepherd of the people   30
and gave him back his whip, and inspired strength into his horses.
Then in her wrath she went on after the son of Admetos
and she, a goddess, smashed his chariot yoke, and his horses
ran on either side of the way, the pole dragged and Eumelos
himself was sent spinning out beside the wheel of the chariot   35
so that his elbows were all torn, and his mouth, and his nostrils,
and his forehead was lacerated about the brows, and his eyes
filled with tears, and the springing voice was held fast within him.

   Then the son of Tydeus, turning his single-foot horses past him,
went far out in front of the others, seeing that Athene   40
had inspired strength in his horses and to himself gave the glory.

The plain of Troy.

After him came the son of Atreus, fair-haired Menelaos.
But Antilochos cried out aloud to his father's horses:
"Come on, you two. Pull, as fast as you can! I am not
trying to make you match your speed with the speed of those others, 45
the horses of Tydeus' valiant son, to whom now Athene
has granted speed and to their rider has given the glory.

But make your burst to catch the horses of the son of Atreus
nor let them leave you behind, for fear Aithe who is female
may shower you in mockery. Are you falling back, my brave horses?   *50*
For I will tell you this, and it will be a thing accomplished.
There will be no more care for you from the shepherd of the people,
Nestor, but he will slaughter you out of hand with the edge
of bronze, if we win the meaner prize because you are unwilling.
Keep on close after him and make all the speed you are able.   *55*
I myself shall know what to do and contrive it, so that
we get by in the narrow place of the way. He will not escape me."
    So he spoke, and they fearing the angry voice of their master
ran harder for a little while, and presently after this
battle-stubborn Antilochos saw where the hollow way narrowed.   *60*
There was a break in the ground where winter water had gathered
and broken out of the road, and made a sunken place all about.
Menelaos shrinking from a collision of chariots steered there,
but Antilochos also turned out his single-foot horses
from the road, and bore a little way aside, and went after him;   *65*
and the son of Atreus was frightened and called out aloud to Antilochos:
"Antilochos, this is reckless horsemanship. Hold in your horses.
The way is narrow here, it will soon be wider for passing.
Be careful not to crash your chariot and wreck both of us."
    So he spoke, but Antilochos drove on all the harder   *70*
with a whiplash for greater speed, as if he had never heard him.
As far as is the range of a discus swung from the shoulder
and thrown by a stripling who tries out the strength of his young manhood,
so far they ran even, but then the mares of Atreides gave way
and fell back, for he of his own will slackened his driving   *75*
for fear that in the road the single-foot horses might crash
and overturn the strong-fabricated chariots, and the men
themselves go down in the dust through their hard striving for victory.
But Menelaos of the fair hair called to him in anger:
"Antilochos, there is no other man more cursed than you are.   *80*
Damn you. We Achaians lied when we said you had good sense.
Even so, you will not get this prize without having to take oath."

*A Greek two-
horse chariot.*

*Fragment of a
Greek painted
vase showing
spectators
watching a
chariot race.*

(The finish:)

… and now Tydeus' son in his rapid course was close on them
and he lashed them always with the whipstroke from the shoulder. His horses
still lifted their feet light and high as they made their swift passage.   85
Dust flying splashed always the charioteer, and the chariot
that was overlaid with gold and tin still rolled hard after
the flying feet of the horses, and in their wake there was not much
trace from the running rims of the wheels left in the thin dust.
The horses came in running hard. Diomedes stopped them   90
in the middle of where the men were assembled, with the dense sweat starting
and dripping to the ground from neck and chest of his horses.
He himself vaulted down to the ground from his shining chariot
and leaned his whip against the yoke. Nor did strong Sthenelos
delay, but made haste to take up the prizes, and gave the woman   95
to his high-hearted companions to lead away and the tripod
with ears to carry, while Diomedes set free the horses.
　　After him Neleian Antilochos drove in his horses,
having passed Menelaos, not by speed but by taking advantage.
But even Menelaos held fast his horses close on him …   100
… At first he was left behind the length of a discus
thrown, but was overhauling him fast, with Aithe
of the fair mane, Agamemnon's mare, putting on a strong burst.
If both of them had had to run the course any further,
Menelaos would have passed him, and there could have been no argument …   105
　　Last and behind them all came in the son of Admetos
dragging his fine chariot and driving his horses before him.

(translation by Richmond Lattimore)

Questions

1 What part do the gods play in Homer's chariot race? In what way does it differ from the part they played in Virgil's boat race?

2 Compare the incident at the "narrow place" (lines 43–82) with the incident at the rock in **Sergestus et Mnēstheus I** and **II** and **victor I**. What are the similarities and differences between the two incidents?

3 What other points of similarity do you notice between Virgil's account of the boat race and Homer's account of the chariot race?

Vocabulary checklist 47

aequor, aequoris, n.	*breeze, air*
careō, carēre, caruī	*lack, be without*
flūctus, flūctūs, m.	*wave*
lābor, lābī, lāpsus sum	*fall, glide; pass by*
laus, laudis, f.	*praise, fame*
mora, morae, f.	*delay*
optō, optāre, optāvī, optātus	*pray for, long for*
parum	*too little*
pondus, ponderis, n.	*weight*
sagitta, sagittae, f.	*arrow*
spatium, spatiī, n.	*space, distance*
vīrēs, vīrium, f. pl.	*strength*

Homer.

NERO ET AGRIPPINA

Stage 48

The two chief characters in this Stage are the Emperor Nero, who ruled from AD 54 to AD 68, and his mother Agrippina. The Latin text is based on the account written by Tacitus in his *Annals* (a history of Rome from the accession of the Emperor Tiberius to the death of Nero).

Agrippina was an able, ambitious, and unscrupulous woman. In AD 54 she arranged the murder of her husband, the Emperor Claudius, by poison. Then with the help of Burrus, the commander of the praetorian guard, she had Nero proclaimed emperor, although he was still only a youth of sixteen.

At first Agrippina enjoyed not only great prestige as the emperor's mother but also considerable power. Possible rivals to the young emperor were removed quickly, efficiently, and ruthlessly. But before long, Agrippina's power and influence were considerably weakened by Burrus and Nero's tutor Seneca, who established themselves as Nero's chief advisers. They handled Nero skillfully, mixing their advice with flattery, and in this way they controlled most of the major decisions about the government of Rome and the empire.

As time went on, however, Nero became more and more interested in getting his own way. He also increasingly hated his mother, partly because he had fallen violently in love with the beautiful Poppaea Sabina, and was determined to marry her, while his mother was equally determined that he should not. In the following pages, the outcome of their struggle is described.

Coin showing Nero and Agrippina.

īnsidiae

I

at Nerō, quī vetustāte imperiī fiēbat iam audācior, amōre Poppaeae magis magisque accēnsus, postrēmō mātrem interficere cōnstituit; ministrōs convocātōs cōnsuluit utrum venēnō an ferrō vel quā aliā vī ūterētur. placuit prīmō venēnum. sī tamen inter epulās prīncipis venēnum darētur, mors cāsuī assignārī nōn poterat, nam similī 5 exitiō Britannicus anteā perierat; atque Agrippīna ipsa praesūmendō remēdia mūnierat corpus. quō modō vīs et caedēs cēlārentur nēmō excōgitāre poterat; et metuēbat Nerō nē quis tantō facinorī dēlēctus iussa sperneret.

vetustāte: vetustās *length, duration*
imperiī: imperium *rule, reign*
accēnsus *inflamed, on fire*
quā: quī *some*
epulās: epulae *feast, banquet*
assignārī: assignāre *attribute, put down to*
Britannicus *Britannicus (the Emperor Claudius' son, poisoned on Nero's orders)*
praesūmendō: praesūmere *take in advance*
caedēs *murder*
metuēbat: metuere *be afraid, fear*
nē quis *lest anyone, that anyone*
dēlēctus: dēligere *choose, select*
sperneret: spernere *disobey, disregard*

tandem Anicētus lībertus, cui Agrippīna odiō erat, cōnsilium   *10*
callidum prōposuit: nāvem posse compōnī cuius pars, in ipsō
marī per artem solūta, Agrippīnam ēiceret ignāram. subrīdēns
Anicētus "nihil" inquit, "tam capāx fortuitōrum quam mare; et sī
naufragiō Agrippīna perierit, quis adeō suspīciōsus erit ut scelerī
id assignet quod ventī et flūctūs fēcerint? mātre dēfūnctā, facile   *15*
erit prīncipī pietātem ostendere templō exstruendō vel ad ārās
sacrificandō."

compōnī: compōnere
    construct
per artem *deliberately, by*
    design
ignārum: ignārus
    unsuspecting
subrīdēns: subrīdēre *smile,*
    smirk
capāx *liable to, full of*
fortuitōrum: fortuita
    accidents
dēfūnctā: dēfūnctus *dead*

ministrōs convocātōs cōnsuluit utrum venēnō an ferrō vel quā aliā vī ūterētur.

Questions

1 What two reasons, according to Tacitus, led Nero to make up his mind to kill his mother?

2 Whose advice did Nero seek? What question did he put to them?

3 What were the two disadvantages of poison? What were the two disadvantages of violence?

4 Who offered a solution to the problem? What plan did he suggest?

5 Why (according to Anicetus) would his plan be unlikely to arouse suspicion? What further
steps did he suggest to convince the people of Nero's innocence?

II

placuit Nerōnī callid24tās Anicētī; praetereā occāsiō optima reī temptandae aderat, nam Nerō illō tempore Bāiās ad diem fēstum celebrandum vīsitābat. illūc mātrem ēlicuit; advenientī in itinere obviam iit; excēpit manū et complexū; ad vīllam eius maritīmam, Baulōs nōmine, dūxit. stābat prope vīllam nāvis ōrnātissima, quasi 5 ad mātrem prīncipis honōrandam; invītāta est Agrippīna ad epūlās Bāiīs parātās, ut facinus nocte ac tenebrīs cēlārētur. rūmōre tamen īnsidiārum per aliquem prōditōrem audītō, Agrippīna incerta prīmō num crēderet, tandem Bāiās lectīcā vecta est. ibi blanditiae sublevāvēre metum: cōmiter excepta, iuxtā Nerōnem ipsum ad 10 cēnam collocāta est. Nerō modo familiāritāte iuvenīlī sē gerēbat, modo graviter loquēbātur. tandem, cēnā multīs sermōnibus diū prōductā, prōsequitur Agrippīnam abeuntem, artius oculīs et pectorī haerēns, vel ad simulātiōnem explendam vel quod peritūrae mātris suprēmus aspectus saevum animum eius retinēbat. 15

Bāiās: Bāiae *Baiae (seaside resort)*
complexū: complexus *embrace*
maritīmam: maritīmus *seaside, by the sea*
Baulōs: Baulī *Bauli (villa owned by Agrippina)*
Bāiīs *at Baiae*
prōditōrem: prōditor *betrayer, informer*
Bāiās (line 9) *to Baiae*
sublevāvēre: sublevāre *remove, relieve*
familiāritāte: familiāritās *friendliness*
iuvenīlī: iuvenīlis *youthful*
prōductā: prōdūcere *prolong, continue*
artius *particularly closely*
haerēns: haerēre *linger, cling*
simulātiōnem: simulātiō *pretense, playacting*
explendam: explēre *complete, put final touch to*
suprēmus *last*
aspectus *sight*
retinēbat: retinēre *restrain, check*

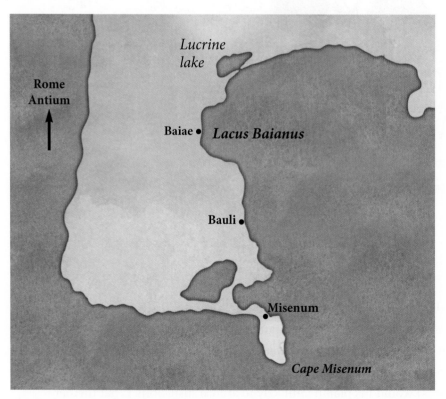

The coast near Baiae.

The gulf of Baiae.

Questions

1 What did Nero think of Anicetus' suggestion? Why did he have a good opportunity to put the plan into operation?

2 What did Nero do when Agrippina arrived? Suggest a reason for his behavior.

3 What method of travel was available to Agrippina at Bauli? What did Nero invite her to do? Why was it important to Nero that his mother's journey to Baiae should take place in the evening?

4 What happened at this point to upset Nero's plan? What was Agrippina's first reaction to the information? How did she eventually travel to Baiae?

5 In what way did her feelings change at Baiae? How was she treated there? How did Nero vary his manner during the feast?

6 How did Nero behave on his mother's departure? What two explanations does Tacitus give for this?

1 From Stage 38 on, you have met sentences like these:

> quid faciam?
> *What am I to do?*
>
> quā tē regiōne requīram?
> *In what region am I to search for you?*
>
> utrum captīvōs līberēmus an interficiāmus?
> *Should we free the prisoners or kill them?*

Questions like these are usually known as **deliberative questions**, because the speaker is "deliberating," or wondering what to do.

Further examples:

a quid dīcam?
b unde auxilium petāmus?
c quō mē vertam?
d utrum abeāmus an maneāmus?

2 You have also met sentences like these:

> prīnceps amīcōs rogāvit quid faceret.
> *The emperor asked his friends what he should do.*
>
> pater nesciēbat quā regiōne fīlium requīreret.
> *The father did not know in what region he was to search for his son.*
>
> incertus eram utrum vī an venēnō ūterer.
> *I was uncertain whether to use violence or poison.*

In each of these examples, a deliberative question is being *reported* or *mentioned*. Examples like these are known as **indirect deliberative questions**.

Further examples:

a difficile est Nerōnī scīre quid respondēret.
b lībertum rogābō quō modō rem administrem.
c mīlitēs incertī erant utrum cēderent an resisterent.
d in animō volvēbāmus quāle dōnum rēgī darēmus.

3 Notice that the verb in a deliberative question, whether direct or indirect, is always subjunctive.

naufragium

I

deī noctem sīderibus illūstrem et placidō marī quiētam praebuēre, quasi ad scelus patefaciendum. nec multum erat prōgressa nāvis, duōbus amīcīs Agrippīnae comitantibus ex quibus Crepereius Gallus haud procul gubernāculō adstābat. Acerrōnia ad pedēs Agrippīnae cubitantis recumbēns paenitentiam fīliī per gaudium commemorābat, cum datō signō ruere tēctum multō plumbō grave. pressus Crepereius statim periit: Agrippīna et Acerrōnia ēminentibus lectī parietibus prōtectae sunt. nec dissolūtiō nāvis sequēbātur, turbātīs omnibus et quod plērīque nautae, sceleris ignārī, eōs impediēbant quī cōnsciī erant. hī igitur cōnātī sunt ūnum in latus inclīnāre atque ita nāvem summergere; nōn tamen eīs erat prōmptus in rem subitam cōnsēnsus, et aliī contrā nītentēs dedēre Agrippīnae facultātem lēniter in mare dēscendendī.

5

10

illūstrem: illūstris *bright*
cubitantis: cubitāre *lie down, rest*
paenitentiam: paenitentia *repentance, change of heart*
per gaudium *joyfully*
ruere = ruit: ruere *collapse*
plumbō: plumbum *lead*
pressus: premere *crush*
ēminentibus: ēminēre *project*
parietibus: pariēs *side*
prōtectae sunt: prōtegere *protect*
dissolūtiō *disintegration, breakup*
turbātīs: turbātus *confused*
inclīnāre *lean*
prōmptus *quick*
in rem subitam *to meet the sudden crisis*
cōnsēnsus *agreement*
contrā *in the opposite direction*
nītentēs: nītī *lean*
facultātem: facultās *opportunity*

Agrippina the Younger.

Acerrōnia autem, dum sē Agrippīnam esse imprūdenter
clāmat utque subvenīrētur mātrī prīncipis, contīs et rēmīs
cōnficitur. Agrippīna silēns eōque minus agnita (ūnum tamen
vulnus umerō excēpit) ad lēnunculōs quōsdam nandō pervenit
quī haud procul erant; deinde in Lucrīnum lacum vecta, ad
vīllam suam dūcitur.

ibi cōgitābat quid faceret; animadverterat enim nāvem neque
ventīs ad lītus āctam, neque saxīs impulsam esse, sed summā suī
parte velut terrestre māchināmentum concidisse. observāns etiam
Acerrōniae caedem, simul suum vulnus aspiciēns, sōlum
īnsidiārum remēdium esse putāvit, sī nōn intellegere vidērētur.
mīsit igitur lībertum quī nūntiāret filiō sē benignitāte deōrum et
fortūnā eius ēvāsisse gravem cāsum; ōrāre ut Nerō, quamvīs
perīculō mātris perterritus, vīsendī cūram differret; sibi ad praesēns
quiēte opus esse. atque interim medicāmenta vulnerī adhibet;
imperat quoque ut testāmentum Acerrōniae requīrātur – hoc sōlum
nōn per simulātiōnem.

15 **imprūdenter** *stupidly, foolishly*
subvenīrētur *help should be brought*
cōnficitur: cōnficere *finish off, murder*
20 **eō** *therefore, for this reason*
agnita: agnōscere *recognize*
lēnunculōs: lēnunculus *small boat*
Lucrīnum lacum: Lucrīnus lacus *the Lucrine lake (a lagoon near Baiae)*
āctam: agere *drive*
summā suī parte *from the top downwards* (literally *from its highest part*)
terrestre: terrestris *on land*
māchināmentum *machine, contraption*
concidisse: concidere *collapse*
observāns: observāre *notice, observe*
ēvāsisse: ēvādere *escape*
quamvīs *although*
vīsendī: vīsere *come to visit*
cūram: cūra *trouble, bother*
ad praesēns *for the present, for the moment*

Questions

1 In what way, according to Tacitus, did the gods take sides (or seem to take sides) in the murder attempt?

2 What was Acerronia doing when the roof fell in? Why does Tacitus mention this?

3 What did the conspirators try to do after the original plan misfired? Why were they again unsuccessful?

4 Why do you think Acerronia shouted out that she was Agrippina? Is there more than one possible explanation for her action?

5 What reasons led Agrippina to realize that the shipwreck had been a deliberate attempt on her life? What did she decide was her only hope of safety?

6 In her message, Agrippina described Nero as **perīculō mātris perterritus**. Is this likely to be true? If not, why did Agrippina describe him in this way?

7 What order did Agrippina give? What do you think her reason was?

8 What impression do you gain from this passage of Agrippina's ability and character?

II

at Nerōnī, nūntiōs patrātī facinoris exspectantī, affertur
Agrippīnam ēvāsisse ictū levī vulnerātam. tum pavōre exanimis et
affirmāns iam iamque adfore mātrem ultiōnis avidam, Burrum et
Senecam statim arcessīvit. longum utrīusque silentium; tandem
Seneca respexit Burrum ac rogāvit num mīlitēs caedem Agrippīnae   5
exsequī iubērentur. ille praetōriānōs tōtī Caesarum domuī
obstrictōs esse respondit: "mīlitēs" inquit, "nihil ātrōx adversus
fīliam Germānicī facere audēbunt; efficiat Anicētus prōmissa." quī
haudquāquam haesitat; poscit summam sceleris. ad haec verba
Nerō profitētur illō diē sibi tandem darī imperium auctōremque   10
tantī mūneris esse lībertum; Anicētō imperāvit ut ad vīllam statim
proficīscerētur dūceretque sēcum hominēs fidēlissimōs.

*Members of the
praetorian guard,
the emperor's
personal
bodyguard* (see
pages 252–253).

patrātī: patrāre	*accomplish, commit*
affertur: afferre	*bring news, report*
ictū: ictus	*blow*
exanimis	*out of one's mind*
iam iamque	*at any moment now*
adfore:	future infinitive of **adesse** *be present, arrive*
exsequī	*carry out*
Caesarum: Caesarēs	*the Caesars* (family of the first Roman emperors)
domuī: domus	*family*
obstrictōs esse: obstringere	*bind (with oath of loyalty)*
ātrōx	*violent, dreadful*
Germānicī: Germānicus	*Germanicus* (Agrippina's father, a popular general and member of the imperial family)
prōmissa: prōmissum	*promise*
summam: summa	*full responsibility, supreme command*
profitētur: profitērī	*declare*

Questions

1 Describe Nero's reaction to the news of Agrippina's escape. Compare it with Agrippina's own reaction to the attempt on her life.

2 Why do you think Seneca and Burrus are so silent and unhelpful (lines 4–8)? Why do you think Anicetus is so eager to carry out the deed (lines 8–9)?

3 How does Nero's mood change after Anicetus has taken charge? Explain his comment **illō diē… esse lībertum** (lines 10–11).

About the language 2: historical infinitives

1 From Unit 1 on, you have met sentences like this:

> Pompēiānī rīdēbant, clāmābant, plaudēbant.
> *The Pompeians were laughing, shouting, and applauding.*

2 In Stage 46, you met a different way of expressing the same idea:

> Pompēiānī rīdēre, clāmāre, plaudere.

Further examples:

> māter ōrāre hortārī iubēre ut fugerem.
> *My mother begged, urged, and ordered me to flee.*

> spectāculum horribile in campīs patentibus – sequī fugere occīdī capī.
> *There was a hideous sight on the open plains – men were chasing, were fleeing, were being killed, and were being captured.*

Notice how the *infinitive* of the verb is used in these examples, instead of an indicative tense such as an imperfect, to describe events happening in the past. This is known as the *historical* use of the infinitive (**historical infinitive** for short). It occurs most often in descriptions of lively and rapid action.

3 Further examples:

a omnēs amīcī bibere cantāre saltāre.
b in urbe maximus pavor; aliī ad portās fugere; aliī bona sua in plaustra impōnere; aliī uxōrēs līberōsque quaerere; omnēs viae multitūdine complērī. (*from the historian Sallust*)

percussōrēs

interim vulgātō Agrippīnae perīculō, omnēs, ut quisque audīverat, dēcurrere ad lītus. hī mōlēs, hī proximās scaphās cōnscendere; aliī, quantum corpus sinēbat, prōcēdere in mare; nōnnūllī manūs extendere; omnis ōra complērī questibus, precibus, clāmōre hominum dīversa rogantium aut incerta respondentium; 5
affluere ingēns multitūdō cum lūminibus, atque ubi incolumem esse Agrippīnam vulgātum est, ad grātulandum sēsē expedīre, dōnec aspectū agminis hominum armātōrum et minantium disiectī sunt. Anicētus vīllam mīlitibus circumvenit, effrāctāque iānuā servōs eōs abripit quī obstant, dōnec ad forēs cubiculī 10
venīret; ibi paucī adstābant, cēterīs terrōre irrumpentium exterritīs. cubiculō modicum lūmen inerat et ancillārum ūna; magis ac magis anxia fiēbat Agrippīna quod nēmō ā fīliō vēnisset. abeunte dēnique ancillā, Agrippīna "tu quoque mē dēseris" inquit; tum respicit Anicētum triērarchō et centuriōne 15
comitātum. "quī estis?" inquit. "dīcite mihi quārē hūc missī sītis." nūllum respōnsum; circumsistunt lectum percussōrēs et prior triērarchus fūstī caput eius afflīxit. deinde centuriōnī gladium ad occīdendum dēstringentī Agrippīna prōtendēns uterum "ventrem ferī" exclāmāvit multīsque vulneribus 20
cōnfecta est.

cremāta est eādem nocte convīvālī lectō et exequiīs vīlibus; num īnspexerit mātrem mortuam Nerō (ut multī affirmant) et fōrmam corporis eius admīrātus sit, incertum est. hunc fore suī fīnem multōs ante annōs crēdiderat Agrippīna contempseratque. 25
nam eī rogantī dē fortūnā Nerōnis respondērunt astrologī illum imperātūrum mātremque occīsūrum; atque Agrippīna "occīdat" inquit, "dum imperet."

"dīcite mihi quārē hūc missī sītis."

percussōrēs: percussor assassin
vulgātō: vulgāre make known
ut quisque as soon as each one
hī … hī some … others
mōlēs: mōlēs embankment, seawall
quantum as far as
sinēbat: sinere allow
questibus: questus lamentation, cry of grief
affluere flock to the spot
sēsē expedīre prepare oneself, get ready
disiectī sunt: disicere scatter, disperse
abripit: abripere remove by force
forēs door
terrōre: terror terror
exterritīs: exterrēre frighten away
triērarchō: triērarchus naval captain
circumsistunt: circumsistere take up position around
fūstī: ablative of fūstis
afflīxit: afflīgere strike
prōtendēns: prōtendere thrust forward
uterum: uterus womb
convīvālī: convīvālis dining
exequiīs: exequiae funeral rites
fore = futūrum esse
contempserat: contemnere disregard
imperātūrum (esse): imperāre be emperor
dum provided that

About the language 3: perfect subjunctive passive

1 In Stage 30, you met the perfect indicative passive:

> duo cōnsulēs creātī sunt.
> *Two consuls have been appointed.*

2 In Stage 48, you have met sentences like these:

> puer stultus nescit quot cōnsulēs **creātī sint**.
> *The stupid boy does not know how many consuls have been appointed.*

> dominus cognōscere vult quanta pecūnia **impēnsa sit**.
> *The master wants to find out how much money has been spent.*

The form of the verb in **boldface** is the **perfect subjunctive passive**.

Further examples:

a incertī sumus utrum Agrippīna servāta an necāta sit.
b dīcite mihi quot hostēs captī sint.
c ignōrō quārē ā centuriōne ēlēctus sim.

3 Compare the indicative and subjunctive forms of the perfect passive of **portō**:

perfect passive indicative	*perfect passive subjunctive*
portātus sum	portātus sim
portātus es	portātus sīs
portātus est	portātus sit
portātī sumus	portātī sīmus
portātī estis	portātī sītis
portātī sunt	portātī sint

Perfect subjunctive passive forms of all conjugations are given on page 273 of the Language information section.

4 Study the following examples:

> tam callidus est mercātor ut magnās opēs **adeptus sit.**
> *The merchant is so clever that he has obtained great wealth.*

> iūdex scīre vult num senī umquam **minātī sīmus**.
> *The judge wants to know whether we have ever threatened the old man.*

The words in **boldface** are perfect subjunctive forms of deponent verbs.

Further examples:

a dīc mihi quid patrōnus tibi pollicitus sit.
b scīre volō quārē nūntiī nōndum profectī sint.

Perfect subjunctive forms of deponent verbs are given on page 278.

Practicing the language

1 Translate each sentence into Latin by selecting correctly from the list of Latin words.

a *I gave money to the boy (who was) carrying the books.*

puerī	librōs	portantī	pecūnia	dedī
puerō	līberōs	portātī	pecūniam	dederam

b *The same women are here again, master.*

eadem	fēminae	simul	adsunt	dominus
eaedem	fēminam	rūrsus	absunt	domine

c *By running, he arrived at the prison more quickly.*

currendō	ad carcerem	celeriter	advēnit
currentī	ā carcere	celerius	advēnī

d *If you do not obey the laws, you will be punished.*

sī	lēgibus	pārueritis	pūnīminī
nisi	lēgī	pārēbātis	pūniēminī

e *Let us force the chiefs of the barbarians to turn back.*

prīncipēs	barbarīs	revertor	cōgimus
prīncipem	barbarōrum	revertī	cōgāmus

f *Men of this kind ought not to be made consuls.*

hominibus	huius	generis	cōnsulem	facere	nōnne	dēbet
hominēs	huic	generī	cōnsulēs	fierī	nōn	dēbent

2 Translate the first sentence. Then, with the help of pages 258–259 and 270–271, express the same idea in a passive form by correctly completing the nouns and verbs in the second sentence. Finally, translate the second sentence.

For example:

> timēbam nē mīlitēs mē caperent.
> timēbam nē ā mīl... caper... .

Translated and completed, this becomes:

> timēbam nē mīlitēs mē caperent.
> *I was afraid that the soldiers would catch me.*
> timēbam nē ā mīlitibus caperer.
> *I was afraid that I would be caught by the soldiers.*

> dīc mihi quārē domina numquam ancillās laudet.
> dīc mihi quārē ancill... numquam ā domin... laud... .

Translated and completed, this becomes:

> dīc mihi quārē domina numquam ancillās laudet.
> *Tell me why the mistress never praises the slave girls.*
> dīc mihi quārē ancillae numquam ā dominā laudentur.
> *Tell me why the slave girls are never praised by the mistress.*

a dominus cognōscere vult num servī cēnam parent.
dominus cognōscere vult num cēn... ā serv... par... .

b tantum erat incendium ut flammae aulam dēlērent.
tantum erat incendium ut aul... flamm... dēlēr... .

c barbarī frūmentum incendērunt ut inopia cibī nōs impedīret.
barbarī frūmentum incendērunt ut inop... cibī imped... .

d in silvā tibi latendum est nē hostēs tē videant.
in silvā tibi latendum est nē ab host... vid... .

e nisi vōs adiūvissem, barbarī vōs circumvēnissent.
nisi vōs adiūvissem, ā barbar... circumven... .

f nescio quārē prīnceps mē relēgāverit.
nescio quārē ā prīncip... relēg... .

The emperor

By AD 59, when the events described in Stage 48 took place, Rome had been ruled by emperors for nearly a century. The Republican system of government (in which two consuls were elected annually as joint heads of state, assisted by other magistrates and the senate) had collapsed in violence and bloodshed at the end of the first century BC. Supreme power in the Roman world was in the hands of a single ruler, the emperor.

To the senate and the people of Rome, the emperor was often known as the **prīnceps** (*chief citizen*); to the soldiers, he was **imperātor** (*commander*). But the word **rēx** (*king*), which might seem a very appropriate title in view of the emperor's great personal power, was deliberately avoided, because the Romans had a long tradition of hatred toward the idea of kings. Kings had ruled Rome in the distant past, and the last one had been so unpopular that he was driven out; four and a half centuries later, when Julius Caesar was suspected of intending to make himself a king, he was assassinated.

The first emperor (Augustus) and most of his successors tried to encourage the belief that in many ways the business of government was being carried out much as before. For example, consuls and other magistrates continued to be appointed, and the senate continued to meet, just as in the days of the Republic. However, the senate, consuls, and magistrates were now much less powerful than before; and they were no longer elected by the people of Rome, but were in many cases appointed directly by the emperor.

The lives and reigns of the emperors in the first century AD are narrated by Tacitus in his *Annals* and *Histories*, and by Suetonius in his *Lives of the Emperors*. They give a vivid and sometimes appalling description of the emperors' immense personal power, the stupidity, greed, lust, extravagance, and cruelty of individual emperors, the frequent plottings and struggles for power that went on among the emperor's advisers and associates, and the savagery and ruthlessness with which emperors treated possible rivals or conspirators.

But even when the emperor was vicious, eccentric, or tyrannical, government of the empire still carried on, and the emperor himself had a crucial part to play; otherwise he risked losing popularity and power. Some emperors behaved sadistically or arrogantly to individuals and still carried out humane and efficient policies in government. For example, Domitian treated the senate with insolence and contempt, and put several of its members to death with little or no excuse, but Suetonius says of him that "he took such great care in supervising the city magistrates and provincial governors that they were more honest and just during his reign than at any other time."

Roman bridge built by Trajan at Alcantara, Spain.

If an emperor was conscientious, his workload was heavy. He took an important and ever-increasing part in administering the law; he chose men for provincial governorships, legionary commands, consulships, the senate, and numerous other positions and privileges; he acted as the commander-in-chief of the Roman army, determining the soldiers' pay, selecting the officers, allocating the legions and auxiliaries to particular parts of the empire, and (in the case of some emperors) leading troops on military campaigns; he received ambassadors from provinces and foreign states who brought him greetings, petitions, complaints, or accusations, to which he would be expected to make an eloquent speech in reply (one of the causes of Nero's dispute with his mother was her attempt to sit at his side, as if she were joint ruler with him, when foreign ambassadors came to see him); he dealt with the problems referred to him by provincial governors (the Bithynia correspondence of Pliny and Trajan provides a good example of this); he often had to care for the plebs or ordinary people of Rome, by providing regular distributions of grain or money to the citizens, putting on splendid and costly shows in the circus and amphitheater, and undertaking large programs of public building to beautify the city and relieve unemployment; he had the power to make law by bringing proposals before the senate; and by holding the post of Pontifex Maximus he was the official head of the state religion.

The Emperor Augustus as Pontifex Maximus presiding at a sacrifice.

The emperor at work

For much of his time, the emperor carried out his responsibilities by receiving and replying to requests, and by hearing and judging disputes. The following examples (based on actual situations and incidents) give some indication of the variety of pleas and problems which he dealt with:

> **The inhabitants of a neighboring town have made a violent attack on us, killing and injuring many innocent people.**

> **Please, will you give Roman citizenship to a doctor who cured me of a dangerous illness.**

> **Several towns in this province have been badly damaged by an earthquake; please, can troops and money be sent.**

> **My husband has been in exile for many years and is now old and ill; I appeal to you to allow him to come back.**

> **There is a serious danger of revolt by the local tribes, and our soldiers urgently need reinforcements.**

> **Please grant our city the privilege of building a temple in honor of your late father.**

> **My neighbor claims his slave is his, but he's a liar; the slave is mine.**

> **Please, will you grant me the honor of the lātus clāvus [broad purple stripe on tunic and toga, indicating membership of the senate].**

> **The governor of our province has illegally tortured and executed Roman citizens; we ask that he be tried and punished.**

Some of the requests and disputes were handled in writing; a constant stream of letters, petitions, appeals, accusations, and other documents poured onto the emperor's desk. He was expected to deal with each one personally, deciding the substance of the reply and in many cases dictating its actual words, occasionally adding a sentence or two in his own handwriting. This correspondence was sometimes carried on in Latin, but often in Greek, especially when dealing with the eastern part of the empire. Other requests and disputes were presented verbally to the emperor in person by the people concerned, some of whom traveled vast distances to do so. An anecdote told by the Greek writer Dio about the

Emperor Hadrian illustrates the way in which a Roman emperor was expected to make himself available to his subjects:

> **When Hadrian was on a journey, he was stopped by a woman who wished to put a request to him. Being in a hurry, he moved on, saying "I'm too busy," whereupon the woman shouted after him, "Then stop being emperor." On hearing this, Hadrian turned around, came back, and listened to her request.**

The emperor's helpers

It was impossible, of course, for one man to govern an empire of fifty million inhabitants single-handed, and although the emperors were reluctant to share power with other people, they needed reliable assistants of various sorts. For military tasks, the emperor could turn to the praetorian guard, who acted as his personal bodyguard and could be immensely important at times of crisis. In Tacitus' account of Nero's attempt to murder Agrippina, one of the first people the emperor sends for when the plot goes wrong is Burrus, the praetorian guard's commander (see page 243, lines 3–4). When the emperor was administering the law or making a decision on which he wanted advice, he could summon his **cōnsilium** (*council*) and ask for opinions of his **amīcī** (*friends*). For assistance in the day-to-day running of government, the emperor could make use of his slaves and (more particularly) his freedmen. These were not official employees of the state, but were members of the emperor's personal household. Some of the freedmen possessed great power and influence; for instance, in the events related in Stage 48, a crucial part was played by the freedman Anicetus, who not only invented a method for carrying out Agrippina's murder (page 237, lines 10–17), but also took control of the situation when the plot misfired (page 243, lines 8–12).

The emperor's freedman Epaphroditus.

The succession

One of the most important questions facing an emperor was to decide who should succeed him. Sometimes the position of emperor was inherited by a son from his father; sometimes an emperor with no sons of his own adopted another member of the family as his heir and successor. Some emperors deliberately looked outside their family in an effort to find the most suitable person; the Emperor Nerva chose an experienced and popular general (Trajan) to succeed him, and adopted him as his heir in preference to any of his own relatives. But on many occasions, the question was settled by force and violence. For example, in

AD 41 the soldiers of the praetorian guard, having murdered the Emperor Caligula, found Caligula's uncle Claudius hiding in the palace and proclaimed him as the new emperor; nobody was in a position to stop them, because they could get their own way by physical force. And in AD 69, which became known as the "year of the four emperors," there was a savage civil war, in which each of several rival candidates, supported by different sections of the Roman army, tried to make himself emperor.

Emperor-worship

At his death, an emperor was normally deified. He received the title **dīvus** (*god*) and was honored with prayers and sacrifices; altars and (sometimes) temples were dedicated to him. Some emperors were worshipped as gods even during their lifetime, especially in the eastern provinces, which had long been accustomed to paying divine honors to their own rulers. For many inhabitants of the empire, worship of this kind was a natural response to the immense power possessed by a Roman emperor.

Carved gem showing the deification of the Emperor Augustus.

Vocabulary checklist 48

caedēs, caedis, f.	murder, slaughter
dōnec	until
ēvādō, ēvādere, ēvāsī	escape
incolumis, incolume	safe
latus, lateris, n.	side
metuō, metuere, metuī	be afraid, fear
mūnus, mūneris, n.	gift
nē quis	in case anyone
nē quid	in case anything
pectus, pectoris, n.	breast, heart
pietās, pietātis, f.	duty, piety (respect for the gods, homeland, and family)
premō, premere, pressī, pressus	press, crush
quisque	each
vel ... vel	either ... or
velut	as if, like
vīs, vis, f.	force, violence

Numbers

ūndecim	eleven
duodecim	twelve
tredecim	thirteen
quattuordecim	fourteen
quīndecim	fifteen
sēdecim	sixteen
septendecim	seventeen
duodēvīgintī	eighteen
ūndēvīgintī	nineteen
trecentī	three hundred
quadringentī	four hundred
quīngentī	five hundred
sescentī	six hundred
septingentī	seven hundred
octingentī	eight hundred
nōngentī	nine hundred

Statue of Tacitus, outside the Austrian parliament in Vienna.

Fragment of an inscription in Domitian's palace. There were once bronze letters set into the marble.

LANGUAGE INFORMATION

Contents

Part One: About the language
Nouns

1

	first declension	*second declension*			*third declension*
GENDER	f.	m.	m.	n.	m.
SINGULAR					
nominative and *vocative*	puella	servus (*voc.* serve)	faber	templum	mercātor
genitive (of)	puellae	servī	fabrī	templī	mercātōris
dative (to, for)	puellae	servō	fabrō	templō	mercātōrī
accusative	puellam	servum	fabrum	templum	mercātōrem
ablative (by, with)	puellā	servō	fabrō	templō	mercātōre
PLURAL					
nominative and *vocative*	puellae	servī	fabrī	templa	mercātōrēs
genitive (of)	puellārum	servōrum	fabrōrum	templōrum	mercātōrum
dative (to, for)	puellīs	servīs	fabrīs	templīs	mercātōribus
accusative	puellās	servōs	fabrōs	templa	mercātōrēs
ablative (by, with)	puellīs	servīs	fabrīs	templīs	mercātōribus

	fourth declension		*fifth declension*	
GENDER	m.	n.	m.	f.
SINGULAR				
nominative and *vocative*	portus	genū	diēs	rēs
genitive (of)	portūs	genūs	diēī	reī
dative (to, for)	portuī	genū	diēī	reī
accusative	portum	genū	diem	rem
ablative (by, with)	portū	genū	diē	rē
PLURAL				
nominative and *vocative*	portūs	genua	diēs	rēs
genitive (of)	portuum	genuum	diērum	rērum
dative (to, for)	portibus	genibus	diēbus	rēbus
accusative	portūs	genua	diēs	rēs
ablative (by, with)	portibus	genibus	diēbus	rēbus

	m.	f.	f.	n.	n.	n.	GENDER
							SINGULAR
eō	cīvis	vōx	urbs	nōmen	tempus	mare	*nominative* and *vocative*
eōnis	cīvis	vōcis	urbis	nōminis	temporis	maris	*genitive (of)*
eōnī	cīvī	vōcī	urbī	nōminī	temporī	marī	*dative (to, for)*
eōnem	cīvem	vōcem	urbem	nōmen	tempus	mare	*accusative*
eōne	cīve	vōce	urbe	nōmine	tempore	marī	*ablative (by, with)*
							PLURAL
eōnēs	cīvēs	vōcēs	urbēs	nōmina	tempora	maria	*nominative* and *vocative*
eōnum	cīvium	vōcum	urbium	nōminum	temporum	marium	*genitive (of)*
eōnibus	cīvibus	vōcibus	urbibus	nōminibus	temporibus	maribus	*dative (to, for)*
eōnēs	cīvēs	vōcēs	urbēs	nōmina	tempora	maria	*accusative*
eōnibus	cīvibus	vōcibus	urbibus	nōminibus	temporibus	maribus	*ablative (by, with)*

2   For the ways in which the different cases are used, see pp. 287–288.

3   Compare the endings of **mare** with those of **nōmen** and **tempus**. Notice in particular the different form of the ablative singular. Other third declension neuter nouns whose nominative singular ends in -**e**, such as **conclāve** (*room*) and **cubīle** (*bed*), form their cases in the same way as **mare**.

4   Give the Latin for the nouns in *italic type* by forming the appropriate case of the word in **boldface**. If necessary, use the tables here and the Vocabulary on pp. 309–352 to help you with the declension and gender of the nouns.

   a   You have a very unusual *name*. (**nōmen**)
   b   The young man took the girl's *hands* in his. (**manus**)
   c   The informer told Epaphroditus an interesting *thing* about the senator. (**rēs**)
   d   The soldiers crossed several *rivers* on their march. (**flūmen**)
   e   The master discovered the *body of the young man* in the well. (**corpus, iuvenis**)
   f   Agricola quickly issued many *orders to the tribunes*. (**iussum, tribūnus**)
   g   Our men were spurred on *by the hope of victory*. (**spēs, victōria**)
   h   Domitian spent many *days* and *nights* thinking about his enemies. (**diēs, nox**)

Adjectives

1 first and second declension

SINGULAR	*masculine*	*feminine*	*neuter*	*masculine*	*feminine*	*neuter*
nominative and *vocative*	bonus (voc. bone)	bona	bonum	pulcher	pulchra	pulchrum
genitive	bonī	bonae	bonī	pulchrī	pulchrae	pulchrī
dative	bonō	bonae	bonō	pulchrō	pulchrae	pulchrō
accusative	bonum	bonam	bonum	pulchrum	pulchram	pulchrum
ablative	bonō	bonā	bonō	pulchrō	pulchrā	pulchrō
PLURAL						
nominative and *vocative*	bonī	bonae	bona	pulchrī	pulchrae	pulchra
genitive	bonōrum	bonārum	bonōrum	pulchrōrum	pulchrārum	pulchrōrum
dative	bonīs	bonīs	bonīs	pulchrīs	pulchrīs	pulchrīs
accusative	bonōs	bonās	bona	pulchrōs	pulchrās	pulchra
ablative	bonīs	bonīs	bonīs	pulchrīs	pulchrīs	pulchrīs

2 third declension

SINGULAR	*masculine and feminine*	*neuter*	*masculine and feminine*	*neuter*
nominative and *vocative*	fortis	forte	fēlīx	fēlīx
genitive	fortis	fortis	fēlīcis	fēlīcis
dative	fortī	fortī	fēlīcī	fēlīcī
accusative	fortem	forte	fēlīcem	fēlīx
ablative	fortī	fortī	fēlīcī	fēlīcī
PLURAL				
nominative and *vocative*	fortēs	fortia	fēlīcēs	fēlīcia
genitive	fortium	fortium	fēlīcium	fēlīcium
dative	fortibus	fortibus	fēlīcibus	fēlīcibus
accusative	fortēs	fortia	fēlīcēs	fēlīcia
ablative	fortibus	fortibus	fēlīcibus	fēlīcibus

third declension continued

SINGULAR	masculine and feminine	neuter	masculine and feminine	neuter
nominative and *vocative*	ingēns	ingēns	longior	longius
genitive	ingentis	ingentis	longiōris	longiōris
dative	ingentī	ingentī	longiōrī	longiōri
accusative	ingentem	ingēns	longiōrem	longius
ablative	ingentī	ingentī	longiōre	longiōre
PLURAL				
nominative and *vocative*	ingentēs	ingentia	longiōrēs	longiōra
genitive	ingentium	ingentium	longiōrum	longiōrum
dative	ingentibus	ingentibus	longiōribus	longiōribus
accusative	ingentēs	ingentia	longiōrēs	longiōra
ablative	ingentibus	ingentibus	longiōribus	longiōribus

Comparatives and superlatives

Adjectives

1

	comparative	*superlative*
longus *long*	longior *longer*	longissimus *longest, very long*
pulcher *beautiful*	pulchrior *more beautiful*	pulcherrimus *most beautiful, very beautiful*
fortis *brave*	fortior *braver*	fortissimus *bravest, very brave*
fēlīx *lucky*	fēlīcior *luckier*	fēlīcissimus *luckiest, very lucky*
prūdēns *shrewd*	prūdentior *shrewder*	prūdentissimus *shrewdest, very shrewd*
facilis *easy*	facilior *easier*	facillimus *easiest, very easy*

2 Irregular forms:

bonus *good*	melior *better*	optimus *best, very good*
malus *bad*	peior *worse*	pessimus *worst, very bad*
magnus *big*	maior *bigger*	maximus *biggest, very big*
parvus *small*	minor *smaller*	minimus *smallest, very small*
multus *much*	plūs *more*	plūrimus *most, very much*
multī *many*	plūrēs *more*	plūrimī *most, very many*

3 The forms of the comparative adjective **longior** are shown on p. 261.

4 Superlative adjectives such as **longissimus** change their endings in the same way as **bonus** (shown on p. 260).

Adverbs

1 Study the way in which comparative and superlative adverbs are formed:

	comparative	*superlative*
lātē *widely*	lātius *more widely*	lātissimē *most widely, very widely*
pulchrē *beautifully*	pulchrius *more beautifully*	pulcherrimē *most beautifully, very beautifully*
fortiter *bravely*	fortius *more bravely*	fortissimē *most bravely, very bravely*
fēlīciter *luckily*	fēlīcius *more luckily*	fēlīcissimē *most luckily, very luckily*
prūdenter *shrewdly*	prūdentius *more shrewdly*	prūdentissimē *most shrewdly, very shrewdly*
facile *easily*	facilius *more easily*	facillimē *most easily, very easily*

2 Irregular forms

bene *good*	melius *better*	optimē *best, very well*
male *badly*	peius *worse*	pessimē *worst, very badly*
magnopere *greatly*	magis *more*	maximē *most, very greatly*
paulum *little*	minus *less*	minimē *least, very little*
multum *much*	plūs *more*	plūrimum *most, very much*

3 Translate the following examples:

a mīlitēs nostrī fortius pugnāvērunt quam barbarī.
b faber mūrum facillimē refēcit.
c ubi strepitum audīvī, magis timēbam.
d optimē respondistī, mī fīlī.

Pronouns I: ego, tū, nōs, vōs, sē

1 **ego** and **tū** (*I, you,* etc.)

	SINGULAR		PLURAL	
nominative	ego	tū	nōs	vōs
genitive	meī	tuī	nostrum	vestrum
dative	mihi	tibi	nōbīs	vōbīs
accusative	mē	tē	nōs	vōs
ablative	mē	tē	nōbīs	vōbīs

2 **sē** (*herself, himself, themselves,* etc.)

	SINGULAR	PLURAL
genitive	suī	suī
dative	sibi	sibi
accusative	sē	sē
ablative	sē	sē

3 Note the adjectives that correspond to the pronouns in paragraphs 1 and 2:

meus, mea, meum	*my*	noster, nostra, nostrum	*our*
tuus, tua, tuum	*your* (s.)	vester, vestra, vestrum	*your* (pl.)
suus, sua, suum	*his own, her own*		
	its own, their own		

These adjectives, like all other adjectives, agree with the nouns they describe in case, number, and gender.

For example:

urbs vestra ā barbarīs mox dēlēbitur.
Your city will soon be destroyed by the barbarians.

domina līberōs suōs semper laudat.
The mistress is always praising her own children.

4 Give the Latin for the words in *italic type* in the following sentences:

a The prisoner was led away *from us.*
b *Our citizens* are very courageous.
c He improved *his own villa*, but not his father's.
d The welfare *of my slaves* is very important.
e They wounded *themselves* to avoid being sent into battle.
f I do not want to give anything *to you* (s.).
g The patron gave money so that the villagers could have *their own temple*.
h *You* (pl.) are rich, but *we* are happy.

Pronouns II: hic, ille, ipse, is, īdem

1 hic (*this, these,* etc.; also used with the meaning *he, she, they,* etc.)

	SINGULAR			PLURAL		
	masculine	*feminine*	*neuter*	*masculine*	*feminine*	*neuter*
nominative	hic	haec	hoc	hī	hae	haec
genitive	huius	huius	huius	hōrum	hārum	hōrum
dative	huic	huic	huic	hīs	hīs	hīs
accusative	hunc	hanc	hoc	hōs	hās	haec
ablative	hōc	hāc	hōc	hīs	hīs	hīs

2 ille (*that, those,* etc.; also used with the meaning *he, she, it,* etc.)

	SINGULAR			PLURAL		
	masculine	*feminine*	*neuter*	*masculine*	*feminine*	*neuter*
nominative	ille	illa	illud	illī	illae	illa
genitive	illīus	illīus	illīus	illōrum	illārum	illōrum
dative	illī	illī	illī	illīs	illīs	illīs
accusative	illum	illam	illud	illōs	illās	illa
ablative	illō	illā	illō	illīs	illīs	illīs

3 ipse (*myself, yourself, himself,* etc.)

	SINGULAR			PLURAL		
	masculine	*feminine*	*neuter*	*masculine*	*feminine*	*neuter*
nominative	ipse	ipsa	ipsum	ipsī	ipsae	ipsa
genitive	ipsīus	ipsīus	ipsīus	ipsōrum	ipsārum	ipsōrum
dative	ipsī	ipsī	ipsī	ipsīs	ipsīs	ipsīs
accusative	ipsum	ipsam	ipsum	ipsōs	ipsās	ipsa
ablative	ipsō	ipsā	ipsō	ipsīs	ipsīs	ipsīs

4 **is** (*he, she, it,* etc.; also used with the meaning *that, those,* etc.)

	SINGULAR			PLURAL		
	masculine	*feminine*	*neuter*	*masculine*	*feminine*	*neuter*
nominative	is	ea	id	eī	eae	ea
genitive	eius	eius	eius	eōrum	eārum	eōrum
dative	eī	eī	eī	eīs	eīs	eīs
accusative	eum	eam	id	eōs	eās	ea
ablative	eō	eā	eō	eīs	eīs	eīs

Notice again how forms of **is** can also be used with the relative pronoun **quī**:

id quod mihi nārrāvistī statim Imperātōrī nūntiābitur.
What you have told to me will be reported at once to the emperor.

eīs quī modo advēnērunt neque cibum neque pecūniam dabō.
To those who have just arrived I shall give neither food nor money.

5 **īdem** (*the same*)

	SINGULAR			PLURAL		
	masculine	*feminine*	*neuter*	*masculine*	*feminine*	*neuter*
nominative	īdem	eadem	idem	eīdem	eaedem	eadem
genitive	eiusdem	eiusdem	eiusdem	eōrundem	eārundem	eōrundem
dative	eīdem	eīdem	eīdem	eīsdem	eīsdem	eīsdem
accusative	eundem	eandem	idem	eōsdem	eāsdem	eadem
ablative	eōdem	eādem	eōdem	eīsdem	eīsdem	eīsdem

Compare the forms of **īdem** with **is** in paragraph 4.

Pronouns III: quī, quīdam

1   The relative pronoun **quī** (*who, which,* etc.)

	SINGULAR			PLURAL		
	masculine	*feminine*	*neuter*	*masculine*	*feminine*	*neuter*
nominative	quī	quae	quod	quī	quae	quae
genitive	cuius	cuius	cuius	quōrum	quārum	quōrum
dative	cui	cui	cui	quibus	quibus	quibus
accusative	quem	quam	quod	quōs	quās	quae
ablative	quō	quā	quō	quibus	quibus	quibus

Notice again the use of the *connecting relative* at the beginning of sentences with the meaning *he, she, it, this,* etc.:

> rēx signum dedit. **quod** simulac vīdērunt, haruspicēs ad āram prōgressī sunt.
> *The king gave a signal. As soon as they saw **it**, the soothsayers advanced towards the altar.*

> cōnsul "captīvīs parcere cōnstituī," inquit. **quibus** verbīs audītīs, senātōrēs plausērunt.
> *"I have decided to spare the prisoners," said the consul. On hearing **these** words, the senators applauded.*

2   From Stage 17 on, you have met various forms of the word **quīdam**, meaning *one, a certain*:

	SINGULAR			PLURAL		
	masculine	*feminine*	*neuter*	*masculine*	*feminine*	*neuter*
nominative	quīdam	quaedam	quoddam	quīdam	quaedam	quaedam
genitive	cuiusdam	cuiusdam	cuiusdam	quōrundam	quārundam	quōrundam
dative	cuidam	cuidam	cuidam	quibusdam	quibusdam	quibusdam
accusative	quendam	quandam	quoddam	quōsdam	quāsdam	quaedam
ablative	quōdam	quādam	quōdam	quibusdam	quibusdam	quibusdam

> quōsdam hominēs nōvī, quī tē adiuvāre poterunt.
> *I know certain men, who will be able to help you.*

> subitō senātor quīdam, celeriter prōgressus, silentium poposcit.
> *Suddenly one senator stepped forward quickly and demanded silence.*

Compare the forms of **quīdam** with **quī** in paragraph 1.

With the help of the table above, find the Latin for the words in *italic type* in the following sentences:

a *Certain* ladies were helping with the wedding preparations.
b *One* young man was addressing the crowd.
c I was staying at the house of *a certain* friend.

Verbs

Indicative active

1

	first conjugation	second conjugation	third conjugation	fourth conjugation
PRESENT	*I carry, you carry, etc.*	*I teach, you teach, etc.*	*I drag, you drag, etc.*	*I hear, you hear, etc.*
	portō	doceō	trahō	audiō
	portās	docēs	trahis	audīs
	portat	docet	trahit	audit
	portāmus	docēmus	trahimus	audīmus
	portātis	docētis	trahitis	audītis
	portant	docent	trahunt	audiunt
IMPERFECT	*I was carrying*	*I was teaching*	*I was dragging*	*I was hearing*
	portābam	docēbam	trahēbam	audiēbam
	portābās	docēbās	trahēbās	audiēbās
	portābat	docēbat	trahēbat	audiēbat
	portābāmus	docēbāmus	trahēbāmus	audiēbāmus
	portābātis	docēbātis	trahēbātis	audiēbātis
	portābant	docēbant	trahēbant	audiēbant
FUTURE	*I shall carry*	*I shall teach*	*I shall drag*	*I shall hear*
	portābō	docēbō	traham	audiam
	portābis	docēbis	trahēs	audiēs
	portābit	docēbit	trahet	audiet
	portābimus	docēbimus	trahēmus	audiēmus
	portābitis	docēbitis	trahētis	audiētis
	portābunt	docēbunt	trahent	audient

2 Translate each word, then change it from the singular to the plural, so that it means *we shall…* or *they will…* instead of *I shall…* or *s/he will…* . Then translate again.

   nāvigābō; mittet; persuādēbit; impediam; monēbō; dūcam.

3 For ways of checking whether a verb ending in **-ēs**, **-et**, etc. belongs to the *present* tense of a *second* conjugation verb like **doceō** or the *future* tense of a *third* conjugation verb like **trahō**, see paragraph 3 on p. 307.

4

	first conjugation	second conjugation	third conjugation	fourth conjugation
PERFECT	*I (have)* *carried* portāvī portāvistī portāvit portāvimus portāvistis portāvērunt	*I (have)* *taught* docuī docuistī docuit docuimus docuistis docuērunt	*I (have)* *dragged* trāxī trāxistī trāxit trāximus trāxistis trāxērunt	*I (have)* *heard* audīvī audīvistī audīvit audīvimus audīvistis audīvērunt
PLUPERFECT	*I had* *carried* portāveram portāverās portāverat portāverāmus portāverātis portāverant	*I had* *taught* docueram docuerās docuerat docuerāmus docuerātis docuerant	*I had* *dragged* trāxeram trāxerās trāxerat trāxerāmus trāxerātis trāxerant	*I had* *heard* audīveram audīverās audīverat audīverāmus audīverātis audīverant
FUTURE PERFECT	*I shall have* *carried* portāverō portāveris portāverit portāverimus portāveritis portāverint	*I shall have* *taught* docuerō docueris docuerit docuerimus docueritis docuerint	*I shall have* *dragged* trāxerō trāxeris trāxerit trāxerimus trāxeritis trāxerint	*I shall have* *heard* audīverō audīveris audīverit audīverimus audīveritis audīverint

The future perfect is often translated by the English present tense:

sī mē portum dūxeris, pecūniam tibi dabō.
If you take me to the harbor, I shall give you money.

Indicative passive

1 In Unit 3, you met the following forms of the *passive*:

	first conjugation	*second conjugation*	*third conjugation*	*fourth conjugation*
PRESENT	*I am (being) carried*	*I am (being) taught*	*I am (being) dragged*	*I am (being) heard*
	portor	doceor	trahor	audior
	portāris	docēris	traheris	audīris
	portātur	docētur	trahitur	audītur
	portāmur	docēmur	trahimur	audīmur
	portāminī	docēminī	trahiminī	audīminī
	portantur	docentur	trahuntur	audiuntur
IMPERFECT	*I was being carried*	*I was being taught*	*I was being dragged*	*I was being heard*
	portābar	docēbar	trahēbar	audiēbar
	portābāris	docēbāris	trahēbāris	audiēbāris
	portābātur	docēbātur	trahēbātur	audiēbātur
	portābāmur	docēbāmur	trahēbāmur	audiēbāmur
	portābāminī	docēbāminī	trahēbāminī	audiēbāminī
	portābantur	docēbantur	trahēbantur	audiēbantur
FUTURE	*I shall be carried*	*I shall be taught*	*I shall be dragged*	*I shall be heard*
	portābor	docēbor	trahar	audiar
	portāberis	docēberis	trahēris	audiēris
	portābitur	docēbitur	trahētur	audiētur
	portābimur	docēbimur	trahēmur	audiēmur
	portābiminī	docēbiminī	trahēminī	audiēminī
	portābuntur	docēbuntur	trahentur	audientur

2 In paragraph 1, find the Latin for:

he is being dragged; you (s.) will be carried; you (pl.) were being heard; we are taught; they will be dragged; we shall be heard.

3 Translate each verb, then change it from the singular to the plural, so that it means *you (pl.)…* or *they…* instead of *you (s.)…* or *s/he…* . Then translate again.

audiēbāris; docēris; trahētur; portābitur; mittēbāris; amātur.

4 Notice how the first and second conjugations form the future passive tense in a different way from the third and fourth conjugations. Compare this with the future active tense on p. 268.

5

	first conjugation	*second conjugation*	*third conjugation*	*fourth conjugation*
PERFECT	*I have been carried, I was carried*	*I have been taught, I was taught*	*I have been dragged, I was dragged*	*I have been heard, I was heard*
	portātus sum	doctus sum	tractus sum	audītus sum
	portātus es	doctus es	tractus es	audītus es
	portātus est	doctus est	tractus est	audītus est
	portātī sumus	doctī sumus	tractī sumus	audītī sumus
	portātī estis	doctī estis	tractī estis	audītī estis
	portātī sunt	doctī sunt	tractī sunt	audītī sunt
PLUPERFECT	*I had been carried*	*I had been taught*	*I had been dragged*	*I had been heard*
	portātus eram	doctus eram	tractus eram	audītus eram
	portātus erās	doctus erās	tractus erās	audītus erās
	portātus erat	doctus erat	tractus erat	audītus erat
	portātī erāmus	doctī erāmus	tractī erāmus	audītī erāmus
	portātī erātis	doctī erātis	tractī erātis	audītī erātis
	portātī erant	doctī erant	tractī erant	audītī erant
FUTURE PERFECT	*I shall have been carried*	*I shall have been taught*	*I shall have been dragged*	*I shall have been heard*
	portātus erō	doctus erō	tractus erō	audītus erō
	portātus eris	doctus eris	tractus eris	audītus eris
	portātus erit	doctus erit	tractus erit	audītus erit
	portātī erimus	doctī erimus	tractī erimus	audītī erimus
	portātī eritis	doctī eritis	tractī eritis	audītī eritis
	portātī erunt	doctī erunt	tractī erunt	audītī erunt

6 The future perfect passive, like the future perfect active, is often translated by an English present tense:

> sī exercitus noster crās victus erit, hostēs oppidum capere poterunt.
> *If our army is defeated tomorrow, the enemy will be able to capture the town.*

7 Translate each example, then change it from the pluperfect to the perfect tense, keeping the same person and number (i.e. 1st person singular, etc.). Then translate each example again.

For example:

> **portātī erāmus** *we had been carried* becomes **portātī sumus** *we have been carried, we were carried.*

doctus eram; audītī erant; missī erātis; accūsātī erāmus; rogātus erās; ducta erat.

Subjunctive active

1

	first conjugation	*second conjugation*	*third conjugation*	*fourth conjugation*
PRESENT	portem	doceam	traham	audiam
	portēs	doceās	trahās	audiās
	portet	doceat	trahat	audiat
	portēmus	doceāmus	trahāmus	audiāmus
	portētis	doceātis	trahātis	audiātis
	portent	doceant	trahant	audiant
IMPERFECT	portārem	docērem	traherem	audīrem
	portārēs	docērēs	traherēs	audīrēs
	portāret	docēret	traheret	audīret
	portārēmus	docērēmus	traherēmus	audīrēmus
	portārētis	docērētis	traherētis	audīrētis
	portārent	docērent	traherent	audīrent
PERFECT	portāverim	docuerim	trāxerim	audīverim
	portāverīs	docuerīs	trāxeris	audīverīs
	portāverit	docuerit	trāxerit	audīverit
	portāverīmus	docuerīmus	trāxerīmus	audīverīmus
	portāverītis	docuerītis	trāxerītis	audīverītis
	portāverint	docuerint	trāxerint	audīverint
PLUPERFECT	portāvissem	docuissem	trāxissem	audīvissem
	portāvissēs	docuissēs	trāxissēs	audīvissēs
	portāvisset	docuisset	trāxisset	audīvisset
	portāvissēmus	docuissēmus	trāxissēmus	audīvissēmus
	portāvissētis	docuissētis	trāxissētis	audīvissētis
	portāvissent	docuissent	trāxissent	audīvissent

Subjunctive passive

1

	first conjugation	*second conjugation*	*third conjugation*	*fourth conjugation*
PRESENT	porter	docear	trahar	audiar
	portēris	doceāris	trahāris	audiāris
	portētur	doceātur	trahātur	audiātur
	portēmur	doceāmur	trahāmur	audiāmur
	portēminī	doceāminī	trahāminī	audiāminī
	portentur	doceantur	trahantur	audiantur
IMPERFECT	portārer	docērer	traherer	audīrer
	portārēris	docērēris	traherēris	audīrēris
	portārētur	docērētur	traherētur	audīrētur
	portārēmur	docērēmur	traherēmur	audīrēmur
	portārēminī	docērēminī	traherēminī	audīrēminī
	portārentur	docērentur	traherentur	audīrentur
PERFECT	portātus sim	doctus sim	tractus sim	audītus sim
	portātus sīs	doctus sīs	tractus sīs	audītus sīs
	portātus sit	doctus sit	tractus sit	audītus sit
	portātī sīmus	doctī sīmus	tractī sīmus	audītī sīmus
	portātī sītis	doctī sītis	tractī sītis	audītī sītis
	portātī sint	doctī sint	tractī sint	audītī sint
PLUPERFECT	portātus essem	doctus essem	tractus essem	audītus essem
	portātus essēs	doctus essēs	tractus essēs	audītus essēs
	portātus esset	doctus esset	tractus esset	audītus esset
	portātī essēmus	doctī essēmus	tractī essēmus	audītī essēmus
	portātī essētis	doctī essētis	tractī essētis	audītī essētis
	portātī essent	doctī essent	tractī essent	audītī essent

2 For ways in which the subjunctive is used, see pp. 291–293.

Other forms of the verb

1

IMPERATIVE	*carry!*	*teach!*	*drag!*	*hear!*
SINGULAR	portā	docē	trahe	audī
PLURAL	portāte	docēte	trahite	audīte

2

PRESENT	*carrying*	*teaching*	*dragging*	*hearing*
PARTICIPLE	portāns	docēns	trahēns	audiēns

Present participles change their endings in the same way as **ingēns** (shown on p. 261), except that their ablative singular sometimes ends in **-e**, e.g. **portante, docente**.

PERFECT PASSIVE	*having been*	*having been*	*having been*	*having been*
PARTICIPLE	*carried*	*taught*	*dragged*	*heard*
	portātus	doctus	tractus	audītus

For examples of perfect active participles, see **Deponent verbs**, p. 279.

FUTURE	*about to*	*about to*	*about to*	*about to*
PARTICIPLE	*carry*	*teach*	*drag*	*hear*
	portātūrus	doctūrus	tractūrus	audītūrus

Perfect passive and future participles change their endings in the same way as **bonus** (shown on p. 260).

For examples of ways in which participles are used, see pp. 289-290.

3

PRESENT ACTIVE INFINITIVE	*to carry* portāre	*to teach* docēre	*to drag* trahere	*to hear* audīre
PRESENT PASSIVE INFINITIVE	*to be carried* portārī	*to be taught* docērī	*to be dragged* trahī	*to be heard* audīrī
PERFECT ACTIVE INFINITIVE	*to have carried* portāvisse	*to have taught* docuisse	*to have dragged* trāxisse	*to have heard* audīvisse
PERFECT PASSIVE INFINITIVE	*to have been carried* portātus esse	*to have been taught* doctus esse	*to have been dragged* tractus esse	*to have been heard* audītus esse
FUTURE ACTIVE INFINITIVE	*to be about to carry* portātūrus esse	*to be about to teach* doctūrus esse	*to be about to drag* tractūrus esse	*to be about to hear* audītūrus esse

For examples of ways in which infinitives are used to express indirect statements, see pp. 294-296.

4

GERUNDIVE	portandus	docendus	trahendus	audiendus

Gerundives change their endings in the same way as **bonus** (p. 260).

For ways in which the gerundive is used, see pp. 299-300.

5

GERUND *(carrying, etc.)*

nominative	(no forms)			
genitive	portandī	docendī	trahendī	audiendī
dative	portandō	docendō	trahendō	audiendō
accusative	portandum	docendum	trahendum	audiendum
ablative	portandō	docendō	trahendō	audiendō

Notice that the gerund changes its endings in the same way as 2nd declension nouns such as **templum**; but it has no nominative case and no plural.

For ways in which the gerund is used, see p. 299.

Deponent verbs

Indicative

1

	first conjugation	second conjugation	third conjugation	fourth conjugation
PRESENT	*I try, I am trying*	*I promise, I am promising*	*I speak, I am speaking*	*I rise, I am rising*
	cōnor	polliceor	loquor	orior
	cōnāris	pollicēris	loqueris	orīris
	cōnātur	pollicētur	loquitur	orītur
	cōnāminī	pollicēmur	loquimur	orīmur
	cōnāminī	pollicēminī	loquiminī	orīminī
	cōnantur	pollicentur	loquuntur	oriuntur
IMPERFECT	*I was trying*	*I was promising*	*I was speaking*	*I was rising*
	cōnābar	pollicēbar	loquēbar	oriēbar
	cōnābāris	pollicēbāris	loquēbāris	oriēbāris
	cōnābātur	pollicēbātur	loquēbātur	oriēbātur
	cōnābāmur	pollicēbāmur	loquēbāmur	oriēbāmur
	cōnābāminī	pollicēbāminī	loquēbāminī	oriēbāminī
	cōnābantur	pollicēbuntur	loquēbantur	oriēbantur
FUTURE	*I shall try*	*I shall promise*	*I shall speak*	*I shall rise*
	cōnābor	pollicēbor	loquar	oriar
	cōnāberis	pollicēberis	loquēris	oriēris
	cōnābitur	pollicēbitur	loquētur	oriētur
	cōnābimur	pollicēbimur	loquēmur	oriēmur
	cōnābiminī	pollicēbiminī	loquēminī	oriēminī
	cōnābuntur	pollicēbuntur	loquentur	orientur

2 In paragraph 1, find the Latin for:

you (s.) speak; we were trying; s/he was promising; they will rise; you (pl.) were speaking; we shall promise.

3 Translate the following examples:

cōnāminī; pollicēberis; oriēbātur; loquentur; precābar; sequimur.

4 Notice the two different ways in which the future tense of deponent verbs is formed and compare them with the future passive forms on p. 270.

5

	first conjugation	second conjugation	third conjugation	fourth conjugation
PERFECT	*I (have) tried*	*I (have) promised*	*I (have) spoken*	*I have risen, I rose*
	cōnātus sum	pollicitus sum	locūtus sum	ortus sum
	cōnātus es	pollicitus es	locūtus es	ortus es
	cōnātus est	pollicitus est	locūtus est	ortus est
	cōnātī sumus	pollicitī sumus	locūtī sumus	ortī sumus
	cōnātī estis	pollicitī estis	locūtī estis	ortī estis
	cōnātī sunt	pollicitī sunt	locūtī sunt	ortī sunt
PLUPERFECT	*I had tried*	*I had promised*	*I had spoken*	*I had risen*
	cōnātus eram	pollicitus eram	locūtus eram	ortus eram
	cōnātus erās	pollicitus erās	locūtus erās	ortus erās
	cōnātus erat	pollicitus erat	locūtus erat	ortus erat
	cōnātī erāmus	pollicitī erāmus	locūtī erāmus	ortī erāmus
	cōnātī erātis	pollicitī erātis	locūtī erātis	ortī erātis
	cōnātī erant	pollicitī erant	locūtī erant	ortī erant
FUTURE PERFECT	*I shall have tried*	*I shall have promised*	*I shall have spoken*	*I shall have risen*
	cōnātus erō	pollicitus erō	locūtus erō	ortus erō
	cōnātus eris	pollicitus eris	locūtus eris	ortus eris
	cōnātus erit	pollicitus erit	locūtus erit	ortus erit
	cōnātī erimus	pollicitī erimus	locūtī erimus	ortī erimus
	cōnātī eritis	pollicitī eritis	locūtī eritis	ortī eritis
	cōnātī erunt	pollicitī erunt	locūtī erunt	ortī erunt

6 In paragraph 5, find the Latin for:

they tried; you (s.) had spoken; we have risen; he will have spoken; you (pl.) had promised; he rose.

7 Translate each example, then change it from the pluperfect to the perfect tense; keeping the same person and number (i.e. 1st person singular, etc.). Then translate the examples again.

For example: **cōnātus erās** *you had tried* becomes **cōnātus es** *you have tried, you tried*.

locūtus erat; cōnāta eram; pollicitī erimus; profectī erātis; adepta erat.

Subjunctive

1

	first conjugation	*second conjugation*	*third conjugation*	*fourth conjugation*
PRESENT	cōner	pollicear	loquar	oriar
	cōnēris	polliceāris	loquāris	oriāris
	cōnētur	polliceātur	loquātur	oriātur
	cōnēmur	polliceāmur	loquāmur	oriāmur
	cōnēminī	polliceāminī	loquāminī	oriāminī
	cōnentur	polliceantur	loquantur	oriantur
IMPERFECT	cōnārer	pollicērer	loquerer	orīrer
	cōnārēris	pollicērēris	loquerēris	orīrēris
	cōnārētur	pollicērētur	loquerētur	orīrētur
	cōnārēmur	pollicērēmur	loquerēmur	orīrēmur
	cōnārēminī	pollicērēminī	loquerēminī	orīrēminī
	cōnārentur	pollicērentur	loquerentur	orīrentur
PERFECT	cōnātus sim	pollicitus sim	locūtus sim	ortus sim
	cōnātus sīs	pollicitus sīs	locūtus sīs	ortus sīs
	cōnātus sit	pollicitus sit	locūtus sit	ortus sit
	cōnātī sīmus	pollicitī sīmus	locūtī sīmus	ortī sīmus
	cōnātī sītis	pollicitī sītis	locūtī sītis	ortī sītis
	cōnātī sint	pollicitī sint	locūtī sint	ortī sint
PLUPERFECT	cōnātus essem	pollicitus essem	locūtus essem	ortus essem
	cōnātus essēs	pollicitus essēs	locūtus essēs	ortus essēs
	cōnātus esset	pollicitus esset	locūtus esset	ortus esset
	cōnātī essēmus	pollicitī essēmus	locūtī essēmus	ortī essēmus
	cōnātī essētis	pollicitī essētis	locūtī essētis	ortī essētis
	cōnātī essent	pollicitī essent	locūtī essent	ortī essent

Other forms

1

IMPERATIVE	*try!*	*promise!*	*speak!*	*rise!*
SINGULAR	cōnāre	pollicēre	loquere	orīre
PLURAL	cōnāminī	pollicēminī	loquiminī	orīminī

2

PRESENT PARTICIPLE	*trying* cōnāns	*promising* pollicēns	*speaking* loquēns	*rising* oriēns
PERFECT PARTICIPLE	*having tried* cōnātus	*having promised* pollicitus	*having spoken* locūtus	*having risen* ortus
FUTURE PARTICIPLE	*about to try* cōnātūrus	*about to promise* pollicitūrus	*about to speak* locūtūrus	*about to rise* oritūrus

3

PRESENT INFINITIVE	*to try* cōnārī	*to promise* pollicērī	*to speak* loquī	*to rise* orīrī
PERFECT INFINITIVE	*to have tried* cōnātus esse	*to have promised* pollicitus esse	*to have spoken* locūtus esse	*to have risen* ortus esse
FUTURE INFINITIVE	*to be about to try* cōnātūrus esse	*to be about to promise* pollicitūrus esse	*to be about to speak* locūtūrus esse	*to be about to rise* oritūrus esse

4

GERUNDIVE	cōnandus	pollicendus	loquendus	oriendus

5

GERUND *(trying, etc.)*

nominative	(no forms)			
genitive	cōnandī	verendī	loquendī	oriendī
dative	cōnandō	verendō	loquendō	oriendō
accusative	cōnandum	verendum	loquendum	oriendum
ablative	cōnandō	verendō	loquendō	oriendō

Irregular verbs

Indicative

1

	PRESENT					
	I am	*I am able*	*I go*	*I want*	*I bring*	*I take*
	sum	possum	eō	volō	ferō	capiō
	es	potes	īs	vīs	fers	capis
	est	potest	it	vult	fert	capit
	sumus	possumus	īmus	volumus	ferimus	capimus
	estis	potestis	ītis	vultis	fertis	capitis
	sunt	possunt	eunt	volunt	ferunt	capiunt

	IMPERFECT					
	I was	*I was able*	*I was going*	*I was wanting*	*I was bringing*	*I was taking*
	eram	poteram	ībam	volēbam	ferēbam	capiēbam
	erās	poterās	ībās	volēbās	ferēbās	capiēbās
	erat	poterat	ībat	volēbat	ferēbat	capiēbat
	erāmus	poterāmus	ībāmus	volēbāmus	ferēbāmus	capiēbāmus
	erātis	poterātis	ībātis	volēbātis	ferēbātis	capiēbātis
	erant	poterant	ībant	volēbant	ferēbant	capiēbant

	FUTURE					
	I shall be	*I shall be able*	*I shall go*	*I shall want*	*I shall bring*	*I shall take*
	erō	poterō	ībō	volam	feram	capiam
	eris	poteris	ībis	volēs	ferēs	capiēs
	erit	poterit	ībit	volet	feret	capiet
	erimus	poterimus	ībimus	volēmus	ferēmus	capiēmus
	eritis	poteritis	ībitis	volētis	ferētis	capiētis
	erunt	poterunt	ībunt	volent	ferent	capient

PERFECT	*I have been, I was*	*I have been able, I was able*	*I have gone, I went*	*I (have) wanted*	*I (have) brought*	*I have taken, I took*
	fuī	potuī	iī	voluī	tulī	cēpī
	fuistī	potuistī	iistī	voluistī	tulistī	cēpistī
	fuit	potuit	iit	voluit	tulit	cēpit
	fuimus	potuimus	iimus	voluimus	tulimus	cēpimus
	fuistis	potuistis	iistis	voluistis	tulistis	cēpistis
	fuērunt	potuērunt	iērunt	voluērunt	tulērunt	cēpērunt
PLUPERFECT	*I had been*	*I had been able*	*I had gone*	*I had wanted*	*I had brought*	*I had taken*
	fueram	potueram	ieram	volueram	tuleram	cēperam
	fuerās	potuerās	ierās	voluerās	tulerās	cēperās
	fuerat	potuerat	ierat	voluerat	tulerat	cēperat
	fuerāmus	potuerāmus	ierāmus	voluerāmus	tulerāmus	cēperāmus
	fuerātis	potuerātis	ierātis	voluerātis	tulerātis	cēperātis
	fuerant	potuerant	ierant	voluerant	tulerant	cēperant
FUTURE PERFECT	*I shall have been*	*I shall have been able*	*I shall have gone*	*I shall have wanted*	*I shall have brought*	*I shall have taken*
	fuerō	potuerō	ierō	voluerō	tulerō	cēperō
	fueris	potueris	ieris	volueris	tuleris	cēperis
	fuerit	potuerit	ierit	voluerit	tulerit	cēperit
	fuerimus	potuerimus	ierimus	voluerimus	tulerimus	cēperimus
	fueritis	potueritis	ieritis	volueritis	tuleritis	cēperitis
	fuerint	potuerint	ierint	voluerint	tulerint	cēperint

2 Subjunctive

PRESENT					
sim	possim	eam	velim	feram	capiam
sīs	possīs	eās	velīs	ferās	capiās
sit	possit	eat	velit	ferat	capiat
sīmus	possīmus	eāmus	velīmus	ferāmus	capiāmus
sītis	possītis	eātis	velītis	ferātis	capiātis
sint	possint	eant	velint	ferant	capiant

IMPERFECT					
essem	possem	īrem	vellem	ferrem	caperem
essēs	possēs	īrēs	vellēs	ferrēs	caperēs
esset	posset	īret	vellet	ferret	caperet
essēmus	possēmus	īrēmus	vellēmus	ferrēmus	caperēmus
essētis	possētis	īrētis	vellētis	ferrētis	caperētis
essent	possent	īrent	vellent	ferrent	caperent

PERFECT					
fuerim	potuerim	ierim	voluerim	tulerim	cēperim
fuerīs	potuerīs	ierīs	voluerīs	tulerīs	cēperīs
fuerit	potuerit	ierit	voluerit	tulerit	cēperit
fuerīmus	potuerīmus	ierīmus	voluerīmus	tulerīmus	cēperīmus
fuerītis	potuerītis	ierītis	voluerītis	tulerītis	cēperītis
fuerint	potuerint	ierint	voluerint	tulerint	cēperint

PLUPERFECT					
fuissem	potuissem	iissem	voluissem	tulissem	cēpissem
fuissēs	potuissēs	iissēs	voluissēs	tulissēs	cēpissēs
fuisset	potuisset	iisset	voluisset	tulisset	cēpisset
fuissēmus	potuissēmus	iissēmus	voluissēmus	tulissēmus	cēpissēmus
fuissētis	potuissētis	iissētis	voluissētis	tulissētis	cēpissētis
fuissent	potuissent	iissent	voluissent	tulissent	cēpissent

3 Other forms of the verb

IMPERATIVE			*go!*		*bring!*	*take!*
SINGULAR			ī		fer	cape
PLURAL			īte		ferte	capite
PRESENT		*being able*	*going*	*wanting*	*bringing*	*taking*
PARTICIPLE		potēns	iēns	volēns	ferēns	capiēns
		potentis	euntis	volentis	ferentis	capientis
PRESENT	*to be*	*to be able*	*to go*	*to want*	*to bring*	*to take*
INFINITIVE	esse	posse	ire	velle	ferre	capere
PERFECT	*to have*	*to have been*	*to have*	*to have*	*to have*	*to have*
INFINITIVE	*been*	*able*	*gone*	*wanted*	*brought*	*taken*
	fuisse	potuisse	iisse	voluisse	tulisse	cēpisse
FUTURE	*to be*		*to be*		*to be*	*to be*
INFINITIVE	*about to*		*about to*		*about to*	*about to*
	be		*go*		*bring*	*take*
	futūrus		itūrus		lātūrus	captūrus
	esse		esse		esse	esse
GERUNDIVE	eundus				ferendus	capiendus
GERUND	eundī				ferendī	capiendī

4 Study the following *passive* forms of **ferō** and **capiō**:

Indicative

PRESENT	*I am brought*	*I am taken*
	feror	capior
	ferris	caperis
	fertur	capitur
	ferimur	capimur
	feriminī	capiminī
	feruntur	capiuntur
IMPERFECT	*I was being brought*	*I was being taken*
	ferēbar	capiēbar
	ferēbāris *etc.*	capiēbāris *etc.*
FUTURE	*I shall be brought*	*I shall be taken*
	ferar	capiar
	ferēris *etc.*	capiēris *etc.*
PERFECT	*I have been brought*	*I have been taken*
	lātus sum	captus sum
	lātus es *etc.*	captus es *etc.*
PLUPERFECT	*I had been brought*	*I had been taken*
	lātus eram	captus eram
	lātus erās *etc.*	captus erās *etc.*
FUTURE PERFECT	*I shall have been brought*	*I shall have been taken*
	lātus erō	captus erō
	lātus eris *etc.*	captus eris *etc.*
PERFECT PASSIVE PARTICIPLE	*having been brought*	*having been taken*
	lātus	captus
PRESENT PASSIVE INFINITIVE	*to be brought*	*to be taken*
	ferrī	capī
PERFECT PASSIVE INFINITIVE	*to have been brought*	*to have been taken*
	lātus esse	captus esse

5 Subjunctive

PRESENT	ferar	capiar
	ferāris	capiāris
	ferātur	capiātur
	ferāmur	capiāmur
	ferāminī	capiāminī
	ferantur	capiantur
IMPERFECT	ferrer	caperer
	ferrēris	caperēris
	ferrētur	caperētur
	ferrēmur	caperēmur
	ferrēminī	caperēminī
	ferrentur	caperentur
PERFECT	lātus sim	captus sim
	lātus sīs	captus sīs
	lātus sit	captus sit
	lātī sīmus	captī sīmus
	lātī sītis	captī sītis
	lātī sint	captī sint
PLUPERFECT	lātus essem	captus essem
	lātus essēs	captus essēs
	lātus esset	captus esset
	lātī essēmus	captī essēmus
	lātī essētis	captī essētis
	lātī essent	captī essent

6 In Stage 42, you met the irregular verb **fīō** (*I am made, I become*, etc.):

	Indicative	Subjunctive
PRESENT	*I become, etc.*	
	fīō	fīam
	fīs	fīās
	fit	fīat
	(fīmus)	fīāmus
	(fītis)	fīātis
	fīunt	fīant
IMPERFECT	*I was becoming, etc.*	
	fīēbam	fierem
	fīēbās	fierēs
	fīēbat	fieret
	fīēbāmus	fierēmus
	fīēbātis	fierētis
	fīēbant	fierent
FUTURE	*I shall become, etc.*	
	fīam	
	fīēs	
	fīet	
	fīēmus	
	fīētis	
	fīent	
PRESENT INFINITIVE	*to become, be made*	
	fierī	

The forms of **fīō** are used as present, future, and imperfect tenses of the passive of **faciō** (*I make, I do*, etc.):

servī nihil faciunt.   nihil fit.
The slaves are doing nothing.   *Nothing is being done.*
                          Or, *Nothing is happening.*

populus mē rēgem faciet.   rēx fīam.
The people will make me a king.   *I shall be made king.*
                          Or, *I shall become king.*

The other tenses of the passive of **faciō** are formed in the usual way:

equitēs impetum fēcērunt.   impetus ab equitibus factus est.
The cavalry made an attack.   *An attack was made by the cavalry.*

Uses of the cases

1 *nominative*

captīvus clāmābat.	*The prisoner was shouting.*

2 *vocative*

valē, **domine**!	*Good-bye, master!*

3 *genitive*

a	māter **puerōrum**	*the mother of the boys*
b	plūs **pecūniae**	*more money*
c	vir **maximae virtūtis**	*a man of very great courage*

4 *dative*

a	**mīlitibus** cibum dedimus.	*We gave food to the soldiers.*
b	**vestrō candidātō** nōn faveō.	*I do not support your candidate.*
c	Note this use of the dative of **auxilium**, **cūra**, and **odium**:	

rēx nōbīs **magnō auxiliō** erat.	*The king was a great help to us.*
dignitās tua mihi **cūrae** est.	*Your dignity is a matter of concern to me.*
Epaphrodītus omnibus **odiō** est.	*Epaphroditus is hateful to everyone.*
	Or, in more natural English:
	Everyone hates Epaphroditus.

5 *accusative*

a	**pontem** trānsiimus.	*We crossed the bridge.*
b	**trēs hōrās** labōrābam.	*I was working for three hours.*
c	per **agrōs**; ad **vīllam**; in **forum**.	*through the fields; to the house; into the forum*

For examples of the accusative used in indirect statement, see pp. 294-296.

6 *ablative*

a	**spectāculō** attonitus	*astonished by the sight*
b	senex **longā barbā**	*an old man with a long beard*
c	**nōbilī gente** nātus	*born from a noble family*
d	**quārtō diē** revēnit.	*He came back on the fourth day.*
e	cum **amīcīs**; ab **urbe**; in **forō**	*with friends; away from the city; in the forum*
f	Note this use of the ablative:	

marītus erat ignāvior **uxōre**.	*The husband was lazier than his wife.*

Compare this with another way of expressing the same idea:

marītus erat ignāvior quam uxor.

g The ablative is used with adjectives such as **dignus** (*worthy*) and **plēnus** (*full*), and verbs such as **ūtor** (*I use*):

magnō honōre dignus	*worthy of great honor*
venēnō ūtī cōnstituit.	*He decided to use poison.*

For examples of ablative absolute phrases, see paragraphs 5-6 on pp. 289-290.

7   Further examples of some of the uses listed above:

    a   satis pecūniae habētis?
    b   theātrum spectātōribus plēnum erat.
    c   septem hōrās dormiēbam.
    d   es stultior asinō!
    e   mīlitēs gladiīs et pugiōnibus ūtēbantur.
    f   Myropnous vōbīs auxiliō erit.
    g   strepitū urbis cōnfectus, ad vīllam rūsticam discessit.
    h   puella parentibus resistere nōn poterat.

8   *locative*

Study the following examples:

    a   **Rōmae** manēbam.   *I was staying in Rome.*
    b   **Londiniī** habitāmus   *We live in London*
    c   **Neāpolī** mortuus est.   *He died at Naples.*
    d   quid **Pompēiīs** accidit?   *What happened in Pompeii?*

The words in **boldface** are in the *locative* case.

The locative case is used only in names of towns and small islands and a small number of other words; it is therefore not normally included in lists of cases such as the table on pp.258-259. In first and second declension singular nouns, the locative case has the same form as the genitive; in third declension singular nouns, it is the same as the dative; in plural nouns, it is the same as the ablative.

Notice the locative case of **domus** (*home*) and **rūs** (*country*):

    e   **domī** dormiēbat.   *He was sleeping at home.*
    f   **rūrī** numquam labōrō.   *I never work in the country.*

Further examples:

    g   hanc epistulam Ephesī scrībō.
    h   Athēnīs manēbimus.
    i   mīlitēs in castrīs Dēvae erant.
    j   rūrī ōtiōsus sum.

Uses of the participle

1   You have seen how participles are used to describe nouns or pronouns:

> clientēs, sportulam **adeptī**, discessērunt.
> *The clients, **having obtained** their handout, departed.*

> centuriō tē in umbrā **latentem** vīdit.
> *The centurion saw you **hiding** in the shadow.*

In the first example, the *perfect active participle* **adeptī** describes **clientēs**; in the second example, the *present participle* **latentem** describes **tē**.

2   Sometimes the noun or pronoun described by a participle is omitted:

> valdē **perturbātus**, ex urbe fūgit.
> ***Having been** thoroughly **alarmed**, **he** fled from the city.*

> **moritūrī** tē salūtāmus.
> ***We, (who are) about to die**, salute you.*

In examples like these, the ending of the verb (**fūgit**, **salūtāmus**, etc.) makes it clear that the participle refers to *he*, *we*, etc.

3   Sometimes the participle refers not to a particular person or thing but more vaguely to *somebody* or *some people*:

> tū faciem sub aquā, Sexte, **natantis** habēs.
> *You have the face, Sextus, **of (someone) swimming** under water.*

> ārea plēna strepitū **labōrantium** erat.
> *The courtyard was full of the noise **of (people) working**.*

4   Notice again how a noun and participle in the dative case may be placed at the beginning of the sentence:

> **Salviō** dē fortūnā **querentī** nūllum respōnsum dedī.
> ***To Salvius complaining** about his luck I gave no reply.*
> Or, in more natural English:
> *When **Salvius complained** about his luck, I gave **him** no reply.*

5   In Unit 3, you met ablative absolute phrases:

> senex, pecūniā cēlātā, fīliōs arcessīvit.
> *After hiding his money, the old man sent for his sons.*

> Epaphrodītō loquente, nūntius accurrit.
> *While Epaphroditus was speaking, a messenger came dashing up.*

6   Further examples:

   a   flammīs exstīnctīs, dominus ruīnam īnspexit.
   b   ubīque vōcēs poētam laudantium audiēbantur.
   c   ā iūdice damnātus, in exilium iit.
   d   fēmina, multōs cāsūs passa, auxilium nostrum petēbat.
   e   servō haesitantī lībertātem praemiumque obtulī.
   f   sōle oriente, lūx fīēbat.
   g   Sparsus mē uxōrem ductūrus est.

Uses of the subjunctive

1   *with* **cum** *(meaning when, since, although)*

   cum prōvinciam circumīrem, incendium Nīcomēdīae coortum est.
   When I was going around the province, *a fire broke out in Nicomedia.*

2   *indirect question*

   mīlitēs cognōscere volunt **ubi senex gemmās cēlāverit**.
   *The soldiers want to find out **where the old man has hidden the jewels**.*

   Sometimes the verb of asking, etc. (e.g. **rogō**, **scio**) is placed *after* the indirect question:

   utrum custōs esset an carnifex, nēmō **sciēbat**.
   *Whether he was a guard or an executioner, no one **knew**.*

3   *purpose clause*

   hīc manēbō, **ut vīllam dēfendam**.
   *I shall stay here, **to defend the villa**.*

   prīnceps Plīnium ēmīsit **quī Bīthȳnōs regeret**.
   *The emperor sent Pliny out **to rule the Bithynians**.*

   tacēbāmus, **nē ā centuriōne audīrēmur**.
   *We kept quiet, **in order not to be heard by the centurion**.*

4   *indirect command*

   tē moneō **ut lēgibus pāreās**.
   *I advise you **to obey the laws**.*

   medicus nōbīs imperāvit **nē ingriderēmur**.
   *The doctor told us **not to go in**.*

5   *result clause*

   barbarī tot hastās coniēcērunt **ut plūrimī equitēs vulnerārentur**.
   *The barbarians threw so many spears **that most horsemen were wounded**.*

6 with **priusquam** *before* and **dum** *until*:

nōbīs fugiendum est, **priusquam custōdēs nōs cōnspiciant**.
*We must run away, **before the guards catch sight of us**.*

exspectābant **dum centuriō signum daret**.
*They were waiting **until the centurion should give the signal**.*
Or, in more natural English:
*They were waiting **for the centurion to give the signal**.*

abībō, **priusquam ā dominō agnōscar**.
*I shall go away, **before I am/can be recognized by the master**.*

dum meaning *while* is used with a *present indicative*.

7 *fearing clauses*

avārus timēbat **nē fūr aurum invenīret**.
*The miser was afraid **that a thief would find his gold**.*

vereor **nē inimīcī nostrī nōn discesserint**.
*I am afraid **that our enemies have not left**.*

8 Further examples:

a senex, cum verba medicī audīvisset, testāmentum fēcit.
b mīlitibus persuādēbō ut marītō tuō parcant.
c latrōnēs mercātōrem occīdērunt priusquam ad salūtem pervenīret.
d tam benignus est rēx ut omnēs eum ament.
e scīre volō quis fenestram frēgerit.
f perīculum est nē occīdāris.
g Domitiānus ipse adest ut fābulam spectet.
h Agricola Britannōs hortātus est ut mōrēs Rōmānōs discerent.
i mīlitēs ēmīsit quī turbam dēpellerent.
j haruspicēs cognōscere cōnābuntur num ōmina bona sint.
k dominus verēbātur nē servī effūgissent.
l ducem ōrābimus nē captīvōs interficiat.

9 *Subjunctives* can also be used in *main clauses* (*independent uses of the subjunctive*):

Hortatory subjunctive

> lūdōs **spectēmus**!   ***Let us watch** the games!*
> nē **morēmur**!   ***Let us** not **delay**!*

Jussive subjunctive

> epistulam statim **recitet**!   ***Let him read out** the letter at once!*
> **caveant** ēmptōrēs!   ***Let** the buyers **beware**!*

Deliberative subjunctive

> quid **faciam**?   *What **am I to do**?*
> quō modō **scīrent**?   *How **were they to know**?*

10 Further examples:

    a   proficīscāmur!
    b   quō fugiam?
    c   Salvius nunc respondeat!
    d   fīat lūx!
    e   utrum loquerentur an tacērent?

11 For examples of the subjunctive in *conditional sentences*, see p. 298.

12 For examples of the subjunctive used in *indirect discourse*, see paragraph 1 on p. 297.

Indirect statement

1 You have met indirect statements, expressed by a noun or pronoun in the *accusative* case and one of the following *infinitive* forms of the verb. Some indirect statements are introduced by a verb in the *present* tense (e.g. **dīcō**, **crēdunt**), while others are introduced by a verb in the *perfect* or *imperfect* tense (e.g. **dīxī**, **crēdēbant**); notice again how this makes a difference to the translation of the infinitive.

a *present active infinitive*

> **crēdō** prīncipem Agricolae **invidēre**.
> *I **believe** that the emperor **is jealous** of Agricola.*

> **crēdēbam** prīncipem Agricolae **invidēre**.
> *I **believed** that the emperor **was jealous** of Agricola.*

(Compare this with the direct statement: prīnceps Agricolae invidet.)

b *present passive infinitive*

> **scit** multās prōvinciās ā latrōnibus **vexārī**.
> *He **knows** that many provinces **are troubled** by bandits.*

> **sciēbat** multās prōvinciās ā latrōnibus **vexārī**.
> *He **knew** that many provinces **were troubled** by bandits.*

(Compare: multae prōvinciae ā latrōnibus vexantur.)

c *perfect active infinitive*

> centuriō hostēs **dīcit cōnstitisse**.
> *The centurion **says** that the enemy **have halted**.*

> centuriō hostēs **dīxit cōnstitisse**.
> *The centurion **said** that the enemy **had halted**.*

(Compare: hostēs cōnstitērunt.)

d *perfect passive infinitive*

> vir uxōrem **servātam esse putat**.
> *The man **thinks** that his wife **has been saved**.*

> vir uxōrem **servātam esse putāvit**.
> *The man **thought** that his wife **had been saved**.*

(Compare: uxor servāta est.)

e *future active infinitive*

> senātōrēs **prō certō habent** cīvēs numquam **cessūrōs esse**.
> *The senators **are sure** that the citizens **will** never **give in**.*

> senātōrēs **prō certō habēbant** cīvēs numquam **cessūrōs esse**.
> *The senators **were sure** that the citizens **would** never **give in**.*

(Compare: cīvēs numquam cēdent.)

The verb of speaking, etc. (e.g. **crēdō**, **dīcit**, **putat**) can be placed either at the beginning of the sentence (as in example **a** above) or in the middle of the indirect statement (as in example **c**), or at the end of the sentence (example **d**).

2 Notice how the verb **negō** is used with indirect statements:

> iuvenis **negāvit** sē pecūniam perdidisse.
> *The young man **denied that** he had wasted the money.*
> Or, *The young man **said that** he had **not** wasted the money.*

3 Compare the following examples:

a Salvius dīcit **sē** in Ītaliā habitāre.
  (Direct statement: in Ītaliā habit**ō**.)
b Salvius dīcit **eum** in forō ambulāre.
  (Direct statement: in forō ambul**at**.)

4 Further examples:

a nauta dīcit sē nāvem mox refectūrum esse.
b nauta dīxit sē nāvem mox refectūrum esse.
c sciō magnum perīculum nōbīs imminēre.
d sciēbam magnum perīculum nōbīs imminēre.
e dux eum discessisse crēdit.
f dux eum discessisse crēdēbat.
g nūntiī vīllās negant dēlētās esse.
h nūntiī vīllās negāvērunt dēlētās esse.
i audiō multōs captīvōs ad mortem cotīdiē dūcī.
j audīvī multōs captīvōs ad mortem cotīdiē dūcī.

5   Further examples:

    a audiō trēs Virginēs Vestālēs damnātās esse.
    b mē putō optimē recitāre.
    c ancilla dīcit dominum in hortō ambulāre.
    d fāma vagātur multa oppida dēlēta esse.
    e ducem auxilium mox missūrum esse spērāvimus.
    f nūntius negāvit sē ad ultimās partēs Britanniae pervēnisse.
    g cūr suspicātus es Salvium testāmentum fīnxisse?
    h fēmina marītum illō carcere tenērī putat.
    i crēdō mīlitēs fidem servātūrōs esse.
    j servus crēdēbat multōs hospitēs invītārī.

6   Sometimes one indirect statement is followed immediately by another:

    rēx dīxit Rōmānōs exercitum parāvisse; mox prīmōs mīlitēs adventūrōs esse.
    *The king said that the Romans had prepared an army; (**he said that**)*
    the first soldiers would soon arrive.

Notice that the verb **dīxit** is not repeated in the second half of the sentence;
the use of the accusative (**prīmōs mīlitēs**) and the infinitive (**adventūrōs
esse**) makes it clear that the sentence is still reporting what the king said.

Further examples:

    a servus nūntiāvit cōnsulem morbō gravī afflīgī; medicōs dē vītā eius dēspērāre.
    b fāma vagābātur decem captīvōs ē carcere līberātōs esse; Imperātōrem enim
       eīs ignōvisse.

7   For examples of the subjunctive used in indirect statements, see paragraphs **1** and **2** on
    p. 297.

Subordinate clauses in indirect discourse

1 The subjunctive is normally used for any verb of a subordinate clause within indirect discourse, i.e. *indirect question*, *indirect command*, and *indirect statement*.

Study the following examples:

   a audiō coquum numquam labōrāre, **quod semper dormiat**.
      *I hear that the cook never works, **because he is always asleep**.*

   b puer rogāvit cūr fūrēs, **postquam canem excitāvissent**, nōn fūgissent.
      *The boy asked why the thieves, **after they had woken the dog**, had not run away.*

   c mercātor servīs imperāvit ut vīnum effunderent **quod īnferrent**.
      *The merchant ordered the slaves to pour the wine **which they were bringing in**.*

2 Translate the following examples:

   a servus dīcit togās, quās ille senex vēndat, sordidās esse.
   b praecō spērābat clientēs, simulac patrōnum salūtāvissent, abitūrōs esse.
   c centuriō mīlitēs rogāvit ubi arma cēlāvissent quae in proeliō cēpissent.
   d Simōn mātrem hortātur nē lacrimīs sē det quamvīs multa mala passa sit.
   e iuvenis nūntiāvit patrem, quod morbō afflīgerētur, domī manēre.
   f iuvenis deōs precātus est ut Modestum quī Vilbiam abstulisset pūnīrent.
   g cīvēs exīstimābant Agricolam, postquam Calēdoniōs vīcisset, iniūstē revocātum esse.
   h Rūfilla scīre vult cūr marītus, quoniam Britannī molestissimī sint, in īnsulā maneat.

Conditional sentences

1 You have met conditional sentences in which *indicative* forms of the verb are used:

   sī valēs, gaudeō.   *If you are well, I am pleased.*

   Notice again that a Latin future perfect (or future) tense in a conditional clause is usually translated by an English present tense:

   sī illud iterum **fēceris**, tē pūniam.
   *If **you do** that again, I shall punish you.*

2 You have also met conditional sentences in which *subjunctive* forms of the verb are used:

   sī dīligentius **labōrāvissem**, dominus mē **līberāvisset**.
   *If **I had worked** harder, the master **would have freed** me.*

   sī Domitiānus nōs adhūc **regeret**, miserrimī **essēmus**.
   *If Domitian **were** still **ruling** us, **we would be** very unhappy.*

   sī hanc medicīnam **bibās**, statim **convalēscās**.
   *If **you were to drink** this medicine, **you would get better** at once.*

   Notice the pattern in English for conditional sentences:

Latin verb tense	"if" clause	main clause
Pluperfect	*... had ...*	*... would have ...*
Imperfect	*... were ...*	*... would ...*
Present	*... were to ...*	*... would ...*

3 Notice again how the word **nisi** is used in conditional sentences:

   nisi Imperātor novās cōpiās mīserit, opprimēmur.
   *If the emperor does **not** send reinforcements, we shall be overwhelmed.*
   Or, ***Unless** the emperor sends reinforcements, we shall be overwhelmed.*

4 Further examples:

   a sī illud putās, longē errās.
   b sī Milō cēterōs āthlētās superāvisset, cīvēs statuam eī posuissent.
   c sī Iuppiter ipse Lesbiam petat, illa eum spernat.
   d sī rēx essem, nōn in hāc vīllā labōrārem.
   e sī mīlitēs urbem oppugnent, facile eam capiant.
   f sī diūtius in urbe morātī essētis, numquam effūgissētis.
   g sī Marcus hodiē vīveret, cum Imperātōre cēnāret.
   h sī forte aurum in Britanniā inveniāmus, dīvitēs fīāmus.
   i nisi ego tuum fundum administrārem, tū pauperrimus essēs.
   j nisi amīcī nōbīs subvēnerint, in carcerem coniciēmur.

Gerunds and gerundives

1 You have met the *gerund*, e.g. **portandum** (*carrying*), **docendum** (*teaching*), etc. Notice again how the various cases of the gerund are used:

genitive

> optimam habeō occāsiōnem **cognōscendī** quid acciderit.
> *I have an excellent opportunity **of finding out** what has happened.*

accusative (with **ad**, meaning *for the purpose of*)

> multī hominēs **ad audiendum** aderant.
> *Many men were there **for the purpose of listening**.*
> Or, in more natural English:
> *Many men were there **to listen**.*

ablative

> prūdenter **emendō** et **vēndendō**, pater meus dīvitissimus fit.
> ***By buying** and **selling** sensibly, my father is becoming very rich.*

The cases of the gerund are listed in full on p. 275.

Further examples:

a senātor ad loquendum surrēxit.
b puer artem cantandī discere cōnābātur.
c decem gladiātōrēs ad pugnandum ēlēctī sunt.
d diū labōrandō, lībertātem adeptus sum.
e senex nūllam spem convalēscendī habēbat.

2 You have also met similar sentences in which the *gerundive* is used, e.g. **portandus**, **docendus**, etc.:

genitive

> optimam habeō occāsiōnem **vēritātis cōgnoscendae**.
> *I have an excellent opportunity **of finding out the truth**.*

accusative

> multī hominēs **ad ōrātiōnēs audiendās** aderant.
> *Many men were there **to listen to speeches**.*

ablative

> prūdenter **vīllīs emendīs** et **vēndendīs**, pater meus dīvitissimus fit.
> ***By buying** and **selling villas** sensibly, my father is becoming very rich.*

Further examples:

a multī clientēs advēnērunt ad nōs salūtandōs.
b erit nūlla occāsiō templī vīsitandī.
c versibus male recitandīs, poēta Mārtiālem vexat.
d cīvēs in theātrum fābulae spectandae causā conveniēbant.
e hī servī nihil dē dominō dēlectandō intellegunt.
f amīcus aquam ad flammās exstinguendās quaerēbat.

3 The *gerundive* is also used with a form of the verb **esse** to indicate that something ought to be done:

>nōbīs vīlla **aedificanda est**.
>*We **must build** a house.*

>mīlitibus **cōnsistendum erit**.
>*The soldiers **will have to halt**.*

When the gerundive is used in this way, it is known as a *gerundive of obligation*.

Further examples:

a tibi novae vestēs emendae sunt.
b pecūnia reddenda est.
c nōbīs in hāc vīllā dormiendum erit.
d exīstimō captīvōs līberandōs esse.
e mihi longum iter faciendum erat.

Part Two: Literary terms and rhetorical devices

The following glossary is not meant to be all-inclusive. In writing a literary appreciation for a piece of literature, it is not enough simply to list literary devices or figures of speech and give examples. Always examine critically each device or figure to see how the writer uses it and what effect is achieved by its use in context.

1 **alliteration:** repetition of the same sound, usually a consonant, at the beginning of two or more adjacent words to draw the reader's attention to those words.

2 **allusion:** a brief reference to details the writer expects the reader to recognize; may be proper nouns; references to customs, geography, history, mythology, etc.

3 **anaphora:** repetition of a word or phrase at the beginning of several successive clauses or phrases.

4 **apostrophe:** a sudden break in the narrative to address the reader or an absent person or thing; often indicates strong emotion.

5 **assonance:** repetition of sound, especially of the same vowel sound, in two or more adjacent words.

6 **asyndeton:** omission of customary connecting words to express lively action, tense excitement, or choking grief.

7 **connotation:** the cluster of implicit or associated meanings of a word as distinguished from that word's denotative or specific meaning.

8 **ellipsis:** omission of word(s) necessary for the grammatical structure of a sentence or clause to give greater brevity, compactness, and force.

9 **euphemism:** using a pleasant expression to replace an unpleasant one.

10 **figurative language:** language that departs from the literal standard meaning in order to achieve a special effect.

   a **metaphor:** an indirect comparison (without "like" or "as").
   b **personification:** the description of an inanimate object or concept in terms of human qualities.
   c **simile:** an expressed comparison often indicated by terms such as **velut, similis, quālis**.
   d **epic simile:** a comparison extended beyond the obvious by further details.

11 **hendiadys:** using two connected nouns rather than a noun modified by an adjective or its equivalent ("two things meaning one").

12 hyperbole: extravagant exaggeration not intended to be taken literally.

13 litotes: affirming something by denying its opposite; an intentional understatement.

14 metonymy: substituting a word for a related word, e.g. cause for effect, container for contained.

15 onomatopoeia: the use of a word or phrase whose sound echoes the meaning; also known as imitative harmony.

16 oxymoron: a rhetorical contrast achieved by putting together two contradictory terms; produces surprise.

17 paradox: a statement that seems contradictory but that reveals a truth.

18 polysyndeton: piling up of connectives; used to create an impressive scene, to stress deliberate action, to emphasize a pathetic enumeration, etc.

19 rhetorical question: a question used for its persuasive effect and for which no answer is expected or for which the answer is self-evident.

20 synecdoche: substituting a part for a whole.

21 tmesis: separating the two parts of a compound word.

22 transferred epithet: the application of a significant modifier to a word other than the one to which it actually belongs.

23 vivid particularization: a concrete or specified description, usually achieved by the use of proper nouns rich in connotations.

24 word order:
  a **chiasmus:** a crisscross arrangement (ABBA).
  b **first and last word positions:** placing an important word at first and last places in a line of poetry.
  c **framing:** a word placed out of its usual order so that it is framed or centered.
  d **interlocking word order/synchysis:** the words of one noun–adjective phrase alternating with those of another (ABAB).
  e **juxtaposition:** two words or phrases set side by side to intensify meaning.
  f **parallelism** or **balanced structure:** the recurrence or repetition of a grammatical pattern.
  g **separation:** separating grammatically related words (e.g. noun–noun; noun–adjective) to produce a word picture of the meaning conveyed by the words.

Part Three: Metrics

Meter or rhythm in poetry

English verse derives its rhythm, or repeated pattern of sound, from the natural stress accent of the English language. For example, Shakespeare's plays are written in iambic pentameter:

x / x / x / x / x /

If music be the food of love, play on.

Latin verse derives its rhythm from the length of time taken to pronounce each syllable. The rhythm depends upon the succession of long and short syllables and, to a lesser degree, upon the word accent. Latin poetry was meant to be read aloud; long and short vowels were clearly distinguished by Roman ears.

1 Finding syllables

A syllable is a single uninterrupted sound unit within a word. For example, **audiāmus** contains four syllables or sound units: **au-di-ā-mus**.

The number of syllables in a Latin word equals the number of vowels or diphthongs (*two vowels pronounced together*). In a syllable a vowel may be by itself or have a consonant(s) before and/or after it (e.g. **do-ce-ō**, **spe-ci-ēs**, **fert**). Latin diphthongs are **ae**, **au**, **oe**.

A consonant is pronounced with the vowel that follows it, e.g. **ro-gā-vit**.

If two vowels or a vowel and diphthong appear together, pronounce them separately, e.g. **di-ēs**, **fī-li-ae**.

If two consonants appear together, pronounce them separately, e.g. **spec-tā-tor**, **sol-li-ci-tus**.

If more than two consonants appear together, pronounce all except the last with the preceding vowel and the last with the following vowel, e.g. **cūnc-tor**.

If the word is compounded, pronounce its original parts separately, e.g. **cōn-sū-mit**.

Notes:
The combination **qu** = **kw**; do not treat the **u** as a vowel.

The letter **i** is a consonant or a vowel. **i** is a consonant if it occurs between vowels (**Trōiae**, **cuius**) or if it begins a word and is followed by a vowel (**iam**, **iungō**).

The letter **u** may be combined with the previous **s** or **g** depending on pronunciation, e.g. **san-guis**, **per-suā-de-ō**, **su-us**, or **ar-gu-ō**.

Divide the following words into syllables: dēligant, suāvis, respondeō, Graecia, quotiēns, audit, Ītalia, init, Britanniae, proelium, coniūrātiō.

2 Length or quantity of syllables

The arrangement of a line of Latin verse is based on a pattern of syllables with long (-) or short (˘) quantities.

A syllable is long by nature if it contains (1) a long vowel or (2) a diphthong, e.g. **dī**-cit, **cae**-ru-le-us.

A syllable is long by position if it contains a short vowel followed by (1) two consonants, one of which may start the next word, e.g. cae-ru-le-**ūs pōn**-tus or (2) a double consonant or **x** or **z**, e.g. īn-fē-**līx**.

A syllable is doubtful (i.e. it can be either short or long as the poet wishes) if it contains a short vowel followed by a consonant and then an **l** or **r** (liquid consonants), e.g. **nēc la**-cri-mīs (Virgil, *Aeneid* V.173) or pāl-mās … **ūt**-rās-que (Virgil, *Aeneid* V.233).

Otherwise a syllable is short.

Mark the long and short syllables in the following: dēligant, respondeō, Graecia, audit, Ītalia, init, Britanniae, proelium, init Graeciam.

3 Word stress (´)

In a word of two syllables, the stress falls on the first syllable, e.g. **á-mō**, **á-mās**.

In a word of three or more syllables, the stress falls on the second last (penultimate) syllable if that syllable is long, e.g. **por-tá-mus**, **cōn-féc-tus**.

In all other words of three or more syllables, the stress falls on the third syllable from the end (antepenultimate).

Mark the stress on the following words: amīcus, ancilla, equus, fīlius, leō, mercātor, monēbant, monent, rēgīna, sacerdōs, trahet.

4 Rhythmic patterns

Each line of Latin poetry is an arrangement of long and short syllables. Each arrangement carries its own pattern composed of a set number of bars or feet (|); e.g. a dactylic foot = - ˘ ˘, a spondaic foot = - -, a trochaic foot = - ˘.

A Scansion of dactylic hexameter

In the dactylic hexameter, there are six feet. The fifth foot is almost always a dactyl. To determine the poetic rhythm of a dactylic hexameter line, divide it into its component feet ( ) using the following pattern:

1	2	3	4	5	6
- ˘ ˘	- ˘ ˘	- ˘ ˘	- ˘ ˘	- ˘ ˘	- ˘
- -	- -	- -	- -	(- -)	- -

For example:

- ˘ ˘	- ˘ ˘	- -	- ˘ ˘	- ˘ ˘	- ˘
tum mihi	caerule	us sup	rā caput	adstitit	imber

Copy the following line and scan it, i.e. mark the rhythm and feet.

errāmus pelagō, totidem sine sīdere noctēs

B Elision

Latin poetry practices elision; in certain circumstances the final syllable of a word is slurred/combined with the first syllable of the next word. On a page you would put parentheses around this final syllable if it (1) ends in a vowel or diphthong before a word beginning with a vowel or **h**, e.g. **dīx-it e-um-qu(e) ī-mīs sub fluc-ti-bus** or (2) ends in a vowel + **m** before a word beginning with a vowel or **h**, e.g. **ax-(em) u-mer-ō tor-quet**. Some of you may be familiar with elision from words such as *l'église* or *l'homme* in French.

Indicate the elisions in the following: rēge hōram, terra ūna, terrae incola, hōram ūna, rēgem hōram, cāsum audiō.

Copy and scan the following:

postquam altum tenuēre ratēs nec iam amplius ūllae

appārent terrae, caelum undique et undique pontus

C Caesura

The ending of a word within a foot is called a **caesura** (cut). The mark for a caesura is ‖. In a hexameter line the main caesura often falls midway.

For example:

tum mihi | caerule | us ‖ sup | rā caput | adstitit | imber

D Scansion of elegiac couplet

The elegiac couplet is comprised of two lines, a dactylic hexameter alternating with a pentameter line, which is actually the first two and a half feet of a hexameter twice.

To determine the rhythmic pattern of an elegiac couplet, divide it into its component feet as follows:

Line 1 | – ⏑ ⏑ | – ⏑ ⏑ | – ⏑ ⏑ | – ⏑ ⏑ | – ⏑ ⏑ | – ⏑
          | – – | – – | – – | – – | | – –

Line 2 | – ⏑ ⏑ | – ⏑ ⏑ | – ‖ | – ⏑ ⏑ | – ⏑ ⏑ | ⏑
          | – – | – – | | | | –

For example:

```
–  ⏑ ⏑ | – –  | –   –  | –     | –  – ⏑ | – –
accipe | frāter | nō mul | tum mā | nantia | flētū,
```

```
–   –  ⏑ | – ⏑  ⏑  |  –  ||  – ⏑ ⏑ | ⏑  ⏑  | –
atqu(e) in | perpetu | um, ‖ frāter, a | v(ē) atque va | lē.
```

Copy and scan the following:

exigis ut nostrōs dōnem tibi, Tucca, libellōs.
   nōn faciam: nam vīs vēndere, nōn legere.

E Scansion of hendecasyllables

The hendecasyllabic line is an arrangement of eleven syllables within five feet.

To determine the rhythmic pattern of a hendecasyllabic line, divide it as follows:

‿ –|– ‿ ‿|– ‿|– ‿|– ‿

For example:

– –|– ‿ ‿|– ‿|– ‿|– –
pas-ser | mor-tu-us | est me- | ae pu- | el-lae,

– –|– ‿ ‿|– ‿|– ‿|– –
pas-ser, | dē-li-ci- | ae me- | ae pu- | el-lae,

– –|– ‿ ‿|– ‿|– ‿|– ‿
quem plūs | il-l(a) o-cu- | līs su- | īs a- | mā-bat.

Copy and scan the following:

vī-vā-mus, me-a Les-bi(a), at-qu(e) a-mē-mus.

mī-rā-ris ve-te-rēs, Va-cer-ra, sō-lōs

nec lau-dās ni-si mor-tu-ōs po-ē-tās.

F Final suggestions

"Scanning" poetry on paper, that is, marking the long and short vowels, is just a way of keeping a record of the rhythm, a device to help you read Latin poetry aloud with an appreciation of the sound effects developed by the Roman poets. A preponderance of dactyls produces a fast pace or light or lilting effect. A preponderance of spondees suggests tension or a slow or difficult movement and produces a more solemn, grand, or ominous effect; several elisions suggest strong emotion.

When you are scanning a line of Latin poetry

- copy the Latin correctly,
- mark elisions and do not count as a syllable,
- mark the syllables you know are long,
- deduce the remaining syllables from the metric pattern,
- read the Latin aloud.

Part Four: Vocabulary

1 Nouns, adjectives, verbs, and prepositions are listed as in the Unit 3 Language information.

2 Verbs such as **crēdō**, **obstō**, etc., which are often used with a noun or pronoun in the dative case, are marked + DAT.

Notice again how such verbs are used:

tibi crēdō.	*I put trust in you.*
	Or, *I trust you.*
turba nōbīs obstābat.	*The crowd was a hindrance to us.*
	Or, *The crowd hindered us.*

3 The *present* tense of *second* conjugation verbs like **doceō** has the same endings (except in the first person singular) as the *future* tense of *third* conjugation verbs like **trahō**.

For example:

	PRESENT		FUTURE	
ACTIVE	doceam	*I teach*	traham	*I shall drag*
	docēs		**trahēs**	
	docet		**trahet**	
	etc.		etc.	
PASSIVE	doceor	*I am taught*	trahar	*I shall be dragged*
	docēris		**trahēris**	
	docētur		**trahētur**	
	etc.		etc.	

The Vocabulary can be used to check which conjugation a verb belongs to, and thus assist in translating its tense correctly. For example, the conjugation and tense of **iubent** can be checked in the following way:

> The verb is listed on page 328 as **iubeō**, **iubēre**, etc., so it belongs to the second conjugation like **doceō**, **docēre**, etc., and therefore **iubent** must be in the present tense: *they order.*

And the conjugation and tense of **dūcent** can be checked like this:

> The verb is listed on page 320 as **dūcō**, **dūcere**, etc., so it belongs to the third conjugation like **trahō**, **trahere**, etc., and therefore **dūcent** must be in the future tense: *they will lead.*

Translate the following words, using the Vocabulary to check conjugation and tense:

a rīdēs, intellegēs   **c** gaudēmus, monēmus   **e** prohibentur, regentur
b dēlent, venient   **d** convertet, ignōscet   **f** dūcēris, iubēris

4 Notice again the difference between the listed forms of deponent verbs and the forms of ordinary verbs:

deponent verbs
cōnor, cōnārī, cōnātus sum *try*
loquor, loquī, locūtus sum *speak*

ordinary verbs
collocō, collocāre, collocāvī, collocātus *place, put*
vēndō, vēndere, vēndidī, vēnditus *sell*

The Vocabulary can be used to check whether a word with a passive ending (e.g. **ēgrediuntur**, **custōdiuntur**) comes from a deponent verb or not.

For example, **ēgrediuntur** comes from a verb which is listed as **ēgredior**, **ēgredī**, **ēgressus sum** *go out*. It is clear from the listed forms that **ēgredior** is a deponent verb; it therefore has an active meaning, and **ēgrediuntur** must mean *they go out*.

custōdiuntur, on the other hand, comes from a verb which is listed as **custōdiō**, **custōdīre**, **custōdīvī**, **custōdītus** *guard*. It is clear from the listed forms that **custōdiō** is not a deponent verb; **custōdiuntur** must therefore have a passive meaning, i.e. *they are being guarded*.

5 Translate the following sentences, using the Vocabulary to check whether the words in **boldface** are deponent verbs or not:

a centuriō mīlitēs **hortābātur**.
b amīcus meus ab Imperātōre **commendābātur**.
c cūr dē fortūnā tuā semper **quereris**?
d cūr ā dominō tuō semper **neglegeris**?
e puer dē perīculō **monitus est**.
f mercātor multās gemmās facile **adeptus est**.

6 All words which are given in **Vocabulary checklists** for Stages 1–48 are marked with the Stage in which they were given. For example:

16 **dēlectō**, **dēlectāre**, **dēlectāvī** *delight, please*

This means that **dēlectō** appeared as a Vocabulary checklist word in Stage 16.

a

A. = Aulus

17,21 ā, ab (+ ABL) — *from; by*

abdūcō, abdūcere, abdūxī, abductus — *lead away, divert*

10 abeō, abīre, abiī — *go away*

abripiō, abripere, abripuī, abreptus — *tear away from*

abrumpō, abrumpere, abrūpī, abruptus — *split, tear apart*

absēns, absēns, absēns *gen.* absentis — *absent*

abstineō, abstinēre, abstinuī — *abstain*

abstulī *see* auferō

6 absum, abesse, āfuī — *be out, be absent, be away*

absurdus, absurda, absurdum — *absurd*

28 ac — *and*

accēnsus, accēnsa, accēnsum — *inflamed, on fire*

25 accidō, accidere, accidī — *happen*

10 accipiō, accipere, accēpī, acceptus — *accept, take in, receive*

accommodō, accommodāre, accommodāvī, accommodātus — *fasten*

accurrō, accurrere, accurrī — *run up*

accūsātiō, accūsātiōnis, f. — *accusation*

accūsātor, accūsātōris, m. — *accuser, prosecutor*

34 accūsō, accūsāre, accūsāvī, accūsātus — *accuse*

ācer, ācris, ācre — *eager, excited*

acerbus, acerba, acerbum — *harsh, disagreeable*

ācriter — *keenly, eagerly, fiercely*

āctus *see* agō

acūtus, acūta, acūtum — *sharp*

3 ad (+ ACC) — *to, at, up to, about*

addō, addere, addidī, additus — *add*

addere gradum — *go forward step by step*

addūcō, addūcere, addūxī, adductus — *lead, lead on, encourage, pull, draw up (to the chest)*

adēmptus, adēmpta, adēmptum — *taken away*

20 adeō, adīre, adiī — *approach, go up to*

27 adeō — *so much, so greatly*

trēs adeō — *as many as three, three entire*

adeptus *see* adipīscor

adest, adfuī *see* adsum

adfīnis, adfīnis, m. — *relative, relation by marriage*

adhibeō, adhibēre, adhibuī, adhibitus — *use, apply*

precēs adhibēre — *offer prayers*

30 adhūc — *now, still*

usque adhūc — *until now, up to this time*

adībō *see* adeō

34 adipīscor, adipīscī, adeptus sum — *receive, obtain*

adiūtor, adiūtōris, m. — *helper*

adiuvō, adiuvāre, adiūvī, adiūtus — *help*

adligō, adligāre, adligāvī, adligātus — *tie*

42 adloquor, adloquī, adlocūtus sum — *speak to, address*

administrō, administrāre, administrāvī, administrātus — *manage*

rem administrāre — *manage the task*

admīrātiō, admīrātiōnis, f. — *admiration*

admīror, admīrārī, admīrātus sum — *admire*

admittō, admittere, admīsī, admissus — *admit, let in, allow*

admoneō, admonēre, admonuī, admonitus — *warn, advise*

adnītor, adnītī, adnīxus sum — *strain, exert oneself*

	adstō, adstāre, adstitī	stand by, stand	
5	adsum, adesse, adfuī	be here, be present, arrive	
	adsūmō, adsūmere, adsūmpsī, adsūmptus	adopt	
	adulātiō, adulātiōnis, f.	flattery	
	adulor, adulārī, adulātus sum	flatter	
	aduncus, adunca, aduncum	curved	
	adūrō, adūrere, adussī, adustus	burn	
13	adveniō, advenīre, advēnī	arrive	
	adventus, adventūs, m.	arrival	
32	adversus, adversa, adversum	hostile, unfavorable, unfortunate, undesirable, opposite	
32	rēs adversae	misfortune	
	adversus (+ ACC)	against, towards	
	advesperāscit, advesperāscere, advesperāvit	get dark, become dark	
13	aedificium, aedificiī, n.	building	
16	aedificō, aedificāre, aedificāvī, aedificātus	build	
	aequātus, aequāta, aequātum	level, side by side	
47	aequor, aequoris, n.	sea	
32	aequus, aequa, aequum	equal, fair, calm	
	āēr, āeris, m.	air	
45	aestās, aestātis, f.	summer	
	aestimō, aestimāre, aestimāvī, aestimātus	value	
	aestus, aestūs, m.	heat	
	aetās, aetātis, f.	age, time	
	aetāte flōrēre	be in the prime of life	
	aeternus, aeterna, aeternum	eternal	
	aethēr, aetheris, m.	sky, heaven	
	afferō, afferre, attulī, adlātus	bring	
30	afficiō, afficere, affēcī, affectus	affect, treat, infect	

	affīgō, affīgere, affīxī, affīxus	attach to, nail to	
	crucī affīgere	nail to a cross, crucify	
40	affirmō, affirmāre, affirmāvī	declare	
	afflīgō, afflīgere, afflīxī, afflīctus	afflict, hurt	
	affluō, affluere, afflūxī	flock to the spot	
35	ager, agrī, m.	field	
43	aggredior, aggredī, aggressus sum	assail, attack, make an attempt on	
15	agmen, agminis, n.	column (of people), procession	
9	agnōscō, agnōscere, agnōvī, agnitus	recognize, acknowledge	
	agnus, agnī, m.	lamb	
4	agō, agere, ēgī, āctus	do, act	
	age!	come on!	
19	grātiās agere	thank, give thanks	
	iter agere	make one's way, travel	
	negōtium agere	do business, work	
	officium agere	do one's duty	
	quid agis?	how are you? how are you doing?	
	triumphum agere	celebrate a triumph	
5	agricola, agricolae, m.	farmer	
	ait	says, said	
	āla, ālae, f.	wing	
	alacriter	eagerly	
	āles, ālitis, m.f.	bird	
	aliquandō	sometimes	
	aliquantō	somewhat, rather	
	aliquī, aliqua, aliquod	some	
14, 25	aliquis, aliquid	someone, something	
15	alius, alia, aliud	other, another, else	
	aliī alia …	some … one thing, some … another, different people… different things	
29	aliī … aliī	some … others	
	in aliud	for any other purpose	
	alō, alere, aluī, altus	encourage	
	altē	high	

13	alter, altera, alterum	the other, another, a second, the second one ... the other		antrum, antrī, n.	cave
	alter ... alter		4	ānulus, ānulī, m.	ring
	usque alter	yet another		anus, anūs, f.	old woman
	altum, altī, n.	deep sea, open sea		anxius, anxia, anxium	anxious
31	altus, alta, altum	high, deep		aper, aprī, m.	boar
	amāns, amantis, m.	lover	25	aperiō, aperīre, aperuī, apertus	open, reveal
30	ambō, ambae, ambō	both	27	appāreō, appārēre, appāruī	appear
5	ambulō, ambulāre, ambulāvī	walk	33	appellō, appellāre, appellāvī, appellātus	call, call out to
	amīca, amīcae, f.	friend, girlfriend, mistress	17	appropinquō, appropinquāre, appropinquāvī (+ DAT)	approach, come near to
40	amīcitia, amīcitiae, f.	friendship		aptus, apta, aptum	suitable
	amīcus, amīca, amīcum	friendly	14	apud (+ ACC)	among, at the house of, with
2	amīcus, amīcī, m.	friend	15	aqua, aquae, f.	water
	amīcī prīncipis	friends of the emperor (the emperor's council)		aquaeductus, aquaeductūs, m.	aqueduct
12	āmittō, āmittere, āmīsī, āmissus	lose		aquilex, aquilegis, m.	water engineer, hydraulic engineer
19	amō, amāre, amāvī, amātus	love, like		Aquilō, Aquilōnis, m.	North wind
22	amor, amōris, m.	love	17	āra, ārae, f.	altar
	amphitheātrum, amphitheātrī, n.	amphitheater		arātor, arātōris, m.	plowman
	amplector, amplectī, amplexus sum	embrace		arātrum, arātrī, n.	plow
	amplius	more fully, at greater length, any more		arbitror, arbitrārī, arbitrātus sum	think
35	an	or, whether	39	arbor, arboris, f.	tree
35	utrum ... an	whether ... or		arca, arcae, f.	strongbox, chest, coffin
2	ancilla, ancillae, f.	slave girl, slave woman	20	accessō, accessere, accessīvī, accessītus	summon, send for
36	animadvertō, animadvertere, animadvertī, animadversus	notice, take notice of, have regard to		architectus, architectī, m.	builder, architect
				arcuātus, arcuāta, arcuātum	arched
	animal, animālis, n.	animal		arcus, arcūs, m.	arch
17	animus, animī, m.	spirit, soul, mind		ardenter	passionately
	in animō volvere	wonder, turn over in the mind	27	ardeō, ardēre, arsī	burn, be on fire
				ārea, āreae, f.	courtyard, construction site
21	annus, annī, m.	year		arēna, arēnae, f.	arena
31	ante (1) (+ ACC)	before, in front of	36	arma, armōrum, n. pl.	arms, weapons
	ante (2)	before, earlier, in front		armātus, armāta, armātum	armed
27	anteā	before		arō, arāre, arāvī, arātus	plow
	antidotum, antidotī, n.	antidote, remedy		arripiō, arripere, arripuī, arreptus	seize

20	ars, artis, f.	art, skill	
	artē	closely	
	artifex, artificis, m.f.	artist, craftsperson	
	artus, artūs, m.	limb	
	as, assis, m.	as (smallest Roman coin)	

29	ascendō, ascendere, ascendī	climb, rise
	ascīscō, ascīscere, ascīvī	adopt
	asinus, asinī, m.	ass, donkey
	aspectus, aspectūs, m.	sight
44	aspiciō, aspicere, aspexī, aspectus	look towards, catch sight of
	assiduē	continually
	assiduus, assidua, assiduum	continual
	assignō, assignāre, assignāvī, assignātus	attribute, put down
	astrologus, astrologī, m.	astrologer
33	at	but, yet
	āter, ātra, ātrum	black
	āthlēta, āthlētae, m.	athlete
28	atque	and
	ātrium, ātriī, n.	atrium, entrance room, hall
	ātrōx, ātrōx, ātrōx gen. ātrōcis	violent, dreadful
	attollō, attollere	lift, raise
	sē attollere	raise itself, rise up
	attollor, attollī	rise
14	attonitus, attonita, attonitum	astonished
	attulī see afferō	
34	auctor, auctōris, m.	creator, originator, person responsible
24	auctōritās, auctōritātis, f.	authority
	auctus see augeō	
29	audācia, audāciae, f.	boldness, audacity
24	audāx, audāx, audāx gen. audācis	bold, daring
18	audeō, audēre, ausus sum	dare
5	audiō, audīre, audīvī, audītus	hear
	audītor, audītōris, m.	listener, (pl.) audience

	audītōrium, audītōriī, n.	auditorium, hall (used for public readings)
26	auferō, auferre, abstulī, ablātus	take away, steal
40	augeō, augēre, auxī, auctus	increase, exaggerate
14	aula, aulae, f.	palace
	auris, auris, f.	ear
	aurum, aurī, n.	gold
39	aut	or
	aut … aut	either … or
25	autem	but
	auxiliāris, auxiliāris, auxiliāre	additional
16	auxilium, auxiliī, n.	help
	auxiliō esse	be a help, be helpful
	avē atque valē	hail and farewell
	avēna, avēnae, f.	reed
	avidus, avida, avidum	eager
	avis, avis, f.	bird
	avunculus, avunculī, m.	uncle
	avus, avī, m.	grandfather

b

	Babylōnius, Babylōnia, Babylōnium	Babylonian, of Babylon
	baculum, baculī, n.	stick, staff
	Bāiae, Bāiārum, f.pl.	Baiae (a coastal resort in Campania)
	balneum, balneī, n.	bath
	barba, barbae, f.	beard
	barbarus, barbara, barbarum	barbarian
	barbarus, barbarī, m.	barbarian
	basilica, basilicae, f.	court building
	bāsiō, bāsiāre, bāsiāvī	kiss
	bāsium, bāsiī, n.	kiss
	beātus, beāta, beātum	prosperous, wealthy, happy
26	bellum, bellī, n.	war
26	bellum gerere	wage war, campaign
	bellus, bella, bellum	pretty
17	bene	well
	bene velle	like, be friendly
	optimē	very well

	benignitās, benignitātis, f.	*kindness, concern, kindly interest*	
17	benignus, benigna, benignum	*kind*	
	bēstia, bēstiae, f.	*wild animal, beast*	
3	bibō, bibere, bibī	*drink*	
	bis	*twice*	
	Bīthȳnī, Bīthȳnōrum, m.pl.	*Bithynians*	
	blanditiae, blanditiārum, f.pl.	*flatteries*	
16	bonus, bona, bonum	*good*	
	bona, bonōrum, n.pl.	*goods, property*	
16	melior, melius	*better*	
	melius est	*it would be better*	
5	optimus, optima, optimum	*very good, excellent, best*	
	Boōtēs, Boōtae, m.	*Herdsman (constellation)*	
	bracchium, bracchiī, n.	*arm*	
33	brevis, brevis, breve	*short, brief*	
	breviter	*briefly*	
	Britannī, Britannōrum, m.pl.	*Britons*	
	Britannia, Britanniae, f.	*Britain*	

c

C. = Gāius		
cachinnō, cachinnāre, cachinnāvī	*laugh, cackle*	
cadō, cadere, cecidī	*fall, die*	
42 caecus, caeca, caecum	*blind; invisible, unseen, impenetrable*	
48 caedēs, caedis, f.	*murder, slaughter*	
caelebs, caelibis, m.	*widower*	
22 caelum, caelī, n.	*sky, heaven*	
caeruleus, caerulea, caeruleum	*blue, from the deep blue sea, dark, dark blue, dark green*	
Calēdonia, Calēdoniae, f.	*Scotland*	
Calēdoniī, Calēdoniōrum, m.pl.	*Caledonians (Scottish tribespeople), Scots*	
cālīgō, cālīginis, f.	*darkness, gloom*	

callidē	*cleverly*	
calliditās, calliditātis, f.	*cleverness, shrewdness*	
10 callidus, callida, callidum	*smart, clever, cunning, shrewd*	
camera, camerae, f.	*ceiling*	
39 campus, campī, m.	*plain*	
candēns, candēns, candēns, gen. candentis	*gleaming white*	
45 candidus, candida, candidum	*bright, shining, gleaming white*	
1 canis, canis, m.	*dog*	
13 cantō, cantāre, cantāvī	*sing, chant*	
cantus, cantūs, m.	*singing*	
cānus, cāna, cānum	*white*	
capāx, capāx, capāx, gen. capācis	*liable to, full of*	
capella, capellae, f.	*she-goat*	
39 capillī, capillōrum, m.pl.	*hair*	
11 capiō, capere, cēpī, captus	*take, catch, capture*	
Capreae, Capreārum, f.pl.	*Capri*	
29 captīvus, captīvī, m.	*prisoner, captive*	
captō, captāre, captāvī, captātus	*try to catch*	
18 caput, capitis, n.	*head; person*	
24 carcer, carceris, m.	*prison*	
44 careō, carēre, caruī (+ ABL)	*lack, be without*	
carīna, carīnae, f.	*keel, ship*	
35 carmen, carminis, n.	*song, poem*	
carnifex, carnificis, m.	*executioner*	
carpō, carpere, carpsī, carptus	*pluck, seize, crop; hasten upon, hasten through, fly through*	
19 cārus, cāra, cārum	*dear*	
casa, casae, f.	*small house, cottage*	
castīgō, castīgāre, castīgāvī, castīgātus	*scold*	
25 castra, castrōrum, n.pl.	*camp*	
cāsus, cāsūs, m.	*misfortune; fall*	
catēna, catēnae, f.	*chain*	
caupō, caupōnis, m.	*innkeeper*	
36 causa, causae, f.	*reason, cause; case (of law)*	

	causā (+ GEN)	*for the sake of*	
	causam dīcere	*plead a case*	
	causam īnferre	*make an excuse, invent an excuse*	
	cautē	*cautiously*	
35	caveō, cavēre, cāvī	*beware*	
	caverna, cavernae, f.	*cave, cavern*	
	cavō, cavāre, cavāvī, cavātus	*hollow out*	
	cecidī *see* cadō		
23	cēdō, cēdere, cessī	*give in, yield*	
	celebrō, celebrāre, celebrāvī, celebrātus	*celebrate; fill, frequent*	
9	celeriter	*quickly, fast*	
	quam celerrimē	*as quickly as possible*	
21	cēlō, cēlāre, cēlāvī, cēlātus	*hide*	
	celsus, celsa, celsum	*high*	
2	cēna, cēnae, f.	*dinner*	
7	cēnō, cēnāre, cēnāvī	*eat dinner, dine*	
28	centum	*a hundred*	
	centuriō, centuriōnis, m.	*centurion*	
	cēnula, cēnulae, f.	*little supper, snack*	
	cēpī *see* capiō		
	cēra, cērae, f.	*wax, wax tablet*	
	certāmen, certāminis, n.	*struggle, contest, fight*	
	certē	*certainly, at least*	
	certō, certāre, certāvī	*compete*	
38	certus, certa, certum	*certain, infallible*	
38	prō certō habēre	*know for certain*	
13	cēterī, cēterae, cētera	*the others, the rest*	
	chorus, chorī, m.	*chorus, choir*	
2	cibus, cibī, m.	*food*	
	cinis, cineris, m.	*ash*	
	circuit = circumit		
21	circum (+ ACC)	*around*	
	circumeō, circumīre, circumiī	*go around*	
	circumflectō, circumflectere, circumflexī, circumflexus	*turn*	
	circumflectere cursum	*turn one's course around*	
	circumsiliō, circumsilīre	*hop around*	
	circumsistō, circumsistere, circumstetī	*take up position around*	

3	circumspectō, circumspectāre, circumspectāvī, circumspectātus	*look around*	
29	circumveniō, circumvenīre, circumvēnī, circumventus	*surround*	
	citō	*quickly*	
11	cīvis, cīvis, m.f.	*citizen*	
	clādēs, clādis, f.	*disaster*	
38	clam	*secretly, in private*	
3	clāmō, clāmāre, clāmāvī	*shout*	
5	clāmor, clāmōris, m.	*shout, uproar*	
23	clārus, clāra, clārum	*famous, distinguished, splendid; clear, bright*	
15	claudō, claudere, clausī, clausus	*shut, close, block, conclude, complete, cut off*	
	clāvus, clāvī, m.	*tiller, helm*	
	cliēns, clientis, m.	*client*	
	clīvus, clīvī, m.	*slope*	
	Cn. = Gnaeus		
	coāctus *see* cōgō		
18	coepī	*I began*	
	coeptum, coeptī, n.	*work, undertaking*	
19	cōgitō, cōgitāre, cōgitāvī	*think, consider*	
	cognāta, cognātae, f.	*relative (by birth)*	
	cognitiō, cognitiōnis, f.	*trial*	
	cognitiō senātūs	*trial by the senate*	
	cognōmen, cognōminis, n.	*surname, additional name*	
18	cognōscō, cognōscere, cognōvī, cognitus	*get to know, find out*	
25	cōgō, cōgere, coēgī, coāctus	*force, compel*	
	collēgium, collēgiī, n.	*brigade, guild*	
	colligō, colligere, collēgī, collēctus	*gather, collect, assemble; suppose, imagine*	
	collis, collis, m.	*hill*	
	collocō, collocāre, collocāvī, collocātus	*place, put*	
	colloquium, colloquiī, n.	*talk, chat*	

colloquor, colloquī,
   collocūtus sum — *talk, chat*

colōnus, colōnī, m. — *tenant farmer; settler, colonist*

27 comes, comitis, m.f. — *comrade, companion*

cōmiter — *politely, courteously*

comitō, comitāre,
   comitāvī, comitātus — *accompany*

34 comitor, comitārī,
   comitātus sum — *accompany*

commemorō,
   commemorāre,
   commemorāvī,
   commemorātus — *talk about, mention, recall*

commendō, commendāre,
   commendāvī,
   commendātus — *recommend*

committō, committere,
   commīsī,
   commissus — *commit, begin*

26 commōtus, commōta,
   commōtum — *moved, upset, affected, alarmed, excited, distressed, overcome*

commūnis, commūnis,
   commūne — *shared (by two or more people)*

19 comparō, comparāre,
   comparāvī, comparātus — *obtain, compare*

compellō, compellere,
   compulī, compulsus — *drive, compel*

complector, complectī,
   complexus sum — *embrace*

12 compleō, complēre,
   complēvī, complētus — *fill*

complexus, complexūs, m. — *embrace*

37 complūrēs, complūrēs,
   complūra — *several*

32 compōnō, compōnere,
   composuī, compositus — *put together, arrange, settle, mix, compose, make up*

compositus, composita,
   compositum — *composed, steady*

24 comprehendō,
   comprehendere,
   comprehendī,
   comprehēnsus — *arrest, seize*

compulsus *see* compellō

cōnātur *see* cōnor

concavus, concava,
   concavum — *hollow*

concidō, concidere,
   concidī — *collapse*

conclāve, conclāvis, n. — *room*

condiciō, condiciōnis, f. — *status*

condō, condere, condidī,
   conditus — *bury; found, establish*

cōnfarreātiō,
   cōnfarreātiōnis, f. — *marriage ceremony*

cōnfectus, cōnfecta,
   cōnfectum — *finished, worn out, exhausted, overcome*

19 cōnficiō, cōnficere,
   cōnfēcī, cōnfectus — *finish*

25 cōnfīdō, cōnfīdere,
   cōnfīsus sum (+ DAT) — *trust, put trust in; be sure, be confident*

44 coniungō, coniungere,
   coniūnxī, coniūnctus — *join*

coniūnx, coniugis, m.f. — *wife, husband, spouse*

coniūrātiō,
   coniūrātiōnis, f. — *plot, conspiracy*

44 coniūrō, coniūrāre,
   coniūrāvī, coniūrātus — *plot, conspire*

34 cōnor, cōnārī,
   cōnātus sum — *try*

cōnscendō, cōnscendere,
   cōnscendī — *climb on, embark on, go on board, mount*

cōnscientia,
   cōnscientiae, f. — *awareness, knowledge*

cōnscīscō, cōnscīscere,
   cōnscīvī — *inflict*
   mortem sibi cōnscīscere — *commit suicide*

cōnscius, cōnsciī, m. — *accomplice, member of the plot*

cōnsecrō, cōnsecrāre,
   cōnsecrāvī,
   cōnsecrātus — *dedicate*

	cōnsēnsus, cōnsēnsus, m.	*agreement*
16	cōnsentiō, cōnsentīre, cōnsēnsī	*agree*
	cōnsequor, cōnsequī, cōnsecūtus sum	*follow, chase*
	cōnsīderātus, cōnsīderāta, cōnsīderātum	*careful, well-considered*
	cōnsīdō, cōnsīdere, cōnsēdī	*sit down*
16	cōnsilium, cōnsiliī, n.	*plan, idea, advice; council*
31	cōnsistō, cōnsistere, cōnstitī	*stand one's ground, stand firm, halt, stop; depend*
	cōnsōlor, cōnsōlārī, cōnsōlātus sum	*console*
	cōnspectus, cōnspectūs, m.	*sight*
7	cōnspiciō, cōnspicere, cōnspexī, cōnspectus	*catch sight of*
34	cōnspicor, cōnspicārī, cōnspicātus sum	*catch sight of*
	cōnstat, cōnstāre, cōnstitit	*be agreed*
	satis cōnstat	*it is generally agreed*
28	cōnstituō, cōnstituere, cōnstituī, cōnstitūtus	*decide; set up, place*
	cōnsuētūdō, cōnsuētūdinis, f.	*custom; companionship*
40	cōnsul, cōnsulis, m.	*consul* (highest elected official of Roman government)
	cōnsulāris, cōnsulāris, m.	*ex-consul*
30	cōnsulō, cōnsulere, cōnsuluī, cōnsultus	*consult, take thought for, give consideration to*
8	cōnsūmō, cōnsūmere, cōnsūmpsī, cōnsūmptus	*eat, destroy*
	cōnsurgō, cōnsurgere, cōnsurrēxī	*jump up*
43	contemnō, contemnere, contempsī, contemptus	*reject, despise*

5	contendō, contendere, contendī	*hurry*
10	contentus, contenta, contentum	*satisfied*
	contineō, continēre, continuī	*contain*
	contingō, contingere, contigī, contāctus	*touch, affect; happen, fall to one's lot*
	contigit nōbīs ut ...	*it was our good fortune that ..., we had the good fortune to ...*
	continuō	*immediately*
	continuus, continua, continuum	*continuous, on end*
33	contrā (1) (+ ACC)	*against*
33	contrā (2)	*in reply, on the other hand*
	contrahō, contrahere, contrāxī, contractus	*draw together, bring together, assemble*
	supercilia contrahere	*draw eyebrows together, frown*
	contrārius, contrāria, contrārium	*opposite, contrary, against*
	contumēlia, contumēliae, f.	*insult, abuse*
	conturbō, conturbāre, conturbāvī, conturbātus	*mix up, lose count of*
	contus, contī, m.	*pole, rod*
	convalēscō, convalēscere, convaluī	*get better, recover*
11	conveniō, convenīre, convēnī	*come together, gather, meet*
32	convertō, convertere, convertī, conversus	*turn, divert*
	sē convertere	*turn*
	convertor, convertī, conversus sum	*turn*
	convīvālis, convīvālis, convīvāle	*for dining*
	convocō, convocāre, convocāvī, convocātus	*call together*

coorior, coorīrī,
coortus sum — *break out, arise, rise*

38 cōpiae, cōpiārum, f.pl. — *troops, forces*

4 coquō, coquere, coxī,
coctus — *cook*

1 coquus, coquī, m. — *cook*

28 corpus, corporis, n. — *body*

corripiō, corripere,
corripuī, correptus — *seize, scold*

14 cotīdiē — *every day*

33 crās — *tomorrow*

11 crēdō, crēdere,
crēdidī (+ DAT) — *trust, believe, have faith in*

crēdulus, crēdula, crēdulum — *trusting*

cremō, cremāre,
cremāvī, cremātus — *cremate, burn, destroy by fire*

creō, creāre, creāvī, creātus — *make, create*

44 crēscō, crēscere,
crēvī, crētus — *grow*

40 crīmen, crīminis, n. — *charge*

crīnēs, crīnium, m.pl. — *hair*

20 crūdēlis, crūdēlis, crūdēle — *cruel*

crūdēliter — *cruelly*

crux, crucis, f. — *cross*

crucī affigere — *nail to a cross, crucify*

6 cubiculum, cubiculī, n. — *bedroom*

cubitō, cubitāre, cubitāvī — *lie down, rest*

cuiuscumque *see* quīcumque

culīna, culīnae, f. — *kitchen*

culmen, culminis, n. — *roof*

41 culpa, culpae, f. — *blame, fault*

illīus culpā — *through his/her fault, thanks to him/her*

35 culpō, culpāre,
culpāvī, culpātus — *blame*

24 cum (1) — *when, since, because, although*

7 cum (2) (+ ABL) — *with*

mēcum — *with me*

cumba, cumbae, f. — *boat*

cūnctor, cūnctārī,
cūnctātus sum — *delay, hesitate*

cūnctus, cūncta, cūnctum — *all*

cupiditās, cupiditātis, f. — *desire*

44 cupīdō, cupīdinis, f. — *desire, ambition*

Cupīdō, Cupīdinis, m. — *Cupid (god of love)*

cupidus, cupida, cupidum — *eager, passionate*

9 cupiō, cupere, cupīvī — *want*

4 cūr? — *why?*

23 cūra, cūrae, f. — *care, concern*

cūrae esse — *be a matter of concern*

cūrātor, cūrātōris, m. — *supervisor, superintendent*

40 cūria, cūriae, f. — *senate-house*

19 cūrō, cūrāre, cūrāvī — *take care of; care for, supervise*

cūrandum est — *steps must be taken*

5 currō, currere, cucurrī — *run, go, fly*

cursus, cursūs, m. — *course, flight*

circumflectere cursum — *turn one's course around*

curvāmen, curvāminis, n. — *curve*

cuspis, cuspidis, f. — *point*

12 custōdiō, custōdīre,
custōdīvī, custōdītus — *guard*

13 custōs, custōdis, m. — *guard*

d

dā, dabō *see* dō

damnātiō, damnātiōnis, f. — *condemnation*

damnō, damnāre,
damnāvī, damnātus — *condemn*

damnōsus, damnōsa,
damnōsum — *ruinous, fatal*

datus *see* dō

11 dē (+ ABL) — *from, down from; about, over*

18 dea, deae, f. — *goddess*

15 dēbeō, dēbēre, dēbuī, dēbitus — *owe; ought, should, must*

dēbilitō, dēbilitāre,
dēbilitāvī, dēbilitātus — *weaken, exhaust, cripple*

33 dēcidō, dēcidere, dēcidī — *fall down*

22 dēcipiō, dēcipere,
dēcēpī, dēceptus — *deceive, trick*

14	decōrus, decōra, decōrum	*right, proper*
	dēcurrō, dēcurrere, dēcurrī	*run down*
	decus, decoris, n.	*ornament*
	dēdecus, dēdecoris, n.	*disgrace*
	dedī *see* dō	
	dēdūcō, dēdūcere, dēdūxī, dēductus	*escort, lead away*
	dēeram *see* dēsum	
29	dēfendō, dēfendere, dēfendī, dēfēnsus	*defend*
	dēfēnsiō, dēfēnsiōnis, f.	*defense*
	dēficiō, dēficere, dēfēcī	*fail, die away*
	dēfīgō, dēfīgere, dēfīxī, dēfīxus	*fix*
	dēfīxiō, dēfīxiōnis, f.	*curse*
	dēflectō, dēflectere, dēflexī	*turn aside, turn off the road*
	dēfōrmis, dēfōrmis, dēfōrme	*ugly, inelegant*
	dēfūnctus, dēfūncta, dēfūnctum	*dead*
	dēhīscō, dēhīscere	*gape open*
	dēiectus, dēiecta, dēiectum	*disappointed, downcast*
	dein = deinde	
16	deinde	*then*
16	dēlectō, dēlectāre, dēlectāvī, dēlectātus	*delight, please*
14	dēleō, dēlēre, dēlēvī, dēlētus	*destroy*
	dēliciae, dēliciārum, f.pl.	*darling*
	dēligō, dēligāre, dēligāvī, dēligātus	*bind, tie, tie up, moor*
	dēmānō, dēmānāre, dēmānāvī	*flow down*
	dēmissus, dēmissa, dēmissum	*low*
30	dēmittō, dēmittere, dēmīsī, dēmissus	*let down, lower*
40	dēmum	*at last*
40	tum dēmum	*then at last, only then*
20	dēnique	*at last, finally*
	dēns, dentis, m.	*tooth, tusk*
	dēnsus, dēnsa, dēnsum	*thick*

	dēpōnō, dēpōnere, dēposuī, dēpositus	*put down, take off, give up, abandon*
	dēprehendō, dēprehendere, dēprehendī, dēprehēnsus	*discover*
	dēprendō = dēprehendō	
	dērīdeō, dērīdēre, dērīsī, dērīsus	*mock, make fun of*
	dēripiō, dēripere, dēripuī, dēreptus	*tear down*
33	dēscendō, dēscendere, dēscendī	*go down, come down*
24	dēserō, dēserere, dēseruī, dēsertus	*desert*
	dēsīderium, dēsīderiī, n.	*loss, longing*
	dēsiliō, dēsilīre, dēsiluī	*jump down*
	dēsinō, dēsinere, dēsiī	*end, cease*
	dēsistō, dēsistere, dēstitī	*stop*
	dēspērātiō, dēspērātiōnis, f.	*despair*
20	dēspērō, dēspērāre, dēspērāvī	*despair, give up*
	dēstinātus, dēstināta, dēstinātum	*determined*
	dēstringō, dēstringere, dēstrīnxī, dēstrictus	*draw out, draw (a sword), unsheathe*
	dēstruō, dēstruere, dēstrūxī, dēstrūctus	*pull down, demolish*
	dēsum, dēesse, dēfuī	*be lacking, be missing, be unavailable*
	dētineō, dētinēre, dētinuī, dētentus	*detain, keep*
	dētrahō, dētrahere, dētrāxī, dētractus	*pull down, take off*
	dēturbō, dēturbāre, dēturbāvī, dēturbātus	*push, send flying*
14	deus, deī, m.	*god*
	dī īnferī	*gods of the underworld*
	dī mānēs	*the spirits of the dead*
	dēvorō, dēvorāre, dēvorāvī, dēvorātus	*devour, eat up*

	dēvoveō, dēvovēre, dēvōvī, dēvōtus	*curse*
	dexter, dextra, dextrum	*right, on the right*
38	dextra, dextrae, f.	*right hand*
	dī *see* deus	
13	dīcō, dīcere, dīxī, dictus	*say*
	causam dīcere	*plead a case*
	dictus, dicta, dictum	*appointed*
	male dīcere	*insult*
	mīrābile dictū	*strange to say*
	sacrāmentum dīcere	*take the military oath*
	dictō, dictāre, dictāvī, dictātus	*dictate*
	didicī *see* discō	
9	diēs, diēī, m.f.	*day*
	diēs fēstus, diēī fēstī, m.	*festival, holiday*
	posterō (diē)	*tomorrow*
	differō, differre, distulī, dīlātus	*postpone, put off*
14	difficilis, difficilis, difficile	*difficult, obstinate*
	diffīdō, diffīdere, diffīsus sum (+ DAT)	*distrust*
37	dignus, digna, dignum (+ ABL)	*worthy, appropriate*
14	dīligenter	*carefully*
	dīligentia, dīligentiae, f.	*industry, hard work*
	dīligō, dīligere, dīlēxī	*be fond of*
	dīluvium, dīluviī, n.	*flood*
	dīmittō, dīmittere, dīmīsī, dīmissus	*send away, dismiss, turn, direct*
	dīrigō, dīrigere, dīrēxī, dīrēctus	*steer*
29	dīrus, dīra, dīrum	*dreadful, awful*
	dīs *see* deus	
18	discēdō, discēdere, discessī	*depart, leave*
	discernō, discernere, discrēvī, discrētus	*distinguish*
36	discipulus, discipulī, m.	*disciple, follower, student*
37	discō, discere, didicī	*learn*
	discordia, discordiae, f.	*strife*
39	discrīmen, discrīminis, n.	*boundary, dividing line, distance; crisis; distinction*
	disiciō, disicere, disiēcī, disiectus	*scatter, disperse*
	dispār, dispār, dispār *gen.* disparis	*of different length*
	dispergō, dispergere, dispersī, dispersus	*scatter*
	dispiciō, dispicere, dispexī, dispectus	*consider*
	displiceō, displicēre, displicuī (+ DAT)	*displease*
	dissentiō, dissentīre, dissēnsī	*disagree, argue*
	dissimulō, dissimulāre, dissimulāvī, dissimulātus	*conceal, hide*
	dissolūtiō, dissolūtiōnis, f.	*disintegration, breakup*
	dissolvō, dissolvere, dissolvī, dissolūtus	*disperse, dissolve*
	distrahō, distrahere, distrāxī, distractus	*tear apart, tear in two*
	distribuō, distribuere, distribuī, distribūtus	*distribute*
	distringō, distringere, distrīnxī, districtus	*distract, divert*
	distulī *see* differō	
17	diū	*for a long time*
	diūtius	*any longer*
41	dīversus, dīversa, dīversum	*different*
30	dīves, dīves, dīves *gen.* dīvitis	*rich*
	dīvidō, dīvidere, dīvīsī, dīvīsus	*divide*
30	dīvitiae, dīvitiārum, f.pl.	*riches*
	dīvortium, dīvortiī, n.	*divorce*
37	dīvus, dīvī, m.	*god*
	dīxī *see* dīcō	
9	dō, dare, dedī, datus	*give, put forward*
26	doceō, docēre, docuī, doctus	*teach*
28	doleō, dolēre, doluī	*hurt, be in pain; grieve, be sad*

29 dolor, dolōris, m. — *pain; grief*

14 domina, dominae, f. — *lady (of the house), mistress*

2 dominus, dominī, m. — *master (of the house), owner*

20 domus, domūs, f. — *home*
    domī — *at home*
    domum Hateriī — *to Haterius' house*
    domum redīre — *return home*
    domum revenīre — *return home*

48 dōnec — *until*

36 dōnō, dōnāre, dōnāvī, dōnātus — *give, present*

14 dōnum, dōnī, n. — *present, gift*

2 dormiō, dormīre, dormīvī — *sleep, sleep through*

37 dubitō, dubitāre, dubitāvī — *hesitate, doubt, be doubtful*
    nōn dubitō quīn — *I do not doubt that*
    dubium, dubiī, n. — *doubt*
    dubius, dubia, dubium — *uncertain, doubtful*
    ducem *see* dux

8 dūcō, dūcere, dūxī, ductus — *lead; consider; extend*
    uxōrem dūcere — *take as a wife, marry*
    dulce — *sweetly*
    dulcis, dulcis, dulce — *sweet, pleasurable*

34 dum — *while, until, so long as, provided that*
    dumtaxat — *not exceeding*

12, 20, 28 duo, duae, duo — *two*

21 dūrus, dūra, dūrum — *harsh, hard*

31 dux, ducis, m. — *leader*
    dūxī *see* dūcō

e

4 ē, ex (+ ABL) — *from, out of*
    eandem *see* īdem

3 ecce! — *see! look!*

43 efferō, efferre, extulī, ēlātus — *bring out, carry out, carry away, bury*
    ēlātus, ēlāta, ēlātum — *thrilled, excited, carried away*

21 efficiō, efficere, effēcī, effectus — *carry out, accomplish*
    efficere ut — *bring it about that, see to it that*

effigiēs, effigiēī, f. — *image, statue*

efflāgitō, efflāgitāre, efflāgitāvī — *demand justice*

effringō, effringere, effrēgī, effrāctus — *break down*

16 effugiō, effugere, effūgī — *escape*

32 effundō, effundere, effūdī, effūsus — *pour out, overflow*
    ēgī *see* agō

4 ego, meī — *I, me*
    est mihi — *I have*
    mēcum — *with me*
    meī locō — *in my place*

34 ēgredior, ēgredī, ēgressus sum — *go out*
    ēgregius, ēgregia, ēgregium — *excellent, outstanding, remarkable*

4 ēheu! — *alas! oh dear!*

33 ēiciō, ēicere, ēiēcī, ēiectus — *throw out*
    eīdem *see* īdem
    ēlābor, ēlābī, ēlāpsus sum — *escape*
    ēlātus *see* efferō
    ēlegāns, ēlegāns, ēlegāns *gen.* ēlegantis — *tasteful, elegant*
    ēliciō, ēlicere, ēlicuī, ēlicitus — *lure, entice*

22 ēligō, ēligere, ēlēgī, ēlēctus — *choose, decide*
    ēmineō, ēminēre, ēminuī — *project*

9 ēmittō, ēmittere, ēmīsī, ēmissus — *throw, send out*

6 emō, emere, ēmī, emptus — *buy*

23 enim — *for*
    ēnsis, ēnsis, m. — *sword*
    ēnumerō, ēnumerāre, ēnumerāvī, ēnumerātus — *count*
    eō — *there, to that place*

11 eō, īre, iī — *go*
    obviam īre (+ DAT) — *meet, go to meet*
    eōdem, eōsdem *see* īdem

Ephesius, Ephesia,
   Ephesium   *of Ephesus*
epigramma,
   epigrammatis, n.   *epigram*
13 epistula, epistulae, f.   *letter*
   epulae, epulārum, f. pl.   *feast, banquet*
24 eques, equitis, m.   *horseman; man of*
                    equestrian rank
   equidem   *indeed*
   equitō, equitāre, equitāvī *ride (a horse)*
15 equus, equī, m.   *horse*
   ērādō, ērādere, ērāsī, ērāsus *erase*
   eram *see* sum
39 ergō   *therefore*
38 ēripiō, ēripere, ēripuī,
   ēreptus   *snatch, tear, rescue,*
                    snatch away
   errō, errāre, errāvī   *make a mistake;*
                    wander
     longē errāre   *make a big mistake*
   ērubēscō, ērubēscere,
   ērubuī   *blush*
   ērudiō, ērudīre, ērudiī,
   ērudītus   *teach*
   ērumpō, ērumpere, ērūpī *break away, break out*
   est *see* sum
3 et   *and; indeed*
33   et … et   *both … and*
15 etiam   *even, also*
    nōn modo … sed etiam *not only … but also*
   Etruscus, Etruscī, m.   *Etruscan*
   etsī   *although, even if*
   euntem *see* eō
48 ēvādō, ēvādere, ēvāsī   *escape*
   ēvānēscō, ēvānēscere,
   ēvānuī   *vanish, die away*
   ēveniō, ēvenīre, ēvēnī   *occur*
   ēvertō, ēvertere, ēvertī,
   ēversus   *overturn*
   ēvolō, ēvolāre, ēvolāvī   *fly out*
   ēvolvō, ēvolvere,
   ēvolvī, ēvolūtus   *unroll, open*
   ēvomō, ēvomere,
   ēvomuī, ēvomitus   *spit out, spew out*
4 ex, ē (+ ABL)   *from, out of*

exanimātus, exanimāta,
   exanimātum   *unconscious*
exanimis, exanimis,
   exanime   *out of one's mind*
exardeō, exardēre, exarsī *blaze up*
33 excipiō, excipere, excēpī,
   exceptus   *receive, take over*
13 excitō, excitāre, excitāvī,
   excitātus   *arouse, wake up,*
                    awaken
10 exclāmō, exclāmāre,
   exclāmāvī   *exclaim, shout*
   excōgitō, excōgitāre,
   excōgitāvī, excōgitātus *invent, think up*
   excruciō, excruciāre,
   excruciāvī, excruciātus *torture, torment*
   excutiō, excutere, excussī,
   excussus   *examine, investigate;*
                    shake off, drive
                    violently off
   exemplum, exemplī, n.   *example, precedent,*
                    pattern of conduct
                    to imitate or avoid
    pertinēre ad exemplum   *involve a precedent*
3 exeō, exīre, exiī   *go out*
   exequiae, exequiārum, f. pl. *funeral rites*
   exerceō, exercēre, exercuī,
   exercitus   *exercise, practice,*
                    train; harass
37 exercitus, exercitūs, m.   *army*
   exigō, exigere, exēgī,
   exāctus   *demand, require, spend*
   exilium, exiliī, n.   *exile*
40 exīstimō, exīstimāre,
   exīstimāvī, exīstimātus *think, consider*
   exit *see* exeō
   exitium, exitiī, n.   *ruin, destruction*
   expediō, expedīre,
     expedīvī, expedītus   *bring out, get out*
     sēsē expedīre   *prepare oneself, get*
                    ready
   expingō, expingere,
     expīnxī, expictus   *paint, put paint onto*
   expleō, explēre,
     explēvī, explētus   *complete, put final*
                    touch to

25	explicō, explicāre, explicāvī, explicātus	*explain*	
	explōrātor, explōrātōris, m.	*scout, spy*	
	expōnō, expōnere, exposuī, expositus	*unload; set out, explain; expose*	
	exsequor, exsequī, exsecūtus sum	*carry out*	
	exspatior, exspatiārī, exspatiātus sum	*extend, spread out*	
3	exspectō, exspectāre, exspectāvī, exspectātus	*wait for*	
	extinguō, extinguere, extīnxī, extīnctus	*extinguish, put out, destroy*	
	exstruō, exstruere, exstrūxī, exstrūctus	*build*	
	exsultō, exsultāre, exsultāvī	*exult, be triumphant, get excited*	
	exta, extōrum, n.pl.	*entrails*	
	extendō, extendere, extendī, extentus	*stretch out*	
	exterreō, exterrēre, exterruī, exterritus	*frighten away*	
25	extrā (+ ACC)	*outside*	
	extrahō, extrahere, extrāxī, extractus	*drag out, pull out, take out*	
36	extrēmus, extrēma, extrēmum	*farthest, final, last*	
	extrēma scaena	*the edge of the stage*	

f

17	faber, fabrī, m.	*craftsman, carpenter, workman, fireman*	
5	fābula, fābulae, f.	*play, story*	
	fābulōsus, fābulōsa, fābulōsum	*legendary, famous*	
	facēs *see* fax		
	faciēs, faciēī, f.	*face*	
8	facile	*easily*	
17	facilis, facilis, facile	*easy*	
	facinus, facinoris, n.	*crime*	
7	faciō, facere, fēcī, factus	*make, do*	

	impetum facere	*charge, make an attack*	
	ō factum male!	*oh dreadfully done! oh awful deed!*	
	quid faciam?	*what am I to do?*	
	factiō, factiōnis, f.	*organized group*	
41	factum, factī, n.	*deed, achievement*	
	factus *see* faciō, fiō		
	facultās, facultātis, f.	*opportunity*	
	fācundē	*fluently, eloquently*	
39	fallō, fallere, fefellī, falsus	*deceive, escape notice of, slip by*	
	fidem fallere	*break one's word*	
	falsum, falsī, n.	*lie, forgery*	
26	falsus, falsa, falsum	*false, untrue, dishonest*	
	fāma, fāmae, f.	*rumor; reputation*	
38	familia, familiae, f.	*household, household servants*	
	familiāris, familiāris, m.	*close friend, relation, relative*	
	familiāritās, familiāritātis, f.	*intimacy*	
	farreus, farrea, farreum	*made from grain*	
	fās, n.	*(that which is morally) right, proper*	
	Fāstī, Fāstōrum, m.pl.	*the list of the consuls*	
	fauce	*by hunger*	
11	faveō, favēre, fāvī (+ DAT)	*favor, support*	
	favor, favōris, m.	*favor*	
	fax, facis, f.	*torch*	
	febricula, febriculae, f.	*slight fever*	
	febris, febris, f.	*fever*	
	fēcī *see* faciō		
	fēcunditās, fēcunditātis, f.	*fertility*	
	fēcundus, fēcunda, fēcundum	*fertile, rich*	
	fēlēs, fēlis, f.	*cat*	
	fēlīciter!	*good luck!*	
	fēlīx, fēlīx, fēlīx *gen.* fēlīcis	*lucky, happy*	
5	fēmina, fēminae, f.	*woman*	
	fenestra, fenestrae, f.	*window*	
	feriō, ferīre	*strike*	
9	ferō, ferre, tulī, lātus	*bring, carry; say*	
6	ferōciter	*fiercely*	

8	ferōx, ferōx, ferōx *gen.* ferōcis	*fierce, ferocious*	
	ferrātus, ferrāta, ferrātum	*tipped with iron*	
	ferreus, ferrea, ferreum	*iron, made of iron*	
	ferrum, ferrī, n.	*iron, sword, weapon*	
13	fessus, fessa, fessum	*tired*	
6	festīnō, festīnāre, festīnāvī	*hurry*	
	fēstus, fēsta, fēstum	*festival, holiday*	
	fīam *see* fīō		
	fictus *see* fingō		
14	fidēlis, fidēlis, fidēle	*faithful, loyal, reliable, trustworthy*	
	fidēliter	*faithfully, loyally, reliably*	
26	fidēs, fideī, f.	*loyalty, trustworthiness, sense of responsibility*	
	medius fidius!	*for goodness sake!*	
43	fīdus, fīda, fīdum	*loyal, trustworthy*	
	fīgō, fīgere, fīxī, fīxus	*fix, fasten, pierce*	
	figūra, figūrae, f.	*figure, shape*	
1	fīlia, fīliae, f.	*daughter*	
1	fīlius, fīliī, m.	*son*	
	fingō, fingere, fīnxī, fictus	*pretend, invent, forge*	
36	fīnis, fīnis, m.	*end*	
37	fīō, fierī, factus sum	*be made, be done, become, occur, happen*	
	firmē	*firmly*	
	firmō, firmāre, firmāvī, firmātus	*strengthen, establish*	
	firmus, firma, firmum	*firm*	
	fistula, fistulae, f.	*pipe*	
12	flamma, flammae, f.	*flame*	
	flammeum, flammeī, n.	*veil*	
	flāvus, flāva, flāvum	*yellow, golden*	
	flectō, flectere, flexī, flexus	*bend, turn*	
45	fleō, flēre, flēvī	*weep (for)*	
	flētus, flētūs, m.	*weeping, tears*	
	flōreō, flōrēre, flōruī	*flourish*	
	aetāte flōrēre	*be in the prime of life*	
16	flōs, flōris, m.	*flower*	
47	flūctus, flūctūs, m.	*wave*	
24	flūmen, flūminis, n.	*river*	

19	fluō, fluere, flūxī	*flow*	
	fluēns, fluēns, fluēns, *gen.* fluentis	*dripping, streaming*	
	foedus, foeda, foedum	*foul, horrible, shameful*	
21	fōns, fontis, m.	*fountain, spring, source*	
	forās	*out of the house, outside, outdoors*	
	fore = futūrum esse (future infinitive of *sum*)		
	forēs, forium, f.pl.	*door*	
	fōrma, fōrmae, f.	*beauty, shape*	
	formīdō, formīdinis, f.	*fear, terror*	
	formīdolōsus, formīdolōsa, formīdolōsum	*alarming*	
	fors	*perhaps*	
18	fortasse	*perhaps*	
19	forte	*by chance*	
6	fortis, fortis, forte	*brave*	
12	fortiter	*bravely*	
	fortuita, fortuitōrum, n. pl.	*accidents*	
	fortūna, fortūnae, f.	*fortune, luck*	
	fortūnātus, fortūnāta, fortūnātum	*lucky*	
	forum, forī, n.	*forum, business center*	
	fossa, fossae, f.	*ditch*	
39	fragor, fragōris, m.	*crash*	
34	frangō, frangere, frēgī, frāctus	*break*	
10	frāter, frātris, m.	*brother*	
	frāternus, frāterna, frāternum	*of a brother, fraternal*	
	fremitus, fremitūs, m.	*noise, din*	
	frēna, frēnōrum, n. pl.	*reins*	
	fretum, fretī, n.	*water, sea*	
	frīgidus, frīgida, frīgidum	*cold*	
	frondēns, frondēns, frondēns *gen.* frondentis	*leafy*	
	frōns, frontis, f.	*forehead, outward appearance*	
31	frūmentum, frūmentī, n.	*grain*	
	fruor, fruī, frūctus sum (+ ABL)	*enjoy*	

12	frūstrā	*in vain*	
	fūdī *see* fundō		
33	fuga, fugae, f.	*escape, flight*	
12	fugiō, fugere, fūgī	*run away, flee (from)*	
	fugitīvus, fugitīvī, m.	*fugitive, runaway*	
	fuī *see* sum		
	fulciō, fulcīre, fulsī, fultus	*prop up, wedge*	
	fulgeō, fulgēre, fūlsī	*shine, shine out, glitter, flash*	
	fulgur, fulguris, m.	*lightning*	
	fulmen, fulminis, n.	*thunderbolt*	
	fulvus, fulva, fulvum	*tawny, light brown*	
	fūmus, fūmī, m.	*smoke*	
22	fundō, fundere, fūdī, fūsus	*pour*	
12	fundus, fundī, m.	*farm*	
	fūnus, fūneris, n.	*funeral, funeral procession*	
6	fūr, fūris, m.	*thief*	
	furēns, furēns, furēns *gen.* furentis	*furious, in a rage, distraught*	
	furor, furoris, m.	*madness, frenzy*	
	fūrtum, fūrtī, n.	*theft*	
	fūstis, fūstis, m.	*club, stick*	
	futūrus, futūra, futūrum	*future*	
	futūrus *see* sum		

g

27	gaudeō, gaudēre, gāvīsus sum	*be pleased, rejoice, be delighted*	
34	gaudium, gaudiī, n.	*joy*	
	gelō, gelāre, gelāvī, gelātus	*freeze*	
	geminus, gemina, geminum	*twin, the two, twofold, double*	
28	gemitus, gemitūs, m.	*groan*	
	gemma, gemmae, f.	*jewel, gem*	
	gena, genae, f.	*cheek*	
	gener, generī, m.	*son-in-law*	
30	gēns, gentis, f.	*family, tribe, race, people*	
42	genū, genūs, n.	*knee*	
39	genus, generis, n.	*race, kind, offspring*	
	genus mortāle	*the human race*	

	Germānī, Germānōrum, m.pl.	*Germans*	
	Germānia, Germāniae, f.	*Germany*	
	Germānus, Germāna, Germānum	*German*	
23	gerō, gerere, gessī, gestus	*wear; achieve, manage; carry on*	
26	bellum gerere	*wage war, campaign*	
	sē gerere	*behave, conduct oneself*	
	Gerūsia, Gerūsiae, f.	*the Gerusia* (club for wealthy, elderly men)	
	gestiō, gestīre, gestīvī	*become restless*	
	gladiātor, gladiātōris, m.	*gladiator*	
8	gladius, gladiī, m.	*sword*	
41	glōria, glōriae, f.	*glory*	
	glōriōsus, glōriōsa, glōriōsum	*boastful*	
	gnātus = nātus		
	gracilis, gracilis, gracile	*graceful*	
	gradus, gradūs, m.	*step, position*	
	addere gradum	*go forward step by step*	
	grāmen, grāminis, n.	*grass*	
	grātiae, grātiārum, f.pl.	*thanks*	
19	grātiās agere	*thank, give thanks*	
	grātificor, grātificārī, grātificātus sum	*do favors*	
	grātulor, grātulārī, grātulātus sum	*congratulate*	
38	grātus, grāta, grātum	*acceptable, pleasing*	
21	gravis, gravis, grave	*heavy, serious, severe*	
17	graviter	*heavily, soundly, seriously*	
	gravō, gravāre, gravāvī	*load, weigh down*	
	gremium, gremiī, n.	*lap*	
	gubernāculum, gubernāculī, n.	*helm, steering oar*	
	gurges, gurgitis, m.	*whirlpool, swirling water*	

h

4	habeō, habēre, habuī, habitus	*have, regard, consider*	
38	prō certō habēre	*know for certain*	

10	habitō, habitāre, habitāvī	*live*	
	haereō, haerēre, haesī	*stick, cling; be fixed*	
	haesitō, haesitāre, haesitāvī	*hesitate*	
	hama, hamae, f.	*fire bucket*	
	harundō, harundinis, f.	*reed, rod, shaft*	
	haruspex, haruspicis, m.	*diviner, soothsayer*	
19	hasta, hastae, f.	*spear*	
34	haud	*not*	
31	haudquāquam	*not at all*	
	haustus, haustūs, m.	*drinking, drinking-place*	

1	hortus, hortī, m.	*garden*
9	hospes, hospitis, m.	*guest, host*
22	hostis, hostis, m.f.	*enemy*
17	hūc	*here, to this place*
	hūc … illūc	*this way … that way, one way … another way, here and there, up and down*

	Helicē, Helicēs, f.	*Big Bear (constellation)*
	hercle!	*by Hercules!*
	hērēs, hērēdis, m.f.	*heir*
7	heri	*yesterday*
	hetaeria, hetaeriae, f.	*political club*
	heu! = ēheu!	
	Hibernī, Hibernōrum, m.pl.	*Irish*
	Hibernia, Hiberniae, f.	*Ireland*
	hībernus, hīberna, hībernum	*wintry, of winter*
33	hīc	*here*
8	hic, haec, hoc	*this*
	hī … aliī	*some … others*
	hic … ille	*this one … that one, one man … another man*
	hiems, hiemis, f.	*winter*
39	hinc	*from here; then, next*
	Hispānia, Hispāniae, f.	*Spain*
5	hodiē	*today*
9	homō, hominis, m.	*person, man*
	homunculus, homunculī, m.	*little man, pip-squeak*
23	honor, honōris, m.	*honor, official position*
	honōrō, honōrāre, honōrāvī, honōrātus	*honor*
21	hōra, hōrae, f.	*hour*
	horrendus, horrenda, horrendum	*horrifying*
	horrēscō, horrēscere, horruī	*shudder*
34	hortor, hortārī, hortātus sum	*encourage, urge*

	humilis, humilis, humile	*low-born, of low class*
	humus, humī, f.	*ground*
24	humī	*on the ground*
	Hymēn, Hymenis, m.	*Hymen (god of weddings)*
	Hymenaeus, Hymenaeī, m.	*Hymen (god of weddings)*

i

12	iaceō, iacēre, iacuī	*lie, rest*
23	iaciō, iacere, iēcī, iactus	*throw*
22	iactō, iactāre, iactāvī, iactātus	*throw, hurl, bring up*
12	iam	*now*
	nec iam	*no longer*
	nunc iam	*now however, as things are now*
3	iānua, iānuae, f.	*door*
18	ibi	*there, then, in those days*
	ībō *see* eō	
	ictus, ictūs, m.	*blow*
31	īdem, eadem, idem	*the same*
	īdem … ac	*the same … as*
	in idem	*for a common purpose, for the same purpose*
31	identidem	*repeatedly*
	ideō	*for this reason*
	ideō … quod	*for the reason that, because*
12	igitur	*therefore, and so*
27	ignārus, ignāra, ignārum	*not knowing, unaware*
8	ignāvus, ignāva, ignāvum	*lazy, cowardly*
36	ignis, ignis, m.	*fire, lightning, heat of the sun*

38	ignōrō, ignōrāre, ignōrāvī	*not know (about)*	
32	ignōscō, ignōscere, ignōvī (+ DAT)	*forgive*	
	ignōtus, ignōta, ignōtum	*unknown*	
	iī *see* eō		
	īlex, īlicis, f.	*oak tree*	
	īlia, īlium, n.pl.	*groin*	
	illāc	*by that way*	
9	ille, illa, illud	*that, he, she*	
	hic … ille	*this one … that one, one man … another man*	
	nē illud deī sinant!	*heaven forbid!*	
	illīc	*there, in that place*	
19	illūc	*there, to that place*	
	hūc … illūc	*this way … that way, one way … another way, here and there, up and down*	
	illūcēscō, illūcēscere, illūxī	*dawn, grow bright*	
	illūstris, illūstris, illūstre	*bright*	
	imāgō, imāginis, f.	*image, picture, bust, death mask; reflection*	
	imber, imbris, m.	*rain, storm-cloud*	
	imitor, imitārī, imitātus sum	*copy, imitate, mime*	
	immēnsus, immēnsa, immēnsum	*vast*	
	immineō, imminēre, imminuī (+ DAT)	*hang over*	
	immītis, immītis, immīte	*cruel*	
	immortālis, immortālis, immortāle	*immortal*	
23	immōtus, immōta, immōtum	*still, motionless*	
15	impediō, impedīre, impedīvī, impedītus	*delay, hinder*	
	impellō, impellere, impulī, impulsus	*push, force*	
	impendium, impendiī, n.	*expense, expenditure*	
	impendō, impendere, impendī, impēnsus	*spend, make use of*	
	impēnsē	*strongly, violently*	

16	imperātor, imperātōris, m.	*emperor*	
	imperfectus, imperfecta, imperfectum	*unfinished*	
10	imperium, imperiī, n.	*power, empire*	
27	imperō, imperāre, imperāvī (+ DAT)	*order, command*	
	impetrō, impetrāre, impetrāvī	*obtain*	
	impetus, impetūs, m.	*attack*	
	impetum facere	*charge, make an attack*	
	implicō, implicāre, implicāvī, implicātus	*implicate, involve*	
	impōnō, impōnere, imposuī, impositus	*impose, put into, put onto*	
	impotēns, impotēns, impotēns gen. impotentis	*helpless, powerless*	
	improbus, improba, improbum	*wicked, relentless*	
	imprōvīsus, imprōvīsa, imprōvīsum	*unexpected, unforeseen*	
	imprūdenter	*stupidly, foolishly*	
	impulī, impulsus *see* impellō		
	īmus, īma, īmum	*lowest, bottom*	
1	in (1) (+ ACC)	*into, onto*	
	in aliud	*for any other purpose*	
	in idem	*for a common purpose, for the same purpose*	
	in mentem venīre	*occur, come to mind*	
	in perpetuum	*forever*	
	in (2) (+ ABL)	*in, on*	
	in animō volvere	*wonder, turn over in the mind*	
	in prīmīs	*in the first place, in particular*	
	in proximō	*nearby*	
40	inānis, inānis, ināne	*empty, meaningless*	
29	incēdō, incēdere, incessī	*march, stride*	
41	incendium, incendiī, n.	*fire, blaze*	
27	incendō, incendere, incendī, incēnsus	*burn, set fire to; enflame, torment*	

incertus, incerta,
 incertum — *uncertain, questionable*

incīdō, incīdere,
 incīdī, incīsus — *cut open*

22 incipiō, incipere,
 incēpī, inceptus — *begin*

incitō, incitāre, incitāvī,
 incitātus — *urge on, encourage*

inclīnō, inclīnāre,
 inclīnāvī, inclīnātus — *lean*

inclūdō, inclūdere,
 inclūsī, inclūsus — *shut up, confine*

incohō, incohāre,
 incohāvī, incohātus — *begin*

48 incolumis, incolumis,
 incolume — *safe*

incurrō, incurrere,
 incurrī — *run onto, collide with, bump into*

35 inde — *then; from this, accordingly*

indicium, indiciī, n. — *sign, evidence*

indignē — *unfairly*

indignor, indignārī,
 indignātus sum — *feel shame, think it shameful*

indulgeō, indulgēre,
 indulsī (+ DAT) — *give way*

inedia, inediae, f. — *starvation*

ineptiō, ineptīre — *be silly, be a fool*

ineptus, inepta, ineptum — *silly*

ineram *see* īnsum

inertia, inertiae, f. — *laziness, idleness*

īnfāns, īnfantis, m. — *baby, child*

21 īnfēlīx, īnfēlīx, īnfēlīx
 gen. īnfēlīcis — *unlucky*

īnferiae, īnferiārum, f.pl. — *tribute to the dead*

īnferior, īnferior,
 īnferius — *lower, further downstream*

20 īnferō, īnferre, intulī,
 inlātus — *bring in, bring on, bring against*

causam īnferre — *make an excuse, invent an excuse*

īnferus, īnfera, īnferum — *of the underworld*

dī īnferī — *gods of the underworld*

īnfestus, īnfesta, īnfestum — *hostile, dangerous*

ingeminō, ingemināre,
 ingemināvī, ingeminātus — *redouble*

ingenium, ingeniī, n. — *character, inclination, talent, idea*

7 ingēns, ingēns, ingēns
 gen. ingentis — *huge*

34 ingredior, ingredī,
 ingressus sum — *enter*

inhorrēscō, inhorrēscere,
 inhorruī — *shudder*

inimīcus, inimīcī, m. — *enemy*

inīquus, inīqua, inīquum — *unfair*

initium, initiī, n. — *beginning*

30 iniūria, iniūriae, f. — *injustice, injury*

iniūstē — *unfairly*

iniūstus, iniūsta, iniūstum — *unjust*

inlātus *see* īnferō

inlēctus, inlēcta, inlēctum — *unread*

innītor, innītī, innīxus sum — *lean on, lean, rest*

innocēns, innocēns,
 innocēns *gen.* innocentis — *innocent*

innocentia, innocentiae, f. — *innocence*

43 inopia, inopiae, f. — *shortage, scarcity, poverty*

inquiētus, inquiēta,
 inquiētum — *unsettled*

4 inquit — *says, said*

 inquam — *I said*

 inquis — *you say*

īnsānus, īnsāna, īnsānum — *insane, crazy*

īnscrībō, īnscrībere,
 īnscrīpsī, īnscrīptus — *write, inscribe*

27 īnsidiae, īnsidiārum, f.pl. — *trap, ambush*

9 īnspiciō, īnspicere,
 īnspexī, īnspectus — *look at, inspect, examine, search*

īnstīgō, īnstīgāre,
 īnstīgāvī, īnstīgātus — *urge on*

īnstituō, īnstituere,
 īnstituī, īnstitūtus — *set up*

īnstō, īnstāre, īnstitī — *be pressing, press on, threaten, harass*

īnstrūmentum,
īnstrūmentī, n. *equipment*
26 īnstruō, īnstruere,
īnstrūxī, īnstrūctus *draw up, set up, equip,
fit (with wings)*
sē īnstruere *draw oneself up*
17 īnsula, īnsulae, f. *island; apartment
building*
īnsum, inesse, īnfuī *be in, be inside*
7 intellegō, intellegere,
intellēxī, intellēctus *understand*
6 intentē *intently*
intentus, intenta, intentum *intent*
16 inter (+ ACC) *among, during*
inter sē *among themselves,
with each other*
24 intereā *meanwhile*
intereō, interīre,
interiī, interitus *wear away, wear out*
13 interficiō, interficere,
interfēcī, interfectus *kill*
interim *meanwhile*
interior, interior, interius *inner*
interpellō, interpellāre,
interpellāvī *interrupt*
interrogō, interrogāre,
interrogāvī, interrogātus *question*
intrā (+ ACC) *inside, during*
intremō, intremere,
intremuī *shake*
2 intrō, intrāre, intrāvī *enter*
intulī *see* īnferō
inultus, inulta, inultum *unavenged*
invalēscō, invalēscere,
invaluī *become strong*
10 inveniō, invenīre,
invēnī, inventus *find*
investīgō, investīgāre,
investīgāvī,
investīgātus *investigate*
invideō, invidēre,
invīdī (+ DAT) *envy, be jealous of,
begrudge, cast an
evil eye*
40 invidia, invidiae, f. *jealousy, envy,
unpopularity*

invidus, invida, invidum *envious*
11 invītō, invītāre, invītāvī,
invītātus *invite*
17 invītus, invīta, invītum *unwilling, reluctant*
involvō, involvere,
involvī, involūtus *envelop, swallow up*
iō! *hurrah!*
iocōsum, iocōsī, n. *moment of fun,
moment of pleasure*

Iovis *see* Iuppiter
14 ipse, ipsa, ipsum *himself, herself, itself;
master, mistress*
28 īra, īrae, f. *anger*
īrāscor, īrāscī,
īrātus sum (+ DAT) *become angry with*
3 īrātus, īrāta, īrātum *angry*
īre *see* eō
irrigō, irrigāre, irrigāvī,
irrigātus *water*
irrumpō, irrumpere,
irrūpī *burst in, burst into*
is, ea, id *he, she, it; that*
id quod *what*
14 iste, ista, istud *that*
it *see* eō
16 ita *in this way*
sīcut … ita *just as … so*
13 ita vērō *yes*
Ītalia, Ītaliae, f. *Italy*
17 itaque *and so*
19 iter, itineris, n. *journey, progress*
iter agere *make one's way,
travel*
9 iterum *again*
nōn iterum *never again*
21 iubeō, iubēre,
iussī, iussus *order*
iūcundus, iūcunda,
iūcundum *pleasant, agreeable,
delightful*
4 iūdex, iūdicis, m. *judge*
iūdicium, iūdiciī, n. *judgment*
46 iūdicō, iūdicāre, iūdicāvī,
iūdicātus *judge*
iūnctus, iūncta, iūnctum *side by side*

38	iungō, iungere, iūnxī, iūnctus	*join*
	Iūnō, Iūnōnis, f.	*Juno (goddess of marriage)*
	Iūnōnius, Iūnōnia, Iūnōnium	*sacred to Juno*
	Iuppiter, Iovis, m.	*Jupiter (god of the sky, greatest of Roman gods)*
	iūrgium, iūrgiī, n.	*argument, dispute, quarrel*
	iūrō, iūrāre, iūrāvī	*swear*
	iūs, iūris, n.	*right, privilege, law*
	iussī *see* iubeō	
27	iussum, iussī, n.	*order, instruction*
	iussū Imperātōris	*at the emperor's order*
	iūstus, iūsta, iūstum	*proper, right, fair*
	iūstius erat	*it would have been fairer, more proper*
	iuvencus, iuvencī, m.	*bullock, young bull*
	iuvenīlis, iuvenīlis, iuvenīle	*youthful*
5	iuvenis, iuvenis, m.	*young man*
39	iuvō, iuvāre, iūvī, iūtus	*help, assist, please*
43	iuxtā (+ ACC)	*next to*

k

	Kal. = Kalendās	
	Kalendae, Kalendārum, f.pl.	*Kalends, first day of each month*

l

	L. = Lūcius	
	labellum, labellī, n.	*lip*
32	labor, labōris, m.	*work, task*
47	lābor, lābī, lāpsus sum	*fall, glide; pass by, slide by*
1	labōrō, labōrāre, labōrāvī	*work*
	lacerō, lacerāre, lacerāvī, lacerātus	*beat, tear, tear apart*

	lacertus, lacertī, m.	*arm, muscle*
22	lacrima, lacrimae, f.	*tear*
7	lacrimō, lacrimāre, lacrimāvī	*weep, cry*
	lacus, lacūs, m.	*lake*
	laedō, laedere, laesī, laesus	*harm*
2	laetus, laeta, laetum	*happy*
	laevus, laeva, laevum	*left*
	laevā parte	*on the left hand*
	lagōna, lagōnae, f.	*bottle*
	langueō, languēre	*feel weak, feel sick*
	lāniger, lānigerī, m.,f.	*woolly one, lamb*
46	lapis, lapidis, m.	*stone*
	lassō, lassāre, lassāvī, lassātus	*tire, weary*
	lātē	*widely*
	latebrae, latebrārum, f.pl.	*hiding-place*
25	lateō, latēre, latuī	*lie hidden*
	Latīnus, Latīna, Latīnum	*Latin*
	latrō, latrōnis, m.	*robber*
	lātrō, lātrāre, lātrāvī	*bark*
48	latus, lateris, n.	*side, flank*
2	laudō, laudāre, laudāvī, laudātus	*praise*
47	laus, laudis, f.	*praise, fame*
	lavō, lavāre (*sometimes* lavere), lāvī, lautus	*wash, bath*
	lectīca, lectīcae, f.	*sedan-chair*
15	lectus, lectī, m.	*couch, bed*
26	lēgātus, lēgātī, m.	*commander, governor*
	lēgem *see* lēx	
26	legiō, legiōnis, f.	*legion*
	lēgō, lēgāre, lēgāvī, lēgātus	*bequeath*
11	legō, legere, lēgī, lēctus	*read; choose, conscript*
	lēniō, lēnīre, lēnīvī, lēnītus	*soothe, calm down*
	lēniter	*gently*
15	lentē	*slowly*
	lentus, lenta, lentum	*supple, pliant*
	lēnunculus, lēnunculī, m.	*small boat*
3	leō, leōnis, m.	*lion*

40	levis, levis, leve	light, slight, trivial, changeable, inconsistent, worthless	
	levō, levāre, levāvī, levātus	raise, lift up	
38	lēx, lēgis, f.	law	
	libellus, libellī, m.	little book	
18	libenter	gladly	
10	liber, librī, m.	book	
11	līberālis, līberālis, līberāle	generous, liberal	
29	līberī, līberōrum, m.pl.	children	
20	līberō, līberāre, līberāvī, līberātus	free, set free	
32	lībertās, lībertātis, f.	freedom	
6	lībertus, lībertī, m.	freedman, ex-slave	
	lībertus Augustī	imperial freedman	
	lībrō, lībrāre, lībrāvī, lībrātus	balance	
	librum see liber		
	lībum, lībī, n.	cake	
44	licet, licēre, licuit	be allowed	
44	mihi licet	I am allowed	
	licet	although	
38	līmen, līminis, n.	threshold, doorway	
	līmes, līmitis, m.	course	
	lingua, linguae, f.	tongue, language	
	līnum, līnī, n.	thread	
	liqueō, liquēre, līquī	flow	
	liquidus, liquida, liquidum	liquid	
	liquō, liquāre, liquāvī, liquātus	strain	
	liquor, liquōris, m.	water	
	līs, lītis, f.	court case	
35	litterae, litterārum, f.pl.	letter (correspondence), letters, literature	
15	lītus, lītoris, n.	seashore, shore	
19	locus, locī, m.	place; occasion, reason	
	meī locō	in my place	
	locus nātālis, locī nātālis, m.	place of birth, native land	
42	longē	far, a long way	
	longē errāre	make a big mistake	

	longus, longa, longum	long	
34	loquor, loquī, locūtus sum	speak	
	lūcem see lūx		
	lūctor, lūctārī, lūctātus sum	struggle	
41	lūdō, lūdere, lūsī, lūsus	play	
33	lūdus, lūdī, m.	game	
41	lūgeō, lūgēre, lūxī	lament, mourn	
46	lūmen, lūminis, n.	light	
	lūmina, lūminum, n.pl.	eyes	
20	lūna, lūnae, f.	moon	
	lupus, lupī, m.	wolf	
	lūscus, lūsca, lūscum	one-eyed	
	lūsus, lūsūs, m.	play, games	
29	lūx, lūcis, f.	light, daylight	

m

	M. = Marcus		
	M'. = Mānius		
	Macedonia, Macedoniae, f.	Macedonia	
	māchināmentum, māchināmentī, n.	machine, contraption	
	madēscō, madēscere, maduī	become wet	
	madidus, madida, madidum	soaked through	
	magister, magistrī, m.	master, foreman	
43	magistrātus, magistrātūs, m.	public official	
	magnificus, magnifica, magnificum	splendid, magnificent	
30	magnopere	greatly	
35	magis	more	
24	maximē	very greatly, very much, most of all	
30	magnus, magna, magnum	big, large, great	
	maior, maior, maius	bigger, larger, greater	
17	maximus, maxima, maximum	very big, very large, very great, greatest	
	Pontifex Maximus	Chief Priest	
35	male	badly, unfavorably	

male dīcere		insult
ō factum male!		oh dreadfully done! oh awful deed!
vōbīs male sit		curses on you
malignus, maligna, malignum		spiteful
29	mālō, mālle, māluī	prefer
	malum, malī, n.	misfortune, evil, tragedy
28	malus, mala, malum	evil, bad
20	pessimus, pessima, pessimum	very bad, worst
23	mandātum, mandātī, n.	instruction, order
28	mandō, mandāre, mandāvī, mandātus	order, entrust, hand over
19	māne	in the morning
9	maneō, manēre, mānsī	remain, stay
	mānēs, mānium, m.pl.	departed spirit
	dī mānēs	the spirits of the dead
	manifestus, manifesta, manifestum	clear, bright
	mānō, mānāre, mānāvī	flow, be wet
	multum mānāns	drenched
18, 27	manus, manūs, f.	hand; band; control (legal term in a marriage)
	in manum convenīre	pass into the hands of
	manus ultima	final touch
15	mare, maris, n.	sea
	margarītum, margarītī, n.	pearl
	maritīmus, maritīma, maritīmum	seaside, by the sea
14	marītus, marītī, m.	husband
	marmor, marmoris, n.	marble
	massa, massae, f.	block
1	māter, mātris, f.	mother
	mātrimōnium, mātrimōniī, n.	marriage
	mātrōna, mātrōnae, f.	lady
	maximē see magnopere	
	maximus see magnus	

	mē see ego	
	medicāmentum, medicāmentī, n.	ointment, medicine, drug
	medicīna, medicīnae, f.	medicine
	medicus, medicī, m.	doctor
	meditor, meditārī, meditātus sum	consider
9	medius, media, medium	middle
	medius fidius!	for goodness sake!
	meī see ego	
	mel, mellis, n.	honey
	melior see bonus	
	mellītus, mellīta, mellītum	sweet as honey
42	meminī, meminisse	remember
	memor, memor, memor gen. memoris	remembering, mindful of
	memoria, memoriae, f.	memory
	mendāx, mendāx, mendāx gen. mendācis	lying, deceitful
	mēns, mentis, f.	mind
	in mentem venīre	occur, come to mind
32	mēnsa, mēnsae, f.	table
39	mēnsis, mēnsis, m.	month
	mēnsor, mēnsōris, m.	surveyor
	mēnsūra, mēnsūrae, f.	measurement
	mentior, mentīrī, mentītus sum	lie, tell a lie
2	mercātor, mercātōris, m.	merchant
41	mereō, merēre, meruī	deserve
	mergō, mergere, mersī, mersum	submerge, drown
	merīdiēs, merīdiēī, m.	noon
	meritus, merita, meritum	deserved, well-deserved
	mēta, mētae, f.	turning point
	metallum, metallī, n.	a mine
48	metuō, metuere, metuī	be afraid, fear
28	metus, metūs, m.	fear
5	meus, mea, meum	my, mine
	mī Lupe	my dear Lupus
	mī Secunde	my dear Secundus

mī = mihi

mihi *see* ego

18 mīles, mīlitis, m.   *soldier*

mīlitō, mīlitāre, mīlitāvī   *be a soldier*

28 mīlle   *a thousand*

28   mīlia, mīlium, n. pl.   *thousands*

minae, minārum, f.pl.   *threats*

11 minimē   *no, least, very little*

minimus *see* parvus

minister, ministrī, m.   *servant, agent*

minor *see* parvus

36 minor, minārī,
    minātus sum (+ DAT)   *threaten*

minus *see* paulum

12 mīrābilis, mīrābilis,
    mīrābile   *marvelous, strange, wonderful*

    mīrābile dictū   *strange to say*

mīror, mīrārī,
    mīrātus sum   *admire, wonder at*

mīrus, mīra, mīrum   *extraordinary*

misellus, misella,
    misellum   *wretched little*

15 miser, misera, miserum   *miserable, wretched, sad*

misericors, misericors,
misericors *gen.*
misericordis   *tender-hearted, full of pity*

12 mittō, mittere,
    mīsī, missus   *send*

moderātiō,
    moderātiōnis, f.   *moderation, caution*

modicus, modica,
    modicum   *ordinary, little*

34 modo   *just, now, only, just now*

45   modo … modo   *now … now, sometimes … sometimes*

    nōn modo … sed etiam   *not only … but also*

23 modus, modī, m.   *manner, way, kind*

22   quō modō?   *how? in what way?*

moechus, moechī, m.   *lover, adulterer*

moenia, moenium, n.pl.   *city walls; city*

mōlēs, mōlis, f.   *the building, the city*

molestus, molesta,
    molestum   *troublesome*

molliō, mollīre,
    mollīvī, mollītus   *soothe, soften*

42 mollis, mollis, molle   *soft, gentle*

22 moneō, monēre,
    monuī, monitus   *warn, advise*

monitus, monitūs, m.   *warning, advice*

12 mōns, montis, m.   *mountain*

    mōns Palātīnus   *the Palatine hill*

    summus mōns   *the top of the mountain*

47 mora, morae, f.   *delay*

21 morbus, morbī, m.   *illness*

mordeō, mordēre,
    momordī, morsus   *bite*

34 morior, morī,
    mortuus sum   *die*

    morere!   *die!*

    mortuus, mortua,
    mortuum   *dead*

35 moror, morārī,
    morātus sum   *delay*

20 mors, mortis, f.   *death*

    mortem obīre   *die*

    mortem sibi cōnscīscere   *commit suicide*

morsus, morsūs, m.   *bite, fangs*

mortālis, mortālis,
    mortāle   *mortal*

    genus mortāle   *the human race*

mortuus *see* morior

mōs, mōris, m.   *custom*

mōtus, mōtūs, m.   *movement*

33 moveō, movēre, mōvī,
    mōtus   *move, influence*

    mōtus, mōta, mōtum   *moved, moving*

9 mox   *soon*

45 mulier, mulieris, f.   *woman*

multitūdō,
    multitūdinis, f.   *crowd*

35 multō   *much*

multum   *much*

    multum mānāns   *drenched*

5	multus, multa, multum	*much*
5	multī	*many*
	plūrēs, plūrēs, plūra	*many, several*
19	plūrimī, plūrimae, plūrima	*very many*
	plūrimus, plūrima, plūrimum	*most*
21	plūs, plūris, n.	*more*
	quid multa?	*in brief, in short*
	quid plūra?	*why say more?*
	mūniō, mūnīre, mūnīvī, mūnītus	*protect, immunize; build*
48	mūnus, mūneris, n.	*gift*
	murmur, murmuris, n.	*roar, rumble*
11	mūrus, mūrī, m.	*wall*
	mūs, mūris, m.f.	*mouse*
	musca, muscae, f.	*fly*
	mūsicus, mūsicī, m.	*musician*
	mūtābili, mūtābilis, mūtābile	*changeable, contradictory*
40	mūtō, mūtāre, mūtāvī, mūtātus	*change*
	vestem mūtāre	*put on mourning clothes*
	mūtus, mūta, mūtum	*silent*

n

18	nam	*for*
	nārrātiō, nārrātiōnis, f.	*narration*
7	nārrō, nārrāre, nārrāvī, nārrātus	*tell, relate*
34	nāscor, nāscī, nātus sum	*be born*
	nātū maximus	*eldest*
	quīndecim annōs nātus	*fifteen years old*
	nat *see* nō	
	nātālis, nātālis, nātāle	*native*
	locus nātālis, locī nātālis, m.	*place of birth, native land*
	natō, natāre, natāvī	*swim*
	nātūra, nātūrae, f.	*nature*

	nātus *see* nāscor	
30	nātus, nātī, m.	*son*
	naufragium, naufragiī, n.	*shipwreck*
15	nauta, nautae, m.	*sailor*
	nauticus, nautica, nauticum	*made by the sailors*
	nāvigātiō, nāvigātiōnis, f.	*voyage*
16	nāvigō, nāvigāre, nāvigāvī	*sail*
3	nāvis, nāvis, f.	*ship*
31	nē	*that … not, so that … not, in order that … not*
48	nē quid	*in case anything, that nothing*
32	nē … quidem	*not even*
48	nē quis	*in case anyone, that anyone, that nobody*
	nebula, nebulae, f.	*mist*
32	nec	*and not, nor*
	nec iam	*no longer*
32	nec … nec	*neither … nor*
	necessārius, necessāria, necessārium	*necessary*
14	necesse	*necessary*
	necessitās, necessitātis, f.	*need, necessity*
7	necō, necāre, necāvī, necātus	*kill*
	nefas, n.	*(that which is divinely) forbidden*
	neglegēns, neglegēns, neglegēns *gen.* neglegentis	*careless*
31	neglegō, neglegere, neglēxī, neglēctus	*neglect*
	neglegentia, neglegentiae, f.	*carelessness*
43	negō, negāre, negāvī, negātus	*deny, say that … not*
17	negōtium, negōtiī, n.	*business*
	negōtium agere	*do business, work*
18	nēmō	*no one, nobody*
	Neptūnus, Neptūnī, m.	*Neptune (god of the sea)*
42	neque	*and not, nor*

24	neque … neque	*neither … nor*	
	nēquīquam	*in vain*	
25	nescio, nescīre, nescīvī	*not know*	
	nēve	*and that … not*	
	nex, necis, f.	*slaughter, murder*	
	nī = nisi		
	Nīcomēdēnsēs, Nīcomēdēnsium, m.pl.	*people of Nicomedia*	
	Nīcomēdīa, Nīcomēdīae, f.	*Nicomedia*	
	nīdus, nīdī, m.	*nest*	
36	niger, nigra, nigrum	*black*	
7	nihil	*nothing*	
	nihil cūrō	*I don't care*	
	nihil opus est	*there is no need*	
	nihilōminus	*nevertheless*	
	nimbus, nimbī, m.	*rain cloud, rain*	
30	nimis	*too*	
23	nimium	*too much*	
33	nisi	*except, unless*	
	nītor, nītī, nīxus sum	*lean*	
	niveus, nivea, niveum	*snow-white*	
	nix, nivis, f.	*snow*	
	nō, nāre, nāvī	*swim*	
30	nōbilis, nōbilis, nōbile	*noble, of noble birth*	
	nōbīs *see* nōs		
27	noceō, nocēre, nocuī (+ DAT)	*hurt*	
	nocte *see* nox		
13	nōlō, nōlle, nōluī	*not want, refuse*	
	nōlī, nōlīte	*do not, don't*	
	nōllem	*I would not want*	
25	nōmen, nōminis, n.	*name*	
	nōminō, nōmināre, nōmināvī, nōminātus	*name, mention by name*	
3	nōn	*not*	
	nōn iterum	*never again*	
	nōn sī	*not even if*	
	nōn tantum	*not only*	
41	nōndum	*not yet*	
16	nōnne?	*surely?*	
21	nōnnūllī, nōnnūllae, nōnnūlla	*some, several*	

	nōnnumquam	*sometimes*	
	nōrat = nōverat		
10	nōs	*we, us*	
	nōscitō, nōscitāre, nōscitāvī	*recognize*	
	nōsse = nōvisse		
11	noster, nostra, nostrum	*our*	
	nōtitia, nōtitiae, f.	*notice*	
26	nōtus, nōta, nōtum	*known, well-known, famous*	
	Notus, Notī, m.	*South wind*	
19	nōvī	*I know*	
	novō, novāre, novāvī, novātus	*change, revolutionize*	
13	novus, nova, novum	*new*	
22	nox, noctis, f.	*night, darkness*	
	nūbēs, nūbis, f.	*cloud*	
38	nūbō, nūbere, nūpsī (+ DAT)	*marry*	
	nūdus, nūda, nūdum	*bare*	
	nūgae, nūgārum, f.pl.	*nonsense, foolish talk*	
13	nūllus, nūlla, nūllum	*not any, no, not at all*	
14	num? (1)	*surely … not?*	
26	num (2)	*whether*	
	numerō, numerāre, numerāvī, numerātus	*count*	
33	numerus, numerī, m.	*number*	
	numerī, numerōrum, m.pl.	*military units; (astrological) calculations*	
17	numquam	*never*	
11	nunc	*now*	
	nunc iam	*now however, as things are now*	
10	nūntiō, nūntiāre, nūntiāvī, nūntiātus	*announce*	
8	nūntius, nūntiī, m.	*messenger, message, news*	
21	nūper	*recently*	
	nūpsī *see* nūbō		
	nūptiae, nūptiārum, f.pl.	*wedding, marriage*	
	nūptiālis, nūptiālis, nūptiāle	*wedding, marriage*	
	tabulae nūptiālēs	*marriage contract, marriage tablets*	

nūptūrus *see* nūbō

35 nusquam   *nowhere*

Nymphae,
 Nymphārum, f.pl. *Nymphs (minor*
         goddesses of
         the woods and
         mountains)

O

obdūrō, obdūrāre,
 obdūrāvī   *be firm*

obeō, obīre, obiī   *meet, go to meet*
 mortem obīre   *die*

obēsus, obēsa, obēsum *fat*

40 obiciō, obicere, obiēcī,
 obiectus   *present, put in the way*
         of, expose to

oblātus *see* offerō

oblīdō, oblīdere,
 oblīsī, oblīsus   *crush*

37 oblīvīscor, oblīvīscī,
 oblītus sum   *forget*

obscūrus, obscūra,
 obscūrum   *dark, gloomy*

observō, observāre,
 observāvī, observātus *notice, observe*

obstinātē   *stubbornly*

obstinātus, obstināta,
 obstinātum   *stubborn*

obstipēscō, obstipēscere,
 obstipuī   *gape in amazement*

18 obstō, obstāre,
 obstitī (+ DAT)   *obstruct, block the*
         way

obstringō, obstringere,
 obstrīnxī, obstrictus *bind (with oath of*
         loyalty)

obstruō, obstruere, obstrūxī,
 obstrūctus   *block the way through*

obstupefaciō, obstupefacere,
 obstupefēcī,
 obstupefactus   *amaze, stun*

obterō, obterere,
 obtrīvī, obtrītus *trample to death*

obtineō, obtinēre,
 obtinuī, obtentus *hold*

obtulī *see* offerō

obviam eō, obviam īre,
 obviam iī (+ DAT) *meet, go to meet*

obvius, obvia, obvium *encountering,*
         meeting

occāsiō, occāsiōnis, f. *opportunity*

28 occīdō, occīdere, occīdī,
 occīsus   *kill*

occidō, occidere, occidī *set*

occupātus, occupāta,
 occupātum   *busy*

occupō, occupāre,
 occupāvī, occupātus *seize, take over*

ocellus, ocellī, m. *poor eye, little eye*

Octōber, Octōbris, Octōbre *October*

28 octōgintā   *eighty*

20 oculus, oculī, m. *eye*

29 ōdī, ōdisse   *hate*

odiōsus, odiōsa,
 odiōsum   *hateful*

37 odium, odiī, n.   *hatred*
 odiō esse   *be hateful*

odōrātus, odōrāta,
 odōrātum   *sweet-smelling*

offendō, offendere,
 offendī, offēnsus *displease, offend*

9 offerō, offerre,
 obtulī, oblātus   *offer*

officium, officiī, n. *duty, task; official use;*
         kindness, service
 officium agere   *do one's duty*

6 ōlim   *once, some time ago,*
         sometimes

omittō, omittere,
 omīsī, omissus   *abandon*

30 omnīnō   *completely*

7 omnis, omnis, omne *all, every*
 omnia   *all, everything*

opera, operae, f.   *work, attention*
 tuā operā   *by your doing,*
         because of you

operiō, operīre, operuī,
 opertus   *cover*

operis *see* opus

28 opēs, opum, f.pl.   *money, wealth; means, power*

opifex, opificis, m.   *inventor, craftsman*

oportet, oportēre, oportuit   *be right*

nōs oportet   *we must*

21 oppidum, oppidī, n.   *town*

oppōnō, oppōnere, opposuī, oppositus   *oppose*

32 opprimō, opprimere, oppressī, oppressus   *crush*

24 oppugnō, oppugnāre, oppugnāvī, oppugnātus   *attack*

optimē *see* bene

optimus *see* bonus

47 optō, optāre, optāvī, optātus   *pray for, long for; choose, select*

30 opus, operis, n.   *work, construction, building*

nihil opus est   *there is no need*

41 opus est (+ ABL)   *there is need of*

ōra, ōrae, f.   *coastline*

ōrātiō, ōrātiōnis, f.   *speech*

ōrātor, ōrātōris, m.   *speaker* (in court), *pleader*

45 orbis, orbis, m.   *globe*

45 orbis terrārum   *world*

orbitās, orbitātis, f.   *childlessness*

orbus, orba, orbum   *bereaved, orphaned*

Orcus, Orcī, m.   *the underworld, Hell*

ōrdō, ōrdinis, m.   *row, line*

Ōrīōn, Ōrīonis, m.   *Orion, the Hunter* (constellation)

38 orior, orīrī, ortus sum   *rise, rise up, arise*

23 ōrnō, ōrnāre, ōrnāvī, ōrnātus   *decorate*

ōrnātus, ōrnāta, ōrnātum   *decorated, elaborately furnished*

31 ōrō, ōrāre, ōrāvī   *beg*

ōs, ōris, n.   *face, mouth*

os, ossis, n.   *bone*

ōsculum, ōsculī, n.   *kiss*

9 ostendō, ostendere, ostendī, ostentus   *show*

32 ōtiōsus, ōtiōsa, ōtiōsum   *idle, on vacation*

45 ōtium, ōtiī, n.   *leisure*

Ovidiānus, Ovidiāna, Ovidiānum   *of Ovid*

ovis, ovis, f.   *sheep*

p

P. = Pūblius

pācem *see* pāx

pacīscor, pacīscī, pactus sum   *exchange, bargain*

pācō, pācāre, pācāvī, pācātus   *pacify, make peaceful*

12 paene   *nearly, almost*

paenitentia, paenitentiae, f.   *repentance, change of heart*

Palātīnus, Palātīna, Palātīnum   *Palatine*

mōns Palātīnus   *the Palatine hill*

pallēscō, pallēscere, palluī   *grow pale*

pallidus, pallida, pallidum   *pale*

palma, palmae, f.   *hand*

pantomīmus, pantomīmī, m.   *pantomime actor, dancer*

pār, pār, pār *gen.* paris   *equal*

parātus, parāta, parātum   *ready, prepared*

22 parcō, parcere, pepercī (+ DAT)   *spare*

parēns, parentis, m.,f.   *parent*

parentēs, parentum, m.,f. pl.   *ancestors, forefathers*

23 pāreō, pārēre, pāruī (+ DAT)   *obey*

pariēs, parietis, m.   *wall*

pariō, parere, peperī, partus   *gain, win; produce*

pariter   *equally, at the same time*

7 parō, parāre, parāvī, parātus   *prepare*

18	pars, partis, f.	*part*	
	laevā parte	*on the left hand*	
47	parum	*too little, not … enough*	
6	parvus, parva, parvum	*small*	
	minor, minor, minus *gen.* minōris	*less, smaller*	
22	minimus, minima, minimum	*very little, least*	
	passer, passeris, m.	*sparrow*	
24	passus, passa, passum	*loose, disheveled*	
	passus *see* patior		
	pāstor, pāstōris, m.	*shepherd*	
24	patefaciō, patefacere, patefēcī, patefactus	*reveal*	
	pateō, patēre, patuī	*lie open*	
1	pater, patris, m.	*father*	
	patientia, patientiae, f.	*patience*	
34	patior, patī, passus sum	*suffer, endure, allow*	
37	patria, patriae, f.	*country, homeland*	
	patrius, patria, patrium	*of the father*	
	patrō, patrāre, patrāvī, patrātus	*accomplish, commit*	
	patrōnus, patrōnī, m.	*patron, defender, advocate*	
17	paucī, paucae, pauca	*few, a few*	
44	paulātim	*gradually*	
	paulīsper	*for a short time*	
37	paulō	*a little*	
46	paulum	*a little, slightly, to a slight extent*	
	minus	*less*	
32	pauper, pauper, pauper *gen.* pauperis	*poor*	
	paveō, pavēre, pāvī	*dread, fear*	
30	pavor, pavōris, m.	*panic*	
10	pāx, pācis, f.	*peace*	
	peccō, peccāre, peccāvī	*do wrong, be to blame, be at fault*	
48	pectus, pectoris, n.	*chest, breast, heart*	
4	pecūnia, pecūniae, f.	*money, sum of money*	
	pedem *see* pēs		
41	peditēs, peditum, m.pl.	*foot soldiers, infantry*	
	pelagus, pelagī, n.	*sea*	

	pendeō, pendēre, pependī	*hang*	
	penes (+ ACC)	*with*	
	penna, pennae, f.	*feather, wing*	
	pepercī *see* parcō		
6	per (+ ACC)	*through, along*	
	percipiō, percipere, percēpī, perceptus	*take hold of, get a grip on*	
	percussor, percussōris, m.	*assassin*	
	percutiō, percutere, percussī, percussus	*strike*	
41	perdō, perdere, perdidī, perditus	*destroy, waste, lose*	
	perditus, perdita, perditum	*completely lost, gone forever*	
	perdūcō, perdūcere, perdūxī, perductus	*bring, carry*	
16	pereō, perīre, periī	*die, perish*	
	perferō, perferre, pertulī, perlātus	*bring, endure*	
29	perficiō, perficere, perfēcī, perfectus	*finish*	
	perfidia, perfidiae, f.	*treachery*	
	perīculōsus, perīculōsa, perīculōsum	*dangerous*	
19	perīculum, perīculī, n.	*danger*	
	periī *see* pereō		
25	perītus, perīta, perītum	*skillful*	
	periūrium, periūriī, n.	*false oath*	
	permisceō, permiscēre, permiscuī, permixtus	*mix with*	
	perōsus, perōsa, perōsum	*hating*	
	perpetuus, perpetua, perpetuum	*perpetual, continual*	
	in perpetuum	*forever*	
	persevērō, persevērāre, persevērāvī	*continue*	
	perstō, perstāre, perstitī	*persist, continue standing*	
20	persuādeō, persuādēre, persuāsī (+ DAT)	*persuade*	
4	perterritus, perterrita, perterritum	*terrified*	

	pertinācia, pertināciae, f.	*obstinacy, determination*	
	pertineō, pertinēre, pertinuī	*concern*	
	pertinēre ad exemplum	*involve a precedent*	
37	perturbō, perturbāre, perturbāvī, perturbātus	*disturb, alarm*	
17	perveniō, pervenīre, pervēnī	*reach, arrive at*	
8	pēs, pedis, m.	*foot, paw*	
	pessimus *see* malus		
5,18	petō, petere, petīvī, petītus	*head for, attack; seek, beg for, ask for*	
	phōca, phōcae, f.	*seal*	
48	pietās, pietātis, f.	*duty, piety, family feeling* (respect for (1) the gods, (2) homeland, (3) family)	
	pinguis, pinguis, pingue	*plump*	
	pīnus, pīnī, f.	*pine tree, boat (made of pine wood)*	
	pīpiō, pīpiāre, pīpiāvī	*chirp, peep*	
	piscis, piscis, m.	*fish*	
	pius, pia, pium	*good, pious, respectful to the gods*	
11	placeō, placēre, placuī (+ DAT)	*please, suit*	
	placidus, placida, placidum	*calm, peaceful*	
	plānus, plāna, plānum	*level, flat*	
5	plaudō, plaudere, plausī, plausus	*applaud, clap*	
	plaustrum, plaustrī, n.	*wagon, cart*	
	plausus, plausūs, m.	*applause*	
21	plēnus, plēna, plēnum	*full*	
	plērīque, plēraeque, plēraque	*most, the majority*	
	plūma, plūmae, f.	*feather*	
	plumbum, plumbī, n.	*lead*	
	plūra, plūrēs, plūs *see* multus		
	plūrimī *see* multus		
25	poena, poenae, f.	*punishment*	

4	poēta, poētae, m.	*poet*	
	pollex, pollicis, m.	*thumb*	
38	polliceor, pollicērī, pollicitus sum	*promise*	
	pompa, pompae, f.	*procession*	
47	pondus, ponderis, n.	*weight*	
16	pōnō, pōnere, posuī, positus	*put, place, put up*	
	pontifex, pontificis, m.	*priest*	
	Pontifex Maximus	*Chief Priest*	
	pontus, pontī, m.	*sea*	
	poposcī *see* poscō		
29	populus, populī, m.	*people*	
8	porta, portae, f.	*gate*	
3	portō, portāre, portāvī, portātus	*carry*	
10	portus, portūs, m.	*harbor, port*	
19	poscō, poscere, poposcī	*demand, ask for*	
	positus *see* pōnō		
43	possideō, possidēre, possēdī, possessus	*possess*	
13	possum, posse, potuī	*can, be able*	
9	post (+ ACC)	*after, behind*	
18	posteā	*afterwards*	
	posterus, postera, posterum	*next*	
6	postquam	*after, when*	
	postrēmō	*finally, lastly*	
	postrēmus, postrēma, postrēmum	*last*	
16	postrīdiē	*(on) the next day*	
8	postulō, postulāre, postulāvī, postulātus	*demand*	
	posuī *see* pōnō		
	potēns, potēns, potēns *gen.* potentis	*powerful*	
	potes *see* possum		
33	potestās, potestātis, f.	*power*	
	in potestātem redigere	*bring under the control*	
	potis, potis, pote	*possible*	
	quī potis est?	*how is that possible? how can that be?*	
	potuī *see* possum		
	prae (+ ABL)	*instead of, rather than; compared with*	

26	praebeō, praebēre, praebuī, praebitus	*provide*
27	praeceps, praeceps, praeceps *gen.* praecipitis	*headlong, rash*
	praeceptum, praeceptī, n.	*instruction*
	praecipiō, praecipere, praecēpī, praeceptus	*instruct, order; take beforehand, receive in advance*
	praecipitō, praecipitāre, praecipitāvī	*hurl*
	praecipuē	*especially*
	praecō, praecōnis, m.	*herald, announcer*
	praecurrō, praecurrere, praecucurrī	*go on ahead, run ahead*
	praedium, praediī, n.	*estate, property*
	praefectus, praefectī, m.	*commander, governor (of an equestrian province)*
	praeficiō, praeficere, praefēcī, praefectus	*put in charge*
27	praemium, praemiī, n.	*prize, reward, profit*
	praesēns, praesēns, praesēns *gen.* praesentis	*present, ready*
36	praesertim	*especially*
	praestō, praestāre, praestitī	*show, display*
	praesum, praeesse, praefuī (+ DAT)	*be in charge of*
	praesūmō, praesūmere, praesūmpsī, praesūmptus	*take in advance*
36	praeter (+ ACC)	*except*
	praetereā	*besides*
	praetereō, praeterīre, praeteriī	*pass by, go past*
	praetōriānus, praetōriāna, praetōriānum	*praetorian* (belonging to emperor's bodyguard)
	praevaleō, praevalēre, praevaluī	*prevail, be uppermost*
	prātum, prātī, n.	*meadow*
34	precor, precārī, precātus sum	*pray (to), plead, plead for*

48	premō, premere, pressī, pressus	*push, press*
	pretiōsus, pretiōsa, pretiōsum	*expensive, precious*
21	pretium, pretiī, n.	*price*
	prex, precis, f.	*prayer*
	precēs adhibēre	*offer prayers*
	prīdiē	*the day before*
	prīmō	*at first*
	prīmum	*first, for the first time*
	cum prīmum	*as soon as*
11	prīmus, prīma, prīmum	*first*
	in prīmīs	*in the first place, in particular*
15	prīnceps, prīncipis, m.	*chief, chieftain, emperor*
	amīcī prīncipis	*friends of the emperor* (the emperor's council)
	prīncipātus, prīncipātūs, m.	*principate, reign*
	prīncipia, prīncipiōrum, n.pl.	*headquarters*
	prior, prior, prius	*first, in front, earlier*
	prīscus, prīsca, prīscum	*ancient*
29	prius	*earlier, before now, first*
34	priusquam	*before, until*
	prīvātus, prīvāta, prīvātum	*private*
18	prō (+ ABL)	*in front of, for, in return for, as, instead of, in accordance with*
38	prō certō habēre	*know for certain*
40	probō, probāre, probāvī, probātus	*prove, examine* (e.g. at time of enrollment), *approve, recommend, make acceptable*
9	prōcēdō, prōcēdere, prōcessī	*advance, proceed*
34	procul	*far off, from afar*
	prōcurrō, prōcurrere, prōcurrī	*project*
	prōdesse *see* prōsum	
	prōditor, prōditōris, m.	*betrayer, informer*

40 prōdō, prōdere,
   prōdidī, prōditus   *betray*
   prōdūcō, prōdūcere,
   prōdūxī, prōductus   *bring forward, bring
                          out*
37 proelium, proeliī, n.   *battle*
34 proficīscor, proficīscī,
   profectus sum   *set out*
   profiteor, profitērī,
   professus sum   *declare*
   prōgeniēs, prōgeniēī, f.   *descendant*
34 prōgredior, prōgredī,
   prōgressus sum   *advance, proceed*
38 prohibeō, prohibēre,
   prohibuī, prohibitus   *prevent*
   prōiciō, prōicere,
   prōiēcī, prōiectus   *cast (as an offering)*
   prōlēs, prōlis, f.   *offspring, brood*
   prōmissum, prōmissī, n.   *promise*
11 prōmittō, prōmittere,
   prōmīsī, prōmissus   *promise*
   prōmptus, prōmpta,
   prōmptum   *quick*
   prōmunturium,
   prōmunturiī, n.   *promontory*
   prōnūntiō, prōnūntiāre,
   prōnūntiāvī,
   prōnūntiātus   *proclaim, preach,
                    announce,
                    pronounce*
   prōnus, prōna, prōnum   *easy*
7 prope (+ ACC)   *near*
   properō, properāre,
   properāvī   *hurry*
   propinquus, propinquī, m.   *relative*
   prōpōnō, prōpōnere,
   prōposuī, prōpositus   *propose, put forward*
   prōpositum, prōpositī, n.   *intention, resolution*
   proprius, propria,
   proprium   *right, proper; one's
                own, that belongs
                to one*
43 propter (+ ACC)   *because of*
   proptereā   *for that reason*
   prōra, prōrae, f.   *prow*

   prōsequor, prōsequī,
   prōsecūtus sum   *follow, escort*
   prōsiliō, prōsilīre, prōsiluī   *leap forward, jump*
   prōsum, prōdesse,
   prōfuī (+ DAT)   *benefit*
   quid prōderit?   *what good will it do?*
   prōtegō, prōtegere,
   prōtēxī, prōtēctus   *protect*
   prōtendō, prōtendere,
   prōtendī, prōtentus   *thrust forward*
   prōtinus   *immediately*
   prōvincia, prōvinciae, f.   *province*
27 proximus, proxima,
   proximum   *nearest, next to, very
                close, last*
   in proximō   *nearby*
   prūdēns, prūdēns, prūdēns
   gen. prūdentis   *shrewd, intelligent,
                      sensible*
   prūdenter   *prudently, sensibly*
   Prūsēnsēs, Prūsēnsium,
   m.pl.   *people of Prusa*
   pūblicō, pūblicāre,
   pūblicāvī, pūblicātum   *confiscate*
   pūblicus, pūblica, pūblicum   *public*
   pudīcitia, pudīcitiae, f.   *chastity, virtue, purity*
   pudīcus, pudīca, pudīcum   *chaste, virtuous*
5 puella, puellae, f.   *girl*
8 puer, puerī, m.   *boy*
   pugiō, pugiōnis, m.   *dagger*
11 pugna, pugnae, f.   *fight*
8 pugnō, pugnāre, pugnāvī   *fight*
9 pulcher, pulchra, pulchrum   *beautiful*
   pulchritūdō,
   pulchritūdinis, f.   *beauty*
6 pulsō, pulsāre,
   pulsāvī, pulsātus   *hit, knock on, whack,
                         punch*
   pūmex, pūmicis, m.   *cliff, volcanic stone*
   pūmiliō, pūmiliōnis, m.   *dwarf*
16 pūniō, pūnīre, pūnīvī,
   pūnītus   *punish*
   puppis, puppis, f.   *stern, poop*
   pūriter   *decently, with clean
               water*

pūrus, pūra, pūrum	pure, clean, spotless	
37 puto, putāre, putāvī	think	

q

Q. = Quīntus		
quā	where	
quadrātus, quadrāta, quadrātum	squared, in blocks	
quadrīga, quadrīgae, f.	chariot	
quaedam see quīdam		
4 quaerō, quaerere, quaesīvī, quaesītus	search for, look for	
quaesō	I beg, i.e. please	
27 quālis, quālis, quāle	what sort of; just like	
14 quam (1)	how	
tam ... quam	as ... as	
10 quam (2)	than	
quam celerrimē	as quickly as possible	
14 quamquam	although, however	
quamvīs	although, however	
35 quandō?	when?	
quandōquidem	seeing that, since	
22 quantus, quanta, quantum	how big	
quantum	as, as much as	
quantum est	as much as there is	
30 quārē?	why?	
quārē	and so	
quārtus, quārta, quārtum	fourth	
34 quasi	as if, like	
quassō, quassāre, quassāvī, quassātus	shake violently	
quater	four times	
quatiō, quatere, quassī, quassus	shake, flap	
20, 28 quattuor	four	
48 quattuordecim	fourteen	
14 -que	and	
-que ... -que	both ... and	
quendam see quīdam		
querēla, querēlae, f.	complaint	
38 queror, querī, questus sum	lament, complain about	

questus, questūs, m.	lamentation, cry of grief	
15 quī, quae, quod	who, which, some	
id quod	what	
quod sī	but if	
15 quī? quae? quod?	which? what? how?	
quī potis est?	how is that possible? how can that be?	
33 quia	because	
quicquam see quisquam		
quicquid see quisquis		
42 quīcumque, quaecumque, quodcumque	whoever, whatever, any whatever	
quid? see quis?		
quid see quis		
32 quīdam, quaedam, quoddam	one, a certain	
35 quidem	indeed	
32 nē ... quidem	not even	
quidquid see quisquis		
quiēs, quiētis, f.	rest	
quiētus, quiēta, quiētum	quiet, peaceful	
quīlibet, quaelibet, quodlibet	anyone at all, anything at all	
quīn	but that, whereby not	
48 quīndecim	fifteen	
20, 28 quīnquāgintā	fifty	
20, 28 quīnque	five	
quīntus, quīnta, quīntum	fifth	
4 quis? quid?	who? what?	
quid agis?	how are you? how are you doing?	
quid faciam?	what am I to do?	
quid multa?	in brief, in short	
quid plūra?	why say more?	
quid prōderit?	what good will it do?	
quis, quid	anyone, anything	
48 nē quid	in case anything, that nothing	
48 nē quis	in case anyone, that anyone, that nobody	

41	sī quid	*if anything*	
41	sī quis	*if anyone*	
28,45	quisquam, quicquam *or* quidquam	*anyone, anything*	
48	quisque, quaeque, quodque	*each one, everyone*	
	usque quāque	*on every possible occasion*	
46	quisquis, quicquid *or* quidquid	*whoever, whatever, whatever possible*	
	quidquid est	*whatever is happening*	
18	quō?	*where? where to?*	
22	quō modō?	*how? in what way?*	
6	quod	*because*	
	ideō quod	*for the reason that, because*	
	quōdam *see* quīdam		
	quodcumque *see* quīcumque		
17	quondam	*one day, once, some time ago, sometimes*	
	quoniam	*since*	
2	quoque	*also, too*	
	quōsdam *see* quīdam		
26	quot?	*how many?*	
35	quotiēns	*whenever*	

r

	rapidus, rapida, rapidum	*rushing, racing, blazing, consuming*	
31	rapiō, rapere, rapuī, raptum	*seize, grab*	
	rārus, rāra, rārum	*occasional*	
	ratiō, ratiōnis, f.	*reason; accounting; procedure, manner*	
	ratiōnēs, ratiōnum, f.pl.	*accounts*	
	ratis, ratis, f.	*boat*	
	rē *see* rēs		
	rebellō, rebellāre, rebellāvī	*rebel, revolt*	
	rēbus *see* rēs		
	recitātiō, recitātiōnis, f.	*recital, public reading*	
35	recitō, recitāre, recitāvī, recitātus	*recite, read out*	

	rēctē	*rightly, properly*	
	rēctor, rēctōris, m.	*helmsman*	
	recumbō, recumbere, recubuī	*lie down, recline*	
18	recūsō, recūsāre, recūsāvī, recūsātus	*refuse*	
4	reddō, reddere, reddidī, redditus	*give back, restore, make*	
	sibi reddī	*be restored to one's senses, be restored to oneself*	
15	redeō, redīre, rediī	*return, go back, come back*	
	redigō, redigere, redēgī, redāctus	*bring*	
	in potestātem redigere	*bring under the control*	
26	referō, referre, rettulī, relātus	*bring back, carry, deliver, tell, report*	
	rēfert, rēferre, rētulit	*make a difference*	
33	reficiō, reficere, refēcī, refectus	*repair*	
33	rēgīna, rēgīnae, f.	*queen*	
	regiō, regiōnis, f.	*region*	
	rēgis *see* rēx		
38	regō, regere, rēxī, rēctus	*rule, guide, advise*	
34	regredior, regredī, regressus sum	*go back, return*	
	relēgō, relēgāre, relēgāvī, relēgātus	*exile*	
20	relinquō, relinquere, relīquī, relictus	*leave*	
	reliquiae, reliquiārum, f.pl.	*remains*	
46	reliquus, reliqua, reliquum	*remaining, the rest*	
	relūcēscō, relūcēscere, relūxī	*become light again*	
	rem *see* rēs		
	remaneō, remanēre, remānsī	*stay behind, remain*	
	remedium, remediī, n.	*cure*	
	rēmigium, rēmigiī, n.	*oars, wings*	
	rēmigō, rēmigāre, rēmigāvī	*row*	
	remittō, remittere, remīsī, remissus	*send back*	

rēmus, rēmī, m.	oar	
renīdeō, renīdēre	grin, smirk, smile	
renovō, renovāre, renovāvī, renovātus	renew, repeat, resume	
repellō, repellere, reppulī, repulsus	repel, push back, rebuff	
repulsus, repulsa, repulsum	repelled, taken aback	

43 repente — *suddenly*

41 reperiō, reperīre, repperī, repertus — *find*

repetō, repetere, repetīvī, repetītus — *seek again, repeat, claim*

reprehendō, reprehendere, reprehendī, reprehēnsus — *blame, criticize*

repudiō, repudiāre, repudiāvī, repudiātus — *divorce, reject*

46 requīrō, requīrere, requīsīvī, requīsītus — *ask, seek, search for, go looking for*

6 rēs, reī, f. — *thing, business*

33 rē vērā — *in fact, truly, really*

rem administrāre — *manage the task*

rem cōgitāre — *consider the problem*

rem nārrāre — *tell the story*

32 rēs adversae — *misfortune*

resecō, resecāre, resecuī, resectus — *cut back, prune*

resīdō, resīdere, resēdī — *sit down*

17 resistō, resistere, restitī (+ DAT) — *resist*

resonō, resonāre, resonāvī — *resound*

resorbeō, resorbēre — *suck back*

respectō, respectāre, respectāvī — *look towards, count on*

respiciō, respicere, respexī — *look at, look upon, look back, look up*

respīrō, respīrāre, respīrāvī — *recover one's breath, get one's breath back*

3 respondeō, respondēre, respondī — *reply*

respōnsum, respōnsī, n. — *answer*

rēspūblica, reīpūblicae, f. — *republic*

restituō, restituere, restituī, restitūtus — *restore*

resūmō, resūmere, resūmpsī, resūmptus — *pick up again*

retineō, retinēre, retinuī, retentus — *keep, hold back*

rettulī *see* referō

reus, reī, m. — *defendant, accused (of)*

9 reveniō, revenīre, revēnī — *come back, return*

revertor, revertī, reversus sum — *turn back, return*

37 revocō, revocāre, revocāvī, revocātus — *recall, call back, recover, make (someone) go back*

revomō, revomere — *vomit up*

14 rēx, rēgis, m. — *king*

rēxī *see* regō

rhētor, rhētoris, m. — *teacher*

3 rīdeō, rīdēre, rīsī — *laugh, smile*

rīdiculus, rīdicula, rīdiculum — *ridiculous, silly*

rīpa, rīpae, f. — *river bank*

rīsus, rīsūs, m. — *smile*

rīte — *properly*

rīvus, rīvī, m. — *stream*

7 rogō, rogāre, rogāvī, rogātus — *ask*

rogus, rogī, m. — *pyre*

Rōma, Rōmae, f. — *Rome*

Rōmānī, Rōmānōrum, m.pl. — *Romans*

Rōmānus, Rōmāna, Rōmānum — *Roman*

rōstrum, rōstrī, n. — *prow*

rubeō, rubēre — *be red*

ruīna, ruīnae, f. — *collapse*

rūmor, rūmōris, m. — *rumor*

rūmōrēs, rūmōrum, m.pl. — *gossip, rumors*

45 rumpō, rumpere, rūpī, ruptus — *break, split, burst, rupture; upset*

13 ruō, ruere, ruī — *rush, charge*

	rūpēs, rūpis, f.	*rock, crag, cliff*
25	rūrsus	*again; on the other hand*
35	rūs, rūris, n.	*country, countryside*
	rūrī	*in the country*
	rūsticus, rūstica, rūsticum	*country, in the country, of a country man*
	vīlla rūstica	*house in the country*

S

	Sabīnus, Sabīnī, m.	*Sabine*
21	sacer, sacra, sacrum	*sacred*
15	sacerdōs, sacerdōtis, m.,f.	*priest, priestess*
	sacerdōtium, sacerdōtiī, n.	*priesthood*
	sacrāmentum, sacrāmentī, n.	*oath*
	sacrificium, sacrificiī, n.	*offering, sacrifice*
	sacrificō, sacrificāre, sacrificāvī, sacrificātus	*sacrifice*
8	saepe	*often*
26	saevus, saeva, saevum	*savage, cruel*
47	sagitta, sagittae, f.	*arrow*
	salsus, salsa, salsum	*salty*
	saltō, saltāre, saltāvī	*dance*
	salūbris, salūbris, salūbre	*comfortable*
29	salūs, salūtis, f.	*safety, health; greetings*
	salūtem dīcere	*send good wishes*
2	salūtō, salūtāre, salūtāvī, salūtātus	*greet*
3	salvē! salvēte!	*hello!*
8	sanguis, sanguinis, m.	*blood*
	sānō, sānāre, sānāvī, sānātus	*heal, cure, treat*
	sapiō, sapere, sapīvī	*be wise*
4	satis	*enough*
	satis cōnstat	*it is generally agreed*
30	saxum, saxī, n.	*rock*
	scaena, scaenae, f.	*stage, scene*
	extrēma scaena	*the edge of the stage*
	scapha, scaphae, f.	*small boat*
	scelerātus, scelerāta, scelerātum	*wicked*

25	scelestus, scelesta, scelestum	*wicked, wretched*
29	scelus, sceleris, n.	*crime*
	scīlicet	*obviously*
31	scindō, scindere, scidī, scissus	*tear, tear up, cut up, cut open, carve*
23	scio, scīre, scīvī	*know*
	scopulus, scopulī, m.	*rock*
6	scrībō, scrībere, scrīpsī, scrīptus	*write*
	sculptor, sculptōris, m.	*sculptor*
	scurrīlis, scurrīlis, scurrīle	*obscene, dirty*
13	sē	*himself, herself, themselves*
	inter sē	*among themselves, with each other*
	sēcum	*with him, with her, with them*
	sēcrētus, sēcrēta, sēcrētum	*secret*
	sector, sectārī, sectātus sum	*chase after*
	secundus, secunda, secundum	*second*
	secūris, secūris, f.	*axe*
	sēcūritās, sēcūritātis, f.	*unconcern, lack of anxiety*
37	sēcūrus, sēcūra, sēcūrum	*without a care*
	secūtus *see* sequor	
4	sed	*but*
1	sedeō, sedēre, sēdī	*sit*
	sēdō, sēdāre, sēdāvī, sēdātus	*quell, calm down*
	seges, segetis, f.	*crop, harvest*
	sēgnis, sēgnis, sēgne	*timid, unenterprising*
	sēiūnctus, sēiūncta, sēiūnctum	*separate*
	sella, sellae, f.	*chair*
	semel	*once*
10	semper	*always*
11	senātor, senātōris, m.	*senator*
	senātus, senātūs, m.	*senate*
	cognitiō senātūs	*trial by the senate*
5	senex, senis, m.	*old man*

	senīlis, senīlis, senīle	*old*	
	senior, senior, senius	*older, elderly*	
	sēnsus, sēnsūs, m.	*feeling, sense*	
	sententia, sententiae, f.	*opinion, sentence*	
12	sentiō, sentīre, sēnsī, sēnsus	*feel, notice*	
42	sepeliō, sepelīre, sepelīvī, sepultus	*bury*	
20,28	septem	*seven*	
	septimus, septima, septimum	*seventh*	
28	septuāgintā	*seventy*	
	sepulcrum, sepulcrī, n.	*tomb*	
	sepultūra, sepultūrae, f.	*burial*	
	sepultus, sepultī, m.	*one who is buried*	
34	sequor, sequī, secūtus sum	*follow*	
	serēnus, serēna, serēnum	*calm, clear*	
	sermō, sermōnis, m.	*conversation*	
	sērō	*late, after a long time*	
10	servō, servāre, servāvī, servātus	*save, look after*	
1	servus, servī, m.	*slave*	
	sēsē = sē		
	sēstertius, sēstertiī, m.	*sesterce (coin)*	
	seu … seu	*whether … or, if … or if*	
	sevērē	*severely*	
	sevēritās, sevēritātis, f.	*strictness, severity*	
	sevērus, sevēra, sevērum	*severe, strict*	
20,28	sex	*six*	
26	sī	*if*	
	nōn sī	*not even if*	
	quod sī	*but if*	
41	sī quid	*if anything*	
41	sī quis	*if anyone*	
	sibi *see* sē		
28	sīc	*thus, in this way, in the same way*	
	siccus, sicca, siccum	*dry, thirsty*	
20	sīcut	*like*	
	sīcut … ita	*just as … so*	
42	sīdus, sīderis, n.	*star*	
	significō, significāre, significāvī, significātus	*mean, indicate*	
	signō, signāre, signāvī, signātus	*sign, seal*	
4	signum, signī, n.	*sign, seal, signal; military service*	
	silentium, silentiī, n.	*silence*	
	sileō, silēre, siluī	*be silent*	
8	silva, silvae, f.	*woods, forest*	
	sim *see* sum		
40	similis, similis, simile (+ DAT)	*similar*	
	simplex, simplex, simplex, *gen.* simplicis	*simple*	
35	simul	*at the same time, as soon as*	
16	simulac, simulatque	*as soon as*	
	simulātiō, simulātiōnis, f.	*pretense, playacting*	
39	simulō, simulāre, simulāvī, simulātus	*pretend*	
34	sine (+ ABL)	*without*	
	sinō, sinere, sīvī, situs	*allow*	
	sīpō, sīpōnis, m.	*fire pump*	
	sistō, sistere, stitī	*stop, halt*	
	sitiō, sitīre, sitīvī	*be thirsty*	
	sitis, sitis, f.	*thirst*	
	socia, sociae, f.	*companion, partner*	
40	socius, sociī, m.	*companion, partner*	
30	sōl, sōlis, m.	*sun, day*	
18	soleō, solēre, solitus sum solitus, solita, solitum	*be accustomed common, usual*	
	sōlitūdō, sōlitūdinis, f.	*lonely place, wilderness*	
	sollemnis, sollemnis, sollemne	*solemn, traditional*	
	sollemniter	*solemnly*	
	sollicitō, sollicitāre, sollicitāvī, sollicitātus	*worry; incite, entice*	
11	sollicitus, sollicita, sollicitum	*worried, anxious*	
10	sōlus, sōla, sōlum	*alone, lonely, only, on one's own*	
	solvō, solvere, solvī, solūtus	*loosen, untie, cast off; destroy*	
46	somnus, somnī, m.	*sleep*	
34	sonitus, sonitūs, m.	*sound*	

sonō, sonāre, sonuī	sound	
sordidus, sordida, sordidum	dirty	
30 soror, sorōris, f.	sister	
sors, sortis, f.	lot, fate, one's lot	
39 spargō, spargere, sparsī, sparsus	scatter, spread	
spatiōsus, spatiōsa, spatiōsum	huge	
47 spatium, spatiī, n.	space, distance	
spē see spēs		
45 speciēs, speciēī, f.	appearance	
8 spectāculum, spectāculī, n.	show, spectacle	
spectātor, spectātōris, m.	spectator	
5 spectō, spectāre, spectāvī, spectātus	look at, watch	
29 spernō, spernere, sprēvī, sprētus	despise, reject, ignore	
31 spērō, spērāre, spērāvī	hope, expect	
28 spēs, speī, f.	hope	
splendidus, splendida, splendidum	splendid, impressive	
spoliō, spoliāre, spoliāvī, spoliātus	deprive	
sportula, sportulae, f.	handout (gift of food or money)	
spūmō, spūmāre, spūmāvī	foam	
st!	ssh! hush!	
stābam see stō		
stabulum, stabulī, n.	cottage, stall	
8 statim	at once	
statua, statuae, f.	statue	
statuō, statuere, statuī, statūtus	set up, establish, build; decide	
46 sternō, sternere, strāvī, strātus	lay low, knock over	
39 stilus, stilī, m.	pen, stylus	
stīva, stīvae, f.	plow handle	
5 stō, stāre, stetī	stand, lie at anchor	
strēnuē	hard, energetically	
strepitus, strepitūs, m.	noise, din	
stringō, stringere, strīnxī, strictus	draw, unsheathe	

44 studeō, studēre, studuī	study	
39 studium, studiī, n.	enthusiasm; study	
11 stultus, stulta, stultum	stupid, foolish	
40 suādeō, suādēre, suāsī (+ DAT)	advise, suggest	
25 suāvis, suāvis, suāve	sweet	
suāviter	sweetly	
27 sub (1) (+ ACC)	under, to the depths of	
sub (2) (+ ABL)	under, beneath	
subeō, subīre, subiī	approach, come up, take over	
subinde	regularly	
6 subitō	suddenly	
subitus, subita, subitum	sudden	
sublevō, sublevāre, sublevāvī, sublevātus	remove, relieve	
subrīdeō, subrīdēre, subrīsī	smile, smirk	
subsellium, subselliī, n.	bench (for prisoner in court)	
subsistō, subsistere, substitī	halt, stop, stay; encounter, face	
suburgeō, suburgēre	drive up close	
32 subveniō, subvenīre, subvēnī (+ DAT)	help, come to help	
successus, successūs, m.	success	
sufficiēns, sufficiēns, sufficiēns gen. sufficientis	enough, sufficient	
sulcō, sulcāre, sulcāvī	plow through	
suī see sē		
1 sum, esse, fuī	be	
est mihi	I have	
summa, summae, f.	full responsibility, supreme command	
summergō, summergere, summersī, summersus	sink, dip	
16 summus, summa, summum	highest, greatest, top	
summus mōns	the top of the mountain	
sumptuōsus, sumptuōsa, sumptuōsum	expensive, lavish, costly	
suōpte = suō		
superbē	arrogantly	
31 superbus, superba, superbum	arrogant, proud	

supercilia,
    superciliōrum, n.pl.   *eyebrows*
    supercilia contrahere   *draw eyebrows*
        together, frown

superior, superior, superius   *higher, further*
        upstream

6 superō, superāre, superāvī,
    superātus   *overcome, overpower,*
        surpass

superpōnō, superpōnere,
    superposuī, superpositus   *place on*
superstes, superstitis, m.   *survivor*
supersum, superesse,
    superfuī   *survive, remain, be*
        left; be excessive

suppliciter   *like a suppliant,*
        humbly

supplicium, suppliciī, n.   *punishment, penalty*
    supplicium ultimum   *death penalty*
supprimō, supprimere,
    suppressī, suppressus   *staunch, stop the*
        flow of

suprā (+ ACC)   *over, on top of*
suprēmus, suprēma,
    suprēmum   *last*
3 surgō, surgere, surrēxī   *get up, rise, grow up,*
        be built up

suscipiō, suscipere,
    suscēpī, susceptus   *undertake, take on*
suspīciō, suspīciōnis, f.   *suspicion*
suspīciōsus, suspīciōsa,
    suspīciōsum   *suspicious*
34 suspicor, suspicārī,
    suspicātus sum   *suspect*
sustulī *see* tollō
susurrō, susurrāre,
    susurrāvī   *whisper, mumble*
10 suus, sua, suum   *his, her, their, his*
        own
    suī, suōrum, m.pl.   *his men, his family,*
        their families

t

T. = Titus
3 taberna, tabernae, f.   *store, shop, inn*

tābēscō, tābēscere, tābuī   *melt*
tablīnum, tablīnī, n.   *study*
tabula, tabulae, f.   *tablet, writing tablet*
    tabulae nūptiālēs   *marriage contract,*
        marriage tablets
10 taceō, tacēre, tacuī   *be silent, be quiet*
    tacē!   *shut up! be quiet!*
7 tacitē   *quietly, silently*
27 tacitus, tacita, tacitum   *quiet, silent, in silence*
23 tālis, tālis, tāle   *such*
20 tam   *so*
    tam … quam   *as … as*
7 tamen   *however*
tamquam   *as, like*
12 tandem   *at last*
36 tangō, tangere, tetigī, tāctus   *touch, move*
tantum   *only*
    nōn tantum   *not only*
27 tantus, tanta, tantum   *so great, such a great*
    tantī esse   *be worth*
    tantum   *so much, such a*
        great number

tardē   *late, slowly*
tardus, tarda, tardum   *late*
taurus, taurī, m.   *bull*
tē *see* tū
46 tēctum, tēctī, n.   *ceiling, roof, building*
45 tegō, tegere, tēxī, tēctus   *cover*
44 tellūs, tellūris, f.   *land, earth*
37 tempestās, tempestātis, f.   *storm, weather*
12 templum, templī, n.   *temple*
20 temptō, temptāre,
    temptāvī, temptātus   *try, put to the test,*
        meddle with
31 tempus, temporis, n.   *time*
tendō, tendere, tetendī,
    tentus   *stretch out*
tenebrae, tenebrārum, f.pl.   *darkness*
tenebricōsus, tenebricōsa,
    tenebricōsum   *dark, shadowy*
15 teneō, tenēre, tenuī,
    tentus   *hold, keep to, hold on*
        to, occupy,
        possess, be upon
tener, tenera, tenerum   *tender, helpless*

45	tenuis, tenuis, tenue	*thin, subtle, shallow*
	tenuō, tenuāre, tenuāvī, tenuātus	*thin out*
	tergum, tergī, n.	*back*
12	terra, terrae, f.	*ground, land*
45	orbis terrārum	*world*
7	terreō, terrēre, terruī, territus	*frighten*
	terrestris, terrestris, terrestre	*on land*
	terribilis, terribilis, terribile	*terrible*
	terror, terrōris, m.	*terror*
	testāceum opus, testāceī operis, n.	*brickwork*
	testāmentum, testāmentī, n.	*will*
	testimōnium, testimōniī, n.	*evidence*
25	testis, testis, m.f.	*witness*
	testor, testārī, testātus sum	*call to witness, swear by, take an oath on*
	tētē = tē	
	tetigī *see* tangere	
	theātrum, theātrī, n.	*theater*
	thermae, thermārum, f.pl.	*baths*
	Tiberis, Tiberis, m.	*Tiber river*
	tibi *see* tū	
	tībia, tībiae, f.	*pipe*
	Tīburs, Tīburtis, m.	*man from Tibur*
12	timeō, timēre, timuī	*be afraid, fear*
	timidē	*fearfully*
	timidus, timida, timidum	*fearful, frightened*
30	timor, timōris, m.	*fear*
	tintinō, tintināre, tintināvī	*ring*
	tīrō, tīrōnis, m.	*recruit*
	toga, togae, f.	*toga*
16	tollō, tollere, sustulī, sublātus	*raise, lift up, hold up; remove, do away with*
	tōnsor, tōnsōris, m.	*barber*
	torpeō, torpēre	*be paralyzed*

	torqueō, torquēre, torsī, tortus	*torture, twist*
	torus, torī, m.	*couch*
19	tot	*so many*
	totidem	*the same number*
8	tōtus, tōta, tōtum	*whole*
	tractō, tractāre, tractāvī, tractātus	*handle, touch*
9	trādō, trādere, trādidī, trāditus	*hand over*
13	trahō, trahere, trāxī, tractus	*drag, draw on, urge on, draw, derive; claim*
	tranquillum, tranquillī, n.	*calm weather*
37	trāns (+ ACC)	*across*
24	trānseō, trānsīre, trānsiī, trānsitus	*cross*
	trānsferō, trānsferre, trānstulī, trānslātus	*transfer, put*
	trānsfīgō, trānsfigere, trānsfīxī, trānsfīxus	*pierce, stab*
48	trecentī, trecentae, trecenta	*three hundred*
	tremō, tremere, tremuī	*tremble, shake*
	tremor, tremōris, m.	*trembling, tremor*
	tremulus, tremula, tremulum	*quivering*
12, 20, 28	trēs, trēs, tria	*three*
	trēs adeō	*as many as three, three entire*
	tribūnus, tribūnī, m.	*tribune* (high-ranking officer)
	tribuō, tribuere, tribuī, tribūtus	*grant, allot, assign*
	triclīnium, triclīniī, n.	*dining room*
	tridēns, tridentis, m.	*trident*
	triērarchus, triērarchī, m.	*naval captain*
20, 28	trīgintā	*thirty*
24	trīstis, trīstis, trīste	*sad*
	triumphus, triumphī, m.	*triumph*
	triumphum agere	*celebrate a triumph*
	trudis, trudis, f.	*pole*
4	tū, tuī	*you* (singular)
	tuba, tubae, f.	*trumpet*
	tueor, tuērī, tuitus sum	*watch over, protect*

	tulī *see* ferō	
6	tum	*then*
40	tum dēmum	*then at last, only then*
	tumidus, tumida, tumidum	*swollen*
	tumultus, tumultūs, m.	*riot*
	tumulus, tumulī, m.	*tomb*
	tunc	*then*
	tundō, tundere	*beat, buffet*
5	turba, turbae, f.	*crowd*
	turbātus, turbāta, turbātum	*confused*
	turbulentus, turbulenta, turbulentum	*rowdy, disorderly, disturbed, muddy*
	turgidulus, turgidula, turgidulum	*swollen*
	turpis, turpis, turpe	*shameful, disgraceful*
22	tūtus, tūta, tūtum	*safe*
6	tuus, tua, tuum	*your* (singular)*, yours*
	tyrannus, tyrannī, m.	*tyrant*

u

5, 14	ubi	*where, when*
	ubicumque	*wherever*
29	ubīque	*everywhere*
43	ulcīscor, ulcīscī, ultus sum	*avenge, take revenge on, take vengeance*
39	ūllus, ūlla, ūllum	*any*
	ulmus, ulmī, f.	*elm tree*
26	ultimus, ultima, ultimum	*farthest, last, final, at the edge*
	manus ultima	*final touch*
	supplicium ultimum	*death penalty*
	ultiō, ultiōnis, f.	*revenge*
46	ultrā	*further, beyond*
	ululātus, ululātūs, m.	*shriek*
	Umber, Umbrī, m.	*Umbrian*
	umbra, umbrae, f.	*shadow, ghost*
	umerus, umerī, m.	*shoulder*
	ūmidus, ūmida, ūmidum	*rainy, stormy*
23	umquam	*ever*

	ūnā	*with him, together*
44	ūnā cum (+ ABL)	*together with*
15	unda, undae, f.	*wave*
21	unde	*from where*
31	undique	*on all sides*
	ūnicus, ūnica, ūnicum	*one and only*
	(mātrōna) ūnivira, (mātrōnae) ūnivirae, f.	*woman who has had one husband*
12, 20, 28	ūnus, ūna, ūnum	*one, a single*
	urbānus, urbāna, urbānum	*chic, fashionable, refined; city-dweller, man from Rome*
5	urbs, urbis, f.	*city*
	urgeō, urgēre	*pursue, press upon*
	ūrō, ūrere, ussī, ustus	*burn*
	usquam	*anywhere*
	usque (1)	*continually*
	usque adhūc	*until now, up to this time*
	usque alter	*yet another*
	usque quāque	*on every possible occasion*
	usque (2) (+ ACC)	*as far as*
	ūsus, ūsūs, m.	*use*
	ūsuī esse	*be of use*
	ūsus *see* ūtor	
28	ut (1)	*as, like, as soon as, when*
26	ut (2)	*that, so that, in order that*
44	uterque, utraque, utrumque	*each, both, each of two*
	utrīque	*both groups of people*
	uterus, uterī, m.	*womb*
	ūtilitās, ūtilitātis, f.	*usefulness*
40	ūtor, ūtī, ūsus sum (+ ABL)	*use*
33	utrum	*whether*
35	utrum … an	*whether … or*
10	uxor, uxōris, f.	*wife*
	uxōrem dūcere	*take as a wife, marry*

V

vacō, vacāre, vacāvī — *be unoccupied*
vacuus, vacua, vacuum — *empty*
vadum, vadī, n. — *water*
vae tē! — *alas for you!*
vāgītus, vāgītūs, m. — *wailing, crying*
vagor, vagārī,
    vagātus sum — *spread, go around, wander*

vagus, vaga, vagum — *wandering*
7 valdē — *very much, very*
11 valē — *good-bye, farewell*
    avē atque valē — *hail and farewell*
valedīcō, valedīcere,
    valedīxī — *say good-bye*
valeō, valēre, valuī — *be well, feel well, thrive, prosper*

37 validus, valida, validum — *strong*
varius, varia, varium — *different, various*
vāstus, vāsta, vāstum — *great, large, enormous*
-ve — *or*
10 vehementer — *violently, loudly*
vehiculum, vehiculī, n. — *carriage*
31 vehō, vehere, vexī, vectus — *carry*
vehor, vehī, vectus sum — *be carried (e.g. by horse or ship), travel*

34 vel — *or; even*
48   vel … vel — *either … or*
velim, vellem *see* volō
48 velut — *like*
vēna, vēnae, f. — *vein*
vēnālīcius, vēnālīciī, m. — *slave dealer*
6 vēndō, vēndere, vēndidī,
    vēnditus — *sell*
23 venēnum, venēnī, n. — *poison*
venia, veniae, f. — *mercy*
5 veniō, venīre, vēnī — *come, come forward*
    in mentem venīre — *occur, come to mind*
vēnor, vēnārī,
    vēnātus sum — *hunt*
venter, ventris, m. — *stomach, womb*
ventitō, ventitāre,
    ventitāvī — *often go, go repeatedly*

28 ventus, ventī, m. — *wind*
Venus, Veneris, f. — *Venus (goddess of love)*
venustus, venusta,
    venustum — *tender-hearted, loving*
22 verbum, verbī, n. — *word*
vērē — *truly*
38 vereor, verērī, veritus sum — *be afraid, fear*
vēritās, vēritātis, f. — *truth*
38 vērō — *indeed, but indeed*
versipellis, versipellis, m. — *werewolf*
versus, versūs, m. — *verse, line of poetry*
vertex, verticis, m. — *top, peak*
16 vertō, vertere, vertī, versus — *turn*
    sē vertere — *turn around*
24 vērum, vērī, n. — *truth*
33 vērus, vēra, vērum — *true, real*
33   rē vērā — *in fact, truly, really*
vespillō, vespillōnis, m. — *undertaker*
Vestālis, Vestālis, Vestāle — *Vestal, belonging to Vesta (goddess of the hearth)*

29 vester, vestra, vestrum — *your (plural)*
34 vestīmenta,
    vestīmentōrum, n.pl. — *clothes*
vestis, vestis, f. — *clothing*
    vestem mūtāre — *put on mourning clothes*

36 vetus, vetus,
    vetus *gen.* veteris — *old*
vetustās, vetustātis, f. — *length, duration*
19 vexō, vexāre, vexāvī,
    vexātus — *annoy, harass*
    vexātus, vexāta, vexātum — *confused, in chaos*
1 via, viae, f. — *street, way*
viātor, viātōris, m. — *traveler*
vicārius, vicāriī, m. — *substitute*
vīcīnia, vīcīniae, f. — *nearness*
vīcīnus, vīcīnī, m. — *neighbor*
victima, victimae, f. — *victim*
victor, victōris, m. — *victor, winner*
victōria, victōriae, f. — *victory*
victus *see* vincō

3	videō, vidēre, vīdī, vīsus	*see; see to it*
40	videor, vidērī, vīsus sum	*seem*
	vigilō, vigilāre, vigilāvī	*stay awake, keep watch*
20, 28	vīgintī	*twenty*
	vīlicus, vīlicī, m.	*overseer, manager*
41	vīlis, vīlis, vīle	*cheap*
	villa, vīllae, f.	*villa, (large) house*
31	vinciō, vincīre, vīnxī, vīnctus	*bind, tie up*
15	vincō, vincere, vīcī, victus	*conquer, win, be victorious, outweigh*
44	vinculum, vinculī, n.	*fastening, chain*
	vindicō, vindicāre, vindicāvī, vindicātus	*avenge; protect*
3	vīnum, vīnī, n.	*wine*
	violentia, violentiae, f.	*violence*
	vīpera, vīperae, f.	*viper*
11	vir, virī, m.	*man, husband*
38	virgō, virginis, f.	*virgin, unmarried woman*
	viridis, viridis, viride	*green*
22	virtūs, virtūtis, f.	*courage, virtue*
40	vīs, vis, f.	*force, violence*
47	vīrēs, vīrium, f.pl.	*forces, strength*
	vīs *see* volō	
	vīsitō, vīsitāre, vīsitāvī, vīsitātus	*visit*
	vīsō, vīsere, vīsī	*come to visit*
3	vīsus *see* videō	
13	vīta, vītae, f.	*life*
41	vitium, vitiī, n.	*sin, fault, failure, vice, weakness*
22	vītō, vītāre, vītāvī, vītātus	*avoid*
6	vituperō, vituperāre, vituperāvī, vituperātus	*find fault with, curse, criticize*
19	vīvō, vīvere, vīxī	*live, be alive*
29	vīvus, vīva, vīvum	*alive, living*
19	vix	*hardly, scarcely, with difficulty*
	vōbīs *see* vōs	
	vōcem *see* vōx	

4	vocō, vocāre, vocāvī, vocātus	*call*
	volātus, volātūs, m.	*flying, flight*
13	volō, velle, voluī	*want*
	bene velle	*like, be friendly*
	velim	*I would like*
	volō, volāre, volāvī	*fly*
	volt = vult	
	volucer, volucris, volucre	*winged, swift*
	volucris, volucris, f.	*bird*
	voluntārius, voluntāriī, m.	*volunteer*
31	volvō, volvere, volvī, volūtus	*turn, turn over, set rolling, turn to billows, send rolling upwards*
	in animō volvere	*wonder, turn over in the mind*
	vōmer, vōmeris, m.	*plowshare*
10	vōs	*you (plural)*
	vōtum, vōtī, n.	*vow*
19	vōx, vōcis, f.	*voice; word*
	vulgō, vulgāre, vulgāvī, vulgātus	*make known, make common*
	vulgus, vulgī, n.	*the ordinary man, common man*
13	vulnerō, vulnerāre, vulnerāvī, vulnerātus	*wound, injure*
20	vulnus, vulneris, n.	*wound*
13	vult *see* volō	
31	vultus, vultūs, m.	*expression, face*

Index of cultural topics

Achilles 230
adultery 43, 95, 201–202
aedile 43–44
Aeneas 138, 162–163, 219–220
Aesop 124–125
Africa 116, 162, 220
Agricola 42, 45, 117–121
Agrippina 235–236, 241, 252
amici principis 42–43, 94, 252
Anchises, father of Aeneas 220
Ara Pacis 29
archaeology 5
Argiletum 78
art, Roman influence on 180–183
Asia (Roman province) 100, 116, 167
Athens 62, 166–167, 220
Atticus 78
augur 44–45
Augustus, emperor 25, 62, 78, 132, 138, 146–147, 161, 249–250, 253
authors 25–27, 63, 78–80, 145–147, 215–217
auxiliaries (auxilia) 118, 250

basilica (court site) 96
birthrate (in Rome) 62
Bithynia 44, 46, 99–100, 116–121, 250
board games 98
books, copying of 25, 27, 78, 217
    physical appearance of 21, 27, 215
    selling of 27, 78, 217
brickwork 37, 81, 107
Britain 45, 116–117, 218
Burrus 236, 252

Caelius 200–203
Caligula, emperor 253
Calpurnia, wife of Pliny 63
Carthage 96, 138, 162, 220
Catullus 126, 147, 186, 197, 200, 203
centumviri, court of 95
children 61–62, 65, 79, 96, 120, 160, 252
Cicero 63, 78, 95–96, 201–203, 216
citizenship, rights of 95, 118–119
civil disputes 95, 251
Claudius, emperor 26, 147, 236, 253
clients 96
Clodia (= Lesbia) 200–203
Clodius, brother of Clodia 200–202
concrete 37, 81
consilium (emperor's council) 42–43, 252
consul 43–45, 117, 249–250
country villas 1, 9–14, 44

courts of law 12, 44, 62–63, 95–97, 118–119
    fairness of 96–97
Crete 116, 138, 166–167, 181, 220
curator 44–45
cursus honorum 43–45, 95, 117

Dacia 116–117
Daedalus 165, 169, 173, 181–182
Dido 138, 162–163
dignitas 78, 217
divorce 61, 160–162
Domitia 70, 94
Domitian, emperor 18, 26, 31, 36–37, 42–44, 61, 70, 78–80, 82, 94–97, 145, 147, 249

education 65, 79, 120, 216
Egypt 116–117,
election bribery 95
elections 62
emperor 42–43, 78, 95, 100, 116–120, 236, 249–253, and *passim*
epic poetry 138, 203, 217, 230
epitaphs 63–64, 148, 154, 156, 216
equestrians 42, 117

farming 5, 7, 12–13
fishing 12, 184
forgery 95
freedmen 25, 64, 124, 132, 252

Gaul 43, 116, 119
governor (legatus) 45, 117, 249–250
    appointment of 117, 250
    duties and powers of 118–120
    misconduct of 95, 251
Greece 100, 116, 167, 181, 220, 230
Greeks 79, 146, 203, 215, 217, 230–233

Hadrian, emperor 9, 252
Homer 231–234
Horace 78–79, 132, 147, 203
hunting 11–12

Icarus 166, 170, 173, 175, 180–183
imagery 146
Italy 100, 116, 126, 132, 138, 163
iuridicus 119

Jesus Christ 21, 117
Jews 117–119
Judea 116–118
judges 95, 118

Julius Caesar 147, 154, 197, 249
jurors 96–97, 202
Juvenal 26, 162

lares 61
laudatio 154
Laurentum, Pliny's villa at 9–11, 16, 215
laws, Roman 43, 60–62, 78, 97, 118–119, 160, 250, 252
lawyers 95–97
legions, Roman 44–45, 104, 108, 117–118, 250
leisure 9–12, 215
Lesbia 186, 200, 203
letters 1, 10–13, 63, 100, 120, 215–218, 251
libraries 27
lyric poetry 145, 203, 217

Maecenas 78–79, 132
magistrate 95, 97, 249
mandata 119
manes 154
Mantua 138
marriage 47, 50, 60–64, 149, 160–163
Martial 12, 25–26, 78, 92, 96, 126, 145, 147
matronae univirae 61, 162–163
Minos 166
murder 95, 200, 202, 252–253
Muses 25, 123
mythology 146, 166, 181–182

Nero, emperor 150, 235–236, 244, 250, 252
Nerva, emperor 252

oratory 12, 79, 92, 95–97, 145, 216–217
Ovid 78–79, 85, 89, 96, 136–137, 147, 166, 181–182

palaces 18, 36–37, 80–82
paterfamilias 60, 65
patrons 25, 27, 78–79, 132
Paul the apostle 118–119
Petronius 150
Phaedrus 124, 147, 150
pirates 118
Plautus 78
plebs 44–45, 250
Pliny the Elder 206, 215
Pliny the Younger 9–13, 25–26, 43–46, 63, 79, 96–97, 100, 117–120, 126, 147, 206, 215–217, 250
poetry 80, 145–147, 182, 203, 230–233
Pompeii 5, 12, 14, 62, 93, 145, 173, 181, 211
Pompey 147, 154
Pontifex Maximus (chief priest) 250
Pontius Pilatus (Pilate) 117
Pontus 100, 116, 121
praefectus 44–45, 117
praetor 43–45, 95, 117–118
praetorian guard 42, 236, 243, 252–253

proconsul 117
provincial government, see Roman empire
publishing trade 25, 27, 217
Pudicitia 162

quaestiones 95
quaestor 44–45
Quintilian 79, 96–97, 145

reading aloud 12, 21, 25, 80
recitationes 16, 25–27, 63, 78
rhetor 79, 95, 145
Rome 9, 13, 18, 27, 36–37, 42, 44–46, 62, 78, 80–82, 94, 97, 100, 116–117, 132, 160–162, 200–201, 217, 220, 236, 249–250
Roman empire
    attitude of provincials towards 120–121
    extent of 100, 116–117, 215, 252
    government of provinces in 42–45, 116–121, 249–253
romanization 120
Russia 100

Salvius 95, 119
Saturnalia 11
Scotland 100, 118–121
senate 12, 43–44, 94–95, 116–117, 249–251
senate-house (curia) 83
senators 29, 42–43, 62, 83, 95, 117
Seneca 26, 236
Sicily 116–117, 201, 220
slaves 10–11, 25–26, 62, 78, 120, 124, 216–217, 252
Spain 116, 129, 249
Subura 78
Suetonius 249–250

Tacitus 26, 120–121, 206, 236, 249, 252, 254
taxation 120
tenant farmers 5, 7, 13
Tiberius, emperor 236
Tibur (Tivoli) 9
Trajan, emperor 26, 43, 100, 104, 109, 116–120, 122, 250, 252
treason 95, 97
tribunes 44–45, 117–118
Troy 220, 230
Turkey 100
Twelve Tables 97, 160

Venusia 132
Virgil 25, 78, 123, 132, 138, 147, 162, 220, 230
Verona 126
Vespasian, emperor 79–80, 94
vigintivir 44–45
voting tablets (in court) 95

water pump 113
writing materials 11, 28, 215

Index of grammatical and literary topics

hendecasyllabic meter 306
hendiadys 301
hic 265
historical infinitive 244
historical present 171, 292
hyperbole 302

īdem 266
ille 265
imperative 190, 274, 279, 283
inceptives 92
indirect command 291, 297
indirect question 159, 291, 297
    see also indirect speech
indirect speech 159, 291, 297
    position of verb of speaking, asking, etc. 159, 291,
       295
    subordinate clauses in 297
indirect statement 6, 34, 39, 51, 57, 88, 159, 294–297
    with forms of **negō** 295
    with future active infinitive 51, 295
    without leading verb (in a series) 296
    with perfect active infinitive 34, 294
    with perfect passive infinitive 39, 294
    with present active infinitive 6, 294
    with present passive infinitive 57, 294
    with **sē** 295
    see also indirect speech
infinitive 6, 13, 45, 49, 51, 57, 275, 279, 283–284, 286,
      294–296
    deponent future 279
    deponent perfect 279
    deponent present 13, 279
    future active 51, 275, 295
    historical 244
    irregular future 283
    irregular perfect 283
    irregular present 284, 286
    perfect active 45, 275, 294
    perfect passive 49, 275, 294
    present active 6, 275, 294
    present passive 57, 275 , 294
ipse 265
is 266

juxtaposition 302

litotes 302
locative case 288

metaphor 301
metonymy 302

nominative case 259, 275, 287
nouns 7, 22–23, 74–76, 142, 146, 228, 258–259, 264,
      289–290, 307
    plural with singular meaning 228

onomatopoeia 302
oxymoron 302

paradox 302
parallelism 146, 302
participles 39, 51, 119, 274, 279, 283–284, 289–290
    as nouns 289
    deponent future 279
    deponent perfect 279
    deponent present 279
    future 51, 274
    perfect passive 39, 119, 274, 284
    present 274, 283
    uses of 289–290
personification 301
poetic plural 265
polysyndeton 302
possum
    indicative 280–281
    subjunctive 27, 282
    see also infinitive, participles
prepositions 22–23, 225, 307
priusquam 292
pronouns 194–195, 264–267, 289–290, 307
    see also **ego, hic, īdem, ille, ipse, is, quī, quīdam,
      sē, tū**
purpose clauses 291

quī (relative pronoun) 194–195, 266–267
quīdam 267

result clauses 291
rhetorical question 302

Time chart

Date	Writing in Latin	Rome and Italy
BC c. 800		Etruscans in central Italy, c. 800
753		Rome founded (traditional date) 753
c. 500	Lapis Niger, Roman Forum	Kings expelled and Republic begins, 509
450	Duodecim Tabulae	Battle of Lake Regillus, 496
c. 289 ff.	Roman coinage	Comitia Centuriata exist, 5th C
c. 210	Livius Andronicus plays, *Odyssey* tr.	Gauls capture Rome, 390
d. 184	Plautus, comedies	Rome controls Italy/Punic Wars, 300–200
239–169	Ennius, epic: *Annales*	Hannibal crosses the Alps, c. 218
c. 160	Cato, *De Agri Cultura*	Rome expands outside Italy, 200–100
c. 160	Terence, comedies	Gracchi and agrarian reforms, 133
106–43	Cicero, speeches and essays	Marius reorganizes the army, 107 ff.
c. 94–55	Lucretius, *De Rerum Natura*	Pompey defeats Mithridates, 66
1st C	Vitruvius, *De Architectura*	Julius Caesar assassinated, 44
c. 84–54	Catullus, poems	Augustus becomes emperor, 27
70–19	Virgil, *Eclogues, Georgics, Aeneid*	Rhine and Danube, Roman frontiers, 9
65–8	Horace, *Odes, Epodes, Satires*	
c. 59–AD 17	Livy, *Ab Urbe Condita Libri*	Tiberius becomes emperor, AD 14
43–AD 17	Ovid, elegies, *Metamorphoses*	Nero emperor, 54–68
d. 50	Phaedrus, *Fables*	Great fire at Rome/Christians blamed, 64
AD 1–65	Seneca, essays and tragedies	Vespasian emperor, 69–79
1st C	Petronius, *Satyrica*	Colosseum begun, c. 72
23–79	Pliny, *Naturalis Historia*	Titus emperor, 79–81
40–104	Martial, epigrams	Vesuvius erupts, 79
c. 100	Suetonius, *De Vita Caesarum*	
40–100	Quintilian, *Institutio Oratoria*	Domitian emperor, 81–96
50–127	Juvenal, satires	Trajan emperor, 98–117
c. 56–115	Tacitus, *Agricola, Annales*	Hadrian emperor, 117–138
61–112	Pliny, *Epistulae*	Septimius Severus dies in Britain, 211
c. 160	Apuleius, *Metamorphoses* (novel)	Constantine tolerates Christianity, 313
160–240	Tertullian, *De Anima*	Empire divided into East and West, 364
c. 385	Jerome, *Vulgata* (Bible in Latin)	Alaric the Goth sacks Rome, 410
c. 400	Augustine, *De Civitate Dei*	Last Roman emperor deposed, 476
d. 524	Boethius, *De Consolatione Philosophiae*	
534	*Codex Justinianus* (laws)	

World history	World culture	Date
Babylonian/Sumerian civilizations		BC c. 3000
Pharaohs in Egypt		c. 3000–322
Indo-European migrations, c. 2100	Maize cultivation, American SW	c. 2000
Hammurabi's Legal Code, c. 1750	Epic of Gilgamesh	post 2000
Minoan civilization at its height, c. 1500	Rig-Veda verses (Hinduism) collected	c. 1500
Israelite exodus from Egypt, c. 1250	Development of Hinduism	c. 1450
Israel and Judah split, c. 922	Phoenician alphabet adapted by Greeks	c. 1000–800
Kush/Meroe kingdom expands	*Iliad* and *Odyssey*	c. 800
	First Olympic Games	776
Solon, Athenian lawgiver, 594	Buddha	c. 563–483
	Confucius	551–479
Persia invades Egypt and Greece, c. 525–400	Golden Age of Greece	500–400
	Death of Socrates	399
Conquests of Alexander the Great		335–323
	Museum founded in Alexandria	290
Great Wall of China built		c. 221
Judas Maccabaeus regains Jerusalem	Feast of Hanukkah inaugurated	165
	Adena Serpent Mound, Ohio	2nd C
Julius Caesar in Gaul, 58	Canal locks exist in China	50
	Glassblowing begins in Sidon	post 50
Cleopatra commits suicide		30
Herod rebuilds the Temple, Jerusalem		c. 20
Roman boundary at Danube, 15	Birth of Jesus	c. 4
	Crucifixion of Jesus	AD c. 29
Britain becomes a Roman province, 43	St Peter in Rome	42–67
	St Paul's missionary journeys	45–67
	Camel introduced into the Sahara	1st C
Sack of Jerusalem and the Temple		70
Roman control extends to Scotland		77–85
	Paper invented in China	c. 100
	Construction at Teotihuacán	c. 100
Roman empire at its greatest extent		98–117
Hadrian's Wall in Britain		122–127
"High Kings" of Ireland		c. 200–1022
Mayan civilization		c. 300–1200
Byzantium renamed Constantinople, 330	Golden Age of Guptan civilization	c. 320–540
	Last ancient Olympic Games	393
Byzantine empire expands		518

Date	Writing in Latin	Rome and Italy
c. 600	Isidore of Seville, encyclopedia	Gregory the Great, pope, 590–604
673–735	Venerable Bede, *Historia Ecclesiastica*	Period of turmoil in Italy, 800–1100
9th/10th C	*Waltharius*, epic, resistance to Attila	Republic of St Mark, Venice, 850
c. 960	Hrosvitha, religious plays b. on Terence	
11th C	Bayeux Tapestry (Norman Conquest)	
c. 1137	Abelard & Heloise, *Historia Calamitatum*	Independent government in Rome, 1143–1455
13th C	*Carmina Burana*, songs and plays	Marco Polo travels to the East, 1271–1295
1225–1274	Thomas Aquinas, *Summa Theologica*	Dante, poet (1265–1321)
13th C	Thomas of Celano, *Dies Irae*, song	Renaissance begins in Italy, *c.* 1400
1304–1374	Petrarch, epic, *Africa* and *Epistulae*	Botticelli, painter (1445–1510)
c. 1505	Amerigo Vespucci, *Mundus Novus*	Leonardo da Vinci (1451–1519)
c. 1511	Erasmus, *Moriae Encomium*	Titian, painter (1489–1576)
1516	Thomas More, *Utopia*	Rebuilding of St Peter's begins, 1506
1525	Zwingli, *De Vera et Falsa Religione*	Michelangelo starts Sistine Chapel ceiling, 1508
1543	Vesalius, *De Humani Corporis Fabrica*	Rome sacked by German/Spanish troops, 1527
1543	Copernicus, *De Revolutionibus …*	Spain controls much of Italy, 1530–1796
1573	T. Brahe, *De Nova Stella* (in Cassiopeia)	Fontana rediscovers Pompeii, 1594
1609	J. Kepler, *Astronomia Nova*	
1610	Galileo, *Sidereus Nuncius*	Galileo invents the telescope, 1610
1620	Francis Bacon, *Novum Organum*	Bernini, architect and sculptor (1598–1680)
1625	H. Grotius, *De Iure Belli et Pacis*	
1628	Harvey, *De Motu Cordis et Sanguinis*	
1596–1650	Descartes, *Cogito ergo sum*	
1608–1674	Milton, poems	
17th C	Hobbes, Locke, Spinoza, philosophers	Vivaldi, composer (*c.* 1678–1743)
1664	DuCreux, *Historiae Canadensis libri X*	Pompeii, systematic excavations, 1763
1687	Newton, *Principia Mathematica*	Carlo Goldoni, dramatist (1707–1793)
1753	Linnaeus, *Species Plantarum*	Napoleon enters Italy, 1796
1739–1798	Galvani, *De Viribus Electritatis*	Verdi, composer (1813–1901)
1745–1827	Volta, *De Vi Attractiva Ignis*	Leopardi, poet, dies, 1837
1835	F. Glass, *Georgii Washingtonii … vita*	Mazzini, Garibaldi, Cavour, active, 1846–1861
		Victor Emmanuel II, united Italy, 1861
		Rome, Italy's capital, 1870
1844–1889	G. Manley Hopkins, poems	Marconi develops wireless telegraphy, 1896
		Mussolini controls Italy, 1922–1945
		Italy a republic, 1946

World history	World culture	Date
	Birth of Muhammad	570
Charlemagne crowned, 800	Arabs adopt Indian numerals	*c.* 771
Vikings reach America, *c.* 1000	*1001 Nights* collected in Iraq	ante 942
Norman invasion of England, 1066	*Tale of Genji*, Japan	1010
First Crusade, 1096	Ife-Benin art, Nigeria	1100–1600
Magna Carta, 1215	Classic Pueblo Cliff dwellings	1050–1300
Genghis Khan (1162–1227)	Al-Idrisi, Arab geographer	1100–1166
Mali empire expands, 1235	Arabs use black (gun) powder in a gun	1304
Joan of Arc dies, 1431	Chaucer's *Canterbury Tales*	ante 1400
Inca empire expands, 1438	Gutenberg Bible printed	1456
Turks capture Constantinople, 1453	Building at Zimbabwe	*c.* 15th C–1750
Moors driven from Spain, 1492	Vasco da Gama sails to India	1497–1498
Columbus arrives in America, 1492		
	Martin Luther writes *95 Theses*	1517
Cortez conquers Mexico		1519–1522
Mogul dynasty established	Magellan names Pacific Ocean	1520
French settlements in Canada, 1534	Copernicus publishes heliocentric theory	1543
Turks defeated, Battle of Lepanto, 1571	Shakespeare	1564–1616
Burmese empire at peak	Muskets first used in Japan	*c.* 1580
Continuing Dutch activity in the East	Cervantes publishes *Don Quixote*	1605
Pilgrims land at Plymouth Rock, 1620	Taj Mahal begun	1632
Manchu dynasty, China, 1644–1912	Palace of Versailles begun	1661
Peter the Great rules Russia, 1682–1725	Newton discovers the Law of Gravity	1682
	J. S. Bach, composer	1685–1750
Industrial Revolution begins, *c.* 1760	Mozart, composer (1756–1791)	*c.* 1760
US Declaration of Independence	Quakers refuse to own slaves	1776
French Revolution begins	Washington, US President	1789
Napoleon defeated at Waterloo	Bolivar continues struggle, S. America	1815
Mexico becomes a republic, 1824	S. B. Anthony, women's rights advocate	1820–1906
American Civil War, 1861–1865	Communist manifesto	1848
Serfdom abolished in Russia		1861
Lincoln's *Emancipation Proclamation*		1863
Canada becomes a Dominion	French Impressionism begins	1867
	Mahatma Gandhi	1869–1948
Cetewayo, king of the Zulus, 1872	Edison invents phonograph	1877
	First modern Olympic Games	1896
First World War, 1914–1918	Model T Ford constructed	1909
Bolshevik Revolution in Russia, 1918	Bohr theory of the atom	1913
	US Constitution gives women the vote	1920
Second World War		1939–1945
United Nations Charter		1945